Stress Response Syndromes

Stress Response Syndromes

Second Edition

Mardi Jon Horowitz, M.D.

JASON ARONSON INC.

Northvale, New Jersey
London

First Softcover Edition 1992

Second Edition Copyright © 1986 by Mardi J. Horowitz
First Edition Copyright © 1978 by Jason Aronson Inc.

ISBN: 0-87668-811-3 (hardcover)
ISBN: 0-87668-298-0 (softcover)

Library of Congress Catalog Number 85-71507

Manufactured in the United States of America. Jason Aronson Inc. offers books and
cassettes. For information and catalog write to Jason Aronson Inc., 230 Livingston.
Street, Northvale, New Jersey 07647

For those strangers who,
roused by a shared sense of humanity,
help those overcome by events,
providing compassion, restoration, and hope

And, more personally, for my mother,
Lillian Horowitz, and in memory of
my father, Morris Horowitz

Contents

Foreword to the First Edition

In 1966, in a review surveying "The Current State of Psychotherapy: Theory, Practice, Research," published in the *Journal of the American Psychoanalytic Association*, I could comfortably (that is, with little risk of effective refutation) quote the sober appraisal of a friendly (non-analyst) psychotherapy researcher, Hans Strupp, that, at least to that date, even with all the burgeoning recent growth in research inquiry into psychotherapy, that very slight influence had as yet been exerted by research upon psychotherapy theory or practice. I quoted approvingly Strupp's bold statement that, "clinical penetration and scientific rigor have varied inversely. . . . If the advances of psychoanalysis as a therapeutic technique are compared with the experimental research contributions, there can be little argument as to which has more profoundly enriched the theory and practice of psychotherapy. To make the point more boldly, I believe that up to the present, research con-

tributions have had exceedingly little influence on the practical procedures of psychotherapy." To put Strupp's argument conversely, the
overwhelming proportion of what clinicians knew and found useful in
conducting clinical work came from impressionistic clinical experience
and apprenticeship training and not from systematic formal psychotherapy research at all.

This book by Dr. Mardi Horowitz on the psychological understanding
and the psychotherapeutic amelioration of specifically circumscribed
psychopathological entities, the Stress Response Syndromes, is an ex-
citing and long needed investigation that reflects the creative interplay
of psychotherapy, research, and practice. It is, after all, of the essence
of the clinical medical and health disciplines, the so-called healing arts,
of which psychotherapy partakes, that continuing advance in understanding and in practice should accrue from the effective and creative
interplay of formal research, basic investigation—in theoretical structure, in experimental laboratory, or in field observation or survey—in
interplay with the clinical experience and clinical reflection of the bed-
side, or in our instance, the consulting room. It is this creative interplay
between research and practice, leading to the enhancement of *both*,
which has been so underdeveloped in our "peculiar" science with its
heretofore essentially one-sided development, sparked by the innova-
tive genius of a Freud, of clinical insight and understanding without
the signal benefit of concomitant growth from the formal and systematic
research side of any comparable insight and understanding.

Mardi Horowitz's book is a multi-faceted model, or rather a series
of models, paradigmatic of a new genre, that brings psychotherapy
research meaningfully into the clinical picture; that is, where each influence furthers the other. What is the nature then of these models?
There is first a model of *problem setting* and *problem delineation* in the field
of psychological understanding and psychological intervention. Through
a sequence (1) of typical clinical *case history* in sufficient detail; (2) of
equally detailed and at the same time wide-ranging *field observation*
and survey drawing upon disaster and extreme circumstance, whether
wartime military combat or peacetime fire or shipwreck, whether such
inhumane extreme circumstances as concentration camps and nuclear
holocaust or more "everyday" circumstance of rape, severe illness,
death and bereavement; and (3) of equally meticulous attention to the
varieties of ingenious analogies to these stress situations, to the extent
that they can be ethically re-created within the *experimental laboratory*
and there be safely studied via controlled manipulation of critical di-

mensions; through this sequencing and drawing of common threads, this book serves as a model for the use of consulting room, of field observation, and of experimental laboratory to throw complementary and therefore incremental illumination upon the essential problem of psychotherapy, the understanding and the possibilities for intervention into the psychological dysfunctions of people.

This volume is secondly a model for the rational description of the *natural history* of a psychopathological syndrome or state, a description, that is, of what Dr. Horowitz calls the "general theory," the psychological explanation of sequentially unfolding phases and the general principles of psychological management and psychotherapeutic intervention specifically and differentially appropriate to the specific developmental phase and state of the disorder. This effort brings some rational order out of what so often looks like a chaotic welter of conflicting claims and competing approaches all vying for consumer acceptance in the unregulated psychotherapy marketplace. And thirdly, really as corollary to the "general theory" that accounts for the understanding and the psychotherapeutic modification of the naturally unfolding stress response syndrome, is the model for differentiated understanding and intervention based on the differing enduring character dispositions of the various *personality types or styles* (the hysterical, the obsessional, and the narcissistic, for example) as they differently mesh with the impositions and implications of the disease state and the requirements and possibilities of the intervention strategies.

And fourthly, the volume is a foretaste of a model for the imposition of *other treatment modes* (in this instance, an essay on the behavioral therapy approach) conceptualized by *its* adherents within an entirely different system of psychological suppositions and meanings, understood and given meaning here within the overall psychodynamic framework of his entire volume—written as it is by a psychoanalyst—and illustrative therefore of how such a differently conceptualized approach can interact more or less effectively with the psychopathological process and be understood (i.e., "explained") in its degree of effectiveness by us in *our* terms. Truly an ambitious program for future study is heralded here!

For that is what the entire volume is, a succession of models for a viable program of psychotherapy research that can become ultimately the labors of many successor volumes—the application to other, less circumscribed, psychopathological formations unfolding in *their* natural histories; the extension to other differentiated personality dispositions or types; the encompassing of more varying therapeutic modes (Gestalt, transactional, existential-humanistic, etc.) as they each varyingly interact with differing personality styles as caught in the web of differing illness states—all reconceptualized for their effect within the framework of psychoanalytic understanding. As such a model, or rather succession of models, this book has created, or at least systematized, methods of psychotherapy research that generate findings that do affect and meaningfully alter practice. In this sense it is a most positive response to Strupp's implied plea and in itself the vehicle of a significant shift in the role that carefully devised therapy study and carefully executed therapy research can play vis à vis the clinical therapy process.

ROBERT S. WALLERSTEIN, M.D.
Professor of Psychiatry
University of California, San Francisco

Preface

Since the publication of the first edition of *Stress Response Syndromes*, additional clinical, field, and experimental research has confirmed the importance of such responses as intrusive thinking and feeling that follow stressful experiences. This type of response has been recognized as a cardinal symptom in a new diagnostic category, Post Traumatic Stress Disorder. The new diagnosis in the official American nomenclature (DSM-III) has further stimulated organized clinical research and continued active debate on such issues as the degree and kind of Post Traumatic Stress Disorders found in the Vietnam War veterans.

In preparing this edition I have attempted to maintain the balance between an essay approach that frames fundamental observations and ideas and a textbook approach that systematically reviews the field.

In this second edition, the most extensive revision is of the chapters on diagnosis, theory, and treatments. The major change in the chapter on diagnosis was the deletion of parts of the historical review now that the concept of stress response syndromes has become part of the official diagnostic system. New additions in that chapter consider the range of stress response syndromes beyond Post Traumatic Stress Disorder and clarify some misconceptions (in my opinion) about PTSD.

The chapter on theory agreed with other investigators' and clinicians' observations and reflections of human psychological response to stress. Nonetheless, it has been tightened, and new sections have added concepts of conscious and unconscious schemata and the controls that regulate thinking and feeling and so form defensive operations.

During the decade since writing the first edition, my colleagues and I have continued to operate the Center for the Study of Neuroses at the Langley Porter Psychiatric Institute of the University of California. This research center contains two major units: the Stress and Anxiety Clinic and the Program on Conscious and Unconscious Mental Processes. The latter program will lead to continued theory development concerning the basic psychological processes as they involve emotion, memory, defense, and motivation. The Stress and Anxiety Clinic has provided the groundwork for psychotherapy research on the treatment of stress response syndromes and, more recently, other anxiety disorders. Through that work of trial, observation, and reformulation, the earlier treatment suggestions have been much expanded, leading to the new chapter on therapeutics of stress response syndromes.

Acknowledgments

In the introduction to the first edition, I thanked my high school chemistry teacher, Mr. Toon, for giving me the gift of wanting to study science, and Jurgen Ruesch for pointing the way in psychiatric research. Many other mentors and colleagues have guided me since then. In this second edition I cannot list all the colleagues, teachers, patients, and students who have made vital contributions. But certainly important among these are my colleagues at the Center for the Study of Neuroses at the University of California, San Francisco: Nancy Kaltreider, Charles Marmar, Robert Wallerstein, Daniel Weiss, and Nancy Wilner. Nancy Wilner, in addition to all her work during her years of association with me, fought her own heroic battles against serious life events. She edited this second edition.

My own efforts at stress research would not have been possible without the support of Mount Zion Hospital and Medical Center and the Langley Porter Psychiatric Institute. A series of two grants from the Research Scientist Awards program of NIMH began all these endeavors, and I am grateful for the support of Betty Pickett, Mary Haworth, David Hamburg, Frederick Worden, Ernest Haggard, Enoch Callaway, Robert Wallerstein, and, in his own special way, Bert Boothe. Grants and Clinical Research Center awards from the National Institutes of Health, the National Heart Lung and Blood Institute, and the National Institute on Aging contributed much to the field, experimental, and clinical investigations framing this book. Finally, work on the second edition was enabled by a fellowship at the Center for Advanced Study in the Behavioral Sciences at Stanford University, supported by a grant from the John D. and Catherine T. MacArthur Foundation. The program on conscious and unconscious mental processes is also fully supported, and was initiated, by the John D. and Catherine T. MacArthur Foundation. I especially thank William Bevan, John Conger, Murray Gell-Mann, and Jonas Salk for their continued vision and encouragement.

Jack Block, Jerome Singer, Richard Lazarus, Irving Janis, Alan Skolnikoff, Norman Mages, George Kaplan, Jerome Oremland, Seymour Boorstein, and Richard Lieberman provided essential consultations. And of course, this book owes much to those colleagues whose assistance is indicated in the Table of Contents.

My children Ariana, Jordan, and Joshua helped with the manuscript at various times but above all softened my own stress responses throughout the time of the work. My thanks to all.

Stress Response Syndromes

Chapter 1

A PARADIGM FOR CLINICAL KNOWLEDGE AND PRACTICE

There is a lag in the development of dynamic psychotherapy that can be counteracted by the clinical theories and observations in certain sectors of conceptualization. These sectors are formed by the problems to be treated, the patients' predispositions, and the therapy's goals.

The aim of short psychotherapies is to resolve specific problems. Characterological revision, the aim in reconstructive work such as psychoanalysis, is not attempted or else is focused on a particular conflict or trait. Nonetheless, characterological styles will be observed in brief, problem-centered therapy, functioning as a resistance to the process of investigation, working-through, and change.

There has been considerable work on managing the resistances and techniques relevant to transference and therapeutic alliance in psychoanalytic therapy but little systematic effort on relating the patient's character, habitual defenses, or cognitive style to the choices and nuances of problem-centered psychotherapeutic technique.

Instead, there has been heavy reliance on "rules of thumb" derived from psychoanalytic technique, especially the principle of interpreting defenses before interpreting what is warded off. It is important to know when this rule is useful and when it is a waste of time, when procedures other than those involving interpretations are useful and when they are not.

STRATEGY

Dynamic psychotherapy needs theory anchored to observables, that is concerned with the relationship between a patient's habitual "style" —and his or her current state and needs—and the rational or "ideal" form of psychotherapeutic technique. This theory must include the following:

1. A statement of the psychopathological or maladaptive states being considered.
2. A statement of at least some typologies of patient styles that organize and process thought and emotion during such states.
3. A clarification of the relationship between the patient's style and state and various modalities and styles of psychotherapy (e.g., even extending to different ways of giving the same interpretation). This clarification must include a theory of how interventions work and why a mode of therapy useful with one patient's style might not be useful with another.

Our approach starts at the existing level of clinical understanding and treatment and works toward progressive clarification and systematization. We have chosen stress response syndromes for close study as the state of maladaption, for the following reasons:

1. The relevant external events are known and recent. Therefore, memories and fantasies can be compared with a consensual reality.
2. The general human response tendencies are also known, phasic, and recognizable. Clinical and experimental studies indicate the existence of general stress response tendencies which take two seemingly opposite forms. One is manifested by intrusive and repetitive thoughts, emotions, and behavior, and the other shows ideational denial, emotional numbing, and behavioral constriction. These general tendencies vary among persons according to cognitive, emotional, and regulatory styles but can be found in some form in patients of any diagnostic or characterologic category.

3. The course of treatment is often short, and the patient's states vary during treatment, allowing clinicians to view the change.
4. The symptoms formed and dissipated after stress events are important throughout the psychopathology. They include loss of control over thought and emotion, denial and numbing, repetitious or maladaptive behavior, assault, extremes of anxiety, general tension and impaired relationships, and psychophysiological disorders.
5. Psychotherapy, often involving some sort of working through and interpretation of defenses and meanings, is frequently the treatment of choice. Within psychoanalytically oriented psychotherapy, there have been various procedures advocated and also called erroneous if badly timed or used with the wrong person (e.g., abreaction versus support and permitted denial). Multiple other types and theories of therapy (e.g., desensitization, guided imagery, abreaction, catharsis, gestalt techniques, and psychodrama) have also been advocated and can be selectively prescribed according to the patient's state and character style.
6. We can thus ask: (a) How does the external stress event interact with the patient's character, cognitive style, and conflicts? The development of clear connections between observation and inference regarding "habitual defenses" is a vital step in this therapeutic work. (b) Where is the patient having difficulty in completing the assimilation of and accommodation to the stress event? (c) How does the patient's relationship with the therapist modify the working-through or warding-off process?

PRELIMINARY TACTICS

In support of the scientific method, Sir Francis Bacon asserted, "The truth will sooner come from error than from confusion." Although this may not be true for dogmatic error, we must nevertheless state our position clearly, even risking reductionistic thinking. To that end, we shall divide the information about a patient into the following three categories:

1. The current phase of his or her response to stress, current symptoms and/or problems, and the relation of current events to past events.
2. His or her disposition regarding personality structure, habitual defenses, cognitive and coping style, behavior patterns, and the relationship of these with his or her family and society.

3. The therapeutic relationship and therapy techniques currently in use or appropriate to prescribe.

To serve these ends the book is divided into sections. Part I describes the investigations into the characteristics of stress response syndromes. Part II explains these general response tendencies and describes the principles of brief treatment for stress-induced symptoms and signs. Part III elaborates on these principles, contrasting three neurotic styles by using a single, manipulated case. We add the current concept of narcissistic personality to the classical patterns of histrionic and obsessional personalities, not so much to span classical and modern dispositional variables as to elucidate three cognitive operations used to ward off emotional pain in states of stress-induced neurotic conflict.

Although we emphasize focused, brief, psychodynamic psychotherapy, this paradigm also permits us to conceptualize the processes, should other forms of therapy be used. An example of this type of treatment variation is behavioral therapy. In Chapter 11, we examine systematic desensitization and implosive variants of behavior therapy as they might be applied to persons with histrionic or obsessional personality styles who develop stress response syndromes.

After describing the relatively universal tendencies and the stylistic variations of these tendencies, Part IV presents six case histories, including transcripts of sections of the psychotherapeutic process, in order to show how personality factors and preexisting conflicts form a patient's reaction to a stressful life event. The final chapter shows how the theory of stress response fits other sectors of clinical knowledge and how it may provide a paradigm that can be extended into other areas.

To avoid the confusion Sir Francis Bacon spoke of, it is necessary to limit our discussion. While formulating what is known about stress response syndromes in terms of phase of response, disposition, and therapeutic approach, it is necessary to indicate what aspects of the topic of stress will be trimmed. There is extensive literature on cross-cultural and sociological patterns of response to stress, on somatic responses, on adult traits set in motion by childhood traumas, and on developmental variation in stress response capacity. But these topics will not be discussed, so that the cognitive and emotional process by which a person assimilates psychologically stressful life experiences can be focused on as clearly as possible.

Part I
Stress Response Syndromes

Chapter 2
INTRUSION AND DENIAL: A PROTOTYPICAL CASE

Intrusive repetitions and denial are labels for two extremes of response to stressful life events, and their meanings are the concern of this book. Because we must use abstract statements and generalizations to explore these meanings, we shall begin with a concrete example, the case of Harry. His unbidden images of a dead woman's body illustrate the intrusive repetition of a horrible sight, and his temporary inability to acknowledge how moved he was by his involvement in her death illustrates a period of denial. Harry is a fictional character, and his history is a composite of characteristics found in studies of real persons. The events of his life are held constant while his character style is molded in various ways in order to contrast the response of different personality styles to the same circumstance.

HARRY

Harry was a 40-year-old truck dispatcher who had worked his way up in a small trucking firm. One night he took a run himself because he was shorthanded. The load consisted of steel pipe, carried in an old truck, and although the truck had armor between the load bed and the driver's side of the forward compartment, it did not fully protect the passenger's side.

Late at night Harry passed an attractive woman hitchhiking alone on a lonely stretch of highway. Impulsively deciding to break the company's rule against passengers of any sort, he picked her up, reasoning that if he did not she might otherwise be molested.

A short time later a car veered across the divider line and entered his lane, threatening a head-on collision. Harry pulled across the shoulder of the road into a clear area but then crashed into a pile of gravel. The pipe shifted, came through the cab of the truck on the passenger's side, and impaled the woman. Harry crashed into the steering wheel and windshield and briefly became unconscious. When he regained consciousness, he was met with the grisly sight of his dead companion.

The highway patrol found no identification on the woman, the other car had driven on, and Harry was taken by ambulance to a hospital emergency room. No fractures were found, his lacerations were sutured, and he remained overnight for observation. His wife, who sat up with him, found him anxious and dazed, talking of the events in a fragmentary and incoherent way.

The next day he left the hospital, and against his wife's wishes and his doctor's recommendation to rest, he returned to work. From then on, for several days, he continued his regular work as if nothing had happened. Harry met with his superiors and with legal advisers and was reprimanded for breaking the rule about passengers but was also reassured that otherwise the accident was not his fault and that he would not be held responsible. It was no secret that other drivers also often broke the "no-passenger" rule.

During this phase of relative denial and numbing of emotional responses, Harry thought about the accident from time to time but was surprised to find how little emotional effect it seemed to have on him. He was responsible and conscientious in his work, but his wife reported that he thrashed around in his sleep, ground his teeth, and seemed more tense and irritable than usual.

Four weeks after the accident he had a nightmare about mangled bodies and he awoke with an anxiety attack. For the next several days he had recurrent, intense, and intrusive images of the dead woman's body. These images, together with his ruminations about her, were accompanied by more and more severe anxiety attacks. Harry even developed a phobia about driving to and from work, and his regular habits of weekend drinking increased to a nightly use of growing quantities of alcohol. He lost his temper over minor frustrations and had difficulty concentrating at work and even while watching television. Harry tried unsuccessfully to dispel his feeling responsible for the accident, and worried about his complaints of insomnia, irritability, and increased alcohol consumption, his doctor referred him for psychiatric treatment.

This phase illustrates intrusive repetition in waking and dreaming thought and emotion. In his psychiatric evaluation, Harry at first was reluctant to talk about the accident. But this resistance subsided relatively quickly, and he reported recurrent intrusive images of the woman's body.

Background

Harry's family lived in a central California city with a population of approximately 100,000. His father worked as a hardware store manager and had a middle-class income. His mother married his father after graduating from high school and had been a housewife and mother since then. Harry had two older sisters and one younger sister.

Harry's father, a strict and moralistic man, had a constricted outlook on life. He had been out of work during the Depression and remained occupied with trying to save money. When this was not possible, he became irritated or worried. Besides his work and family, Harry's father valued his men's club activities and his trout fishing. He was never overtly affectionate but did praise the children when they were good. He also took Harry on occasional fishing trips but remained fairly remote. He consistently displayed a rigorous sense of morality and was a strict disciplinarian. As we shall see, Harry internalized these standards of behavior, which contributed to his guilty feelings after the accident.

Harry's mother struggled to provide a good home for her children, making sure that the house was clean, the meals were on time, and the laundry was done. She sometimes cried and belittled herself when she was unable to complete these tasks. Harry felt that his father did not appreciate his mother and that his father did not help her enough.

While his father sat in a chair during the evening, his mother continued working, with Harry sometimes helping. Harry's mother favored him and generally was lenient about what he did.

One older sister resented Harry's favored position with their mother and periodically teased and tormented him. But the other two sisters shared their mother's feeling that he was the special one. Harry felt especially close to his younger sister but was not closely attached to the others.

Harry was one of the more intelligent and gifted children in his high school class, and some of his teachers encouraged him to go to college. But he fell in love with a girl in his class, and gradually, with considerable guilt over each new step in their sexual intimacy, they had an affair. Late in their senior year of high school, she became pregnant. They decided they were in love and should therefore get married and have the child. Harry found a job working for a local store which led to his entering the truck-driving field. Periodic promotions followed until he reached the position of chief dispatcher a few years before the accident. He worked hard, valued the esteem of the other men, but felt bored and limited. His resulting desire for something more contributed a certain impulsiveness to his life, such as his readiness to break the rules to pick up the hitchhiking woman.

Harry and his wife had three children, two boys and a girl. Although Harry occasionally felt dragged down by the amount of time the children demanded from him in the evenings and on weekends, he was an attentive and loving father. He worked at this and consciously wanted to be a better husband and father than his father had been. His resentment of his wife occasionally surfaced, however, for he also wanted independence from what he saw as her demands. He believed that if he had not had to marry her, he could have gone to college, developed his potential, and found more interesting and remunerative work.

For two years, Harry had served in the military, and his wife and family were able to accompany him to a stateside base. He remembered this as one of the happier periods of his life because of the variety of experience and the comaraderie with other men. He had felt occasionally depressed since then.

When he was feeling morose, instead of coming home for dinner, Harry would go to a local bar with some of the men from work. He generally returned home three or four hours later, moderately intoxicated. His wife reacted with coldness, tears, or an angry attack. He counteracted by feeling either upset, guilty, apologetic, or angry in return, criticizing his wife's faults and shortcomings. Once he hit her during such an altercation; she threatened to leave him, and the physical abuse was never repeated. After the accident he feared that his wife would react to his picking up the woman with similar coldness, accusation, and anger.

Following such outbursts, Harry tended to carry a grudge against his wife for several weeks. But to his surprise, she recovered the same day. Her main grievance was that she felt unappreciated for all her devotion as his wife and the mother of his children. Although their sex life was intermittently active, she accused him of being less interested in her, and herself of being less interesting. Even though Harry did not tell her, he agreed. He had been sexually interested in women at work, but this had not gone beyond flirtations and kissing at office parties. But his sexual fantasies had been activated by seeing the woman alone on the highway.

Harry's main leisure activities were picnicking and camping with his family and trout fishing with his father. The two had developed a kind of distant but affectionate relationship around this activity. In addition, Harry liked to read. He tended to select recent novels and had also purchased a set from a "great books" series that he was determined to read from beginning to end.

Treatment

During his psychotherapy, Harry worked through several complexes of ideas and feelings linked associatively to the accident and his intrusive images. The emergent conflictual themes included guilt over causing the woman's death, guilt over the sexual ideas about her that he had fantasied before the accident, guilt that he felt glad to be alive when she had died, and fear and anger that he had been involved in an accident and her death. There was also a magical belief that the woman had "caused" the accident by her hitchhiking, and his associated anger toward her that then fed back into his various guilt feelings.

His symptoms gradually diminished. At first he was able to sleep better, and gradually he felt less anxious, tense, and irritable. He reduced his alcohol intake to an occasional social drink. Later, the image symptoms stopped, and his relationships returned to about the same level as before the accident, except that he felt closer to his wife, whom he credited with helping him through a difficult period.

Each of the complexes of ideas and feelings were activated not only by the accident but also by Harry's state before the conflict. Friction and sexual disinterest in his wife had led to fantasies about other women and activities that resulted in themes of guilt. Such guilt was connected with his feelings after the accident, just as his anger with his wife was related to the theme of his anger with the woman hitch-hiker. Thus the stress event led to a period of stress that combined internal and external elements.

We shall consider these various elements and combinations as the case of Harry evolves in subsequent chapters. What is important here is the concrete illustration of Harry's signs and symptoms after the accident. The recognition of such signs as the denial period, the free interval when Harry functioned well at work after the accident, and the symptom of intrusive images is enhanced by a knowledge of the theory of the psychological response to stress and how this relates to clinical psychopathology. Without this knowledge, the free period might look like normal adaptiveness, and the intrusive images might not have been explored or might have been regarded as unimportant.

Chapter 3

CLINICAL OBSERVATIONS AND DIAGNOSES

Physical injuries following physical traumas have a variety of diagnoses, and the classification of such disorders has been a part of medicine throughout recorded history. Psychological injuries after psychological traumas have been observed for as long a period, but in a far less systematic and consensually accepted form. The major efforts at agreeing on clinical psychological syndromes began with observations of signs and symptoms following disasters such as train wrecks and wars that exposed many to the same type of experience. "Railroad spine," for example, was a common disability after railway accidents

---

Some of the ideas used in this chapter appeared in a different form in my "Stress, Post-traumatic and Adjustment," a chapter in J. Cavenar et al., eds., *Textbook of Psychiatry*. Philadelphia: Lippincott (in press); and in my "Post-traumatic stress disorders," *Behavioral Sciences and the Law* 1:9–23, 1983.

(Trimble, 1981). Although the threat of litigations was a motivation, it became quite clear to neurologists that conscious malingering was not the reason for many of the functional symptoms that persisted long after the disasters.

Post-traumatic neuroses concerned not only the clinical problem of diagnosis and etiological formulation but also the legal problem of compensation when the traumatic events were seen as the potential responsibility of others. That is why the industrial era, with its development of railroad systems run by transportation boards, led to a clearer observation of post-traumatic neuroses. There were many legal arguments among experts on both the plaintiff's and the defendant's sides. In the latter part of the 19th century and into the 20th century, these arguments concerned the degree to which a patient's distress and functional impairment was related to (1) aims to get compensation; (2) hysterical conversion reactions precipitated by trauma; (3) physical impairments in various organ systems such as the brain, spine, and peripheral nerves; and (4) stress specific responses such as special psychological signs and symptoms induced by psychic trauma.

The implication of nonconscious, psychological motivational factors in symptom formation was a topic of considerable controversy. Hysteria in human behavior had a history of 4,000 years and was thought to be a syndrome based on heredity, emotional predisposition, and psychological responses to current situations, including stressful life events (Veith, 1965, 1977; Luisada, Peele, and Pittard, 1974). Charcot demonstrated the unconscious derivation of hysterical symptoms and suggested its relation to trauma. He also discussed its presence in men as well as women. But the clearest relationship between hysterical symptoms and earlier psychological and physical traumas was presented by Breuer and Freud in their "Studies on Hysteria" (1895).

Using the early methods of psychoanalysis, Breuer and Freud explored hysterical symptoms in terms of associated memories and fantasies and found that earlier psychological traumas provided the contents that were reenacted symbolically or indirectly in the symptoms of hysteria. These traumatic events often involved a sexual situation in which the person was involuntarily aroused, in which such excitement was both excessive and incompatible with moral standards. Emotions and impulses to act were strong, yet warded off by defenses. The pressure for expression, together with defensive distortions of expression, was seen as the cause of symptoms that emerged long after the evocative life situation. An emotionally charged recollection of the traumatic memories and a working-through of previously incompatible ideas relieved the symptoms.

COMPULSIVE REPETITIONS

Breuer and Freud noted the psychological traumas that could precipitate such diverse hysterical symptoms as recurrent visual hallucinations, emotional outbursts, paralyses, compulsive movements, and other sensory or motor disturbances. They also discovered that there was frequently a latent period between the occurrence of a stressful event and the onset of symptoms. Once symptoms formed, however, there was a remarkable tendency toward recurrence or persistence long after the event's termination and its immediate effects. In addition, there was often a bland denial of the meaning of symptoms, which was called *la belle indifference*.

Freud made many theoretical revisions after the initial psychoanalytic discoveries of the traumatic basis of hysterical symptoms. He was at first dismayed to find that memories of childhood seduction, the primary trauma in his theory, were not always true memories but occasionally fantasy elaborations of childhood situations (Jones, 1953). Thus, the traumatic event did not always represent an external stress alone. It also involved internal components and might produce virtually any symptomatic picture, not just hysterical syndromes (Freud, 1920).

Through the elaborations and corrections of the theory, the concept of trauma became generalized. And as psychoanalysis developed, trauma and familial strain were regarded as the causes of various symptoms, conflicts, fixations, character traits, defenses, and adaptive and maladaptive cognitive and affective developments (Bibring, 1943; Fenichel, 1945). This generalization of trauma as an explanatory concept necessitated the description of its many variations. An array of terms resulted, including multiple, strain, cumulative, screen, bad-object, fantasy, and retrospective traumas (Glover, 1929; Sears, 1936; Freud, 1937; Greenacre, 1952; Fairbairn, 1954; Stern, 1961; Furst, 1967; and Sachs, 1967). Despite this diffusion of terminology and theory, clinicians did agree on some key findings. One of these discoveries was the phenomenon that after a traumatic event there is a compulsive tendency to repeat some aspect of the experience (Freud, 1914b, 1920; Schur, 1966; Horowitz, 1976). This involuntary repetition includes the recurrence of thoughts and especially images about the stress event, of feelings related to the original experience, and of behavioral reenactments of parts of the experience itself. Repetitions in thought may take many forms, including nightmares, dreams, hallucinations, pseudohallucinations, recurrent unbidden images, illusions, and recurrent obsessive ideas. Harry's images of the dead woman's body, as discussed in Chapter 2, are one example. Emotional repetitions may occur with or without clear conscious awareness of their conceptual associations. Behavioral reenactments range from compulsive verbalizations of the event through recurrent expressions of it in gesture, movement, or artistic productions, to patterning of interpersonal relations. The trauma may be symbolically repeated over and over again. Finally, there are several repetitive physiological responses to stress: behavioral or cognitive repetitions may include recurrence of stress-related physiological responses such as sweating, tremor, palpitations, or other autonomic symptoms.

Involuntary repetitions may occur despite conscious efforts to avoid and suppress them, but they are not necessarily static replicas of the original experience. A series of successive revisions in content and form is frequently noted in clinical studies. Such repetitions may eventually lose their intrusive and involuntary nature; the change in content and reduced intrusiveness indicates that there has been a progressive mastery of the experience. But unfortunately this does not always happen, and in some persons these intrusive repetitions persist indefinitely.

DENIAL

The involuntary repetition of stress-relevant contents may be a sharp contrast with its ostensible opposite; the massive ideational denial of the event and general emotional numbness. Menninger called this hypersuppression the most normal and the most prevalent of defenses (1954). Warding off thoughts about the stress event or its implications may alternate with intrusive repetitions in a variety of phasic relationships. Denial and numbness may occur over a given time span of hours or days, alternating with phases of ideational intrusion and emotional pangs. There also may be intrusive repetitions of one aspect of a stress event, with simultaneous denial and numbing of another implication of the event (intrusion of fearful themes, for example, with inhibitions of the experience of guilty themes).

To recapitulate, clinical studies indicate that major stress events tend to be followed by involuntary repetition in thought, emotion, and behavior. Such responses tend to occur in phases and to alternate with periods of relatively successful warding off of repetitions, as indicated by ideational denial and emotional numbness.

COMMON THEMES

Any event is appraised and assimilated in relation to the past history and the current cognitive and emotional set of the person who experiences it, and therefore it produces idiosyncratic responses. Human beings are as similar as they are different, however, and there seem to be certain, fairly universal conflicts between wishes and realities after stress events such as accidental injuries, illnesses, and losses. Clinical studies reveal at least nine themes as common problems during the process of working through stressful life events (Chart 3-1). Such thematic contents may occur as intrusive ideas, deliberately contemplated ideas, or warded-off ideas.

Fear of Repetition

Any event that occurs once may recur; yet the anticipation of repeating painful stress events conflicts with the wish to avoid displeasure. Persons not only fear a real repetition; they also fear repetition in thought and emotion.

Chart 3-1
Common Concerns after Stressful Life Events

- Fear of repetition
- Fear of merger with victims
- Shame and rage over vulnerability
- Rage at the source
- Rage at those exempted
- Fear of loss of control of aggressive impulses
- Guilt or shame over aggressive impulses
- Guilt or shame over surviving
- Sadness over losses

The range of states of mind colored by fear are much like those states of mind colored by anxiety, as observed in bodily sensations and felt emotions. The main difference between the two sets of states is the nature of the thoughts and how they appraise external situations. When an external situation is judged in reality to be very threatening or dangerous, then the emotional quality may be labeled as fear; when the situation is judged as not really threatening, the affect is labeled as anxiety. Matters become complex because persons fear anxiety and are anxious about fear. And they become even more complex in regard to who judges how threatening the external situation really is to the particular individual or to the average individual.

It is in this context of the fear of repetition that the problems of diagnosing anxiety disorders develop. Many of the same signs and symptoms that characterize a phobic disorder may be found in a post-traumatic stress disorder. The fear of repetition leads persons to develop a phobic anxiety with any stimulus that can be associated to the previous traumatic event and to engage in a variety of marked withdrawal procedures. A person who has had an accident on the street may develop a phobic reaction not only to the specific street corner but also to any street corner and to traffic and may even withdraw into his or her home and be labeled as agoraphobic.

Sometimes a peripheral stimulus present during the traumatic event, such as the fragrance of flowers that was noticed at the scene of a previous attack in the park, may trigger a sudden fear response when the fragrance is smelled again. This may lead to a panic attack, with full-blown symptoms of pounding heart, weak knees, and choking sensations. At other times, there is no sudden acceleration of alarm responses but, rather, a constant sense of foreboding, impending doom, and a nameless dread constituting chronic anxiety. Sometimes the specific fear of repetition is relatively unconscious; only the dread seeps into conscious awareness. Then the anxiety is not associated with the memory of the stressful life event or the concern that it might be repeated.

Fear of Merger with Victims

Like the fear of repetition, there can also be a fear of the reenactment of events in which the injured person is now the self rather than the other person. For example, if one sees a suicide, one may fear committing suicide oneself.

Shame and Rage over Vulnerability

The expectation of personal omnipotence or total control is unrealistic but is nonetheless a universal hope and sometimes a deeply felt personal belief. Both the failure to prevent a stress event such as an accident and the weakness that may follow an event such as an illness are regarded as a loss of control and conflict with the wish for power and mastery. Persons who have had a heart attack or back injury, for example, may apologize profusely because they cannot carry out garbage cans, or they may unwisely carry them out to avoid a sense of shame for either shirking their duty or feeling useless. After a fire has burned down the family house, parents may feel deflated in the eyes of their children because their life is now uncomfortable, with smaller quarters and economic difficulties. Magical thinking often extends such irrational attitudes so that the inability to master a stressful event is regarded as equivalent to a regression to infantile helplessness.

Rage at the Source

Rage is a natural response to frustration. One important theme after stress events is anger with any symbolic figure who can be construed as responsible, however irrational this may seem. A patient may become angry with a doctor who tells him or her the bad news that a diagnostic study has revealed a serious and unexpected illness. A mother who cuts her finger while slicing meat may feel an impulse to say to a nearby child, "See what you made me do." Asking why it happened and why me, after a stress event, is usually associated with the need to find out who is to blame and who should be punished.

Rage frequently will conflict with a sense of social morality. For instance, a person may feel rage toward a friend who has fallen ill; and this rage conflicts with the recognition that the illness is not the friend's fault and that he or she needs help, not blame.

A less obvious but often important instance of rage at the source is the theme of resentment toward a person who has died. At an unconscious level, the deceased may be regarded not as a passive agent who has died but, rather, as an active agent who has deliberately abandoned the survivor. Thoughts directed toward the deceased are expressed as "How could you have left me now?" Knowing consciously and intellectually that the death was not deliberate may not prevent such an emotional and transient response. These themes may be based in part on unconscious views from childhood that parental figures will always be there, are omnipotent, and so can prevent bad things from happening to themselves if they really wanted to.

Rage at Those Exempted

If one has suffered a loss, perhaps the death of a loved one, it is possible to feel angry with those others—no matter how sympathetic they may be—whose loved ones remain alive. Such responses can range from envy to hatred and destructive wishes, even though such ideas seem irrational, undesirable, and unthinkable to the person who experiences them.

Fear of Loss of Control of Aggressive Impulses

There is another conflict between the destructive fantasies mentioned above and the wish to remain in control, and that is the fear that one will impulsively act out one's fantasies in an out-of-control manner. For example, a soldier traumatized by repeated combat experiences often fears, upon his return to civilian life, that he will physically attack persons who only slightly provoke him.

Guilt or Shame over Aggressive Impulses

The rage alluded to above often extends to destructive fantasies directed toward anyone symbolically connected to the stressful event. When violence is a part of the event, this itself seems to stimulate generalized aggression. The aroused hostility conflicts with a sense of conscience and leads to feelings of guilt or shame.

The urgent need to stare at a potential threat is another impulse that can evoke guilt or shame. This instinctive investigative gesture would seem to be free of conflict, but when other persons are the victims, it is not. For example, there may be severe bodily damage to others killed in an accident, in which both social convention and natural revulsion dictate looking away from maimed bodies or covering them up. Staring at dead bodies seems, to the person who does it, to be an unwarranted aggression. The memory of such episodes of compulsive looking can lead to anxiety or guilt if the person feels that he or she was morbidly curious and thus fails to recognize the presence of an intrinsic need to gain information about a potential threat.

Guilt or Shame over Surviving

When others have been injured or killed, it is a relief to realize that one has been spared. Once again, at a level of magical thinking there is a common irrational belief that destiny chooses an allotment of victims, as in the placation of primitive gods through human sacrifice. If one has eluded the Fates, it may seem to have been unfairly at the expense of other victims. The wish to be a survivor conflicts with moral attitudes toward sharing social pain, leading to self-castigation for being selfish.

Sadness over Losses

Any painful stress event contains an element of loss that conflicts with the universal wish for life permanence, safety, and satisfaction. The loss may be another person, an external resource, or an aspect of the self. Naturally, some losses are both symbolic and real. A person who has been laid off from work, not for personal reasons, but because a plant has closed, may suffer a loss of self-esteem because he or she has been prevented from working.

EMERGENCE OF THEMES

The frequency of these stress-related themes can be determined for stressed populations by defining their ideational and emotional components and independently rating their occurrence in clinical material, as described by Krupnick and Horowitz, 1981. Such studies indicate these themes' presence in many kinds of traumatic life events.

As mentioned earlier, these nine themes provide the ideational and emotional contents that are commonly warded off in periods of denial or are intrusive in periods of compulsive repetition. Any one of these themes merges the current stress event with earlier conflicts over previous stress events. Guilt over hostile impulses is too common in everyone's past history to be a theme unique to a current trauma. Rather, the current event will be emotionally associated to previous memories and fantasies of guilt over excessive hostility. Such blending of themes leads to a diagnostic dilemma requiring determination of how much of a given problem is due to the recent life event, however stressful, and how much is due to earlier developments.

DIAGNOSTIC PROBLEMS

Psychodynamic investigations of syndromes occurring after stressful life events demonstrate the intermingling of elements from earlier unresolved conflicts with response elements related to the recent experience (Windholz, 1945; Greenacre, 1952; Murphy, 1961; Solomon et al., 1971). Given that all psychological manifestations are determined by multiple causes, the question of diagnosis becomes one of the relative weights of possible etiological factors. The main problem is the existence, nature, and etiological importance of general stress response tendencies, as contrasted with idiosyncratic or person-specific variations in response to stress. This problem has proved to be so difficult that before DSM-III there was no really adequate diagnostic category for Traumatic Neuroses in the formal nomenclature.

In the official (1952) American psychiatric nomenclature (DSM-I) and in the 1968 revision (DSM-II), neuroses that followed major external stress events were classified according to their presenting symptoms, as were other types of neuroses, such as anxiety neurosis, obsessive compulsive neurosis, or hysterical neurosis. In DSM-I, symptomatic responses to very stressful experiences could also be classified as Gross Stress Reactions, but this category was later deleted in the DSM-II of 1968. The appropriate categorization became Transient Situational Disturbances, with subheadings of adjustment reaction of adult, adolescent, or childhood life.

Despite such vague official diagnostic definitions in the psychiatric literature, courtrooms, and case conferences, the diagnosis of traumatic neurosis was used frequently, and most agreed on what the term meant (Keiser, 1969). For example, in Hinsie's and Campbell's *Psychiatric Dictionary* (1960), traumatic neurosis was defined as having the following features:

> (1) fixation on the trauma with amnesia for the traumatic situation which may be total or partial; (2) typical dreamlife (dreams of annihilation, aggression dreams where the patient is the aggressor but is defeated, frustration or Sisyphus dreams, and occupational dreams in which it is the means of livelihood rather than the body-ego which is annihilated); (3) contraction of the general level of functioning, with constant fear of the environment, disorganized behavior, lowered efficiency, lack of coordinated goal activities, and profoundly altered functioning in the autonomic motor, and sensory nervous system; (4) general irritability; and (5) a proclivity to explosive aggressive reactions. (p. 497)

The term "fixation on trauma" in the preceding definition refers to the same phenomena that are labeled in Moore's and Fine's *Glossary of Psychoanalytic Terms* (1968) as "repetition compulsion," in the following psychoanalytic definition of traumatic neurosis:

> Traumatic Neurosis: A neurosis in which overwhelming tension and painful affects, such as anxiety or guilt related to a traumatic experience, can be mastered by the usual defenses of the ego. Pathological and archaic ego mechanisms are set in motion which determine a clinical picture dominated by somatic features and a repetition compulsion forcibly bringing to mind the original trauma. Symptoms include marked emotional lability, with uncontrollable discharges of anxiety, fear, or rage; severe disturbances of sleep, with typical dreams in which the trauma is painfully re-experienced; and mental repetitions in the waking state of the traumatic situation, in whole or in part, in the form of fantasies, thoughts, or feelings. Psychological mastery of the trauma is usually accompanied by recession of the traumatic elements and increasing prominence of psychoneurotic symptoms. (p.94)

These kinds of clinical summations and the reviews of evidence presented in the first edition of this work (Horowitz, 1976) and in many other journal articles, led to the DSM-III's inclusion of the diagnosis of Post Traumatic Stress Disorder. The diagnostic criteria are summarized in Chart 3-2, and at this writing, the revision of DSM-III is under way, and changes in the criteria's contents are being discussed.

Chart 3-2
Official Diagnostic Criteria for Post Traumatic Stress Disorder (DSM-III)

A. Existence of a recognizable stressor that would evoke significant symptoms of distress in almost anyone.
B. Reexperiencing of the trauma as evidenced by at least one of the following:
  (1) recurrent and intrusive recollections of the event
  (2) recurrent dreams of the event
  (3) sudden acting or feeling as if the traumatic event were recurring because of an association with an environmental or ideational stimulus
C. Numbing of responsiveness to or reduced involvement with the external world, beginning some time after the trauma, as shown by at least one of the following:
  (1) markedly diminished interest in one or more significant activities
  (2) feeling of detachment or estrangement from others
  (3) constricted affect
D. At least two of the following symptoms that were not present before the trauma:
  (1) hyperalertness or exaggerated startle response
  (2) sleep disturbance
  (3) guilt about surviving when others have not, or about behavior required for survival
  (4) memory impairment or trouble concentrating
  (5) avoidance of activities that arouse recollection of the traumatic event
  (6) intensification of symptoms by exposure to events that symbolize or resemble the traumatic event

---

Any diagnosis involves judgments about the intensity, frequency, timing, and relativity of various signs and symptoms. In the clinical observation of people after serious life events, there is a series of signs and symptoms that occur more or less together and have an overall quality referred to as *intrusion* in this text. They are summarized in Chart 3-3.

During the *intrusive* state, mental images in any sensory modality (visual, auditory, olfactory) may form as if they were real perceptions (Horowitz, 1983). A variety of imagery experiences are quite important in post traumatic stress disorders (Brett and Ostroff, 1985). In a *hallucinatory* experience, the person has sensations that he or she interprets as real but that have no external basis. In a *pseudohallucination*, the person sees the vivid subjective images as false signals of external reality but nonetheless responds emotionally as if they were real. These *unbidden images*, whether hallucinatory, pseudohallucinatory, illusory, or mnemonic, include sensing the presence of others who may have died during the traumatic event. And these images may be the source of paranormal phenomena, such as seeing or hearing ghosts of the deceased.

Such unbidden images tend to occur most frequently when the person relaxes, lies down to sleep, or closes his or her eyes to rest. Vivid sensory images occurring during periods of rest or relaxation constitute a *hypnagogic* phenomenon. A similar occurrence when awakening is

---

Chart 3-3
Symptoms and Signs Related to Intrusive Experience and Behavior

- Hypervigilance, including hypersensitivity to associated events
- Startle reactions
- Illusions or pseudohallucinations, including sensation of recurrence
- Intrusive-repetitive thoughts, images, emotions, and behaviors
- Overgeneralization of associations
- Inability to concentrate on other topics because of preoccupation with event-related themes
- Confusion or thought disruption when thinking about event-related themes
- Labile or explosive entry into intensely emotional and undermodulated states of mind
- Sleep and dream disturbances, including recurrent dreams
- Sensations or symptoms of flight or flight readiness (or of exhaustion from chronic arousal), including tremor, nausea, diarrhea, and sweating (adrenergic, noradrenergic, or histaminic arousals)
- Search for lost persons or situations, compulsive repetitions

---

called a *hypnopompic* phenomenon. These frightening experiences may lead to *anticipatory anxiety* about their recurrence or to *secondary anxiety* if the subject interprets the phenomenon as a sign of losing control or "going crazy."

Patients can immediately be reassured that hypnogogic phenomena and other unbidden perceptual and other imagery experiences are not serious portents of psychosis but are common in those who have experienced traumatic events. Reassurance is especially useful if denial states have created a latency period before the onset of an intrusive phase of response. In such instances, intrusive experiences come as a major surprise to a person who believes that he or she has already "mastered" the stressful life event.

Similarly, there is a set of signs and symptoms that often comprise a state of mind that can be labeled by the denial (not necessarily the defense mechanism) of the implications of a stressful life event. These experiences of a denial phase are summarized in Chart 3-4. In regard to perception and attention, the daze and selective inattention of the denial states contrast with the excessive alertness and startle reactions of the intrusive states. Denial experiences may include staring blankly into space, and even avoiding the faces of others who can provide emotional support. There may also be a narrowing of focus and a failure to react appropriately to new stimuli, with a sometimes stubborn adherence to tasks and stimuli considered important before the new and drastic changes in the life situation occurred. As well, there may be an accompanying inner sense of clouding of perception, with a feeling that the world has become gray, less colorful than before. This clouding of consciousness may include a diminished awareness of bodily sensations, even a feeling of being "dead in life" (Lifton, 1967).

This brings us to two important phenomena: (1) the sense of numbness that may be present during the denial phase and (2) its opposite, pangs of strong emotion that may characterize an intrusive phase. Numbness is not simply an absence of emotions; it is a sense of being "benumbed." The individual may actually feel surrounded by a layer of cotton or insulation. This emotional blunting may alter patterns of interaction with support systems, affecting family life, friendship, and work relationships. Members of the support network may be offended by this alteration in the nature of their relationship with the patient and so withdraw, reducing the person's support just when he or she most needs it.

These kinds of experiences or signs do not sharply differentiate the normal or abnormal responses to serious life events. Rather, along with

Chart 3-4
Symptoms and Signs Related to Denial or Numbing Experiences and Behavior

- Daze
- Selective inattention
- Inability to appreciate significance of stimuli
- Amnesia (complete or partial)
- Inability to visualize memories
- Disavowal of meanings of stimuli
- Constriction and inflexibility of thought
- Presence of fantasies to counteract reality
- A sense of numbness or unreality, including detachment and estrangement
- Overcontrolled states of mind, including behavioral avoidances
- Sleep disturbances (e.g., too little or too much)
- Tension-inhibition responses of the autonomic nervous system, with felt sensations such as bowel symptoms, fatigue, and headache
- Frantic overactivity to jam attention with stimuli
- Withdrawal from ordinary life activities

the diagnosis of mental disorder, they are a matter of degree and, to some extent, of personal as well as social value judgment and labeling. Chart 3-5 illustrates the relationship among common routes of response to serious life events and the pathological intensifications of each phase, which leads, in some instances, to the diagnosis of a mental disorder such as Post Traumatic Stress Disorder. Note that the route indicated suggests a general phasic tendency between denial and intrusions, across populations and types of stress events. This general tendency toward phases of response is reinforced by empirical findings when studied in groups but has many individual and situational variations (Horowitz, Wilner, Kaltreider, and Alvarez, 1980; Zilberg, Weiss, and Horowitz, 1982). The phases are described in more detail in Figure 3-1 (p. 41).

The frequency and intensity of these intrusive and denial signs and symptoms can be examined quantitatively, by obtaining a self-report form, using common assertions, and asking any new subject to agree whether or not that assertion could be made about his or her experiences during the past week. Clinicians can also judge the presence or intensity of a sign or symptom by using a rating scale. The Impact of Event Scale (Horowitz, Wilner, and Alvarez, 1979; Zilberg, Weiss, and Horowitz, 1982) measures the former, and the Stress Response Rating Scale (Horowitz, Wilner, Kaltreider, et al., 1980; Weiss, Horowitz, and Wilner, 1984) measures the latter.

Using these instruments on a series of 66 consecutive cases in our clinic treatment of stress response syndromes, we summarized the comparative frequencies and intensities of the various intrusive and denial experiences and manifest patterns. These data are summarized in Tables 3-1 and 3-2.

Both the self-report and the clinician's rating scale allow separate scores for intrusive and avoidance or denial experiences. In another study, we compared the mean scores of 38 patients for whom the inciting serious life event for a stress response syndrome was exposure to violence directed at the self and 43 cases for whom the inciting event was the death of a close relative or very close friend. There were no significant differences in the group mean scores on intrusion or avoidance in these groups, thus agreeing with the assertions made in this book that these are general stress response tendencies. But there were a few differences on specific items: The group exposed to violence reported more efforts to remove the event from conscious remembrance and more efforts not to allow their thoughts to turn to the event. The group who had experienced deaths often reported that they felt

---

Chart 3-5
Common Poststress Experiences and Their Pathological Intensification

COMMON ROUTES OF RESPONSE TO SERIOUS LIFE EVENTS	PATHOLOGICAL INTENSIFICATIONS
Event and immediate coping ⟶	Overwhelmed, dazed, confused
↓	
Outcry ⟶	Panic, dissociative reactions, reactive psychoses
↓	
Denial experiences ⟶	Maladaptive avoidances (withdrawal, drug or alcohol abuse, counterphobic frenzy, fugue states)
↑↓	
Intrusion experiences ⟶	Flooded and impulsive states, despair, impaired work and social functions, compulsive reenactments
↓	
Working through (blocked) ⟶	Anxiety and depressive reactions, physiological disruptions
↓	
Relative completion (not reached) of response ⟶	Inability to work, create, or feel emotions as a distortion of character

Table 3-1. Impact of Event Scale: Experiences Reported by 66 Subjects with Stress Response Syndromes (from Horowitz, Wilner, Kaltreider, et al., 1980)

	%[a]	GROUP MEAN[b]	SD
Intrusion Items			
I had waves of strong feelings about it.	88	3.8	1.9
Things I saw or heard suddenly reminded me of it.	85	3.7	1.9
I thought about it when I didn't mean to.	76	3.3	2.2
Images related to it popped into my mind.	76	3.2	2.2
Any reminder brought back emotions related to it.	76	3.0	2.1
I have difficulty falling asleep because of images or thoughts related to the event.	64	2.6	2.4
I had bad dreams related to the event.	44	1.7	2.2
Avoidance Items			
I knew that a lot of unresolved feelings were still there, but I kept them under wraps.	71	3.0	2.2
I avoided letting myself get emotional when I thought about it or was reminded of it.	70	2.8	2.1
I wished to banish it from my store of memories.	65	2.8	2.3
I made an effort to avoid talking about it.	61	2.2	2.0
I felt unrealistic about it, as if it hadn't happened or as if it wasn't real.	58	2.2	2.3
I stayed away from things or situations that might remind me of it.	53	2.2	2.3
My emotions related to it were kind of numb.	59	2.1	2.1
I didn't let myself have thoughts related to it.	50	1.8	2.2

[a]Percent positive endorsement.
[b]On a scale of intensity where 5 is severe; 3, moderate; 1, mild; 0, not at all (within the past seven days).

as if the event had not been real, or at least not completely real. Similarly, on the clinician's ratings, the group exposed to actual or severely threatened violence was rated as having more symptoms of hypervigilance, startle reactions, and more impairing bad dreams. Again, on most items there were comparably high scores that did not differentiate the groups. The data for these findings are presented in Tables 3-3 and 3-4. The scales are worded exactly as given to patients and clinicians. The stress response rating scale has been expanded to 40 signs and symptoms. The additions go beyond intrusive items (the 12 signs in Table 3-4) to include denial items and general stress reactivity. Table 3-5 lists the additional items.

Table 3-2. Stress Response Rating Scale: Signs and Symptoms Reported by Clinicians for 66 Subjects with Stress Response Syndromes (from Horowitz, Wilner, Kaltreider, et al., 1980)

	%[a]	GROUP MEAN[b]	SD
Intrusion Items			
Pangs of emotion	95	3.1	1.3
Rumination or preoccupation	90	2.9	1.4
Fear of losing bodily control or hyperactivity in any bodily system	82	2.6	1.5
Intrusive ideas (in word form)	77	2.3	1.5
Difficulty in dispelling ideas	74	2.1	1.6
Hypervigilance	69	1.6	1.4
Bad dreams	54	1.6	1.7
Intrusive thoughts or images when trying to sleep	51	1.6	1.8
Reenactments	57	1.5	1.5
Intrusive images	51	1.4	1.6
Startle reactions	34	0.6	1.0
Illusions	26	0.6	1.1
Hallucinations, pseudohallucinations	8	0.2	0.8
Denial Items			
Numbness	69	1.8	1.5
Avoidance of associational connections	69	1.7	1.4
Reduced level of feeling responses to outer stimuli	67	1.7	1.5
Rigidly role adherent or stereotyped	62	1.5	1.5
Loss of reality appropriacy of thought by switching attitudes	64	1.4	1.2
Unrealistic narrowing of attention, vagueness, or disavowal of stimuli	52	1.2	1.3
Inattention, daze	48	1.2	1.5
Inflexibility or constriction of thought	46	1.0	1.2
Loss of train of thoughts	44	0.9	1.2
Loss of reality appropriacy of thought by sliding meanings	41	0.8	1.2
Memory failure	34	0.8	1.2
Loss of reality appropriacy of thought by use of disavowal	25	0.6	1.2
Warding off trains of reality-oriented thought by use of fantasy	15	0.3	0.8

[a]Percent positive endorsement.
[b]On a scale of intensity where 5 is major; 3, moderate; 1, minor; 0, not present (within the past seven days).

Table 3-3. Impact of Event Scale: Self-Reports

On _____ you experienced _____.
    (date)   (life event)

Below is a list of comments made by people after stressful life events. Please check each item, indicating how frequently these comments were true for you *during the past seven days.* If they did not occur during that time, please mark the "not at all" column.

	MEAN ENDORSEMENT	
	VIOLENCE GROUP (n = 38)	DEATH GROUP (n = 43)
1. I thought about it when I didn't mean to.	3.39	3.64
2. I avoided letting myself get upset when I thought about it or was reminded of it.	3.32	2.88
3. I tried to remove it from memory.	3.50	1.95[a]
4. I had trouble falling asleep or staying asleep.	3.00	2.67
5. I had waves of strong feelings about it.	3.95	3.60
6. I had dreams about it.	1.87	1.09[b]
7. I stayed away from reminders of it.	2.66	2.12
8. I felt as if it hadn't happened or it wasn't real.	1.18	2.05[a]
9. I tried not to talk about it.	2.59	2.33
10. Pictures about it popped into my mind.	3.35	3.39
11. Other things kept making me think about it.	3.29	3.53
12. I was aware that I still had a lot of feelings about it, but I didn't deal with them.	3.16	3.52
13. I tried not to think about it.	3.34	2.40[a]
14. Any reminder brought back feelings about it.	3.78	3.77
15. My feelings about it were kind of numb.	2.26	2.53

Note: Intrusion subset = 1, 4, 5, 6, 10, 11, 14; avoidance subset = 2, 3, 7, 8, 9, 12, 13, 15. Mean scores on each item are based on a 5-point scale, where 0 = not experienced, 1 = rarely experienced, 3 = sometimes experienced, and 5 = often experienced during the last week.
[a]Value significantly different from value in violence group.
[b]Value marginally significantly different from value in violence group.

POST TRAUMATIC STRESS DISORDERS

As defined in DSM-III, the Post Traumatic Stress Disorders have criteria beyond symptoms and signs. As shown earlier, the first criterion (A) has a situational feature, the occurrence of an event that is "generally outside the range of human experience." This criterion also

Table 3-4. Stress Response Rating Scale: Clinicians' Ratings

Directions: Please judge the degree to which the following signs and symptoms describe the patient *within the last seven days only*. Do not spend too much time deciding about any one item. Base your judgments on either the history as reported, or your own observations. Check the appropriate line for each item. If you have absolutely no information for a particular item, and the not present response might inaccurately describe the subject's condition, then use the no information response, but use it sparingly. Scores are based on degree of presence with 0 = not present, 1 = minor, 3 = moderate, 5 = major.

| | MEAN ENDORSEMENT | |
| | VIOLENCE GROUP (n = 38) | DEATH GROUP (n = 41) |
SIGN OR SYMPTOM		
1. Hypervigilance: Excessively alert, overly scanning the surrounding environment, overly aroused in perceptual searching, tensely expectant.	2.38	0.56[a]
2. Startle reactions: Flinching after noises, unusual orienting reactions, blanching or otherwise reacting to stimuli that usually do not warrant such responses.	1.09	0.42[a]
3. Illusions or misperceptions: A misappraisal of a person, object, or scene as something or someone else (e.g., a bush is seen for a moment as a person; a person is misrecognized as someone else).	0.57	0.52
4. Intrusive thoughts or images when trying to sleep: Unwelcome and unbidden mental contents that may be difficult to dispel; include trains of thought that begin volitionally but develop an out-of-control quality.	2.22	1.43
5. Bad dreams. Any dreams experienced as unpleasant, not just the classical nightmare with anxious awakenings.	2.11	1.13[a]
6. Hallucinations, pseudohallucinations: A emotional reaction to imagined stimuli, experienced as if it were real, regardless of the person's belief in its reality. "Felt presences" of others as well as sensations of smell, taste, touch, movement, sound and vision are included, along with out-of-body experiences.	0.29	0.75
7. Intrusive images while awake: Unbidden sensations which occur in a nonvolitional manner either in visual or other sensory systems. Awareness of these images is unwanted and occurs suddenly.	2.06	2.31
8. Intrusive thoughts or feeling while awake: Unwilled entries of simple ideas or trains of thought and feeling taking unwilled directions.	2.08	2.68

(continued)

Table 3-4. *(Continued)*

SIGN OR SYMPTOM	MEAN ENDORSEMENT	
	VIOLENCE GROUP (n = 38)	DEATH GROUP (n = 41)
9. Reenactments: Any behavior that repeats any aspects of the serious life event, from minor tic-like movements and gestures to acting out in major movements and sequences, including retelling the event. Repeated enactments of personal responses to the life event, whether or not they actually occurred at the time of the event.	0.94	0.77
10. Rumination or preoccupation: Continuous conscious awareness about the event and associations to the event that go beyond ordinary thinking through. The key characteristic is a sense of uncontrolled repetition.	2.77	2.90
11. Difficulty in dispelling thoughts and feelings: Once a thought or feeling has come to mind, even if it was deliberate, awareness of it cannot be stopped.	2.2	2.68
12. Pangs of emotion: A wave of feeling that increases and then decreases rather than remaining constant.	2.89	3.08

^aValue significantly different from value in violence group.

asserts that the stressful event is "likely to produce significant symptoms of distress in most people" and is generally "beyond the range of such common experiences as a simple bereavement, chronic illness, business loss, or marital conflict." Yet because of some people's predisposition and situational circumstances, these eliminated events can produce the characteristic symptom pattern of overwhelming intrusion and maladaptive denial. This pattern may be similar to the symptom patterns in persons with stress events acceptable by DSM-III criteria, such as rape, assault, military combat, floods, earthquakes, car accidents with serious physical injury, airplane crashes, large fires, bombing, torture, death camps, and accidental man-made disasters. Some life events are not "outside the range of human experience" but are shocking and uncommon experiences for the individual who undergoes them for the first time.

The intrusive thoughts and feelings that may characterize a stress-induced disorder are not unique to the post traumatic stress disorders. They are a sign of strain to psychological systems in general and may occur in a variety of disorders, following internal stressful events such

Table 3-5. Other Signs and Symptoms of Stress for Clinician Rating on the Stress Response Rating Scale

13. Fears or sensations of losing bodily control: Sensations of urinating, vomiting, or defecating without will, fear of suffocating, fear of being unable to control voluntary behavior as well as somatic responses such as sweating, diarrhea, tachycardia.

14. Inattention, daze: Staring off into space, failure to determine the significance of stimuli, flatness of response to stimuli.

15. Memory failure: Inability to recall expectable details, sequences of event, or specific events.

16. Loss of train of thought: Temporary or micromomentary lapses in continuation of a communication, or report of inability to concentrate on a train of thought.

17. Numbness: Sense of not having feelings, or being "benumbed." (Note: Either patient report or your inference is acceptable here.)

18. Sense of unreality: Experiences of depersonalization, derealization, or altered sense of time and place.

19. Withdrawal: Feelings or actions indicating social isolation, or experiences of being isolated and detached.

20. Misdirection of feelings: Displacement of positive or negative feelings.

21. Excessive use of alcohol or drugs: Avoidance of implications of the event by increased usage. Alcohol: excessive usage. Drugs: abuse of prescription agents, as well as abuse of other drugs, legal and illegal.

22. Inhibition of thinking: Attempts to block thinking about the event. Success or awareness of the attempt is not a consideration.

23. Unrealistic distortion of meanings: Effects of the event on day-to-day living are inaccurately appraised.

24. Excessive sleeping: Avoidance of implications of the event by increased sleeping as well as by simply staying in bed.

25. Avoidance of reminders: Staying away from certain places, foods, or activities; avoiding photographs or other mementos.

26. Seeking of distracting stimulation or activity: Avoidance of the implications of the event by seeking excessive exposure to external stimuli or activities such as television, loud music, fast driving, sexual activity, voracious reading, or other diversions.

27. Hyperactivity: Fidgeting, markedly increased pace of activity, inability to slow down or stop sequences of actions; periods of frenzied activity.

28. Retarded pace of actions: Psychomotor retardation; clear slowing, either continuous or episodic, of thought or behavior.

29. Tremors or tics: Tremors or tics, including about the eyes and mouth. (Note: Basis of tremor or tic as neurological or characterological is irrelevant.)

30. Clumsiness or carelessness: Dropping objects, bumping into furniture, actions that are more than awkward.

31. Autonomic hyperarousal: Sweating, palpitations, frequent urination, altered skin color, altered pupil size, or other autonomic signs.

32. Troubled sleep: Inability to fall and stay asleep; bad feelings about or during sleep.

(continued)

Table 3-5. *(Continued)*

33. Restlessness or agitation: Report of inner sensations of agitation or action and behavior which is restless or agitated.
34. Excited states: Thought and action is dominated by excessively high rate of arousal, information processing, and expression. May include excessively high levels of sexuality, creativity, productivity, exercise.
35. Self-hatred: Uncontrollable suicidal preoccupation or gestures, self-loathing, or hostility toward a part of the body.
36. Rage at others: Uncontrollable hostility and anger, even if the target is unclear.
37. Panic or disintegration: Periods of high pressure, confusion, chaos, anxiety, and purposelessness.
38. Sadness: Uncontrollable sadness or grief; floods of despair, longing, pining, or hopelessness.
39. Guilt or shame: Out-of-control experience of remorse, sense of wrongdoing, or exposure of personal evil or defectiveness.
40. Irritability or touchiness: Relations with peers, children, or strangers that are either inwardly irritating or outwardly abrupt, hostile, and bristling.

as a shocking dream or nightmare. Intrusive thinking also may increase, with upsets caused by increases in internal conflict.

The Adjustment Disorders (another DSM-III category) and the Post Traumatic Stress Disorders are not etiologically distinguished, and the diagnosis of one or the other is made by balanced judgment. When an external event has been shocking to the individual and has been followed by intrusive thinking as well as the other cardinal symptoms, then the diagnosis of post traumatic stress disorder is probably the most specific. An example is a car accident such as Harry's in which a passenger is killed. This may be a common life event—to be in an automobile accident in which one is not hurt—but the trauma may cause the person to develop intrusive thinking with themes of guilt over being spared the fate of the passenger.

Similarly, the death of a loved one is an experience that all of us have to endure and is regarded as a common life event. An unexpected and possibly traumatic death is not a common experience, however. It requires readjustment and may be considered a possible precipitant of a post-traumatic stress disorder. Some persons may be more predisposed than others to such pathological states. By understanding the transactive etiology and combining predisposition and fairly universal psychological stress response tendencies, clinicians can make individual diagnoses. Some of these problems are illustrated in the following example (Horowitz, 1983).

THE CASE

Following his graduation from college, a 24-year-old man lived with his mother while working sporadically at jobs that he did not like. He occasionally dated but had never lived with a woman or with other roommates. He and his mother occasionally had loud verbal fights about domestic issues such as who would keep the apartment clean, and on occasion they had even been warned by the landlord that other tenants had complained about the noise.

One evening, after such an argument, his mother had crushing chest pains and shortness of breath. The young man called their family physician but reached an answering service. After some frustration, he was advised to call an ambulance to take his mother to the nearest emergency room. He became increasingly frantic when she lost consciousness and the ambulance had not yet arrived. He therefore took her to an emergency room in his own car and stayed at her side as she was wheeled to the intensive care unit. Shortly after intravenous treatment was started, monitors indicated a cessation of heartbeat. The woman was defibrillated and an airway passed into her trachea. Her son refused to leave and was pushed aside by the resuscitation team. Several urgent medical orders were given and then rescinded, and the young man wondered whether his mother was receiving adequate care.

Despite the resumption of heartbeat with defibrillation, there was again a cardiac arrest, and after a time his mother was pronounced dead. The young man wept, received some support from the emergency room staff, and then returned alone to his apartment.

For the next several days he remained at home by himself, felt sad, and occasionally cried. He then resumed his job and apparently worked well for two months but then began to function less well and was laid off. Within a few weeks he consulted a community mental health center because of depression. After the initial interview, a diagnosis of major depressive disorder was made because he had difficulty sleeping, had lost weight, had no appetite, had a loss of sexual interest, felt morose, and brooded most of the time.

After a few interviews it became apparent that his depressive symptoms seemed to be clearly related to the event of his mother's death. He reported that he had difficulty sleeping because of intrusive and repetitive images of his mother's head being yanked back while a laryngoscope was being forced, as he saw it, down her throat. He was enraged at the emergency room staff, who he felt had provided incompetent care. He blamed himself for not taking his mother more quickly to a better emergency room, without the telephone delay or waiting for an ambulance. In continued psychotherapy, he worked on the conflicting relationship with his mother, in which his ambivalence toward her before her death was also a prominent feature.

He remained angry about the care of his mother in the emergency room, sought legal advice, and brought suit against the hospital. Records of her treatment at the hospital emergency room were subpoenaed, and the defense counsel for the hospital obtained documents about the young man's treatment at the community mental health center, including the process notes of the therapeutic interviews.

In the ensuing trial, the relationship between the patient and his mother, the competency of her care in the emergency room, and the patient's reaction thereafter were the issues of concern. The following is an analysis of each of these points.

It was clear that the young man had had a somewhat turbulent relationship with his mother, with feelings of ambivalence toward her, as she had toward him, in the period before her death. This may have complicated his mourning process. In addition, the young man's personality characteristics, which included difficulty in relating to women, becoming independent, and making decisions, had led to previous episodes of depression, although he had never received a formal psychiatric diagnosis or treatment for a depressive disorder. He had, however, sought previous psychiatric consultations and had made some imcomplete starts on psychotherapy in college. His emotional pain following his mother's death was partly due to these preevent characteristics in his personality and to the ambivalence and guilt in his relationship with his mother.

In the process notes, the therapist at the community health center had recorded an interpretation made to this young man in which she had said that his anger with the hospital emergency room staff was an attempt to displace his anger with himself. This anger with himself was due to guilt over his argument with his mother and his own sense of having failed her. The therapist encouraged him to review more realistically the events leading to the death and to feel an appropriate level of remorse but not an exaggerated guilt. Even though this interpretation may have been accurate, it only indicates that there were complex themes involved in the development of this man's stress response syndrome with its phasic components of intrusion and denial.

The competency of medical care as an issue in the suit included both the degree of damage to the mother's chances of survival and the degree of damage done to the young man, as he witnessed the trauma of the treatments as well as his mother's death. In reviewing the mother's treatment in the emergency room, it was established that there had been some procedural errors and omissions but that these had been rapidly corrected and were not deemed to have caused her death. There was some impression of violence in the treatment, as in the passage of the laryngoscope, but the impact of this on the young man was partly due to his refusal to follow the staff's instructions to leave the room. In this case, the actions witnessed contributed to his syndrome but not to his mother's death. Although the perceptions led to memories intrusively recalled, it was felt that the inappropriate actions by the hospital staff were not significant in causing his reaction.

If this case had turned out differently, if the hospital had been found in some way responsible for precipitating some of the young man's psychological responses, an expert opinion might then have tackled the diagnostic problems. There might have been a debate among experts on post-traumatic stress disorders, about whether this patient warranted that diagnosis. After all, his initial diagnosis in the community mental health center was that of a depressive disorder, not a post-traumatic disorder or an adjustment disorder. His experience could also be seen as a simple bereavement, once the connection to the death of his mother was established, as most people do have to sustain at some time the death of one or both parents.

The arguments for this individual's being diagnosed as having a Post Traumatic Stress Disorder are that (1) the initial diagnosis of major depressive disorder was not based on the full information, (2) the death of the young man's mother was associated with visual traumatizations that had been shocking to him, and (3) his symptoms of repetitive and intrusive recollection of the emergency room scene were prominent. His reaction did involve preevent conflicts, invariably the case to some degree, but the context of the event was of sufficient severity to warrant the diagnosis.

From this case, we find that premorbid personality is involved even with reactions to shocking, unusual, and disastrous experiences. It is especially pertinent to how a person works through these experiences and when the person emerges from a period of symptomatology. Life events that seem commonplace, such as the death of a parent, are not necessarily simple bereavements but may have traumatic features for the individual. Finally, diagnoses are not mutually exclusive; a person may satisfy several diagnoses according to the DSM-III's criteria and clinical criteria. Thus, complex bereavements may be considered to be post-traumatic stress disorders.

OTHER TYPES OF DIAGNOSES

Post-traumatic Stress Disorder, Chronic Type

The diagnosis of post-traumatic stress disorder, acute type, is made when the onset of symptoms occurs within 6 months of the trauma and has lasted for less than 6 months. For example, the emergence of nightmares and unbidden images regarding a rape 5 months after the assault itself and continuing up to 11 months afterward is still considered an acute post-traumatic stress disorder according to the DSM-III's criteria. This should be differentiated from a chronic post-traumatic stress disorder in which the symptoms have lasted for 6 months or more. The duration of symptoms should also include the period of denial symptoms, when there has been a markedly diminished interest in activities, or feelings of detachment, estrangement, or constricted or numbed emotions. If, for example, the rape occurred in January, with a period of denial and numbing until August, followed by the onset of intrusion in September, and leading to diagnosis because of continued symptoms in October, then the situation is, according to the DSM-III's criteria, a chronic post-traumatic stress disorder. Despite the label chronic, there may be little difference between the chronic syndrome and an acute post-traumatic stress disorder.

Delayed Post-traumatic Stress Disorder

A delayed post-traumatic stress disorder, according to the DSM-III, refers to an onset of symptoms at least 6 months after the trauma. This latency period is common because defensive mechanisms may restrict association to the event until the person feels at some safe distance from it. Paradoxically, this sense of now being safe, often coupled with some perceptual reminder of the event, can trigger the onset of an intrusive phase of symptoms. This period may emerge first in the form of dreams about the event and then spill over to unbidden images in the daytime. Diagnosis is made more complicated because the person's wish to deny the association to the event may impede full expression of the association of ideas and feelings, so that the current symptomatology may not be related clearly to the event now more distant in time.

Chronicity

Despite the DSM-III's differentiation of acute, chronic, and delayed post-traumatic stress disorders, the actual clinical experience of them may be similar, whether or not the symptoms reach prominence within the first 6 months following the trauma, the second 6 months, or thereafter. Anniversary reactions, exactly one year after the event, may also evoke the beginning of an apparent post-traumatic stress disorder. The issue of chronicity arises when the disturbance goes on for several years or emerges after a delay of several years. In such instances, there is an even more complex compounding of personality characteristics and the response to the particular serious life event, and very severe life events may lead to further character changes beyond those that occur during adolescence and early adulthood. When a decade or so has passed since a single traumatic event, especially when time has passed since a string of traumatic experiences (as in combat or concentration camps), then the syndrome may be so complex that multiple diagnoses need to be made and carefully formulated in order to understand that individual.

Organic Brain Syndromes

In making both differential and comprehensive diagnoses, it is important to consider the possibility of concussion in acute physical traumas or malnutrition in prolonged stress responses. Very mild concussions may leave no immediate apparent neurologic signs but have residual long-term effects on mood and concentration (Trimble, 1981). Malnutrition during extended stressful periods may also lead to organic brain syndromes.

Persons with post-traumatic stress disorders commonly cope in ways that may lead to other disorders, such as turning to an excessive use of tobacco, alcohol, narcotics, sedatives, or food. If they present a mixed syndrome combining organic and psychological factors, one should make a diagnosis of each disorder concurrent with the diagnosis of post-traumatic stress disorder.

Adjustment Disorders

Adjustment disorders are defined by the DSM-III as maladaptive reactions to identifiable psychosocial pressures. For this to be the correct diagnosis, signs and symptoms should emerge within 3 months of the onset of the change in life circumstances. The signs and symptoms include a wide variety of disturbances in interpersonal and work functions as well as maladaptive extremes of anxiety, depression, rage, shame, and guilt. According to the DSM-III, if these signs and symptoms meet the criteria for another Axis I mental disorder, such as anxiety disorder or depressive disorder, the diagnosis of adjustment disorder should not be made.

The identifiable psychosocial pressures that may precipitate adjustment disorders include such changed life circumstances as divorce, difficulties with child rearing, illness or disability, financial difficulties, a new form of work, graduation, moving, retirement, and cultural upheaval.

The DSM-III lists subcategories for adjustment disorders, organized by the patient's predominant complaint about his or her subjective experience. Among the subtypes are depressed or anxious mood, other out-of-control emotional states (i.e., rage, shame), disturbance of social conduct, work or academic inhibition, and withdrawal from others. This is an open-ended diagnostic entity, with subtypes classified by surface phenomena.

Neither post-traumatic stress disorder nor adjustment disorder should be regarded as a minor mental disorder. In either instance, suicidal ideation may be high and severe dysfunction found in such areas as work, social life, and parenting. Although both disorders may cause high levels of personal distress, the prognosis for full recovery is usually excellent.

Brief Reactive Psychoses

Another diagnosis related to traumatic events is that of brief reactive psychoses. These conditions have a sudden onset immediately following exposure to stressful events.They may last for a few hours or for as long as two weeks. The clinical picture includes emotional turmoil and the presence of at least one gross psychotic symptom such as expressed delusions. This is what primarily differentiates a brief reactive psychosis from a post-traumatic stress disorder and an adjustment disorder.

To be diagnosed as having a brief reactive psychosis, the patient should have experienced a recent traumatic life event that lies outside the range of usual human experiences. Observations suggest that brief reactive psychoses are less common than are post-traumatic stress disorders.

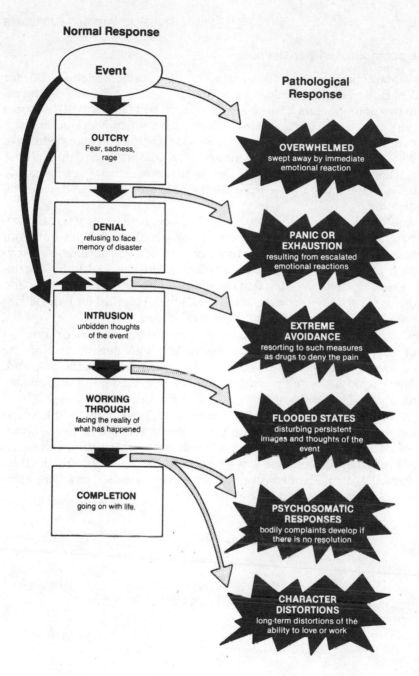

Figure 3-1. Normal and Pathological Phases of Poststress Response

Uncomplicated Bereavement

Many persons react to bereavement in a resilient manner. But for others, bereavement leads to a period of turbulent distress lasting up to two or more years (Osterweiss, Solomon, and Green, 1984). At some time during the year following a death, a person may episodically experience signs and symptoms that would constitute a major depressive disorder were they not transient and clearly connected to grief. These reactions may constitute a disorder, in that professional treatment may be indicated, but in the DSM-III they are not considered a mental disorder.

Medical disorders may be part of the bereavement reactions. Clinicians should take a careful history for increased alcohol consumption, being alert for cirrhosis of the liver, organic brain syndrome, and accident proneness. They should also ask about suicidal impulses, increased cigarette smoking and its cardiorespiratory consequences, and the use of sedatives or tranquilizers with their potential for habituation, paradoxic wakefulness, and other side effects.

Some circumstances are likely to increase the severity or duration of grief reactions, including a preexisting high dependency on the deceased, preexisting frustration or anxiety in relating to the deceased, unexpected or torturous deaths, a sense of alienation or antagonism to others, a history of multiple earlier or simultaneous losses that have not been integrated, and real or fantasied responsibility for the suffering or death itself. When several of these factors are present, a complicated bereavement reaction may result that warrants diagnosis as one of the anxiety or depressive disorders (including post-traumatic stress disorder), an adjustment disorder, reactive psychosis, or a flare-up of a preexisting personality disorder.

Chapter **4**

FIELD STUDIES ON THE
IMPACT OF LIFE EVENTS

With the assistance of Nancy Wilner

The clinical studies are of patients who present themselves spontaneously for treatment, and field studies are necessary to determine the generality of phenomena. Without field studies, one cannot know if the clinical observations are pertinent only to rare instances of "falling ill" or indicate general response tendencies.

MILITARY COMBAT

Field studies of stress require the natural occurrence of the same kind of disaster in a more or less extensive population. War, unfortunately, provides such conditions. The threat of death, maimed bodies, and the loss of comrades are common, and people often commit acts of violence and/or witness the consequences for others. Oddly enough,

43

even though there have been so many wars, psychological stress response syndromes were not fully recognized until World War II, as they had to be forced past considerable resistance. Physical causes were preferred as a basis for the theory, because psychological causation sounded too much like weakness, cowardice, or a lack of patriotism.

But the immense number of psychological casualties among combat soldiers, sailors, and airmen in World War I forced the recognition of some type of syndrome. Earlier observations had been made, such as De Costa's description of "soldier's heart" in the American Civil War, but they lacked psychological descriptors. Instead of calling them coronary symptoms due to the strains of combat, in World War I the presence of daze, fear, trembling, nightmares, and inability to function were sometimes attributed to brain damage. The cause was postulated to be cerebral concussions and the ruptures of small blood vessels caused by exploding shells, hence the then common term for traumatic war neuroses of *shell shock*. This organic focus led to a concentration on expectable symptoms such as those known to characterize acute and chronic brain syndromes. Earlier, at the end of the 19th century, traumatic neuroses after derailments and other train wrecks had been attributed to spinal concussions (Trimble, 1981).

Multiple observations eventually revealed that physical traumas were not invariably antecedents of combat reactions. Anyone exposed to constant death threats and terrible sights might respond with prolonged symptoms, even if he or she emerged physically unharmed and was exposed only once. Symptoms also appeared frequently in persons exposed to extended combat, with antecedent physical traumas not necessarily the cause.

The vast populations presenting symptomatic responses to psychologically traumatic events in World War II forced phenomenological studies of the symptoms' relative frequency (Archibald and Tuddenham, 1965). A good example is the study of combat reactions by Grinker and Spiegel (1945), whose summary of the 19 most common symptoms that persisted long after the soldiers were removed from combat are shown by rank order in Chart 4-1. The organization of tabulation, as in most phenomenological studies, is according to frequency of occurrence.

These symptoms are typical of those found in other studies of military combat. After World War II, Lidz (1946), Fairbairn (1952), and Brill and Beebe (1955) each described nightmares as significant signs of combat neuroses. More recent work by Haley (1974) on patients' reports of atrocities described Vietnam veterans who were depressed, anxious,

Chart 4-1
Most Common Signs and Symptoms of Operational Fatigue as Found by Grinker and Spiegel (1945) (in rank order by frequency)

1. Restlessness	11. Tremor
2. Irritability or aggression	12. Difficulty concentrating, confusion
3. Fatigue on arising, lethargy	13. Alcoholism
4. Difficulty falling asleep	14. Preoccupation with combat
5. Anxiety, subjective	15. Decreased appetite
6. Frequent fatigue	16. Nightmares
7. Startle reactions	17. Psychosomatic symptoms (e.g., vomiting, diarrhea)
8. Feeling of tension	
9. Depression	18. Irrational fears (phobias)
10. Personality change and memory loss	19. Suspiciousness

sad, rageful, and despairing. He saw their delayed reactions as including denial and leading toward intrusions, which also took the form of sleep disturbances and nightmares.

De Fazio (1975) also pointed to nightmares as a frequent psychological problem for Vietnam veterans. In 1982, Langley reported symptoms of guilt, depression, alienation, irritability, high stress, nightmares, flashbacks, and startle response in a group of Vietnam combat veterans who developed the additional problems of substance abuse and marital, legal, and vocational difficulties. In 1984, Silver and Iacono reported a study of 405 Vietnam veterans that supports the DSM-III's Post Traumatic Stress Disorder symptoms of intrusions, sleep disturbance, and difficulty concentrating. Similar important findings were also compiled by Figley (1978, 1979, 1984; Figley and Leventman, 1980) and Kolb (1982, 1983, 1984).

The categories of symptoms that Grinker and Spiegel slated for observation and codification may reflect the theory of that time. In his studies of post-traumatic neuroses of World War I veterans, Freud (1920) emphasized nightmares, one form of intrusive and repetitive thought, but had played down a similar phenomenon—recurrent unbidden images of frightening scenes that occur in waking thought:

> Now dreams occurring in traumatic neuroses have the characteristic of repeatedly bringing the patient back into the situation of his accident, a situation from which he wakes up in another fright. . . . I am not aware, however, patients suffering from traumatic neurosis are much occupied in their waking lives with memories of their accident. Perhaps they are more concerned with *not* thinking of it (p. 13).

Freud was partly incorrect, for recurrent memories such as unbidden images while awake are a much more common occurrence than Freud believed.

Wilson and Krauss (1982) made a systematic study of Vietnam veterans with and without post-traumatic stress disorder (see also Wilson, 1980; Hendin and Haas, 1984). Their results indicate that the best predictor of a post-traumatic stress disorder in Vietnam veterans is knowing the degree to which the person was involved in combat, felt stress during combat, was exposed to injury and death, and felt psychologically isolated upon returning home from the war (see also Vander Kolk, Blitz, Burr, et al., 1984). In a multiple regression analysis of the best predictors of seven post-traumatic symptoms such as intrusive imagery, depression, and problems of anger and rage, Wilson and Krauss found that the best predictive exponential variables for subsequent intrusive imagery were exposure to scenes of injury and/or death and psychological isolation upon coming home. Psychological isolation, but not injury and death, was the best predictive variable for the other six symptoms of post-traumatic stress disorder. This indicates that the intrusive and repetitive imagery from experiences of violence and death threats is often a specific stress response.

The expression "everyone has his or her breaking point" evolved from experience with reactions to combat. It suggests that every person, when exposed to enough stress, may show an acute stress response syndrome. Persons with certain latent neurotic conflicts or predispositions to certain stress triggers and alarm reactions may respond to lower levels of external stress (Hendin et al., 1983; Hendin, Hass, Singer, et al., 1983). Persons with a higher stress tolerance will not "break down" until the level of stress is higher. Brill (1967) observed that soldiers with preexisting neuroses had a seven-to-eight-times greater chance of psychiatric reactions than did those with more normal predispositional characteristics.

In a lengthy review of the literature, Hocking (1970) verified the hypothesis that individuals adjust differently to differing degrees of stress. In his view, prolonged, extreme stress results in neurotic symptoms in virtually every person exposed to it. He noted that of 303 individuals in military combat during World War II, more than half suffered from subsequent depression, insomnia, nightmares, anxiety, tension, irritability, startle reactions, impairment of memory, and obsession with thoughts of wartime experiences. Significant numbers of men were also observed to deny trauma by channeling their emotional difficulties into psychosomatic symptoms (see also the comprehensive review by Lewis and Engel, 1954).

Despite efforts to distinguish among the symptoms and signs of acute and chronic reactions (Kardiner and Spiegel, 1947), extended field studies indicate that these stress responses are not necessarily disparate, the main difference being the temporal onset or maintenance of the syndrome. It is clear that the phases of symptoms and signs may begin shortly after the stress event, may persist for a long period, or may begin only after a long latency period (Cobb and Lindemann, 1943; Baker and Chapman, 1962; Friedman and Linn, 1957; Popovic and Petrovic, 1965; Parkes, 1964; Davis, 1966; Horowitz, Wilner, Kaltreider, et al., 1980; Archibald and Tuddenham, 1965; Archibald et al., 1962).

CONCENTRATION CAMPS

Additional evidence regarding the duration of stress responses and the frequency of occurrence of stress symptoms arose from the most deplorable circumstances imaginable. Studies of concentration camp victims indicated that profound and protracted stress may have chronic or permanent effects no matter what the predisposition of the prestress personality. This evidence was found in the decades of studying the survivors of the Nazi concentration camps (Eaton, Sigal, and Weinfeld, 1982). Study after study, as reviewed in two workshops (Krystal, 1968; Krystal and Niederland, 1971), confirm the occurrence of stress response syndromes, persisting for decades, in major proportions of those populations who survived protracted concentration camp experiences. As just one example, 99 percent of the 226 Norwegian survivors of a Nazi concentration camp in World War II had some psychiatric disturbances when intensively surveyed years after their return to normal life. Of the total population studied, 87 percent had cognitive disturbances such as poor memory and inability to concentrate, 85 percent had persistent nervousness and irritability, 60 percent had sleep disturbances, and 52 percent had nightmares (Eitinger, 1969). It should be noted that the hideousness of these concentration camps also meant severe malnutrition and physical maltreatment that could have caused brain injury.

In addition to such general stress symptoms as recurrent intrusive memories, concentration camp survivors may have special symptoms and signs because of the protracted duration of their stress and the intensity of their dehumanization by the Nazis. Such signs as the synecdoche of success, the bleaching away of childhood memories, and the altered schemata of self- and object relationships may distinguish the survivor syndrome of concentration camp victims from stress response syndromes in general (Ostwald and Bittner, 1968; Krystal, 1968; Furst, 1967; Lifton, 1967).

The effects of being a victim of a concentration camp can lead to changes in personality and so to changes of interpersonal patterns, including those of parenting. The result is that the effects of the concentration camp may be visited onto the children of the victims and perhaps to succeeding generations (Krystal, 1985). These generations of families thus become carriers of conscious and unconscious values, myths, fantasies, and beliefs as well as actual interpersonal transactive styles that may have been forcibly changed by the violent life experiences of one generation (Danieli, 1982).

To recapitulate, though not negating the powerful influence of pre-stress personality configurations, findings from large groups of persons exposed to the most severe stress indicate that stress response syndromes are not necessarily limited to any subgroup of the exposed populations. There is no doubt, then, that some general stress response tendencies can be found.

THE CONCEPT OF PHASES OF STRESS RESPONSE

War and concentration camps produce extraordinary strain, but even so there seem to be phases of response in which denial or intrusive symptoms and signs may predominate.

Shatan (1973), in a study of Vietnam veterans 24 months after combat, noted the presence of intrusiveness in the form of insomnia, nightmares, and restlessness that may not have surfaced during combat and demobilization, when denial and numbing may have predominated. Shatan observed that the delay in the manifestation of these symptoms caused the government physicians to assume that the Vietnam War produced fewer psychiatric casualties than may actually have been the case. Horowitz and Solomon (1975, 1978) described the differences between soldiers under great protracted combat stress during World War II and those in Vietnam. Soldiers in combat in World War II went initially into a period of denial and numbing, but they did, nonetheless, remain at the front. The stress mounted, and when it exceeded the person's ability to maintain denial, then experiences characteristic of intrusive and repetitive feelings emerged.

In Vietnam, because of repeated rotation to relative safety, Horowitz and Solomon presumed it was possible for many soldiers to enter and remain in the denial phase. Other elements, such as the availability of drugs, the lack of group fidelity, and the opposition to the war, contributed to a state of alienation characterized by depersonalization and isolation.

Upon return to the United States, there would be a period of relief and well-being, and the denial and numbing would continue for a while. Ultimately, with the relaxation of defensive and coping operations, the person might then enter the painful phase of intrusive recollection (Egendorf et al., 1981).

For whatever combination of reasons, during the combat period of the Vietnam War, there was a general impression that levels of traumatic disorders were lower than they were during World War II. A period of controversy followed the combat period as to the prominence of Post Traumatic Stress Disorders in veterans, succeeded by a growing recognition of relatively widespread problems in the veterans. One issue was the emergence, after the Vietnam War, of a new official nosology, DSM-III, with the diagnostic composition of Post Traumatic Stress Disorder, as we have discussed.

It may be more useful in some cases to think in terms of Post Traumatic Character Disorders, although there is no official inclusion of such a term in the nomenclature. The reason is that wars are often fought by combat troops in late adolescence or very early adulthood. Identity is not completely consolidated, and the traumatic experiences of the war become incorporated into self schemata and concepts of the relationship of self to the world. A confusing situation, including the domestic unpopularity of the war, faced the veterans returning from Vietnam and alienated many of them. This situation combined with predisposition before the war, the war itself, and atrocities observed or committed to alter personality while it was being formed and re-formed during an important developmental phase. Problems resulted in self definition, self coherence, and self articulation to domestic society.

Excessive adherence to official diagnostic labels may inhibit individualized case formulations along these lines. Character development occurs throughout adult life, and massive trauma or prolonged strain affects this process. Prolonged denial or intrusion phases become, in some, new features of personality.

Concentration camp survivors sometimes exhibit such effects. Chodoff (1970) observed a sequence of reactions to concentration camp life in his studies of these victims and described this sequence in terms of stages. First was the universal response of shock and terror upon arriving at the camp. This fright reaction was generally followed by a period of apathy and often by a longer period of mourning and depression. The apathy was psychologically protective, by providing a kind of emotional hibernation. Lifton (1967) suggested that this kind of depression might, in part, be characterized as a delayed mourning reaction, as the victims were unable to engage in a ceremonial mourning for their dead. Gorer too, (1965), emphasized the connection between ritual and mourning and the maladaptions that may result if distress is not worked through in this personal and expressively social form.

As an adaptive measure, regression was a stage noted in many prisoners of war, as the result of overwhelming pressures. Docility and submissiveness were the products of the victims' dependency on their masters. Some identification with the aggressor was observed, and irritable behavior was discharged in petty fights with other prisoners.

The most important defenses among concentration camp inmates during their imprisonment were denial and isolation of affect. Chodoff named the most distinctive, long-term consequence of Nazi persecution observable over a 30 year period as the "concentration camp syndrome." Invariably present in this syndrome is some degree of felt anxiety, along with irritability, restlessness, apprehensiveness, and startle reactions. These anxiety symptoms are worse at night, accompanied by insomnia and nightmares, which are simple or slightly disguised intrusive repetitions of the traumatic experience.

Lifton pointed out the significance of psychic numbing in the behavior of Jews in Nazi camps, stating that anyone encountering such massive death will experience a cessation of feeling, a desensitization or psychic numbing. An element of this kind of denial is the need to "see nothing," for if it is not "seen," it is not happening. Added to this is the severing of human bonds of identification. "I see you dying, but I'm not related to you in your death." Lifton also described two kinds of numbing—the apathy of the "walking corpse," or the "know nothing" who acts as though death does not exist.

From this a collaborative numbing emerges, an equalizer between the victim and the victimizer, in which the Jew, the victim, does not exist, and the Nazi, the victimizer, is omnipotent but denies the human consequences of his or her actions. Such numbing and denial may be followed, even years later, by a phase of the intrusive repetition of ideas and feeling related to the earlier warded-off events.

NUCLEAR HOLOCAUST

Based on interviews with 75 survivors, made 17 years after the United States dropped an atomic bomb on Hiroshima, Japan, Lifton (1967) described the experience as a permanent encounter with death, consisting of four phrases. This first was an overwhelming immersion in death, a "death in life" feeling similar to that of the concentration camp victims. This phase was dominated by elements of extreme helplessness in the face of threatened annihilation and surmounted by an extremely widespread and effective defense mechanism which Lifton called "psychic closing off," a cessation of feeling within a very short period of time. The unconscious process was described as closing oneself off from death, the controlling fantasy being "If I feel nothing, then death is not taking place." It is thus related to the defense mechanisms of denial and isolation, as well as to the behavioral state of apathy, and is distinguished by its global quality, a screen of protection against the impact of death in the midst of death and dying. This response to an overall exposure to death merges with longer-term feelings of depression and despair, mingled with feelings of shame and guilt. The guilty fantasy "I am responsible for his death; I killed him" is interwoven with the shameful fantasy "I should have saved him or helped him."

The second phase of the Hiroshima encounter with death is called the "invisible contamination," in which symptoms of radiation sickness appeared at unpredictable intervals of weeks or months after the bomb had been dropped. There was a fear of epidemic contamination, a sense of individual powerlessness in the face of an invisible agent, and a denial of illness when the symptoms did appear.

The third phase, which occurred after many years, with the experience of later radiation effects, was an undercurrent of imagery of an endless chain of potentially lethal impairments that, if not evident that year or five years later, would appear in the next generation.

The fourth phase was that of a lifelong identification with death and dying, which Lifton explained as the survivors' means of maintaining life. Because of the burden of guilt they carry for having survived, the survivors' obeisance before the dead is their best means for justifying and maintaining their own existence and is a continued preoccupation.

Lifton also described the survivors' residual problems, especially those of psychological imagery, which manifest themselves in various ways. Among them he noted a profound impairment of the sense of invulnerability; a sense of being among the "elite" who have mastered death and, paradoxically, a sense of vulnerability to it at any time. Many victims carried with them, 17 years later, intrusive images of the horror of that day and the days immediately after and talked of still seeing pictures in their minds of people walking slowly in the streets, their skin peeling off.

A profoundly ambivalent pattern emerged of both seeking help and resenting it. Working through this event, Lifton felt, was a reformulation, a way of establishing an inner ideology as a means of dealing with overwhelming feelings, creating a new reality within which the victims could understand and master their experiences and their feelings of shame and existential guilt. Faced with this form of guilt, with resistance to establishing trust in the human order, the survivors of concentration camps, of atomic bombing, and of Vietnam need a new identity, a sense of connection with people, and meaning and significance for their life, in order to come to terms with the past disaster and the world in which they continue to live.

DISASTERS

The term *post-traumatic neurosis* was coined by those physicians who studied and treated victims of railway accidents late in the 19th century. The general signs and symptoms that followed derailments were more severe than those noted in persons knocked down in the streets by horses or carts, despite the absence of neurologically diagnosed physical injury, and this was thought to be due to the unusual fear and dread involved. As well reviewed by Trimble (1981) the term *traumatic neurosis* was first used in this situation by Oppenheim, who wrote in 1905 a major text on neurology, noting that the syndrome might appear after any injury or surgical operation. He wrote that traumatic neurosis was clearly different from hysteria, although this differentiation was disputed by other leading physicians. Gradually, studies of natural and man-made disasters indicated that although stress might precipitate a variety of syndromes, including post-traumatic psychoses and dissociative episodes, the post-traumatic stress disorders were noted in discrete. neurotic-level forms (Keiser, 1968).

The signs and symptoms characterizing both the denial and the intrusion phases of stress response syndromes have been noted in modern studies of disaster (Green, 1982). These symptoms are found more frequently and prominently in those persons exposed to a disaster who have had the greatest levels of shock, injury, or loss (Green, Grace, and Glesser, in press). Treatment by psychotherapy helps reduce these symptoms (Lindy, Green, Grace, and Titchner, in press). Premorbid culture and the social environment—whether supportive or neglectful, benign or hostile—also influence the course of recovery from stress response syndromes (Green, Wilson, and Lindy, 1985; Boehnlein, Kinzie, Ben, and Fleck, 1985).

For example, the skywalk of a prominent hotel in Kansas City fell to crush, injure, or threaten hundreds below in a crowded social gathering. Wilkinson (1983) studied the 102 survivors during the five months following the disaster. Of these, 88 percent had a significant degree of intrusive episodes of thought and feeling. Repeated recollections of the disaster were reported as symptoms in 83 percent of the 52 men and in 94 percent of the 50 women studied. Recurrent feelings, usually of anxiety and depression, were found in 54 percent of the sample, again more in women (60 percent). Difficulty concentrating was found in 44 percent of the sample. The victims and observers of the falling skywalk suffered more often from such symptoms as intrusion and ease of startle than did those persons in the sample who served as rescuers. Themes of survivor guilt were prominent in the bereaved, and many needed to talk over and over again about what happened. Post-traumatic symptoms may also be found in secondary disaster victims, those who recover and sort human remains (Jones, 1985).

Similar findings were noted in several studies of the survivors of the Buffalo Creek Disaster. The Buffalo Creek Disaster occurred when a large upstream body of water was suddenly released, forming a gigantic wave that tore through a West Virginia town, killing 125 people and rendering the entire population of 5,000 homeless. Erickson (1976) described these survivors in some of the same terms used by Lifton to describe the survivors of Hiroshima. Some were demoralized, disoriented in terms of life plans, and apathetic. In a separate study of some of the same people, Titchner and Kapp (1976) found post-traumatic neurotic symptoms in 80 percent of the group interviewed, with a prominence of unresolved grief, survivor shame and guilt, and feelings of impotent rage and hopelessness even two years after the traumatic event.

Children, with their varied mind development at rapidly changing stages, may have some of the same, or different, characteristics of responses. An example is Terr's (1981, 1983) reports on the responses of the Chowchilla survivors. This study is about 23 to 25 of the 26 children who in 1976 were kidnapped from their Chowchilla, California, school bus. Three kidnappers drove them for about 11 hours in two vans with blackened windows and then buried them alive in a truck-trailer under the ground in a covered hole. The children and their bus driver remained there for 16 hours, uncertain of their fate, until two of the kidnapped boys dug a tunnel out to summon help. Terr was able to follow these children and to report their status four years later.

Every one of the 25 child victims suffered from persistent fears, although after four years, 19 reported spontaneous resolution of some of these fears. Eighteen of the 25 youngsters, mostly between 10 and 15 years of age, suppressed any thoughts about the kidnap experience. Although the children had visual memories of the events, they were like daydreams and not accompanied by signs of acute distress or a sense of intrusiveness (except when they occurred as nightmares or hallucinations). Misperceptions and perceptual overgeneralizations led to startle reactions.

Unexpected, sudden reminders could evoke sensory memories and precipitate extreme anxiety in some of these children. Although five children had terrifying dreams in the first year after the kidnapping, 12 described them in later follow-up interviews, after more than two years had passed. Sometime during the four years, 18 of the children had played out repetitively some theme clearly related to the traumatic events. Some of the children denied the post-traumatic symptoms, but, Terr felt that every child she studied suffered from a post-traumatic stress response syndrome but that the numbing, amnesias, and intrusive, dysphoric flashbacks seen in traumatized adults were not prominent in this population.

Because there are variations in predisposing character and culture, post-traumatic social and environmental influences, and age and status, it is hard to predict how many members of a given population will develop what type of stress response syndrome after a disaster. Some indication is offered, however, by epidemiological studies that sample a large population containing persons who have and have not been exposed to a given event. Robins and colleagues (Robins, Smith, Cottler, et al., 1985) studied a group of 43 persons exposed to flood, tornado, or toxic contaminations and compared their responses to those of a well-selected group of 325 similar people who had not been exposed. Over half of the exposed persons had three or more symptoms of Post Traumatic Stress Disorder, although only 2 of the 43 warranted a diagnosis as circumscribed in DSM-III. This contrasted with 10 persons, about 3 percent, of the sample of unexposed persons, one of whom warranted the diagnosis of Post Traumatic Stress Disorder. Of the exposed group, 8 percent warranted the diagnosis of phobic disorder, compared with 4 percent of the unexposed group. In addition, 27 percent of the exposed group reported their health to be only fair to poor, contrasted with 8 percent of the nonexposed group. The more directly exposed persons in such samples, as already mentioned, tend to exhibit greater morbidity (Smith, Robins, Cottler, et al., 1985). The best predictors of post-trauma symptoms were degree of exposure and the number of symptoms the individual subject experienced before the event. Sex differences were not noted.

In similar studies, Shore, Tatum, and Vollmer (1985) found that persons involved in the Mount St. Helen's volcanic eruption disaster had significant elevations in the frequency of three psychiatric disorders when compared with an epidemiologically similar group. These disorders were Post Traumatic Stress Disorders, Generalized Anxiety Disorders, and single epidoses of Major Depressive Disorder. In this sample females showed higher incidences of the conditions than did males, and morbidity increased between year one and year three after the disaster. Women between 36 and 50 years of age seemed the most susceptible (Tatum, Vollmer, and Shore, 1985).

To recapitulate, such field studies confirm the findings of clinical investigations of the psychological response to external stress events. As in clinical observation, a phasic tendency was noted. Intrusive repetitions may coexist or alternate with periods of denial and numbness. Like repetitions, the periods of numbness and denial are relatively involuntary. Finally, these phases are perhaps most clearly seen in bereaved persons, whether the bereavement comes from the loss of another or the threat of one's own death.

BEREAVEMENT

Much of the literature on bereavement was summarized by Parkes (1964), later expanded through his own studies (1970, 1972; Parkes and Weiss, 1983), and has been reviewed recently by Raphael (1983) and Osterweiss, Solomon, and Green (1984). Bowlby (1961, 1969, 1980) has also reviewed the material.

Parkes referred to the now-classic paper by Lindemann (1944) on the varieties of reactions to bereavement found in a mixed group of psychiatric and nonpsychiatric patients. He noted that Lindemann did not show the relative frequency of the various syndromes that he described, nor did he indicate how long after bereavement his interviews took place. Lindemann defined acute grief as a definitive syndrome with psychological and somatic symptomatology, which may appear immediately after a crisis or may be delayed. He described it as uniform, in that it is expressed by waves of anxiety and panic that are defended against by denial of the event and by avoidance (i.e., of visits from others, of mentioning the deceased, or of expressions of sympathy by others). He explained the use of denial as motivated by

fear of loss of control and emphasized the importance of the possibility of underreaction as well as overreaction.

Parkes felt that although Lindemann's studies gave a fair picture of
the overall reaction, they failed to reveal the relationships between the
phases described and the variations of each phase over a period of time.
They particularly did not explain how long the various phases of grief
could be expected to last, nor did they delineate what was a pathological, as opposed to a normal, variant of grief.

To answer some of these questions, Parkes (1970) interviewed 22
London widows at 3-month periods for 13 months after their bereavement. These widows were felt to be showing typical grief reactions: of
the 22, only 6 felt that they had fully accepted the news when they were
told that their husbands would die; 8 frankly disbelieved it. As a result
of these interviews, Parkes was able to find phases of reaction.

Denial-Numbing

The initial, immediate reaction is described by Parkes as a state of
numbness, often preceded by an expression of great distress. Although
this sense of numbness was a relatively transient phenomenon, some
form of denial of the full reality of what had happened often persisted.
One year later, 13 widows said there were still times when they had
difficulty believing in the reality of their husbands' deaths. Bowlby, too
(Bowlby and Parkes, 1970), had revised his classification of the phases
of mourning to introduce numbness as the initial phase. This is re-
flected, in Parkes's study, in affective reports of one group that showed
little or no affect in the first week, not much in the second, but moder-
ate-to-severe disturbance by the third month.

A second group showed a steady increase in affect over a period of
time, and a third group, which showed moderate or severe affect in
the first week, tended to remain disturbed during the first two months
but improved thereafter. Each widow seemed to have her own way of
mitigating her feelings. These included a blocking out or denial of affect, partial disbelief, an inhibition of painful thoughts and evocation
of pleasant ones, and an avoidance of reminders.

In 1960, Lindemann noted another form of mitigation that he called
selective forgetting. In this phenomenon the image of the deceased person is lost from consciousness. This observation was supported by
Parkes and illustrated by a woman in his sample who could not recall
the face of her husband during the first month after his death, although
in ensuing months she had a clear visual memory.

Intrusive Repetitions

Parkes indicated the presence of intrusive thinking, often in the form of misidentification illusions (seeing the deceased in a stranger) or of hypnogogic hallucinations (Marris, 1958). For example, one woman felt initially stunned and angry after the death of her husband. For the next few days she kept busy, and then, five days later, she said that something invaded her; a presence almost "pushed her out of bed." It was her husband, and the experience was "terribly overwhelming." During this period, the widows' feelings were seldom admitted fully to consciousness, and their minds were often distracted from the loss, but there were periodic breakthroughs.

Bowlby called the second phase, the one following numbing, "yearning" or "protest." Parkes emphasized this phase as well, indicating four components: (1) pining and preoccupation, (2) direction of attention toward places and objects associated with the lost person, (3) development of a perceptual set for the deceased, and (4) crying for him or her. Parkes pointed out, too, that hallucinations and illusions occurred and noted that they have always occupied a prominent place in folklore, especially in the form of ghosts and in the concept of being haunted.

Parkes postulated that a widow who had fully accepted bereavement and made a good adjustment would be able to look back on the past with pleasure and into the future with optimism. But after 13 months, only 3 widows satisfied his criteria, 6 found the loss too painful to think about, 9 found it more pleasant than unpleasant, and 7 had mixed feelings.

In Lindemann's earlier account (1944) he stated that after eight to ten interviews within a period of four to six weeks, in which psychiatrists facilitated grief work, it was possible to complete the working-through of ordinary, uncomplicated grief reactions. He was referring to families of victims of the Coconut Grove fire, who suffered no anticipatory grief, who participated in "group mourning," and received much sympathy and support. Lindemann's statement had caused Parkes to underestimate the duration of uncomplicated and oftentimes anticipatory grief; he ultimately determined that it was necessary to follow the bereaved for a two- to three-year period.

Parkes (1970) interpreted his study as confirming Bowlby's belief that grief is a phasic process, although transitions from one phase to another are seldom distinct. In 1972, Parkes distinguished seven phases of mourning: (1) initial denial and avoidance of loss; (2) alarm reactions such as anxiety, restlessness, and physiological complaints; (3) searching, an irrational urge to find the lost person; (4) anger and guilt; (5) feelings of internal loss; (6) adoption of traits or mannerisms of the deceased; and (7) acceptance and resolution, including appropriate changes in identity.

Grayson (1970) found a similarity between the grief reactions to the loss of real objects and the loss of intangibles, particularly missed experiences and relinquished hopes. The process of diminishing the force of these wishes requires the same working through to completion as does the mourning process (Lewis, 1961; Rees, 1970). Grayson found abreaction and catharsis to be valuable discharges of affect without which decathecting would take longer and be less complete. He emphasized the need for persons to break through the phase of denial in order to face the painful reality of the missed experience.

Gorer (1965) also agreed with the theory of phases, having studied 35 bereaved people who sought psychiatric help because they suffered from prolonged grief, delayed reaction, vivid nightmares, or an absence of grief that signified that all was not well. Gorer described the most characteristic feature of grief not as prolonged depression but as acute and episodic pangs or episodes of severe anxiety and psychological pain that begin within a few hours or days after bereavement and reach a peak of severity within two weeks. At first they are frequent and spontaneous, but as time passes, they become less frequent and occur only when something brings the loss to mind.

Gorer noted the phenomenon of searching that fills the gap between aim and object and gives a sense of the deceased's continued presence. He explained avoidance of the full reality of the loss as a way of mitigating the pain of grieving and as a necessary part of distancing so that implications could be slowly worked through and dealt with cognitively. Gorer also observed the presence of two opposing tendencies: an inhibitory tendency that, by means of repression, avoidance, and postponement, holds back or limits the perception of disturbing stimuli; and a facilitating or reality tendency that enhances perception of and thoughts about disturbing stimuli. He pointed out that over a period of time, an individual will often oscillate between the two tendencies so that periods of intense feeling will alternate with periods of conscious or unconscious avoidance. He also found no clear ending to grief but, rather, a turning point that reflects the abandonment of old modes of thought and behavior.

Glick, Parkes, and Weiss (1975) found that widows in the first year after their husbands' death usually could not enter into a new relationship without concomitant feelings of disloyalty toward the dead spouse.

This indicated a sex difference, as the widowers in their study did not feel that a new relationship would conflict with the memory of commitment and fidelity to the deceased wife. Instead, widowers often established a new quasi-marital relationship within a few months of their wife's death and expected sympathy from the new companion for their continued grieving for their dead wife.

In addition to sexual differences, there are cultural differences in response to bereavement that may be related to different views of the meaning of death, different patterns of attachment, different rituals and responses to loss, and other factors (Eisenbruch, 1984; Windholz et al., 1985). Nonetheless, tendencies toward intrusive experiences, including hallucinatory experiences of the deceased, and toward denial experiences, including denial of the fact of death itself, are found in some individuals cross-culturally. Across cultures, intense grief and mourning responses are expected to last up to a year after the death, often with a ritual at that time to mark a return to social availability (Rosenblatt et al., 1976).

Life events questionnaires, as reviewed by Horowitz et al. (1977), are a way of surveying the distress experienced by groups of individuals after a variety of events. The most devastating life event is usually thought to be the death of a child. As just one example of many studies, marital discord and divorce were reported in 50 to 70 percent of families whose child died from cancer (Kaplan, Grobstein, and Smith, 1976; Strauss, 1975).

DEATH OF A PARENT

By selecting a specific type of bereavement, such as the death of a parent, it is possible to compare the experiences of persons who do and do not seek help in dealing with the trauma and their responses to it. The death of a parent is a common event, one that most adult children of living parents come to expect with the advancing age of their mothers and fathers. Yet such deaths have an impact, as both the current loss and the past meaning of the relationship are reconsidered, with concomitant reflection on self-concepts. In some persons, intrusive and denial phases may be prominent.

In a series of papers, our own research group reported on the quantitative and clinical studies of field subjects who experienced a parental death and went through 2-, 6-, and 13-month evaluation sessions of their responses, and of patients who sought brief psychotherapy because of neurotic-level symptoms precipitated by the death of a parent (Horowitz, Wilner, Marmar et al., 1980; Horowitz, Krupnick, Kaltreider et al., 1981; Horowitz, Marmar, Weiss et al., 1984; Horowitz, Weiss, Kaltreider et al., 1984; Horowitz, Marmar, Krupnick et al., 1984; Kaltreider, Becker, and Horowitz, 1984; Kaltreider and Mendelson, 1985).

In the initial evaluations, intrusion levels were high on the self-report in 33 percent of the field subjects and at medium levels in 39 percent. High levels were defined clinically as the level of signs and symptoms that merited concern, that diagnostic, evaluative, or treatment procedures were clearly warranted, and that the person was more likely to be in a problem or pathological category. Medium levels were defined as a clinical level of concern with complaints or signs that gave a global indication of a condition that warranted further diagnostic, evaluative, or treatment procedures, even though the severity was not marked. Though the patient sample had higher levels of distress, as shown in Table 4-1, there was a subpopulation among the field subjects that was also high in distress, as shown in Table 4-2. Table 4-3 shows the same data 13 months after the death of the parent.

Table 4-1. Differences between Groups at First Evaluation

| | MEAN (SD) | | | | |
PRIMARY DISTRESS VARIABLES[a]	PATIENTS (N = 31)	FIELD SUBJECTS (N = 36)	t	P	ω^{2}[b]
Self-rating					
Intrusion (IES)	21.52 (7.99)	13.83 (9.05)	3.66	.001	.16
Avoidance (IES)	20.74 (9.64)	9.69 (9.66)	4.67	.000	.24
Depression (SCL-90)	1.75 (1.00)	0.81 (0.78)	4.30	.000	.21
Anxiety (SCL-90)	1.22 (0.84)	0.69 (0.78)	2.62	.011	.08
Total symptoms (SCL-90)	1.12 (0.63)	0.57 (0.59)	3.68	.000	.16
Clinician rating					
Intrusion (SRRS)	18.53 (11.05)	8.36 (10.72)	3.79	.000	.17
Total neurotic signs and symptoms (BPRS)	16.48 (4.68)	10.64 (6.83)	4.13	.000	.19

[a]IES indicates the Impact of Event Scale; SCL-90, the Symptom Checklist-90; SRRS, the Stress Response Rating Scale; and BPRS, the Brief Psychiatric Rating Scale.
[b]This is an index of the proportion of variance accounted for by group variance.
Source: Horowitz, M. J., Krupnick, J., Kaltreider, N., Wilner, N., Leong, A., and Marmar, C. Initial psychological response to parental death. *Archives of General Psychiatry* 38:316–323, 1981.

Table 4-2. Percentages of Persons at Three Levels of Distress on Initial Evaluation after the Death of a Parent

PRIMARY DISTRESS VARIABLES[a]	PATIENTS (N=31)			FIELD SUBJECTS (N=36)			x^2	P
	LOW	MEDIUM	HIGH	LOW	MEDIUM	HIGH		
Self-rating								
Intrusion (IES)	3	36	61	28	39	33	8.98	.011
Avoidance (IES)	10	32	58	61	17	22	19.02	.001
Depression (SCL-90)	7	32	61	46	31	23	15.23	.001
Anxiety (SCL-90)	23	26	51	65	6	29	13.32	.001
Total symptoms (SCL-90)	23	23	54	66	17	17	13.68	.001
Clinician rating								
Intrusion (SRRS)	17	40	43	67	19	14	16.91	.001
Total neurotic signs and symptoms (BPRS)	3	52	45	42	47	11	17.56	.001

[a]IES indicates the Impact of Event Scale; SCL-90, the Symptom Checklist-90; SRRS, the Stress Response Rating Scale; and BPRS, the Brief Psychiatric Rating Scale.

Source: Horowitz, M. J., Krupnick, J., Kaltreider, N., Wilner, N., Leong, A., and Marmar, C. Initial psychological response to parental death. *Archives of General Psychiatry* 38:316–323, 1981.

Table 4-3. Percentages of Persons at Three Levels of Distress at 13 Months

PRIMARY DISTRESS VARIABLES[a]	PATIENTS[b]			FIELD SUBJECTS[b]			x^2	p
	LOW	MEDIUM	HIGH	LOW	MEDIUM	HIGH		
Self-rating								
Intrusion (IES)	57	33	10	69	19	12	1.72	NS
Avoidance (IES)	73	17	10	75	19	6	.31	NS
Depression (SCL-90)	55	26	19	66	22	12	.87	NS
Anxiety (SCL-90)	68	19	13	85	6	9	2.88	NS
Total symptoms (SCL-90)	77	13	10	81	13	6	.26	NS
Clinician rating								
Intrusion (SRRS)	53	37	10	90	7	3	10.04	.007
Total neurotic signs and symptoms (BPRS)	43	47	10	47	53	0	3.17	NS

[a]IES indicates the Impact of Event Scale; SCL-90, the Symptom Checklist 90; SRRS, the Stress Response Rating Scale; and BPRS, the Brief Psychiatric Rating Scale.

[b]Numbers vary from 32 to 30.

Source: Horowitz, M. J., Krupnick, J., Kaltreider, N., Wilner, N., Leong, A., and Marmar, C. Initial psychological response to parental death. Archives of General Psychiatry 38: 316–323, 1981.

Those persons who felt in some way responsible for, guilty over, or ashamed of the events leading up to, during, and following the parental death had more prolonged symptoms. The loss of the mother produced more prolonged symptoms over time than did the death of the father. The more the persons experienced other negative life events, the more they tended to have persisting symptoms related to the themes of the parental death. Those persons judged to have more developed self-organizational capacities had the sharpest rate of decline in symptoms over time.

PERSONAL ILLNESS, DYING, AND THE THREAT OF DEATH

In her study of 400 dying patients in a Chicago hospital, Kübler-Ross (1969) pioneered investigations into the psychological effects of the process of dying. After first having difficulty in getting these people to talk to her, she discovered the denial of impending death not only by the patients but also by the doctors and nurses. The medical staff coped with the difficulty of confronting the dying patient by the defensive maneuvers of selective withdrawal and inaccessibility. Thus when human contact was needed most, it was less available because of avoidance behavior. According to Kübler-Ross's report, patients go through five stages between their awareness of serious illness and their death:

1. *Shock and denial* when told that they have a serious illness, with a few maintaining this defense until the very end. Aldrich (1974) mentioned the impact of ambivalence on anticipatory grief. The dying person grieves in anticipation of the loss of his or her loved ones and resents being the one to die. The dying person finds it difficult to cope with this ambivalence, which increases the likelihood of denial. Aldrich noted that denial will prevail until the patient's disengagement and withdrawal have progressed to a point from which he or she can face death and loss with relative equanimity.

2. *Anger*, directed toward family, nurses and doctors, and those who epitomize health, functioning, and life itself, and remind them of what they are attempting to deny. The patients are, in effect, asking "why me?" and, by expressing their rage or anger, receive some comfort.

3. *Bargaining for time*, for example, to see a son graduate from college or a grandchild born. The patient is now saying, "Yes, me, *but*. . . "

4. *Depression*, which may be of two kinds: one is a reactive depression manifested by simultaneous crying and talking about the loss that lies ahead; the other is a quiet depression in which there is crying but

no talk. Encouraging the grieving and mourning over the impending loss allows for the emergence of anticipatory grief and leads the patient into the last phase.

5. *Acceptance*, a period when the patient separates from those people he or she will leave behind. The unfinished business has been finished.

RAPE

Rape, or attempted rape, is a different kind of event from those previously discussed, although it, too, can be life threatening. It is not anticipated; there is no long period of time to deal with its possibilities; but it certainly demands a period of time to work through its effects (Veronen and Kilpatrick, 1983). Its victims also indicate a phasic response to this kind of episode.

In a study of "rape trauma syndrome," during a one-year period, Burgess and Holmstrom (1974) followed 146 women who were seen at the emergency ward of Boston City Hospital. Their results were essentially similar to those of an earlier study of 13 women by Sutherland and Scherl (1970) in which they noted phasic responses. The rape trauma syndrome is described as "an acute phase and a long-term reorganization process that occurs as a result of forcible rape or attempted forcible rape" (p. 508). These behavioral, somatic, and psychological responses are an acute stress reaction to a life-threatening situation. In the acute phase, there may be a wide range of emotions, characterized by disorganization of the victim's life-style. Shock and disbelief are often expressed, and two emotional styles emerge in equal number. One is the expressed style, in which feelings of fear, anger, and anxiety are evidenced by crying, smiling, restlessness, and tension. The other is the controlled style, in which feelings were masked or hidden and the victim appeared calm.

In the second phase, which was found to begin about two or three weeks after the attack, motor activity changes, and nightmares and phobias are especially evident. Dreams and nightmares are very upsetting and are of two types, one in which the victim is being attacked, wishes to do something, but wakens before acting. In the second type of dream, also of an attack, which occurs after a longer period of time, the victim masters the situation and fights off the assailant. There were some instances in which the victim woke up crying, though she had been unable to cry during daytime hours. There was also a phobic reaction to this traumatic situation, much like the "traumatophobia" described by Rado (1948) in his paper on the treatment of war victims. The phobia develops as a defensive reaction to the stressful event. There were fears connected with the setting in which the rape occurred (outdoors, indoors, being alone), sexual fears, fears of crowds, and fears of being followed.

In a later publication on crisis intervention with victims of rape, Sutherland-Fox and Scherl (1975) described a third phase in which the patient feels depressed and wants to talk. It is during this phase that two central issues must be worked though: the victim's feelings about herself and her feelings about the assailant. Some go through a period of guilt and self-punishment as a first step toward integrating the experience. Initial feelings of anger or denial—suppressed or rationalized during the second phase—now reappear for resolution. The third phase is relatively brief, and if after several weeks, the experience has not been integrated and taken its appropriate place in the past, Sutherland-Fox and Scherl suggest that further help be sought.

A "silent rape reaction" was also observed. A number of women in the sample stated that they had been raped or molested at earlier periods of their lives and that the current rape reawakened their reaction to the earlier experience. It became clear that because they had not talked about and worked through the effects of the previous rape, the syndrome had continued to develop and remained unresolved. Emphasis was placed on the victim's need for support and comfort, for a working-through from the acute phase to reorganization to completion, and a return to normal functioning as quickly as possible.

In a monograph sponsored by the American Psychiatric Association Committee on Women, Hilberman (1976) described four clinical phases of response to such a crisis: (1) an anticipatory or threat phase in which there is a need to protect the illusion of invulnerability; (2) an impact phase that includes anxiety, numbness, disorganization of thought, and loss of control; (3) a recoil phase in which the individual becomes more aware of adaptive or maladaptive responses to the stress and can experience either increased self-confidence or damage to self-esteem, depending on her perception of her behavior during the stress; and (4) a post-traumatic phase in which a successful response includes assimilation of the experience and spontaneous recovery, whereas a maladaptive response may result in a permanently impaired self-concept with evidence of continuing anger, guilt, nightmares, and impaired capacity to function.

Burgess and Holstrom (1976) elaborated on the fourth phase in explaining the victim's coping strategy before and during the assault as an issue to be confronted after the assault. For example, they asserted that there might have been intense guilt for the woman who submitted to rape in response to physical threats, whereas the victim who was beaten to insensibility and then raped may have suffered differently. Rape, of course, is used here as an extreme example of many other types of assault such as mugging, battery, burglary, and bullying. Any of these episodes of violence, threat, or fright can lead to stress response syndromes.

MEDICAL ILLNESSES

Medical illnesses and disabilities can also instigate the life events that lead to stress response syndromes. Kaltreider, Wallace, and Horowitz (1979) found that a substantial minority of women who have had a hysterectomy manifested a related stress response syndrome in the months that followed the operation. Mourning problems may also occur after an abortion. Often a new pregnancy diminishes the mourning process, and reactions may not occur until after the birth of a healthy baby (Bourne and Lewis, 1984). During the period between a perinatal death and a subsequently healthy pregnancy, the person may be relatively unwilling to look at all the implications of the perinatal death.

Life-threatening illnesses such as myocardial infarctions are even more likely to be associated with early denial and later intrusive thinking. The early denial may even ameliorate certain problems, as it can reduce emotional arousal at a time of cardiac irritability, when arrhythmias, with fatal consequences, may occur (Bilodeau and Hackett, 1971; Hackett and Cassem, 1970). Broncoscopy, burn treatment, spinal cord malfunction, renal dialysis, stroke, chronic pain, and other illnesses all may provide a major stressor with profound psychological as well as physical consequences (Krueger, 1984).

Even the news of being at risk for premature death may set in motion a stress response syndrome. Interventions to inform people of risk factors are now more and more common; perhaps the most common is telling persons that they are at risk for premature heart disease because of high cholesterol, patterns of heavy cigarette smoking, or elevated blood pressures. In a large study of men so informed, intrusive thinking was found at higher levels in those given repeated reminders than in an informed group with less systematic reminders of the causes for early death from heart attacks. Elevated levels of intrusive thinking were found at yearly intervals, including the time period of three years after the news of risk. At the third year, 7 percent of a group of nearly 1,500 men reported they were more than "quite a lot upset" by this news (Horowitz, Simon, Holden et al., 1983). An additional 11 percent were at "moderate" to "quite a lot upset" about this news, meaning that 18 percent of men were substantially upset for a period of three or more years after receiving such news. Having intrusive thoughts and being constantly upset about the news is not the same, however, as having a diagnosable stress response syndrome, as indicated in the previous chapter. This suggests that physicians should ask about psychological consequences for a considerable time after a patient has an illness or has been told that he or she is at risk of illness. Although stress response syndromes are less frequent in such situations than after disasters or personal traumas, they may nonetheless occur and impede adaptation to medical conditions (Dimsdale and Hackett, 1982).

Medical procedures can be embedded in a cascading series of stress events that characterize illnesses and modern treatment practices. Pain but, even more, the fear of pain, loss of control, or medical error can add to the psychological stress.

MENTAL ILLNESS AS A STRESS EVENT

Other mental disorders also may create a cascading series of stress events, while at the same time impair coping capacity. The individual who has a psychotic reaction, is hospitalized and treated, and then is to be discharged may also be regarded as having a stress response syndrome involving the memories (and fantasies) along this pathway of experience. If manic behavior occurred at work, there may be memories of the episodes that lead to a dreadful anticipation of social scorn on returning to the work place. If violent or bizarre behavior threatened loved ones during a paranoid reaction, the person who has now recovered to rational levels of interpersonal functioning may still have intrusive thoughts about the illness episodes. Witnessed struggles with staff or demented episodes of other patients in the hospital may also have been stressful events, during a period of relative "copelessness." The kind of brief psychotherapy to work through stressful life events, which will be discussed later, should also be considered as part of the overall approach to patients who have had such psychotic disorders or relevant nonpsychotic medical and psychiatric disorders.

CONCLUSIONS

Phases of stress response found in clinical studies of individuals who seek evaluation and treatment are also found in populations who sustain similar stress events and who are then evaluated as part of field study research. Intrusive thinking and denial characterize these phases. The generality of intrusive thinking as a stress response tendency led to the type of experiments to be described in the next chapter, as a further examination of the generality of this type of response in the experimental laboratory where many variables may be systematically controlled.

Chapter 5

EXPERIMENTAL FINDINGS

With the assistance of Stephanie Becker and Nancy Wilner

Clinical and field studies agree regarding findings of general human responses to stress, which include a central tendency toward intrusive repetition and a counteractive tendency labeled as denial. The idea of a general tendency has another meaning beyond "pertaining to many people," and that is that it may occur after stress events of varying magnitude. Clinical and field studies are of persons after major stress events; minor events do not usually motivate persons to seek help. The study of responses to stress events that range from minor to moderate in intensity can, however, be examined in the laboratory. Such experimental studies are advantageous for several reasons: the degree of generality across kinds of events and kinds of persons can be examined under controlled circumstances, and the precise operational definitions necessary for experimental work may sharpen theoretical reflection.

All experiments summarized here used volunteer subjects who reported their conscious experiences before and after viewing a variety of stressful films. The findings indicated that intrusive and repetitive thought tended to follow this more moderate, nontraumatic kind of stress and that positive affect–inducing films and depressing films produced effects equivalent to those produced by a film that threatened bodily injury. These data will be summarized in this chapter; the details have been published previously.

EXPERIMENTAL BACKGROUND

Films afford a well-studied and replicable laboratory device for providing visual stress events (Lazarus, 1966; Lazarus and Opton, 1966; Nomikos et al., 1968; Goldstein et al., 1965). Intrusive and repetitive thought can be defined and then quantified using self-report and content analysis procedures. Aside from the stress film method, the experimental literature on stress research provides few leads relevant to this paradigm (Higbee, 1969). Fortunately, there is now a return to measuring conscious experience fostered by dream and hallucinogen research and most recently by interests in altered states of consciousness (Hartman, 1967; Barr et al., 1972; Tart, 1969). Lazarus (1966) developed a cognitive paradigm for experimental research on the impact of stressful films. Several teams have studied the effects of stress films on subsequent dreams (Breger, Hunter and Lane, 1971; Witkin and Lewis, 1965; Witkin, 1969; Cartwright et al., 1969). In brief, these studies indicate that the stressful experience incurred while awake is repeated later while in dreaming sleep. The repetition often occurs in covert forms. Contrary to clinical observations of response to traumas, nightmares were not noted. This omission of observation was due perhaps to the mildness of the experimental stress events or the heightened defensiveness of subjects in a laboratory setting. Intrusive thoughts were not measured in these studies.

METHODS

A Series of Experiments

The hypothesis states that after a visually perceived stress event imposed by film, subjects from a variety of population groups, given a variety of instructional sets, will report more intrusive thoughts, more repetitions of film contents, and more visual images than after a less stressful contrast film. This hypothesis was first tested in a pilot study, and when significant positive results were found, a series of replications with additional controls was conducted. The series varied the subject populations, the instructions and demand set given to the subjects, and the contents and order of the stress films. An outline of sequence and references is found in Figure 5-1.

Design

In a prototypic experiment, groups of subjects saw a stress film and a neutral contrast film in counterbalanced order. Before and after each film, measurements were taken to obtain baseline, postneutral film (referred to as neutral) and poststress film (referred to as stress) scores on selected variables.

Subjects

The volunteers in the different experiments were college students and enlisted men in military service.

Film Stimuli

The stress films were (1) *Subincision*, which depicts circumcision as part of a puberty rite; (2) *It Didn't Have to Happen*, a film showing woodshop accidents; and (3) an auto accident film. The neutral contrast film used was *The Runner*, which shows a man running through the countryside meeting people along the way. All films were silent and edited to run from six to nine minutes.

Signal Detection Task and Mental Content Reports

The periods for reporting mental contents were interspersed between segments of a signal detection task that, though boring, demanded continuous attention as subjects judged whether a tone was higher, lower, or the same as the preceding tone. At the end of each segment, during a two-minute break, subjects wrote a report of their mental contents, defined as any thoughts, feelings, visual images, other images, observations, "flashes," memories, or anything else that occurred in the mind during the tone task (Horowitz, 1969, 1970; Horowitz and Becker, 1971c).

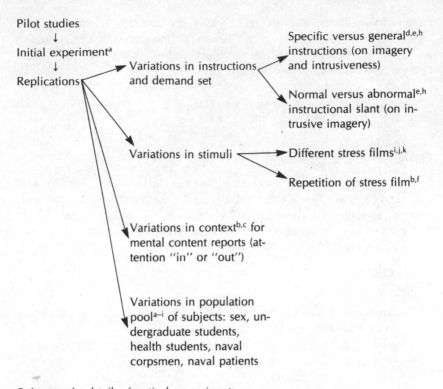

Pilot studies
↓
Initial experiment[a]
↓
Replications

Variations in instructions and demand set

Specific versus general[d,e,h] instructions (on imagery and intrusiveness)

Normal versus abnormal[e,h] instructional slant (on intrusive imagery)

Variations in stimuli

Different stress films[i,j,k]

Repetition of stress film[b,f]

Variations in context[b,c] for mental content reports (attention "in" or "out")

Variations in population pool[a–i] of subjects: sex, undergraduate students, health students, naval corpsmen, naval patients

References for details of particular experiments

a. Horowitz (1969)
b. Horowitz (1970)
c. Horowitz & Becker (1971a)
d. Horowitz & Becker (1971b)
e. Horowitz & Becker (1971c)
f. Horowitz, Becker & Moskowitz (1971)

g. Horowitz, Becker, Moskowitz & Rashid (1972)
h. Becker, Horowitz & Campbell (1973)
i. Horowitz & Becker (1973)
j. Horowitz & Wilner (1976)
k. Wilner & Horowitz (1975)

Figure 5-1. The Sequential Organization of the Series of Experiments

Self-ratings of Affect

The affect ratings consisted of 11 mood words that the subjects rated on a 9-point scale to indicate their feelings at different points in the experiment. The negative affect words included anger, contempt, disgust, fear, nervousness, pain, sadness, and surprise, and the positive affect words included happiness, interest, and pleasantness.

Quantification of Data on Conscious Experience

The raw data from the mental contents reports were content analyzed by judges for intrusive thoughts, film references, and several other variables of less relevance here. The Spearman rank difference correlations for the two or three judges used in the separate experiments ranged from 0.85 to 0.94 for intrusions and 0.91 to 0.99 for film references.

Briefly, an *intrusive thought* was defined as any thought that implies nonvolitional entry into awareness, requires suppressive effort or is hard to dispel, occurs perseveratively, or is experienced as something to be avoided. A *film reference* was defined as any thought that refers directly to the film, film setting, or film experience, and it includes anticipations of seeing the film.

Instructional Demand

The different experiments varied according to the demand sets incorporated into instructions to subjects, because in studying conscious experience, such variables have been found to exert significant effects (Rosenthal, 1966; Orne, 1962). The main instructional variances, as indicated in Figure 5-1, were to suggest to some subjects that intrusive images were minor equivalents of a pathological process, such as that leading to hallucinations, and to other subjects that such images were an unconsciously motivated normal process aimed at mastering a stress event.

Data Analysis

Recent computer implementation of the Finn Multivariate Analysis of Variance for a nonorthogonal design enabled the cross-experimental data analysis reported here (Finn, 1972). The analysis was divided into stages, because not every variable was scored for every experiment and not every design included baseline, neutral, and stress conditions. The main variables, scored for every experiment, were subjected to an analysis of variance for 133 subjects who had data in all three conditions. Included as potential sources of variance for this analysis were the subject groups; the demand set incorporated in the instructions; the order in which films were viewed; the baseline, neutral, and stress conditions; interaction effects; and variances among and within subjects.

RESULTS

The hypothesis that intrusive and repetitive thought would occur most frequently in the stress condition was confirmed.

Intrusions and Film References

Tables 5-1 and 5-2 report an ANOVA and adjusted means for the effects of all factors and conditions on intrusions and film references. The population consisted of 133 subjects in various experiments who each had data on the variable in all conditions (baseline, neutral and stress). At the $p < .05$ cutoff level, only the change in conditions exerts a significant effect on both intrusions (MS = 57.5, df = 2, F = 20.70, $p < .001$) and film references (MS = 146.5, df = 2, F = 49.1, $p < .001$). Population differences (health sciences students, college students, military personnel), film order (stress or neutral first), sex of subjects, and instructional demand (general, specific, abnormal, normal slants) did not exert a significant effect. Intrusions and film references correlated positively in the stress condition ($r = .51$, $p < .001$, $n = 133$).

The adjusted means in Table 5-2 indicate deflections of a content analysis item from a norm of zero, with zero computed as the expectable level based on word length alone. Positive scores indicate the number of intrusions per subject above expectation, and negative scores indicate lower than expectable levels. The significant condition effect for intrusions is accounted for by the stress film. Baseline film references are, of course, especially low because no film has yet been seen, and only occasional anticipatory remarks have been made. The neutral and stress condition film reference levels are significantly different. Overall, 77 percent of the subjects were scored by two or three judges as having at least one episode of intrusions in the stress condition.

Intrusions Correlating with Degree of Reported Stress

In the stress condition, persons who rated themselves high on negative emotions tended also to report high levels of intrusions. The adjusted intrusion scores, in 133 subjects who made the same affect report measure during the stress condition, correlated significantly and positively with a composite of negative affects ($r = .27$, $p < .001$) and significantly and negatively with a composite of positive effects ($r = -.16$, $p < .05$). The highest correlation with specific individual affects was with

Table 5-1. Analysis of Variance Data for Intrusion and Film References Considering All Factors and Conditions for 133 Subjects

	INTRUSIONS			
Sources of Variance	MS	df	f	p
Among Subjects				
Population of Sample	7.46	2	1.01	<.37
Instructional Demand	16.16	3	2.18	<.09
Sex	16.84	1	2.27	<.13
Order of Films	1.14	1	.15	<.70
Among-subjects Error	7.42	117		
Within Subjects				
Condition	57.51	2	20.69	<.001
Cond. X Pop.	6.39	2	2.30	<.10
Cond. X Instruc.	1.67	3	.60	<.50
Cond. X Sex	3.13	1	1.13	<.30
Cond. X Order	1.05	1	.38	<.50
Within-subjects Error	2.78	234		
	Film References			
Among Subjects				
Population	32.75	2	2.11	<.13
Instruct	1.16	3	.07	<.97
Sex	1.73	1	.11	<.74
Order	4.52	1	.29	<.59
Among-subjects Error	15.51	117		
Within Subjects				
Condition (s)	146.51	2	49.08	<.001
Pop. X Cond. (s)	14.04	2	2.57	<.10
Instruc. X Cond. (s)	6.93	3	1.27	<.20
Sex X Cond. (s)	5.72	1	1.05	<.30
Order X Cond. (s)	12.01	1	2.20	<.20
Within-subjects Error	5.47	234		

Table 5-2. Combined Means on Intrusions and Film References as Adjusted According to Report Length

Factor	N	INTRUSIONS			FILM REFERENCES		
		Base	Neutral	Stress	Base	Neutral	Stress
Population							
Military Inpts.	23	−.44	−.16	.41	−1.69	−.88	−.08
Civil. Students	82	−.83	−.40	1.38	−2.14	−.23	1.51
Health Students	28	−.50	−.11	.39	−1.53	.08	1.61
Sex							
Male	99	−.66	−.33	.55	−1.81	−.13	.98
Female	34	−.80	−.20	2.33	−2.29	−.69	2.05
Instructional Demand							
Normal	24	−.72	−.30	1.73	−2.26	−.53	2.44
Abnormal	25	−.63	.02	1.79	−1.96	−.25	1.65
Specific	16	−.49	.01	.93	−1.70	.07	.86
General	68	−.76	−.49	.49	−1.86	−.28	.78
Order							
Stress 1st	51	−.67	−.20	.57	−1.82	.16	.86
Neutral 1st	82	−.71	−.36	1.27	−2.00	−.55	1.50
Overall	133	−.69	−.30	1.00	−1.23	−.29	1.23

pain ($r = .38$, $p < .001$) and surprise ($r = .35$, $p < .001$). With large numbers of subjects, some low-levels of correlation (e.g., $r = −.16$) may reach statistical levels of significance but indicate only a small size of effect.

A group of 77 subjects also rated themselves after the stress film on a 1-100 "thermometer" scale for emotional and physical stress, following Stevens's method (1966). Both scales correlated significantly and positively with intrusion levels. For emotional stress, the correlation was $r = .39$, $p < .01$, and for physical stress, $r = .34$, $p < .01$.

MIXED AFFECT EXPERIMENT

The previous series of experiments indicated that the tendency toward intrusive thought is general in that it occurs even after the mild to moderate stress of seeing a silent film and is thus not restricted to traumatization or overwhelming stress. However, the theme of each stress film used was one of bodily injury, a topic usually evoking fear.

Though fear is highly relevant to the concept of stress and trauma, it is a specific and limited emotion. If intrusive repetitiousness is a general response tendency, it can be expected after the arousal of other types of emotion associated with other sets of information. This includes prediction of intrusive episodes even after arousal of positive affects.

To test this hypothesis, four stimulus conditions were used to evoke fearful, sad, pleasant, and comparatively neutral states. To maintain coherence with the previous series of studies, equivalent designs and measures were used. It was predicted that the three affect arousal states all would lead to intrusive and repetitive thought and that these responses would be significantly greater than those resulting from the comparatively neutral stimulus.

METHODS

Design

The subjects were drawn from the same population pool. They were ranked for emotional responsivity according to pretest data on their usual responses to horror, pornographic, and tragic films. Following their ranked order, they were evenly assigned to view films depicting either the separation of a small child from his parents, nude erotic interactions, or bodily injury, or the neutral film used in the previous experiments. After collecting the data, as described earlier, the subjects were informed of an investigator's interest in qualities of thought and were taught how to rate themselves retrospectively for frequency and intensity of intrusive and repetitive thought. The data were analyzed by groups designated according to the particular film stimulus. There were eight film showings, two at each of four experimental sessions. Each of the four films was shown as the first film during one session and as the second film during another session.

Films

All of the films were silent and edited to run between six and nine minutes. The woodshop film provided the bodily injury stimulus, the runner film the neutral stimulus. For a separation theme, *John*, a documentary (1969), was edited by us and depicts an 18-month-old boy whose mother has just died. His father places him in a foundling home and makes occasional brief visits. The film portrays John's initial gregariousness, his subsequent angry, crying, and searching behavior, and finally, his lethargy, despair, and withdrawal. There are poignant close-ups of his facial expressions, some as he is rejected by his father, but no such shocking scenes as in the other negative affect film with its depiction of bodily injury. The basic theme of this film is the sadness of separation.

Erotic Film

The erotic film depicts a loving heterosexual couple enjoying fore-play and intercourse. The film is pleasurable and erotically arousing, with no hints of perversion. The erotic arousal, supplemented by ac-tivation of voyeuristic-exhibitionistic themes, is regarded as stressful because of the absence of immediate means to reduce this arousal.

Subjects

The subjects were 75 health science students.

Data Analysis

The direct means for each subject, derived by averaging the scores given by three judges, were used to analyze the mental content data, as the word length of reports was noted to be consistent among the subject subgroups. Analyses of variance were used to determine the significance of film, order, and sex effects. T-tests were used to examine the significance of differences among particular cells of data.

RESULTS

Film Effects

As predicted by the main hypothesis, intrusions and film references were high after the erotic, separation, and bodily injury films and low after the neutral film. This variation in films contributed the main ef-fect, according to an analysis of variance (see Tables 5-3, 5-4).

The bodily injury film, least evocative of intrusions of the three stress films, differed significantly from the neutral film ($t = 3.5$, $df = 78$, $p < .001$). The greatest differences among the three stress films was between the separation film (more intrusions) and the bodily injury film (fewer in-

Table 5-3. Intrusions: Analysis of Variance and Means by Sex and Film

Source of Variance	df	MS	F	p
Order (1st or 2nd)	1	6.01	2.24	.14
Sex	1	8.93	3.33	.07
Film (Content)	3	18.31	6.82	.0003
Sex X Film	3	3.91	1.46	.23
Film X Order	3	4.39	1.63	.18
Between S's Error	134	2.68		

COMBINED MEANS

	Erotic	Neutral	Separation	Injury	
Males	1.68	.62	1.42	1.58	1.27
Females	1.98	.68	2.98	1.74	1.83
	1.81	.64	2.23	1.65	

NUMBER OF SUBJECTS

	Erotic	Neutral	Separation	Injury	
Males	22	27	15	20	84
Females	17	17	16	16	66
	39	44	31	36	150

trusions), but this difference was not significant. The stress films did not differ significantly for film references. The lowest film reference scores after a stress film were also those after the bodily injury film. This level was significantly higher than that noted after the neutral film ($t = 2.47$, df $= 78$, $p < .02$). Persons with high levels of intrusions tended to have high levels of film references after the separation film ($r = .61$, $p < .01$), the bodily injury film ($r = .49$, $p < .01$), and the neutral film ($r = .36$, $p < .05$) but not after the erotic film ($r = .16$, $p = NS$).

These content analysis variables had significant and positive correlations with the self-ratings completed by the subjects during the retrospective phase of the experiments, except for frequency and intensity of film repetitions after the erotic film (see Table 5-5).

Table 5-4. Film References: Analysis of Variance and Means by Order and Film

Source of Variance	df	MS	F	p
Order (1st or 2nd)	1	49.54	2.74	.10
Sex	1	25.02	1.39	.24
Film (Content)	3	81.99	4.54	.0046
Sex X Film	3	14.03	.78	.51
Film X Order	3	44.02	2.44	.07
Between S's Error	134	18.06		

COMBINED MEANS				
	Erotic	Neutral	Separation	Injury
Order 1	3.94	3.16	5.32	3.12	3.80
Order 2	5.92	1.50	6.28	6.24	5.00
	5.26	2.48	5.72	4.68	

Table 5-5. Correlation of Content Analysis and Self-report Variables

CONTENT ANALYSIS VARIABLES	SELF-REPORT VARIABLES					
	Frequency of Nondeliberate Film Repetitions			Intensity of Nondeliberate Film Repetitions		
INTRUSIONS	Erotic	Separation	Bodily Injury	Erotic	Separation	Bodily Injury
Erotic	.32[a]			.42[b]		
Separation		.62[c]			.49[b]	
Bodily Injury			.71[c]			.68[c]
FILM REFERENCES						
Erotic	.25			.15		
Separation		.60[c]			.47[b]	
Bodily Injury			.54[c]			.36[a]

[a] $p < .05$
[b] $p < .01$
[c] $p < .001$

Table 5-6. Frequency and Intensity of Film Repetitions by Self-report. Group Means on a 1 (Low) to 9 (High) Scale for Frequency and Intensity

	EROTIC	NEUTRAL	SEPARATION	BODILY INJURY
Frequency of Repetition	4.23	2.06	3.77	3.75
Intensity of Repetition	4.38	2.11	4.06	4.03

Affects

The data on affects conform to what one would expect from the films' themes. In analyses of variance, the film effects dominated and were highly significant for every affect (p values < .0001). Pleasantness, interest, and happiness were greatest after the erotic film. Sadness and anger were greatest after the separation film, and contempt was rated equally high for the bodily injury and the separation films. Fear, nervousness, physical sensations, pain, and disgust were greatest after the bodily injury film.

Correlations of selected individual affects with levels of intrusions after the separation film were positive between intrusions and sadness, greater than that of any other affect. Intrusions after the bodily injury film correlated positively but not significantly with reports of nervousness and physical sensations during the film. Intrusions after the erotic film also correlated positively and significantly with both physical sensations and happiness and nervousness.

Self-report of Intrusions and Repetitions

The self-ratings of nondeliberate film repetitions during the signal detection task, and the intensity of these repetitions, were significantly affected by the kind of film seen before the task (f = 4.15, df = 110, p < .008 for repetitions, F = 4.87, df = 110, p < .003 for intensity). This difference was due to the mild effects of the neutral film, as opposed to the films evocative of strong emotions, as shown in Table 5-6.

CONCLUSION

The tendency toward intrusive and repetitive thought after stressful events was observed in clinical, field, and experimental modes of investigation. This concept is clear and can be quantified. Both the field and experimental studies supplemented the clinical understanding by indicating that the tendency is a general one, found across divergent populations. The experimental studies also revealed another aspect of the generality of this pattern. Intrusive and repetitive thoughts usually occurred after stress that varied in the emotion that was aroused and in the intensity of that emotion in a range from mild to moderate to severe.

Part II
General Theory

Chapter 6

PHASES OF DENIAL AND INTRUSION

The basic experimental, field, and clinical findings regarding stress response syndromes can be summed up as a list of observations to be accounted for by any theory:

1. There are general response tendencies to stressful events. Although people vary in resiliency, areas of vulnerability, and available supports, those subjected to enough stress may be expected to show some stress responses.
2. The response tendencies are also general in that they may appear after a variety of stress events differing in quantity and quality. (Different kinds of stress events may result in additional particular responses.)
3. Many stress responses persist long after termination and resolution of the external event. Some responses to external stress begin only after an interval of extended relief.

4. After termination of the external stress event, one of the main observations in clinical, field, and experimental studies is of intrusive repetition in thought, emotion, and/or behavior. A set of related but antithetical responses, including ideational denial, emotional numbness, and behavioral avoidances, is also frequently noted.
5. These stress response tendencies of intrusion and denial are inclined to occur in temporal phases, at least after major stress events. Phases may overlap, and persons may vary in their entry into and emergence from a phase and in their sequence and termination of phases. One person may function in different phases with regard to different complexes of ideational and emotional responses. Abstracting a general stress response tendency from a wide range of variation in individuals and kinds of stress events, one arrives at the following cognitive and emotional sequence:
   a. Phase of initial realization that a stress event has occurred, often with a sharply accelerated expression of reactive emotion.
   b. Phase of denial and numbness.
   c. Mixed phase of denial and intrusive repetition in thought, emotion, and/or behavior.
   d. Phase of further ideational and emotional processing, working through, and acceptance (or stable defensive distortion), with a loss of either the denial or the peremptory recollection of the stress event.

In this chapter we shall present the early psychoanalytic, contemporary psychodynamic, and cognitive models for explaining general stress responses. A fuller explanation of personality variations with case examples can be found in *States of Mind* (Horowitz, 1979) and *Personality Styles and Brief Psychotherapy* (Horowitz, Marmar, Krupnick, et al., 1984).

PSYCHOANALYTIC MODEL

In his later theoretical model of psychic trauma, Freud (1920) hypothesized that traumas occur when excessive stimuli overexcite the mind. He accounted for the different responses to the same kind of life event by hypothesizing variations in a "stimulus barrier." This barrier against stimulation was a theoretical construct to account for the regulation of the perceptual entry of information and energy from external events into the psychic apparatus. Freud also conceptualized the motive for altering this stimulus barrier. Signals of danger, fear, or anxiety are activated as an external stress event is anticipated or sampled by the initial perception (Freud, 1926). As the anxiety increases, the stimulus barrier is raised and so accepts less input.

The term *anxiety*, as used here, is a theoretical construct and not necessarily a felt emotion. The term *stimulus barrier* also refers to a theoretical construct. Though widely used in the early psychoanalytic literature, the term has unfortunate concrete implications. Reduction and augmentation functions are performed by multiple processes at various levels of stimulus processing. The concept of regulation is thus relevant, but to avoid the concrete metaphor of a barrier, we shall substitute the term *modulation* of stimulus input. This modulation can occur, as external events are appraised, at any step of the information processing. This regulation includes both inhibitions and facilitations of representation and sequencing.

Freud's theoretical model conceptualized a feedback loop. Suppose that there is a continuous perceptual sampling of an ongoing external stress event and that the degree of processing of this information can be regulated. The degree of this modulation, in turn, depends on the magnitude of aroused emotions such as fear or anxiety. Initially, as the information input increases, signal emotions, such as anxiety, also increase. The anxiety encourages an increase in defensive inhibitions, and so there is a reduction in information processing. And when the anxiety decreases as a result of these controls, the emotional motive for modulation also decreases. With less modulation there is then more information processing and so the anxiety or other emotional arousal increases again. If such a dynamic system is unstable at its extremes, the feedback loop and transactional arrangement may lead to phases in which there is a decrease from higher levels of anxiety and an increase from lower levels. In information-processing models this is called *marginal instability*.

Freud's clinical theory of traumatization was developed during his observation and training with Charcot, the French scholar of hysteria and hypnosis, and in his subsequent work with Breuer on hysteria (Breuer and Freud, 1895). The Breuer–Freud theory of the traumatic etiology of hysterical symptoms emphasized not only the role of external stress events but also the importance of repressing certain ideas and emotions triggered by the event and by contributors to the earlier internal stress events. As Breuer and Freud stated, persons with hysterical symptoms actually suffer from reminiscences because they cannot remember and they cannot *not* remember. When they try to remember, they have either partial amnesia or an overwhelming uncontrolled recollection. And when they try not to remember, they have intrusive "breakthroughs" such as unbidden images.

In these early formulations, repression is a control concept, related to memories, associated ideas, and event-reactive emotions and impulses. The difference between Freud's theory of repression and that of the stimulus barrier is that in repression the inhibition is directed against traumatic memory rather than against traumatic perceptions. The classical psychoanalytic theory of control over the contents of consciousness is a system of dual entry of information from internal and external sources with a feedback loop allowing for defensive regulation of both sources. Symptoms of amnesia are explained in this model as the products of overextensive inhibitory control. Intrusions are failures of defensive inhibition in the face of impulsive facilitations. In later formulations this thesis was complicated by the need to include other unconscious defensive operations involved in the formation of symptoms, which earlier had been explained as instances of repressive failure.

CONTEMPORARY MODELS OF COGNITIVE PROCESSING

Evocation of a stress state requires that the person register and interpret incoming stimuli as cues of threat. One reason for the variance in individual responses to stress events is that persons differ in registration and interpretation as well as in styles and capacities for coping with threats. In recent decades psychologists have worked increasingly with cognition and have attempted to model the place of cognitive mediation in the sequence from stress event to stress response. Their theoretical contributions led to the expansion of the early psychoanalytic model.

Lazarus, an influential experimentalist and theoretician in the psychology of cognitive aspects of response to stress (Lazarus, 1966; Lazarus and Folkman, 1984), emphasized the importance of appraisal in coping with threat. Very simply, he considers emotions as responses to concept-forming operations. A person views environmental cues as threatening or nonthreatening through primary and secondary appraisals and reappraisals. The degree of threat appraised and reappraised leads to variations in emotions such as fear, anger, depression, euphoria, and elation. Tomkins (1978) views such emotions as ways of increasing the motivation to respond, as amplifications of the response tendencies activated by threats, or as tension reductions.

Lazarus explained that secondary appraisals compare the threat with the coping resources and with several reappraisals of threat to see whether it exceeds the coping capacity. The discrepancy between the degree of threat and the available coping capacities thus accounts for the emotion activated. An initial emotional response such as fear or anger may be reduced when a benign reappraisal of threat is made through cognitive processing.

A cognitive elaboration of the psychoanalytic model of stress response was developed by Janis, another leading psychological theorist and investigator (Janis, 1958, 1962, 1967, 1969; Janis and Leventhal, 1968; Janis and Mann, 1977). Janis and Lazarus agree on the importance of cognitive processing, although Janis emphasized emotions as motives, in contrast with Lazarus, who emphasized cognitive processing as a precursor and cause of emotional responses (Lazarus, Averill, and Opton, 1969). But these positions are not incompatible, as there may be many levels of conscious and unconscious information processing, with emotional responses serving as both cause and effect at different levels of representation (see Horowitz, Marmar, Krupnick, et al., 1984).

Janis followed and elaborated the classical psychoanalytic model while emphasizing the distinctive motivational properties of what he called "reflective fear." He joined the word *reflective* to fear to obtain a term more precise than the hypothetical construct *signal anxiety*. The word *reflective* indicates that both threat and information from cognitive processing affect the magnitude of this kind of emotional response to danger. When aroused, reflective fear can lead to three modes of adjustment of the stress state. Janis called these adjustments increased needs for vigilance or reassurance or fusions into a compromise of the two divergent tendencies.

Vigilance needs strengthen the cognitive processing of the other cues, relevant or not, and may lead to the misinterpretation of cues and unwarranted increases in reflective fear. Startle reactions from the list of intrusive symptoms given in Chapter 3 are one example. Reassurance needs may motivate thought processes that lead to either appropriately or inappropriately reassuring ideas. In pathological degrees, reassurance needs lead to "blanket reassurance," a reduction in reflective fear, and, hence, to unwarranted and perhaps maladaptive complacency. In extreme forms, then, reassurance contains elements of denial and numbness.

The difference in emphasis on emotions as motives or as responses can be resolved in a manner implied in the extended written theories of Freud, Janis, and Lazarus. That is, emotions, thoughts, and controls can be considered as they interact. Emotions are responses to thought processes, thus providing a circuit for the equilibration of levels of emotional arousal.

Additional support for such transactional models and the central importance of ideational processes is found in field studies of response to surgery as related to clinically rated levels of fear before the operation (Johnson, Leventhal, and Dabbs, 1971; Cohen and Lazarus, 1973). The findings failed to replicate Janis's findings that anticipatory fear reduces postoperative distress. Johnson and his colleagues therefore rejected the Janis theory that fear is drivelike in its motivation of cognition, as in his concept of the "work of worrying." Instead, like Lazarus, Johnson and his colleagues modeled emotion as a response. Saltz (1970) supported this model in his review of experimental research on anxiety and threat, showing that the data do not sustain the theories that anxiety functions as if in a drive state (Taylor and Spence, 1952; Spielberger, 1966).

Nonetheless, emotions such as anxiety can have motivational functions when they influence the controls, which in turn modify the cognitive processes. Low levels of emotion may themselves act as new information, for example, as bodily sensations, and these sensations may increase associations to memories related to similar bodily-sensory states. This may influence and promote a working-through process. Janis's formulations and findings thus remain viable and useful. At high levels of emotional arousal, however, inhibitory controls may be activated, and a reverse effect may occur, constricting the associational width and inhibiting the ideational processing. The reason for this heightened control lies in part in the motives to avoid accelerating anxiety, to avoid entering into highly fearful states of mind, or to be able to exit from them.

TERMINATION OF STRESS STATES BY ACTION

Action is the prototypic terminator of stress states because action changes events. The knight who slays an attacking dragon terminates the threat. He also discharges (or changes) the state of his own rage and rage-action plans as activated by the effrontery of the dragon's attack. The knave who runs faster than the dragon can, also cancels the stress of the attack and discharges (or changes) his fear and fear-action plans. In either case, successful action terminates the stress event. Emotions such as fear of the dragon or rage at it also are reduced by successful action. Such termination of states of emotional appetite, as Dahl suggested (1977), can be conceptualized in two ways. The traditional view is that there is a discharge of aroused emotions through action. The cognitive view is that there is a reduction of emotion because of the completion of a script, the discharge of an intention, or else because of the following sequence: The action alters events; the alteration of events alters representation; the alteration of representations alters cognitive processing; and the alteration of cognitive processing alters emotional responses.

With the addition of this concept of terminating external stress events, a model can be developed showing that internalized action plans can be terminated by means of cognitive processing in the absence of externally expressed actions. Such a model is relevant to understanding the symptomatic responses to stress that persist or begin after the external stress events are terminated, a time when external action may seem relevant. The internalized action plan shows how representations of threat, loss, or injury are incorporated into existing schemata of how the self relates to the outside world.

TERMINATION OF STRESS STATES BY COGNITIVE COMPLETION

None of the foregoing models completely explains the persistence and periodicity of responses to stress. Nor do they explain how and when compulsive repetitions may be terminated. As mentioned earlier, psychoanalysis has offered two additional and relevant theories. One theory hypothesizes a need for mastery and predicts cessation of repetitions when mastery has occurred. The second theory states that the repetition compulsion is, in part, instinctive and will terminate when there is a sufficient degree of drive discharge.

Concept of a Repetition Compulsion

Freud noted compulsive repetitions in persons with psychoneuroses and persons exposed to external stress events. As mentioned in Chapter 4, the repetitions of combat experiences in nightmares occur in veterans for decades after wars are over. Freud noted this in the years after World War I. Such an extremely painful type of dream life could not, it seemed to Freud, be explained by the principle that dreams were wish fulfillments. This observation led him to revise his theory of instinctual drives, and to write "Beyond the Pleasure Principle" (1920). To his conception of a sexual drive he added the postulate of a fundamental aggressive drive. Indeed, Freud used the compulsive repetition observations as a springboard for further speculation on the possibility of a death instinct that contributed a component of the aggressive drive, but he also posited the need to master the traumatic event as a motive for compulsive repetitions (Freud, 1920).

Later theorists also considered the concept of compulsive repetition to have two aspects. The "id aspect" was the instinctual compulsion, and the "ego aspect" resulted from interaction between the impulse and ego functions such as thinking and memory. They regarded the id components as the reproductive tendencies and the ego functions as attempts to work off or work through the internal stimulation activated by the painful experience (Hartmann, 1939; Bibring, 1943; Waelder, 1964). Schur (1966) clarified the matter further when he suggested that trauma leaves the ego with "an incomplete task," in the sense illustrated by the Zeigarnik effect (the tendency to remember incomplete tasks better than completed tasks). The incomplete task leads to an ego wish to complete the task by means of thinking.

Our argument will follow Schur regarding the motives for the repetition of ideas and emotions related to the stressor life events. However, his concept of an ego wish will be replaced with the idea of a completion tendency as a specific property of cognitive process.

Completion Tendency

The need to match new information with inner models based on older information, and the revision of both until they agree, can be called a *completion tendency* (Horowitz, 1976). The assumption of a completion tendency is not new. Festinger (1957) described similar forms of cognitive processing as part of a need to reduce cognitive dissonance, and French (1952) explained conceptual shifts as ideas passed through integrative fields. Mandler (1964) observed a completion tendency in a complex series of interrupted behavioral responses. After an organized response system has been interrupted, it usually resumes later and continues until the initial plan has been completed. Mandler followed Miller, Galanter, and Pribram (1960) in attributing this effect to a built-in tendency to execute successive steps, as in a computer program. Script theory elaborates this point of view (Schank and Abelson, 1977).

A similar avoidance of postulating instincts by means of information-processing models was suggested by Peterfreund (1971). For example, suppose that a task plan is interrupted; thus the incomplete portion automatically remains stored in working memory. The problem is to explain how and when a given plan is terminated (Mandler, 1964; Miller, 1963).

In an earlier but parallel theory, Lewin (1935) stated that any intention to reach a goal produces a tension system that is preserved until a goal is reached. It was this theory that led to the prediction of the Zeigarnik effect. Mandler (1964) suggested that in addition to the completion tendency of initiated plans, interruption may lead to a state of increased arousal that is distressing and is maintained until the plans have been completed. The organism thus favors completion in order to end this distress.

In his theoretical model of peremptory ideation, Klein (1967) further developed this concept of the completion tendency and the distress-reduction tendency of plans or programs. He added this concept of conscious and unconscious plans for processing thought and also the concept of defense as an interruption mechanism used when there is a threat of distress if the plan were to go forward unchecked. When inhibition is lessened or when motives increase, the cycle resumes operations and follows the interrupted plan. Thus the tendency toward cognitive completion is emphasized in various theoretical approaches.

The Completion Principle

The completion principle summarizes the human mind's intrinsic ability to continue to process new information in order to bring up to date the inner schemata of the self and the world. This continual revision of relatively enduring structures of meaning is necessary to bring these inner models into accord with current reality so that they can guide decisions toward the next most effective possible actions. Persons in a healthy mental state maintain a variety of inner working models or "cognitive maps" of basic factors in their lives. These factors include their body image, various other self-concepts, role relationship models, scripts and agendas, spatial layouts of their repeated environmental circumstances, and other schemata that help them organize their perceptions and plan their next moves.

A stressful life event is, by definition, one that is not fully in accord with a person's usual inner working models. It contains either too much or too little of some familiar situation, but more often, it is not the familiar situation but something else that threatens equilibrium and the expectation that things will remain constant. When this happens, the news of the event must be reappraised so that it either conforms to inner models or is reappraised as unimportant, or else inner schemata must be revised so that they match the changed circumstances.

After deaths, personal injuries, and other serious life events, the inner model must be revised. Such processes require considerable cognitive change and extended time for the necessary information processing, and therefore, the point of completion cannot be achieved at once. In addition, every recognition of the discrepancy between the new state of affairs and the inner habitual model may bring emotional responses that are sufficiently painful so as to interrupt the information processing necessary to reach the completion point. Until completion, we assume that there is some type of memory that retains the important but incompletely assessed set of memories and responses, presenting this complex of memories, ideas, and feelings whenever opportunity and inner choice permit.

Repetition as a Property of Active Memory Storage

A key assumption is a type of memory with motivational properties that tends to instigate a next step in processing. Because of this intrinsic property, it will be labeled as *active memory*. The assertion is that active memory storage has an intrinsic tendency to repeat the representation of contents. This repetition will cease when the contents held in active memory have been terminated by the completion of cognitive processing.

Active memory storage, with a tendency toward repeated representation in thought, is contrasted with inactive memory. *Active* and *inactive* memory can also correspond to current usage of the terms *short-term* and *long-term memory*, respectively. But the term active memory is preferable here to short-term memory because intrusive stress-event recollections may occur for a long time. This assumption of an active memory with special properties of recurrent representation is compatible with experimental findings in the fields of perception, attention, and memory. For example, Broadbent (1971) summarized this research and developed a model that has several forms of short-term memory that occur after sensory registration and before transformation of information into long-term memory.

Broadbent includes three kinds of short-term memory. One is a "buffer storage" that holds images for a while after the sensory registration ceases. The second is a "rehearsal buffer" that retains important images for longer periods than does the rapid decay of information in buffer storage. The third is "primary memory by slots" in which certain memories remain in a kind of active information bank. It is of greatest relevance to our formulation that information is retained in the primary memory slots until it is terminated by replacement with other, presumably more important, information. Stress-related information is, by definition, very important and hence is not terminated until it is assimilated.

Processing Stressful and Nonstressful Events

The recurrence of a familiar nonstressful event is likely to be quickly and automatically assimilated. The cognitive processing will be completed, and the information in active memory storage will be rapidly terminated. The information in novel and stressful events, however, cannot be processed rapidly. Thus the point of relative completion is not achieved, and so the active memory retention is not terminated, with relevant codings of information remaining in active memory.

Assuming a limited capacity for processing, such codings will remain stored in active memory even when other programs (those used for processing other sets of information) have greater priority in the hierarchy of claims for channels. These actively stored contents, however, will generally be repeatedly represented. Each episode of representation will trigger a resumption of processing. Thus, whenever this set of information achieves a high-enough priority, representation and processing will resume. If the contents are interrupted by controls that regulate priorities, they will remain in coded form in active memory.

Incongruity

Completion requires the resolution of differences between new information and enduring mental models. Thus, news of the death of a loved one is incongruent with an entire world picture that includes not only wishes and hopes but also habits and routine roles and self-images. Cognitive processing is reinitiated when representation occurs and may evoke unpleasant emotions such as fear or anxiety. Every repetition is a confrontation with a major difference between what is and what was and what was gratifying and may invoke various responsive emotional states such as fear, anxiety, rage, panic, or guilt. If these emotional responses are likely to increase beyond the limits of toleration, the result may be distraught, overwhelmed states of mind. To avoid entry into such states of mind, therefore, controls are activated that will modify the cognitive processes (Horowitz, 1979). For example, the path from active memory storage to representation and processing can be inhibited. This reduction in processing reduces anxiety and, in turn, reduces the motivation for controls. With the reduction in control, the tendency of active memory toward representation then reasserts itself. Other immediate programs may be interrupted with the repeated representation of the stress-related information. The processing of the stress-related information resumes; the anxiety increases, the control increases; and the cycle continues.

The simple model leads to states of high and low emotion, high and low degrees of representation, and continuation and cessation of processing. The oscillation continues because of the intrinsic tendency of active memory to repeat the representation until the point of completion. Only stable controls or absent controls lead to a steady state, a situation seldom encountered in human psychology.

With each "on" phase of information processing, more and more alterations of inner working models and plans for adoptive action are accomplished. This process continues until completion. With the relative completion of information processing, the cycle terminates, because the relevant contents are cleared from active memory storage. The "new" information has now been integrated with the inner mental models and organized memories. Inner models or schemata are now relatively congruent with the new information about the self and the world, and with the actual external situation to the extent that it is represented accurately in that new information.

Information Processing

One aspect of the processing of traumatic perceptions and memories can be conceptualized as a series of matchings of different types of representations. For example, new stimuli are matched with expectancies based on current needs or fears; new information about the world is matched with schematic representations of the world; current body sensations are related to body images, images are matched with relevant labels such as words; new demands are matched with available coping strategies; and so forth.

When there is not an immediate good fit between the new information and the existing schemata, further information processing is instigated. This then leads to progressive modifications of the meaning of the recently acquired information and/or to progressive modifications of the preexisting models. This processing for fit leads to a series of approximating representations of the stress event and the relevant inner schemata.

When there is a limited channel capacity for processing and when these channels are "claimed" by problems with greater priority, then the progressive series of representations that do not yet "fit" together is stored in active memory. This set of information mixes information from the life event with preliminary associations to it. It will be represented again when it has relatively high priority (e.g., when it is associatively triggered or primed or when more urgent business is finished, as when the driver of a car finds a place to stop after calmly driving through a nearly disastrous accident, then reconsiders the events and only then has a panic reaction).

A single traumatic event may set in motion several trains of thought and feeling. It may need to be associated with different constellations of memories, personal agendas, and varied schemata of self and relationships. The matching between inner sets of organized meaning and the traumatic event may lead to varied emotional states. A specific traumatic event may lead to an appraisal of the self as being too weak to cope; this might activate strong emotional responses of fear. The event might also be associatively linked to previous themes of personal blame, and activate usually latent schemata of the self as a bad person. The strong emotion of guilt might result if the information was processed along that route. To reduce the fear or the guilt, the processing of the given theme might be interrupted.

The activation of emotion begins as ideas are processed, and emotion is itself both represented and anticipated. These anticipations of emotional states are a part of both unconscious thinking and unconscious automatic processes. The person may have learned to interrupt processing of themes that lead to emotional states that feel particularly out of control, overwhelming, and unbearable. Although such interruption may prevent entry into intrusive, emotionally flooded states of mind, it also prevents completion of the work of integrating the stressful life event with that particular theme. Some themes may be worked through relatively completely at a given time; other themes may be warded off. In the latter case they have a "dynamic unconscious" property: preserved in active memory, they tend toward repeated representation and processing. When they are represented, it may be with an intrusive quality. When inhibited, a sense of numbing and avoidance may be present, or denial may be a totally unconscious mechanism without reflection in immediate consciousness.

CONSCIOUSNESS, UNCONSCIOUS
PROCESSING, AND ADAPTIVE CHANGE

Information about events, emotions, and defenses can become a conscious experience only when the encoded information is translated into representational form. Although only representations can become conscious experience, not all representations necessarily attract this special form of attention. Representational and prerepresentational thinking may proceed unconsciously, and many of the processes already mentioned proceed as unconscious computations. Even when representations become conscious, there are varieties and degrees of awareness, intensity, quality, duration, and memory for episodes of awareness. Their quality ranges from representation by action and sensory images to representation by word meanings (Horowitz, 1970, 1983).

Theoreticians such as Hartmann (1939) and Kubie (1958) assumed a range of thought from automatic and relatively nonconscious forms of representational processing to conscious and nonautomatic processing. Roughly, the more conscious the thought is, the greater will be the probability of solving problems, but the slower will be the thought process. When information can be processed by habitual and automatic routes, then time is saved by doing so, and with a minimum of conscious awareness. This is what Lazarus meant by automatized coping. It thus follows that consciousness is most useful for working over representations that have high relevance and that do not fit well into habitual organizations of information or schemata. Suppose that consciousness is the experiential product of "recognizers" of representations that have high relevance but are not matched successfully with schemata. Stress events would then be more apt to reach conscious levels of awareness than would nonstress events because stress events are, by definition, of high relevance and out of the ordinary. Routine expectations and intentions are disrupted, and representations associated with stress events that are difficult to process to completion are also recognized. The recognizer function would be a kind of conceptual enlargement, as suggested by Tomkins (1962, 1979), or some method of reduplication, increased intensity, or spatial expansion of information. This enlargement then would produce a conscious experience of the representation.

The recurrent stress-event representations, often reported as intrusive and unusually vivid when compared with ordinary conscious experience, would be caused by the propulsion to consciousness by the recognition that the theme was important to the self and that its unconscious processing was stymied. The entry of these representations into conscious awareness may be experienced as intrusive for several reasons: the association of the thematic content with the threat and emotional pain of the states of mind during the traumatic events, the unusual vividness of representations derived from memories and traumatic perceptions, the intuitive knowledge that the representational process has been opposed by inhibitory controls, and the emergence of representations unconnected to the immediately previous and intended train of thought.

Despite the conscious experience of intrusiveness, however, the end result may be adaptational, because the conceptual processes initiated by the conscious representation may lead to revising the automatic processing of such information, to revising the relevant schemata, to inventing new solutions, and to completing the processing of the stressful information.

In the psychotherapy of stress response syndromes, the process of using conscious awareness for change is of central importance. The interventions of the therapist and the safe relationship established with the patient are aimed at altering the controls by which the stress-related ideas are warded off and the intolerable emotional states that threaten to emerge if the ideas are not warded off are controlled. Consciousness for the sake of awareness alone is not the goal; rather, conscious contemplation is used as a tool for unlearning automatic associations and resolving seemingly irreconcilable conflicts. Change is accomplished by a combination of conscious and unconscious processes, by the revisions, learning, and the creation of new solutions required by the altered situation. In other words, change can be explained as decisions, both conscious and unconscious, that revise inner schemata and plans for action. The goal is continuity of the traumatic experience with other life memories, and the reintegration of personal aims.

RECAPITULATION

The mind operates to maintain inner schemata that relate the self to others and the surrounding world. One interprets new information by means of those schemata and revises them to remain true to current reality. Serious life events such as a loss or injury present news that will eventually change the inner models. But the change is slow; time is essential to reviewing the implications of the news and the available options for response. The mind continues to process important new information consciously and unconsciously until the situation or the models change and the reality and the schemata of that reality reach an accord. This tendency can be called a *completion tendency*.

Until completion occurs, the new information and the reactions to it are stored in active memory. According to this theory, the active memory contents will be transformed into representations whenever that process is not actively inhibited. Only when the storage of those contents in active memory has been terminated will this repeated representation end. For very important contents, termination will not occur with decay but will occur only when the information processing is complete. At that point, the news will be part of the revised inner schemata.

As ideas related to the stress event are represented, there will be a natural comparison of the news with relevant and assorted enduring attitudes. Because a stress event is, by definition, an important change, there will be a discrepancy among the news, its implications, and the enduring, slowly changing schemata. This discrepancy between the new ideas and the schemata evokes emotion: Serious life events are so different from one's inner models of oneself, one's attachment to others, and one's inner world view that very painful emotional responses result, threatening emotional states of such power that controls are activated to prevent their occurrence or continuation.

Perceptions and immediate responses to serious life events remain stored in active memory because on first encounter the meanings are recognized as having high personal importance. Because the contents are strongly coded in active memory, they tend to be represented intensely and frequently. With each recurrence of the information, the comparisons are made again, and the emotional activation increases. Emotional responses are also represented and so become part of the constellation stored in active memory. When other tasks are more immediately relevant or when emotional responses such as fear, guilt, rage, or sorrow are a threat, the controls are initiated. This feedback thus modulates the flow of information and reduces emotional response.

Excessive controls interrupt the process, change the state of the person, and may prevent completion. Failures of control lead to the excessive levels of emotional flooding, and retraumatization. Optimal controls slow down recognition processes and so provide tolerable doses of new information and emotional responses. In this optimal condition, some intrusiveness will occur with repeated representation, and some denial will occur when the controls operate more pervasively, but the overall result will be adaptive in that the reaction to the stressful life event will eventually be mastered and completed. The schemata will also eventually conform to the new reality, as in the process of completing mourning.

At any given time, different sets of meanings of a stress event will be at different stages and levels of processing. The degree and effectiveness of controls of themes may vary. For example, fear of repetition or fear of merger with a victim may be a recurrent intrusive experience, whereas survivor guilt themes may be totally inhibited from conscious experience. Later, in situations of greater safety, the warded-off guilt theme may surface as an intrusive experience.

This model accounts for the phases of intrusion and denial and the eventual resolution of stress response syndromes. Although general stress response tendencies can be abstracted in this way, persons also respond in unique ways. This is due in part to how their developmental history colors their personal meanings of an event and in part to how their current life tasks and environment are affected by the event. Individual variations in response to the same kind of life event are also due in part to variations in their habitual style of defense and coping.

CONTROL: DEFENSE MECHANISMS

Control theory in psychodynamics has been historically discussed in terms of the defense mechanisms (A. Freud, 1936). Yet the names of defense mechanisms indicate *what* is accomplished rather than *how* it is accomplished. Wallerstein (1967) pointed out this hiatus in the existing theory of defenses and defense mechanisms and defined *defense mechanism* as a theoretical construct used to denote a functioning of the mind, a way of warding off or modulating impulses, ideas, and feelings. *Defenses* are the actual thoughts, feelings, and acts that serve defensive purposes. Complex configurations of defense are called *defensive maneuvers*. Similarly, attempts have been made to detail coping strategies (Pearlin and Schooler, 1978; Lazarus and Folkman, 1984). Again, the available combinations of processes and actions complicate any limited or comprehensive categorization, although there are several coping styles (see also Coelho, Hamburg, and Adams, 1974; Moos, 1976; Monat and Lazarus, 1977).

As Haan (1977) pointed out, a specific mental process may have various end results, including coping and defensive functions, as well as the failure to meet adaptive aims. It seems to me that a theory of defense, of coping, and of succumbing to stress (defensive or coping ''failure'') can be reformulated by considering the controls most used to modulate emotional reactions to serious life events. Understanding the inhibitions, facilitations, distortions, and deflections involved in the processing of information is useful also in formulating techniques of psychotherapeutic treatment of stress response syndromes. The aim is to help the person reverse a course of succumbing to stress, to use those operations that lead to coping, and to set aside those control operations that are so defensive as to impede adaptation.

Controls maintain a state of mind and determine the transition from one state of mind to another. The basic controls are inhibition and facilitation, but it is helpful to be more specific about what is inhibited or facilitated. To do so, we shall separate controls into the following three levels: (1) selecting the overall topic and mode of thinking about it; (2) selecting schemata such as the self-concepts, role relationship models, and agendas or scenarios that will organize the examination of this topic; and (3) selecting the information to be used and skirted in sequences of thought and feeling about the topic. Any phenomenon, such as a recurrent and intrusive image of a dead body weeks after seeing it during an automobile accident, will be a consequence of the operation of many controls at all three levels.

MENTAL SET: SELECTING THE TOPIC AND MODE OF THOUGHT

Mental set is a broad level of abstraction that refers to the choice of topic, the mode of thinking on that topic and, in a general way, to the activation or excitation level. Within this level of abstraction, the control operations most relevant to modulating responses to stress are summarized in Table 6-1. Listed first is the conceptual area selection, an operation that determines the next constellation of information for conceptual processing. While working through serious news, the topic or an aspect of the event may be inhibited or facilitated, resulting in the experience of time on and time away from considering that constellation. This operation can lead to coping experiences, such as when a person doses the recognition of a threat with time off from facing unpleasant realities in order to regain composure. An end result called defensive rather than coping might be total inhibition with no time ''on'' any aspect of the topic. An inability to inhibit a stress event topic may lead

Table 6-1. Controls of Mental Set

PROCESSES	SAMPLE OUTCOMES		
	Coping	Defense	Succumbing to Stress
Selection of next topics for thought	Dosing (periods of time on and off topic)	Denial of importance of an important topic	Amnestic states, intrusion of topics
Mode of organization: temporal set (viewing theme by short or long time orientation)	Looking at only one step at a time, relating the event to a life span	Denial of urgency of threat	Distraught states such as panic
Mode of organization: sequential set (problem solving versus reverie modes)	Thinking only about what to do next, restoring fantasies of lost situations	Workaholism, obsessive rumination and doubting, fantasy preoccupation, faith in unrealistic views	Confusion
Mode of organization: representational set (words, images, muscles, autonomic nervous system, hormones)	Solving problems in words because images evoke too many emotions (intellectual analysis)	Denial of emotional responses to threat, isolation of topics into one mode of representation (words without images, images without words, ideas without emotion)	Emotional flooding
Mode of organization: locus set (external or internal sources of information)	Making restorative changes of activity and contemplation	Compulsive action to avoid thought, fantasy to avoid action	Illusions, hallucinations, felt presences
Activation Level (excitation or dampening various systems, regulating rate of information flow)	Creating cycles of working and resting	Hypervigilance, avoidant sleeping	Exhaustion

103

to feelings of being flooded and dazed, a result that can be called succumbing to stress.

Another set of controls to format selects the mode of organizing information. One such operation is separating into long or short segments the time period to be considered. Extremes of such controls are common during responses to serious life events. One frequent end result is concentration on extremely short time intervals as a person handles a seemingly overwhelming situation by breaking it down into a series of steps, dealing with them one at a time, and describing only what should be done in the next minute or two, or by taking things "one day at a time." Another common response is to scan unusually long sweeps of time in order to place a bitter moment of suffering into a stretch of time that allows it to pale in significance or renders it meaningful in some larger, even cosmic, plan. Thoughts that suffering is a chance to "build character" or "expiate sin" are one result.

Another control over organizing stress-related information is selecting a sequential set. This sequential set determines the kind of flow from one bit of information to another. For example, problem solving is a mode in which bits of information are arranged by principles of logic and by fidelity to real probabilities. A quite different set is used in fantasy or experiential flows in which the next bits of information can be associatively linked to preceding bits by sensory similarities and to congruencies of wish or fear rather than probability or accuracy. This is sometime called primary process.

Heightening such controls after a serious life event leads to common responses. For instance, after being raped, a woman may find herself thinking only of what to do next, whom to call, what to say, and where to shower and rigorously avoiding any experiential reliving in memory of the terrifying event or any similar past experience. Another result of such control is noted when after a rape, for example, the woman may only fantasy an unlikely revenge and avoid thinking about what she has to do next, such as telling someone who can help and support her. Similarly, after a death, the person may fantasy restoration of the lost object and avoid thinking of the implications of the event and the life functions that he or she must now assume. In such failures of control, the result may be an intrusion of fantasy during problem-solving thought or an intrusion into the awareness of real problems, either of which may lead to emotional flooding.

Control of representational set is another way to modulate expression of thought. These controls determine whether the flow of information will proceed in lexical, image, or enactive (motoric) forms. By using such controls, some persons think back on a serious life event, such as a car accident, only in words and block images to avoid emotional arousal from quasi-perceptual thought. Such operations help coping and also may provide defenses such as isolation and intellectualization. The episodes of intensive images of a bloodied body that may occur weeks after an accident are seen as a combination of the impetus of active memory, other motives, and the relative failure of the controls.

Likewise, other controls set the locus, as on the search for or relative acceptance of internal or external sources of information. The end results may be a successful search for relevant external information that also wards off the feelings that will emerge when personal implications are contemplated. The levels of activation of various systems can also be controlled, leading to various altered states of consciousness and also to physiological responses ranging from hyperarousal to hypoarousal (Fischer, 1971).

CONTROLS THAT SELECT SCHEMATA
OF SELF, OTHERS, AND RELATIONSHIPS

Controls that select schemata of self, others, and relationships choose how the self and others will be conceptualized. Every person has not just one self-schemata or version of interaction between the self and others, but multiple inner models of roles and relationship sequences. The dominant model used to organize a train of thought influences the concepts and emotions that occur during the thought sequence.

Controls also select which of a person's several possible self-schemata will organize a series of ideas (Horowitz, 1979; Horowitz and Zilberg, 1983). The results include the various progressions and regressions of identity that commonly occur after serious life events such as the death of a parent. The failure to select or stabilize a self-concept or the loss of a supraordinate self-schema may lead to experiences such as chaotic lapses in identity, as indicated in Table 6-2. Similarly, a person can decide whether to experience a given self-concept as a subject or an object, leading to a variety of common stress responses such as either unusually heightened states of self-actualization or depersonalization, or role reversals.

Another way to reduce emotional response levels while examining implications of a serious life event is to alter the governing model of role relationship between the self and others. A common coping response is to see oneself as more than usually in need and to seek help

Table 6-2. Controls of Schemata as Organizers of Information

| | | SAMPLE OUTCOMES | |
PROCESSES	Coping	Defense	Succumbing to Stress
Altering which self-schema is an activated self-concept	Heightened sense of identity by using the most competent self-concept in the subject's repertoire of self-views	Omnipotent denial of personal vulnerability, "as-if" self-concepts, regressions to earlier self-concepts	Depersonalization, chaotic lapse of identity, annihilation anxiety
Altering dominance hierarchy of available role relationship models and scripts	Seeking help, sublimation	Dissociations and splitting, passive-dependent expectations	Sensation of helplessness, separation anxiety
Altering dominance hierarchy of available world views	Increased sense of unity or ideological commitment, altruism, increased sense of reality, sublimation	Altruistic surrender, increased self-centeredness	Sense of meaninglessness or derealization

and support, or to become dependent on others. Common defensive responses are to adopt illusions of self-sufficiency, to split relationships into those that are all-good and all-bad, or to heighten introjective experiences in order to maintain an illusion of attachment. When these controls fail, a panicky state of mind with ideas of helplessness and emotions related to vulnerability and despair may result. All of these coping, defensive, and adaptive failure responses are well known to every psychotherapist. The point here is to indicate the need of going somewhat beyond managing the results of controls to recognizing the selection process itself, as a therapist's interventions can prevent inappropriate selections and maladaptive consequences.

INFORMATION FLOW SELECTION

The most familiar controls are those that govern the flow of ideas and responsive feelings, because these controls accomplish the common defenses of denial, repression, undoing, and projection. The main controls of information flow are (1) facilitating; (2) inhibiting of representation; (3) switching among sets of information, a process of facilitation as well as inhibition; (4) sliding meaning; (5) shifting the locus of meaning, as from within the self to within another; (6) rearranging information, as in problem solving; (7) seeking new information; (8) revising preexistent goals and inner models; and (9) practicing to make revisions automatic rather than volitional efforts. The results of these controls are summarized in Table 6-3. The results are based on the interaction of many controls and other formative factors and are offered only to show emphasis. The most common impediments to working through the stress induced by a serious life event are inhibition, switching, and sliding meanings.

BIOLOGICAL FACTORS

Activation of the neural systems into extremely high arousal or into special types of alarm and shock may interfere with the consolidation of memory traces. This in turn may lead to memory impairments so that amnesias occur during denial phases that are not only the consequence of temporary defensive operations.

Christianson and Nilsson (in press) reported four experiments in which normal and horribly disfigured faces were presented to experimental subjects. Data from physiological measurements and postex-

Table 6-3. Controls of Ideas and Sequences

PROCESSES	SAMPLE OUTCOMES		
	Coping	*Defense*	*Succumbing to Stress*
Controlling Ideas by			
Facilitation	Contemplation of implications	Rumination	Inability to think clearly
Inhibition	Dosing, modulated arousal, selective inattention	Denial, repression, suppression, isolation, numbing, dissociations, use of drugs, flight, or suicide as avoidance	Intrusions and emotional flooding
Sequencing Ideas by			
Seeking information	Understanding, learning new skills	Intellectualization	Apathy
Switching among attitudes	Emotional balancing	Undoing	Indecision
Sliding meanings and valuations	Humor, wisdom	Reaction formation, exaggeration or minimization, displacement	Intrusions and emotional flooding
Arranging information into decision trees	Problem solving	Denial by rationalization	Inanition
Revising schemata	Adaptation, identifications, acceptance	Inappropriate role reversals by externalization or introjection	Giving up and hopeless states
Practicing new modes of thinking and acting	Deautomatization of outmoded linkages, automatization of new ways	Counterphobic rehearsals	Lack of preparedness for repetition of threat

perimental interviews indicated that negative emotions were aroused by the presentation of the disfigured faces. Each face was accompanied by four verbal descriptors, and amnesia was discovered for those items associated with the traumatic events. Various analyses of their data suggested that this amnesia was developed by limited encoding of the memory trace rather than by problems in retrieval or reconstruction. Such limitations on encoding traumatic perceptions probably have a biological basis.

Other biological factors found in these post-traumatic amnesias may be due to head trauma. Even if there are no positive X-ray or electro-encephalographic findings, the postconcussion syndrome may include general mental deterioration as well as particular memory disturbances and amnesias for a short period of time (Richardson, 1979). These amnesias often include both retrograde and anterograde amnesia, lasting from minutes to months, in which the anterograde amnesia is usually more pronounced. Upon recovery, the retrograde amnesia gradually proceeds to cover the period of just a few seconds or minutes before the trauma and head injury (Whitty and Zangwill, 1977). This phenomenon has been referred to as a recovery of "islands of memory." The entire issue of organic factors in the production of signs and symptoms of post-traumatic stress disorders pertaining to historical diagnostic issues, including the problem of malingering, was reviewed by Trimble (1981).

A third type of biological response may be the consequence of disruptions in attachment to another person, as is the case with bereavement. There may be several hormonal and immunological changes, and this psychological, neurological, and immunological circuit may lead to increased vulnerability to disease, though this has not yet been proved (see Osterweiss, Solomon, and Green, 1984). Such changes in the biological systems, such as neurotransmitters, can also affect psychological capacities, such as feedback, and change a person's ability to exert regulatory operations, such as those pertaining to defense mechanisms.

These psychoneuroimmunological transactions are additions to the biology of how external threat stimuli activate the endocrine system's flight, fight, and conservation responses (e.g., Selye, 1976; Engel, 1967). These involve not only the adrenal cortex and the noradrenergic system of neurotransmitters but other electrochemical messenger systems as well. Facilitations, inhibitions, and dysinhibitions may occur at synapses along particular pathways, and the mechanisms may change the configuration of protein molecules in different ways along neural pathways. Hormones may determine which genes in a neuron's nucleus will form the template for protein synthesis. This in turn will affect the vesicles near the synaptic cleft that contain neurotransmitters, and that may affect the synaptic potentials and information transfer (Kandel, 1983). The brain under stress may also have an altered functional capacity, but the brain-to-mind connection of such factors is not completely understood. One may speculate that enduring psychological change, as in chronic fear arousal or extended despair, can set in motion a pathological brain state such as depression, which then secondarily impairs the kind of information processing emphasized here. Such factors would be in addition to the concomitant physical effects of certain traumas, such as head concussions during automobile or other accidents, or the malnutrition and sleep loss from some disasters.

Persons vary in their genetic inheritance and in how their basic neural systems are organized during development. Some persons may be predisposed to certain vulnerabilities that are then noted only in situations of stress. Biological predispositions—to a "short supply" of certain neurotransmitters, disruptive alarm reactions, or stabilization of a maladaptive state—may be different for those who can work through a stress response syndrome and those who may develop chronic symptoms.

SUMMARY

Everyone fears the inevitable loss of life and the trauma of capricious disaster. When these serious life events occur they can shatter a person's reality, and the inner models of the world that have sustained the person must now be changed to accord with the new situation. Such revisions take time. Recognition of the loss to oneself by accident or the loss of another by death evokes themes of guilt, fear, sadness, and rage. Avoiding recognizing these themes can numb the emotions, but that can create a discord between external reality and what the person believes. There is an interval of time before both the violent emotional pangs of recognition and the avoidance of recognition subside in favor of realistically accepting the new situation. During this interval, characteristic control processes help a person modulate his or her stress responses. This capacity for control is probably determined by biological as well as psychological factors.

Chapter 7
GENERAL TREATMENT PRINCIPLES

If a recent traumatic event is the inciting cause or is a primary factor in developing a stress response syndrome, then the anticipated treatment will usually be brief and focal. The aim is to restore the person to preevent levels of functioning and to foster further development, if that is possible, by working on the focus pertinent to the current reaction to a serious life event. The technique of treatment is aimed at facilitating the patient's own healing tendencies, such as the completion tendency described in Chapter 6. This technique also involves working with the patient's control operations, to enhance regulatory processes in a person who has failing defensive operations and to help the person modulate excessive defenses by making them less necessary as a way of avoiding the threat of distraught, overwhelming states of mind.

Because the treatment is focal, it is important to formulate that focus for both the traumatic events and the highly personal individual reactions. This formulation will often include biological and social factors and individual psychological factors. The process of working through the formulated problems to a more adaptive solution or developmental plane will also include communication and a relationship in which that communication is emotionally contained and sustained.

Modifying excessive controls, altering pathological defensive stances, and supporting weak regulatory capacities all are part of the treatment of stress response syndromes. These coping and defensive conditions are set in motion by the impact of the stressor events; yet they are also a product of long-standing personality styles. The patient's character also includes enduring schemata of self, others, and relationships, as well as persistent life agendas encompassing unconscious scenarios of how the person hopes life will turn out. The treatment invariably involves work with coping and defensive strategies, as well as with the repertoires mentioned above, whether or not these levels of immediate reaction or personality are interpreted. Thus the treatment is both specific and general.

HARRY IN PSYCHOTHERAPY

As you will recall from our case example of Harry, four weeks after the truck accident he had a nightmare in which mangled bodies appeared. He awoke with an anxiety attack. Throughout the following days he had recurrent, intense, and intrusive images of the dead woman's body, and these images, together with ruminations about the woman, were accompanied by anxiety attacks of growing severity. Harry also developed a phobia about driving to and from work. His regular habits of weekend drinking had increased to a nightly use of more and more alcohol; he had temper outbursts over minor frustrations; and he had difficulty concentrating at work and even while watching television.

Harry tried unsuccessfully to dispel his guilty feelings about the accident. Worried about his complaints of insomnia, irritability, and increased alcohol consumption, his doctor referred him for psychiatric treatment. In the psychiatric evaluation, Harry was initially resistant to talking about the accident. But this resistance subsided relatively quickly, and he reported recurrent intrusive images of the woman's body.

During Harry's psychotherapy, he worked through several complexes of ideas and feelings linked associatively to the accident and his intrusive images. The emergent conflictual themes included guilt over causing the woman's death, guilt over the sexual ideas he fantasied about her before the accident, guilt that he felt glad to be alive when she had died, guilt for having broken company rules, and fear and anger that he had been involved in an accident and her death. To a small extent, he also had a magical or primary process belief that the woman had "caused" the accident by her hitchhiking, as well as associated anger with her, which then fed back into his various guilt feelings.

Before continuing with those conflicts triggered by the accident, it is helpful to consider the ideal route of conceptualization that Harry should follow. To reach a point of adaptation to this disaster, he should perceive the event correctly, translate these perceptions into clear meanings, relate these meanings to his enduring schemata, decide on appropriate actions, and revise his memory, attitude, and belief systems to fit this new development in his life. This would lead to a point of relative completion. During this information processing, Harry should not ward off implications of the event or relevant associations to the event, as to do so would impair his capacity to understand and adapt to new realities.

But human thought does not follow this ideal course. The accident has many meanings that sharply contrast with Harry's previous world picture and self-organization. The threat to himself, the possibility that he had done harm, the horrors of death and injury, and the fear of accusation by others sharply differ from his wishes for personal integrity, his current self-concepts, and his view of his life role. This dichotomy between his new conceptualizations and his enduring schemata arouses strong painful emotions that threaten to flood his awareness. To avoid such unbearable feelings, Harry limited the processes to elaborating both the real and the fantasy meanings of the stressful event. Thus the general task of psychotherapy was to work through these various meanings in the context of Harry's tolerance for emotional responses.

The six problematic themes of Harry's psychotherapy can now be reconsidered as ideational-emotional structures in schematic form. These themes will also provide a concrete referent during our later discussion of character-style variations in Chapters 8, 9, and 10. Table 7-1 represents each theme as a match between a current concept and an enduring schema or attitude. Because there is an incongruity between the new and the old, the elicited emotion is also listed.

Table 7-1. Themes Activated by the Accident

CURRENT CONCEPT	Incongruent with ⟶	ENDURING SCHEMATA OR BELIEF ⟶	EMOTION
A. Self as "aggressor"			
a1. Relief that she and not he was the victim.		Social morality	Guilt
a2. Aggressive ideas about the woman.		Social morality	Guilt
a3. Sexual ideas about the woman.		Social morality	Guilt
B. Self as "victim"			
b1. Damage to her body could have happened to him.		Invulnerable self.	Fear
b2. He broke rules.		Responsibility to the company.	Fear (of accusations)
b3. She instigated the situation by hitchhiking.		He is innocent of any badness; the fault is outside.	Anger

Three themes cluster under the general idea that Harry saw himself as the aggressor and the woman as the victim. For example, he felt relief that he was alive when someone "had to die." The recollection of this idea elicited survivor guilt because it contradicted social morality, which holds that one should share the good and bad with companions or social group members.

Harry also felt that he had caused the woman to die. This idea was based on his wish to live, combined with a primitive concept that someone had to fill the role of dying and a belief in his magical power to choose who would fill that role. Similarly, his sexual ideas about the woman before the crash were recalled and were incongruent with his sense of sexual morality and marital fidelity. All three themes are associated with guilty feelings. The first two, survivor guilt and guilt over aggressivity, are common poststress themes, as discussed earlier. The third is a more idiosyncratic response to the particular situation.

Three other themes center on an opposite conceptualization of himself, this time as the victim. Harry was appalled by the damage to the woman's body, for by extension his body could also have been damaged. This forceful idea interfered with his usual denial of personal vulnerability and was inconsistent with his wishes for invulnerability. The result was fear.

Harry also conceived of himself as a victim when he remembered that he had broken company rules by picking up a passenger. Because the violation resulted in a disaster and differed from his sense of what the company wanted, he believed that accusations would be justified and was frightened. "Harrys" with varying character pathology would experience this same theme in different ways. A Harry with a paranoid style might project the accusation theme and suspect that others were now accusing him. He might use such externalizations to make himself feel enraged rather than guilty. If Harry had a histrionic, hysterical character style that featured repression and the inhibition of ideas, he might have uncontrolled experiences of dread or anxiety without a clear representation of the instigating recollections and associations. If he had a preexisting compulsive, rigid, obsessional character style, Harry might ruminate about the rules, about whether they were right or wrong, whether he had or had not done his duty, what he ought to do next, and on and on, without any decisive conclusion.

The last theme cited in Table 7-1 places Harry as a victim of the woman's imagined aggression. His fantasy, here, was that she made the disaster happen by appearing on the highway, which matched his enduring concept of personal innocence in a way that provoked his anger. These angry feelings are then represented as a current concept, and the responses to these concepts again transform Harry's state. His felt experience of anger and his concept of the woman as aggressor did not mesh with his sense of reality. The accident was not her fault, and so as his state of ideas changed, his emotional experience (or potential emotional experience) changed, and he felt guilty for having irrational and hostile thoughts about her.

With this switch from the feelings of a victim to the feelings of an aggressor, there has been a change in emotions from anger to guilt and, in state, from b3 to a2 as diagrammed in Table 7-1. Two of these three themes, fear of identification or merger with the victim and aggression at the source, are also common after stress events. The third theme, fear of accusation from the company, is partially idiosyncratic to this specific situation.

All six themes might be activated by the accident. In "Harrys" of different character styles, some themes might be more important or conflictual than others. In a histrionic or hysterical Harry, sexual guilt themes (a3) might predominate and influence his bad dreams, intrusive images, and pangs of emotion. In an obsessional Harry, aggression-guilt (a2) and concern for duty (b2) might predominate in recurrent thoughts, ruminations, and spasms of self-doubt and anxiety. In a narcissistic Harry, "self as an innocent victim" themes (b3) and fears of body vulnerability might be central. In a borderline character, dissociations of views of the relationship between himself and the woman into all-good and all-bad sets with themes of chaotic bodily and psychic disintegration might prevail. Guilt over being a survivor (a1) and fear of the trauma's repetition (not tabulated) seem to occur universally (Furst, 1967; Lifton, 1967; Krupnick and Horowitz, 1981).

The important point is that generally, there will be many themes connected with the stress event while the associated information is processed to a point of completion. Any given self-concept, as either a victim or an aggressor, and any emotional experience, such as guilt, fear, or anxiety, will be overdetermined, in that not one but several themes may be linked to form the concept or affect. No stress response syndrome is ever a single conflicted train of ideational and affective response; rather, there are always many factors resulting from the mind's tendency to seek similarities and integrations.

Harry experienced a period in which he more or less denied and felt numb about all of these themes. Later, at various times after the accident, some themes were repressed, others emerged, and eventually some were worked through so that they no longer aroused intense emotion or motivated defensive efforts. The first emergent themes were triggered by the nightmare of mangled bodies and the daytime recurrent unbidden images of the woman's body. The themes of bodily injury and survivor guilt (a1 and b1) were no longer completely warded off but rather occurred in alternation, with periods of both intrusion and relatively successful inhibition. In psychotherapy these intrusive themes required early attention; the other themes, such as sexual guilt, emerged later.

Psychotherapy was aimed at resolving the conflicts in all of the relevant themes, in the approximate order of their emergence. That is, an effort was made to bring each theme to a point of completion, and this task used all the usual techniques of psychotherapy.

General strategies have been suggested for working through the various meanings and the complex interplay of impulsive and avoidance aims in stress response syndromes. An inspection of a phenomenology of the main treatments advocated in the past shows that they correspond to the main phases of stress response. Some treatments aim at reliving, analyzing, and working through the stress event; others at suppressing and moving away from the stress event. The first set of treatments is analogous to intrusive repetitions, although the techniques may be used to counteract the opposite phase of signs and symptoms, that is, denial numbing. The latter "rest" treatments are analogous to denial numbing, although they are usually prescribed to end intrusive symptoms.

Historical Review of Treatment Strategies

Combat neuroses presented a massive treatment problem in World Wars I and II, as already mentioned. In World War I, the German army's medical corps recognized the psychological nature of the many cases of "shattered nerves" and "shell shock." Some military physicians reasoned that these cases were caused by fear of bodily damage or death in the trenches. They thus decided to counteract that rational fear with a greater threat of real pain. The "nerve cases," or stress response syndromes as they would now be termed, were given excruciatingly painful electric shock treatment.

As these military doctors hoped, many soldiers returned to the front to escape the "treatment," but others committed suicide to avoid either disaster. After the war, Freud was part of a commission to study complaints of such treatment. This experience probably contributed to his writing "Beyond the Pleasure Principle" (1920), his key work on trauma and the repetition compulsion. In more technical approaches to the psychoanalytic treatment of psychological trauma, Freud (1914b) consistently emphasized the importance of remembering, repeating, understanding, and working through.

The aim was to overcome resistance to emotional expressions and repression, and to assimilate the experience. In this treatment approach, the patient's task is to remember both the external and internal events of subjective experiences. One of the therapist's first tasks is reconstructive. By basing inferences on historical information and observations of the patient's current associations and behavior, the therapist fills in the gaps in the patient's memory (Freud, 1937). The next task is interpretation based on the reconstructions, by working through conflicts until they are resolved.

Memories of traumas are, in the reconstructive process, regarded as having some psychological, but not necessarily historical, reality. The process of change in memories is an important clinical observation, in that early versions are often found to be organizers as well as "screens" that both filter out and admit elements of the objective event (Freud, 1899; Greenacre, 1949; Fenichel, 1954; Reider, 1953; Sachs, 1967; Glover, 1929).

ABREACTION AND CATHARSIS

In World War II, the Allies used an abreactive and cathartic treatment using hypnosis and narcohypnosis that was based on Freud's
ideas. Because of time pressures, and possibly ignorance of some of
Freud's later writings, the dramatic aspects of abreaction received more
emphasis than did the lengthier, harder process of working through.
The hypnotic state was induced in order to skirt the defensive avoidances, to reenact the inciting trauma in full detail of the external events
and internal reaction, and to work through the emergent conflicts.
Posthypnotic sessions were used to complete the working-through
process.

The purpose of treatment was to resolve, as soon as possible after
they occurred, incompleted reactions and conflicts activated by the
stressful events of warfare (Zabriskie and Brush, 1941). Hypnosis, with
or without the aid of amytal or pentothal, was seen as a very rapid treatment. Indeed, the drugs were so effective in reducing defenses and getting at the event that they gained the mystery-magic title of "truth
serum." The reliving of these events was believed to instigate two main
therapeutic processes:

> *Abreaction:* The events were recalled with florid detail and hence made
> known to the treatment team. This communication itself was therapeutic
> because it was a social process. It worked through fears of personal aliena-
> tion, especially if "selfish" thoughts had occurred on seeing a comrade
> killed or if the patient had wished to escape from danger and these wishes
> seemed unfair to other members of his unit. In addition, the therapist could
> respond in a way that facilitated a sense of social acceptance of the warded-
> off memories.
> *Catharsis:* The emotions, ideas, and motoric associations triggered by the
> events could be discharged, thus completing a cycle, much as an orgasm
> completes the cycle of erotic arousal.

During wakeful consciousness following the amytal or hypnotic
state, therapy sessions were held to process further the information that
had been elicited (Kubie, 1943). The resocialization of persons who had
accused themselves of "bad" and "selfish" thoughts was empirically
found to be an important therapeutic factor. Group therapy became a
valuable approach during World War II, not only because it used professional labor hours economically, but also because it filled an observed
need to restore group ties (Bartheimer et al., 1946).

Although resocialization appeared effective, it was determined that
narcohypnosis, regarded as a revelatory or "dramatic trick," was not

as therapeutic as had been originally hoped. For example, no statistically significant difference was found in 200 cases of combat exhaustion treated with narcoanalysis and 200 treated with other methods, including slower, wakeful, and associative approaches to abreaction (Bartheimer et al., 1946).

Even without "truth serums," abreaction was not a cure-all for traumatic symptoms. As Lidz (1946) put it, "the pit seemed fathomless." Abreaction led to more abreaction, to seemingly endless accounts, all related to the traumatic neurosis but with little apparent improvement. Abreaction may relieve anxiety, but this effect can be nonspecific and transient. To obtain durable improvement, it seems necessary to understand the individual patient, the meaning of the experience in relation to the continuum of his life, and to revise discrepancies in self-object representations and other organizing constructs. Rest, recreation, and resocialization were found to be necessary additions, probably as techniques for reducing intrusive and repetitive syndromes and associated psychosomatic symptoms and for reassuring the person that he was not ostracized by his peers. Finally, support of the coping and defensive processes appeared to be important in the acute phases (Hoch, 1943; Bion, 1940; Rioch, 1955).

Abreaction and catharsis, in retrospect, seemed useful for restarting the processing of incompletely integrated stress events. It must be remembered, however, that the goals of treatment in combat medicine were often social rather than individual. That is, the cohesiveness of combat groups and return to duty were as or more important than individual adaptation. In the Korean, Vietnam, and Arab-Israeli wars, for example, a brief period of support, rest, and sedation was considered the best treatment for most stress response syndromes, as it returned more men to action (Glass, 1953, 1954; Bourne, 1970). Exploration of fears of bodily injury or personal guilt might not lead to motivation to return to combat, although it might be necessary at a later time for maximum individual recovery. The long-term effects of suppressive treatment are still being debated (Lifton, 1973; Shatan, 1973; Horowitz and Solomon, 1975; Bourne, 1970).

When using rest, with or without sedation, to treat acute stress response syndromes during military combat, the patient was told that his syndrome was not unusual, was temporary, and could be relieved quickly with an expected return to the unit of service. This was accomplished in aid stations very close to front lines.

Such policies of sedation, rest, reassurance, and return to action accomplish the military's aim of not losing personnel to the rear. The individual who returns to combat duty will often continue without a relapse of the stress response syndrome. True, after a latency period he may again develop a stress response syndrome: perhaps after a return home, with an increasing sense of safety and a relaxation of warding-off defensive maneuvers such as repression and dissociation of experience from the context of the self. Then there may be a delayed stress response syndrome, and the psychotherapeutic help not given initially may be strongly indicated.

EARLY TREATMENT

If treatment is not instituted early, recent traumas have a greater likelihood of producing pathological reactions. For example, persons will act to end any state of crisis, even if this means using the "universal defense" of general inhibition. The results range from a healthy temporary denial, which may actually help heart attack victims to survive, to a dazed and frozen state with a reduced capacity to adapt in general (Kardiner and Spiegel, 1947; Maskin, 1941; Hackett and Cassem, 1970). In addition, a morbid blend of responses to the recent stress and pretraumatic neurotic conflicts may become fixated as character attitudes rather than as ideas and feelings in current flux.

Hypnosis

But even with rapid treatment, it was found that the hypnotic approach to abreaction and catharsis was complicated, as the experiences relived so vividly were sometimes inaccurate. As Freud had found using equivalent methods to "cure" traumatic hysteria, additions were derived from earlier memories and fantasies, and elaboration continued in waking memories (Kubie, 1943; Solomon et al., 1971). Dreamlike states often do produce experiences that, because of their hallucinatory vividness, are then accepted by the subject as authentic memories of external events (Horowitz, 1974a).

Further limitations on the effectiveness of treatment by abreaction, however conscious and extended in time, were noted in the treatment of survivors of the German concentration camps of World War II. For some the damage appeared irreversible; the horror was too great, and the treatment could become only a reliving but not a dispelling of nightmares (Straker, 1971; Koranyi, 1969; Ostwald and Bittner, 1968).

It is tragic to say that a true and full mourning of such a prolonged and total holocaust may be impossible for some individuals.

Crisis Intervention

The rapid treatment of civilian crises was the next development in the history of treating stress response syndromes. As already discussed, the treatment of combat neurosis was necessarily brief. The immediacy of the crisis, the simple goal of symptom relief, and the patients' relative ego strength were thought to contribute to the success of these brief approaches. Such brief psychotherapy, again focusing on resolving sectors of conflicts, was found to be successful in several civilian crisis situations (Knight, 1971; Berliner, 1941; Deutsch, 1949; Lindemann, 1944; Sterba, 1951). The key feature was a careful concentration on the most important current conflict (Stone, 1951; Socarides, 1954; Malan, 1976). Other sectors of function, however conflicted, had to be omitted (Pumpian-Mindlin, 1953; De La Torre, 1972) or given only an incomplete or inexact interpretation (Glover, 1931). And very disturbed patients seemed to respond less well to such brief approach strategies (Kernberg et al., 1972).

Lindemann's (1944) important paper on the management of loss had a major influence on all subsequent brief treatment approaches. He alerted clinicians to delayed or frozen grief and described techniques for reinstigating the "work of grieving." Caplan (1961) also helped develop the crisis-oriented brief therapy, by viewing a crisis as a period of special fluidity, one in which psychic change might even be easier or faster than during times of stability.

The work of Lindemann and that of Caplan (1964), spurred by the development of community mental health centers and the need for detailed rationales for brief and inexpensive treatment, led to the concept of crisis intervention. The stress model of crisis intervention views the onset of the crisis as a precipitatory event (or series of events) that is enough to exceed a person's ordinary coping capacity. In this model, crises are seen as quite time limited. Although there may be turbulent societies, times, or persons, a particular crisis will evoke reaction in a person, possibly in a pathological way. As in military psychiatry, the person must be treated before fixed response sets are solidified (Parad et al., 1976); otherwise the treatment task may be more difficult and take longer.

Jacobson (1974) extended the crisis model into a formula for treatment. The patient comes, it is believed, because of a "cognitive impasse" in response to a "hazard." The therapist's goal is thus to find the hazard and solve the impasse. The hazard is situated in the changes in the person's life space, and a chronological outline helps the therapist discover the stressful external events that a patient may avoid mentioning in a less directive interview.

This is an important point. Just as a surgical patient "guards" his or her abdomen to avoid pain from the hands of an examining physician, patients under stress may ward off pain by skirting around consideration of decisive events. The technique suggested by Jacobson is both diagnostic and therapeutic because it helps the patient understand the determination of his or her current state. In addition to locating critical events in time, the therapist uses the common methods of requesting details, fantasies, and associations in order to find the psychological meaning of the event, usually in terms of loss or threat of loss of some life need. Jacobson established a time period of 6 visits to deal with these meanings. Sifneos (1972) and Mann (1973) used 10 to 12 interviews. The brevity is to prevent dependency and diffuse exploration and to suggest early change. The definite end point encourages both the therapist and the patient to begin to deal with the important issue of separation from each other during the middle phase of the contact.

At the end of that time period, the patient is not necessarily terminated but may be referred to another therapist, in order to adhere to the original agreement. This latter aspect of this approach has the advantages cited above, but also the disadvantages of external caveat and of fitting patients to a mold that may not meet their needs. Thus the safety of an extended relationship may be necessary for some types of psychological change.

MODERN PHASE-ORIENTED TREATMENT

Although the various treatment techniques suggested in the past have had their efficacy, they also have had their hazards. Too often the techniques were applied by therapists in a stereotyped rather than a patient-specific manner. In World War II, psychoanalytically oriented psychiatrists tended to use abreactive hypnosis, and "directive organic" types of psychiatrists, as they were then called, tended to use rest and sedation. We now understand the importance of orientation to treatment not by schools but by the immediate situation as well as the phase of response and the character of the patient.

Phases are often determined by the current degree of control over a tendency toward repetition. In general, the rest and support types of treatment try to supplement relatively weak controls. The treatment staff takes over some aspects of control operations, and they reduce the likelihood of emotional and ideational triggers to repeated representations. In contrast, the abreactive-cathartic methods reduce controls through suggestion, social pressure, hypnosis, or hypnotic drugs. The long-range goal of the abreactive-cathartic treatment is not to reduce controls, however, but to reduce the need for controls by helping the patient complete the cycle of ideational and emotional responses to a stress event.

Such generalities orient understanding but do not help in the prescription of person-specific treatments. Any individual treatment is constructed by selecting many specific maneuvers from the repertoire of available techniques. This selection is based on clinical inference about the patient's immediate state and guided by theory. Unfortunately, the repertoire of available techniques and theories has never been well classified, though a rudimentary attempt at phase-specific technique classification is presented in Table 7-2, the goal being to convey a general idea not to recommend particular treatment forms.

Completing integration of an event's meanings and developing adaptational responses are the goals of treating a stress response syndrome. One knows that this achievement is near when the person is freely able to think about, or not think about, the event. These goals can be broken down according to immediate aims that depend on the patient's current state. When the stress event is ongoing, aims may center on fairly direct support. When the event's external aspects are over, but the person swings between paralyzing denial and intolerable attacks of ideas and feelings, then the immediate aim is to reduce the amplitude of these swings. Similarly, if the patient is frozen in a state of inhibited cognitive-emotional processing, then the therapist must both induce further thought and help package these responses into tolerable doses (see Table 7-3).

General Problems Treating Acute Patients in an Intrusive Phase of Response

Most patients seek help for stress response syndromes when they are overwhelmed with intrusive ideas and emotions. The reality of the traumatic events usually contributes, with the patient's sense of urgent need, to the therapist's wish to react rapidly and to provide help. For

Table 7-2. Treatments for Stress Response Syndromes

STATES	
Denial-Numbing Phase	*Intrusive-Repetitive Phase*
Reduce controls —interpret defenses and attitudes that make controls necessary —suggest recollection	Supply structure externally —structure time and events for patient when essential —organize information Reduce external demands and stimulus levels Rest Provide identification models, group membership, good leadership, orienting values Permit temporary idealization, dependency
Encourage abreaction Encourage description —association —speech —use of images rather than just words in recollection and fantasy —conceptual enactments, possibly also role playing and art therapy Reconstructions to prime memory and associations	Work through and reorganize by clarifying and educative interpretive work Differentiate —reality from fantasy —past from current schemata —self-attributes from object attributes Remove environmental reminders and triggers, interpret their meaning and effect Teach "dosing," e.g., attention on and away from stress-related information
Encourage catharsis Explore emotional aspects of relationships and experiences of self during event Supply support and encourage emotional relationships to counteract numbness	Support Evoke other emotions, e.g., benevolent environment Suppress emotion, e.g., selective use of antianxiety agents Desensitization procedures and relaxation

many physicians and psychiatrists, this urgency may translate into prescribing antianxiety or sedative agents. Although this is sometimes indicated, the availability of the care provider and the establishment of a treatment program are often sufficient. The act of talking about the events and personal reactions during an extended session often markedly reduces the sense of being overwhelmed. When insomnia is producing fatigue and lowering coping capacity, sedation with one of the antianxiety agents may be used on a night-by-night basis. Smaller doses of the same agent may be prescribed during the day, again on a dose-

Table 7-3. Priorities of Treatment

PATIENT'S CURRENT STATE	TREATMENT GOAL
Under continuing impact of external stress event.	—Terminate external event or remove patient from contiguity with it. —Provide temporary relationship. —Help with decisions, plans, or working-through.
Swings to intolerable levels: —Ideational-emotional attacks. —Paralyzing denial and numbness.	—Reduce amplitude of oscillations to swings of tolerable intensity of ideation and emotion. —Continue emotional and ideational support. —Selection of techniques cited for states of intrusion in Table 7-2.
Frozen in overcontrol state of denial and numbness with or without intrusive repetitions.	—Help patient "dose" reexperience of event and implications that help remember for a time, put out of mind for a time, remember for a time, and so on. Selection of denial techniques from Table 7-2. —During periods of recollection, help patient organize and express experience. Increase sense of safety in therapeutic relationship so patient can resume processing the event.
Able to experience and tolerate episodes of ideation and waves of emotion.	—Help patient work through associations: the conceptual, emotional, object relations, and self-image implications of the stress event. —Help patient relate this stress event to earlier threats, relationship models, self-concepts, and future plans.
Able to work through ideas and emotions on one's own.	—Work through loss of therapeutic relationship. —Terminate treatment.

by-dose basis, if the patient's severely distraught, anxious states of mind challenge adaptive functioning.

The patient and persons close to the patient should be cautioned against using multiple mood control agents, especially against combining alcohol with prescribed medications. Alcohol in small doses may be a sufficient soporific and calming agent without additional medication, but for some patients it may lead to excessive self-dosages. Antidepressive agents should not be prescribed to relieve immediate sadness and despondent responses to loss, but they may be used for prolonged pathological reactions that meet the necessary diagnostic criteria for the major depressive disorders, if psychotherapy alone is not leading to clear, rapid, and progressive improvement.

In addition, in the acute phase of responding to a traumatic event, the patient may be advised, for a time, to avoid driving, operating machinery, or engaging in tasks in which alertness is essential to safety. The reason is that persons already under stress are more likely to have accidents because they have lapses of attention, concentration, and sequential planning or because they have startle reactions that disrupt motor control.

During the intrusive phase, relatives and colleagues may also offer support. Advice that has been useful in the past to the patient can be extended directly or through such social support networks. The following list, which restates some of the principles already discussed, may be helpful:

1. Remember that the victim remains vulnerable to entering a distraught state of mind, even in states of safety and even weeks after the event. Such distraught states as pangs of searing grief, remorse, terror, or diffuse rage are attenuated or are less likely to occur if the victim is surrounded by supportive companions. The companions should be aware that being there is doing a lot and that helping may not require doing the impossible. Persons who have sustained the same type of trauma are sometimes especially helpful companions, and that is why self-help groups contain persons who are at different phases of dealing with similar situations.

2. The more the person has been traumatized, the longer the phases of response will be. After a major loss, considerable revision is necessary in both daily life and inner views of life. This revision may mean that the person is not even relatively back to normal, in terms of usual mood patterns, for a year or two. This contrasts with the expectation in many work environments that the traumatized person should be back to usual functional levels within a week or two. The work place

may provide sustaining interests and social supports so that the victim is not left isolated or encapsulated; yet some modulation of what is expected should extend for longer periods than has become the case in a society driven by work productivity and advancement.

3. Sleep disruption is a common part of post-traumatic stress disorders. The victim comes to associate efforts to relax and sleep with episodes of panic or vivid unpleasant imagery associated with the trauma, especially if it has occurred at times when one's guard has been lowered or one's concentration on daytime activities is reduced. It may be helpful to change habit patterns in whatever way strengthens the sense of safety that permits restful sleep. This may include leaving the room lights on or sleeping with a pet or with another person. In extreme cases, rest can be encouraged by telling the victim that a companion will stay awake and watch over him or her during sleep.

4. The person who has been traumatized may have cognitive impairments of which he or she is not aware. The victim may feel more effective, alert, and reflexively responsive than is actually the case and may be more at risk of accidents while driving or operating machinery. Any kind of drug, such as a single drink of alcohol, may have a more impairing effect on such persons than would usually be the case. For these reasons, not letting the victim drive or providing nonhazardous work tasks is advisable even when the victim insists this is not necessary. Thus it must be done tactfully so as to avoid anything that might encourage a transition to incompetent self-concepts.

5. Right after a traumatic event, the victim's relatives and friends rightfully cluster around and want to know all about it. The victim, often alone at the time of the event, now recounts the story again and again to each new arrival. There is here a paradox, because later on the victim will want to retell the story again and again but now, early, is when it is demanded. These many early repetitions may lead to an exhausting reliving of the still-vivid experience with all its violent emotional responses. Later the relatives and friends may behave as if they were tired of hearing about it and may counter with their own similar tales of mishap and woe. The victim may then feel pent up with the need to repeat the traumatic experience and to communicate his or her conceptual and emotional responses to it. It is at these later stages that empathic listening, without trying to short-circuit the conversation, may be very useful. Then gradually the victim's attention can be brought first to the present and then the future.

6. The victim expects to be upset after a trauma, and so when responses come later, after a period of restored good functioning, they

come as a surprise and may lead to a fear of losing mental control and unnecessary doubts about recovery. Knowledge about the normal phases, including a return of intrusive ideas and emotions after a period of denial, can be very useful for the victim at this point. Sometimes, however, the victim will have a correct intuitive sense of being blocked in working through a trauma. This subjective sense may be usefully echoed by a relative or friend who also recognizes that the reaction is too intense, prolonged, complicated, or impacted. That social communication, in the context of a calm and straightforward discussion, may enable the victim to seek professional help when it is indicated.

In evaluating a patient in an acute, probably intrusive phase of response to a traumatic life event, the clinician should specifically inquire about intrusive experiences, as the patient may find them difficult to describe on his or her own. The clinician then may label this symptom as a normal response to stress in order to reassure the patient that he or she is not losing control of his or her mind. When the patient describes what is intruding into his or her experience, the clinician should encourage him or her to expand on the topic in order to develop further the meaning of the event. Usually nonspecific statements are helpful in encouraging this elaboration; for example, one may ask, "Can you tell me more about that?" "Is there anything else?" "What was it like for you?" and so forth.

While listening to the patient expand on the topic, the clinician should be alert to blocks in thinking or feeling in the next step in a sequence that might lead to some kind of acceptance or closure of the event. For example, thinking about the event's implications may lead to ideas of what caused it. The patient may think that he or she did something that caused the event, which would lead to feelings of intense guilt, and so he or she may then block off this train of thought at that moment in order to avoid experiencing the guilt.

When the clinician discovers a block to working through reactions to a stressful event, he or she may help the patient by looking at the differences between realistic appraisal and fantasy appraisal. For example, if a patient feels that he has brought on a heart attack by harboring angry thoughts toward his boss, it may be important to indicate to him that this was not the cause of the coronary occlusion and that he does not have to blame himself for it. This is not meant to complete the therapy in a single visit but to move toward a hopeful focus for the treatment.

The clinician does not have to be a figure who restores what has been lost. But it is important to the patient that the clinician represent a person who is not overwhelmed by thinking about the implications of some illness, injury, or loss. The very presence of the clinician as a person who is able to contemplate these events and to think about them logically is often extremely reassuring to the patient during an intrusive phase. The denial phase is also an especially important one to consider in relation to treatment interventions. Denial may serve adaptive purposes, allowing the person to restabilize, but it may also interfere with important decisions that may have to be made at once because of time pressure. Health care choices are one example, as with a patient with gangrene from an electrical burn during an accident who has to decide at once on the degree of amputation that he will permit.

Time Pressure during a Denial Phase

Intellectualization may be openly advised for the patient as a way to make immediate decisions. For example, the patient may be told that although there will be many emotional reactions to the situation, for the time being it might be best to consider only those problems requiring an immediate choice and to talk them over in terms of advantageous and disadvantageous outcomes. The processes involved in denial may also be labeled so that the patient can understand why it is difficult to concentrate on making a decision. Sometimes it is necessary to accept the patient's inability to make a fully rational decision at the moment because of the specific stress disorder and to explain both the denial phase and the information pertinent to decision making to another person who is accepted by the patient as serving his or her best interests. When this is the case, the physician should realize that this is a transient assignment, not one that should continue for a long time. Later the patient should be told how and why these decisions were reached.

No Time Pressure during a Denial Phase

Patients may be told that they are pushing away recognition of the event's implications and that this is a normal adaptive reaction. This should be done in a noncritical manner, indicating the acceptability of such defensive avoidances. If patients are not, on their own, progressing through a period of denial and numbness, it may be helpful to remind them of the need to make the next adaptive move. The patients may be encouraged to allow a conscious review of memories and to experience ideas and feelings related to what has passed.

Patients may be urged to take a one-dose-at-a-time approach, contemplating the most immediate consequences of what has happened and perhaps putting off the next considerations for a short period of time. This kind of reassurance indicates to the patients that they can tolerate some aspects of what has seemed intolerable but that they do not have to confront everything all at once. Patients may also be given realistic reassurance that they will eventually be able to tolerate what now seems overwhelming. The example of mourning may be given, that it seems intolerable to accept a loss that has just occurred but that people come to accept it over a period of a year or two. It is often helpful in this regard for the clinician to indicate that he or she will remain available to the patient as a support until the patient works through and accepts his or her experience.

TIME-LIMITED BRIEF DYNAMIC PSYCHOTHERAPY FOR STRESS DISORDERS

At the Center for the Study of Neuroses, University of California, San Francisco, my colleagues and I developed a brief psychotherapy for stress response syndromes (Horowitz, 1973, 1976; Horowitz and Kaltreider, 1979; Horowitz, Marmar, Krupnick, Wilner, Kaltreider, and Wallerstein, 1984). This procedure uses a time limit of 12 sessions which can be varied as required by individual circumstances, characteristics, and responses. A sample of what tends to happen in such therapies is given in Table 7-4.

When a person seeks help, the therapist establishes a working alliance through which he or she assists the patient in working through his or her reactions. In addition, efforts may be directed at modifying preexisting conflicts, developmental difficulties, and defensive styles that made the person unusually vulnerable to traumatization by this particular experience.

Therapy begins by establishing a safe and communicative relationship. This, together with specific interventions such as an analysis of defensive avoidances and an identification of warded-off contents, alters the status of the patient's controls. The patient can then proceed to reappraise the serious life event and the meanings associated with it and make the necessary revisions of his or her inner models of the self and the world. As this reappraisal and revision take place, the person moves into a position to make new decisions and to engage in adaptive actions. The patient can follow any altered behavioral patterns until they become automatic. As he or she is able to achieve new levels of awareness, this process is repeated and deepened. That is, as the pa-

Table 7-4. Sample 12-Session Dynamic Therapy for Stress Disorders

SESSION	RELATIONSHIP ISSUES	PATIENT ACTIVITY	THERAPIST ACTIVITY
1	Initial positive feeling for helper	Patient tells story of event	Preliminary focus is discussed
2	Lull as sense of pressure is reduced	Event is related to previous life	Takes psychiatric history. Gives patient realistic appraisal of syndrome
3	Patient testing therapist for various relationship possibilities	Patient adds associations to indicate expanded meaning of event	Focus is realigned; resistances to contemplating stress-related themes are interpreted
4	Therapeutic alliance deepened	Implications of event in the present are contemplated	Defenses and warded-off contents are interpreted, linking of latter to stress-event and responses
5		Themes that have been avoided are worked on	Active confrontation with feared topics and reengagement in feared activities are encouraged
6		The future is contemplated	Time of termination is discussed
7–11	Transference reactions interpreted and linked to other configurations Acknowledgment of pending separation	The working-through of central conflicts and issues of termination, as related to the life event and reactions to it, is continued	Central conflicts, termination, unfinished issues, and recommendations all are clarified and interpreted
12	Saying good-bye	Work to be continued on own and plans for the future are discussed	Real gains and summary of future work for patient to do on own are acknowledged

tient can relate more closely, he or she can modify controls further and assimilate more warded-off thoughts about the current stress. There is then the necessity of working through the reactions to the approaching loss of the therapist and the therapy.

Within the time limits of a brief psychotherapy, the therapist works to establish conditions that will help process the painful event. There is an early concern by the patient for both the safety of the relationship and the therapist's ability to help him or her cope with the symptoms. These symptoms can seem less overwhelming when the therapist offers support, suggests some immediate structuring of time and events, and prescribes medication if anxiety or insomnia are too disruptive.

Introducing plans for terminating the therapy several sessions before the final one leads to a reexperience of the loss, often with a return of the symptoms. But this time, the loss can be faced gradually, actively rather than passively, and within a communicative and helping relationship. Specific interpretations of the link of the termination experience to the stress event are made, and the final hours center on this theme. At termination, the patient will usually still have symptoms, both because of the time needed to process a major loss and because of anxiety about the loss of the relationship with the therapist.

Patients sometimes become aware during these brief therapies of a particular style they have for *not* thinking about events, and they are able deliberately to alter that avoidance. It may be possible for them, by continued work on their own after therapy, to live out changes that may gradually modify their habitual defenses and attitudes. In this manner, the brief therapy of stress response syndromes follows the techniques of focal dynamic therapy, as described by Malan (1979), Basch (1980), Strupp and Binder (1984), and Luborsky (1984), and may also use special imagery techniques, as described by Singer and Pope (1978) and Horowitz (1983).

When people experience the impact of a serious life event, such as a loss or injury, their most advanced, adaptive role relationships can be threatened. They may regress to earlier role relationships, or the meaning of the event itself may create some new role relationship, perhaps with unattractive, dangerous, or undesirable characteristics. Such persons may then enter a series of painful, strongly affective states based on altered self-concepts and role relationship models. As a consequence of the therapeutic facilitation of normal processes, these disturbing role relationships or self-concepts can once again be subordinated to more adaptive, mature self-concepts and role relationships. Intensive work using this type of brief therapy model may change the symptomatic response to a stressful life event and may facilitate further progress along developmental lines.

Realignment of Focus during a Brief Therapy

Patients will usually have presented painful symptomatology or problematic states as the chief complaint or motivation for seeking help. The first focus or agreement between patient and therapist will be to help attenuate these symptoms or states or to avoid reentry into them. Problematic states will be seen in relation to other states of experience and behavior. A broader analysis of the situation with the patients will include examining the reasons for entering the problem states and other, even more threatening states that are warded off. As painful symptoms are ameliorated, the emphasis may shift to exploring when and why the patient enters these painful states. This revised focus often pertains to particular self-concepts and inner models of relationships. If this shift in focus is not made at the right time, the patient may move toward termination or avoidance of treatment when he or she achieves enough control to enter a relatively stable denial phase. Separation from treatment at this time may be an error because the patient has not worked through some of the most difficult parts of his or her stress response and may not do so on his or her own.

CLINICAL EXAMPLE FROM A BEREAVEMENT CASE. The patient was a young woman in her mid-twenties. She sought help because of feelings of confusion, intense sadness, and loss of initiative six weeks after the sudden, unexpected death of her father. Her first aim was to regain a sense of self-control. This was accomplished within a few sessions, because she found a substitute for the idealized, positive relationship with her father in the relationship with the therapist and realistically hoped that she could understand and master her changed life circumstances.

As she regained control and could feel pangs of sadness without entering flooded, overwhelmed, or dazed states, she began to wonder what she might further accomplish in the therapy and if the therapy was worthwhile. The focus gradually shifted from recounting the story of her father's death and her responses, to understanding her past and current inner relationship with her father. The focus of therapy became her vulnerability to entering states governed by defective, weak, and evil self-concepts. These self-concepts related to feelings that her father had scorned her in recent years because she had not lived up to his ideals. He died before she could accomplish her goal of reestablishing a mutual relationship of admiration and respect through her plan to convince him that her own modified career line and life-style would lead to many worthwhile accomplishments.

This image of herself as bad and defective was matched by a complementary image of her father as scornful of her. She felt ashamed of herself and angry with him for not confirming her as worthwhile. In this role relationship model, she held him to be strong, even omnipo-

tent, and in a magical way she saw his death as his deliberate desertion of her. These ideas had been warded off because of the intense
humiliation and rage that would occur when they were clearly represented. But contemplation of such ideas in therapy allowed her to
review and reappraise them, revising her view of herself and of him.

Every person has many self-images and role relationship models.
In this patient, an additional important self-image was of herself as a
person too weak to tolerate the loss of a strong father. As is common,
no life event occurs in isolation from other life changes but is almost
invariably part of a cluster of events and effects. After this woman
returned from her father's funeral, she turned to her lover for consola-
tion and sympathy. She had selected a lover who, like her father, was
superior, cool, and remote. But when she needed compassionate attention, he was unable to provide it, and they separated. Establishing a
therapeutic alliance thus provided much needed support, but its termination threatened her once again with the loss of a sustaining figure.
In the mid-phase of therapy, it therefore was necessary for her to focus
on those weak self-images in order to test them against her real capabili-
ty for independence.

To recapitulate, early in therapy this patient rapidly established a
therapeutic alliance around a working focus to relieve her of the acute
distress of the intrusive phase of a stress response syndrome, in this
case an adjustment disorder. This alliance led to a rapid attenuation
of the problematic states of mind. With this symptom reduction, the
focus shifted to the aim of working through various aspects of her relationship with her father. In addition to the primary meanings of her
grief, that is, the loss of a continued relationship with her father and
the hope of changing it, she had to work through several additional
themes: herself as scorned by her father, herself as too weak to survive without her father, and herself as evil and partly responsible for
his death.

These important self-concepts, present before the death, were worked
on during the mid-phase of therapy. They were related to role relationship models that pertained not only to her father but also to other past
figures (mother and siblings), current social relationships, and transference themes. As she contemplated and worked with these themes,
her focus expanded from past and current versions of these constellations to include additional issues. Were she to maintain these self-
concepts and views of role relationships, she might either reject men
altogether or continue with a neurotic repetition of efforts to regain her
father and convert him to the ideal figure she remembered from early

adolescence. This prospective work also included examining her reaction to separation from the therapist and how she would in the future interpret that relationship.

Interpreting Defenses and Transference for a Particular Event

All patients will have a combination of reactions to stress events and their prestress problems. Therapists therefore should attend to the manifestations of characteristic defensive styles and the emergence of transference even during the comparatively brief treatment of a stress response syndrome. What do therapists do with this information? Do they interpret defenses, interpret and try to work through transference? Or do they work around defense and transference to bring the stress-event reactions to a point of completion? Each patient–therapist pair can arrive at a satisfactory end point by means of different routes. Nonetheless, "using the gestalt of the stress event" can be one of the guiding principles.

This means that defensive modifications and self-object dyad interpretations can be made and that they can be centered on the specific contents of the stress-event memories.

EXAMPLE OF CONNECTION-FORMING INTERVENTIONS. A young woman had attacks of incapacitating anxiety for months after she was raped. She had flirted with the man and encouraged his advances, but when she wished to go no further in the sexual encounter, he forced her, with threats of violence, to have intercourse. She decided not to report the matter to either the police or a physician. She came for help later because of increased anxiety.

The first work involved her telling the story of how she was traumatized by this man's vicious behavior. This, plus the establishment of a therapeutic relationship, helped reduce her anxiety, but an unclear sense of her own participation remained and required further therapeutic attention.

During psychotherapy she was generally vague in her verbal communication. Nonverbally, there were gestures in her bodily movements to which the therapist did not respond but found somewhat erotically stimulating. When the therapist failed to show interest in her physical attributes and movements, the patient seemed to feel hurt, looked dejected, withdrew, and talked in a self-depreciating manner. Despite this reactivity, the patient did not appear to be conceptually aware of either her bodily "gambits," the therapist's lack of attention to them, or her "hurt" responses.

Through many such observations of process, the therapist made two inferences. One was that she had a repressive-denying and dissociative style. The other concerned a pattern for interpersonal relationships in which she offered an erotic surrender to a domineering other person and expected attention and care in return.

These inferences were not interpreted directly or in terms of the transference manifestations. Instead, they were used as information to help reconstruct the rape and preceding events. The rape was seen as a pattern contributed to by the real but unrecognized assaultative nature of the man involved, her general pattern of relating to men, and her method of avoiding appraisal of this particular man.

In this way, some aspects of the fear, anger, guilt, and shame evoking ideas about the event were worked through. In addition, the therapeutic process allowed some progressive change in her self- and object concepts. For example, one unconscious attitude present before the stress event was that an erotic approach was the only way to get attention because she herself was so undeserving. She must give her body in order to get attention. In work on the meaning of the rape, she became aware of this defective self-concept and related rescue fantasies. She was able to revise her attitudes, including her automatic and unrealistic expectations that dominant others would feel guilty about exploiting her and then be motivated by guilt to be concerned and tender.

The relatively clear contents of the stress-event memories provided a concrete context for this work. The focus of discussion was outside the therapeutic relationship, although there was a tendency toward a compulsive repetition of the "raper–rapee" relationship in the transference situation. The therapeutic alliance was maintained but might have been disrupted by the anxiety that would have occurred if interpretation of the same self-object transactions were directed to the transference situation.

At some point, if advisable, it may be possible to extend recognition of the same patterns to the transference, to childhood relationships, and to current interpersonal relationships. That is, this focus on the stress events does not mean that the interpretation of transference is omitted from a stress-focused treatment. But there is no intent to allow a transference neurosis to evolve, and transference interpretations will usually focus on negative responses that are likely to impede therapy.

EXAMPLE OF A BLEND OF TRANSFERENCE RECOGNITION FOCUSING ON A RECENT STRESSFUL EVENT. A young woman patient broke her leg in a fall from a ladder while helping her father paint his house. A partial paralysis complicated matters and disrupted her plans to accept an available teaching position on graduation from college. She came for therapy because of a reactive depression. One of the dormant psychological complexes activated by her injury was hostility toward her father for not taking good-enough care of her. The relevant theme of the stress event was anger that her father had given her a rickety, second-class ladder while he used a good one. She had, in the past, been unable to recognize her own ambivalence toward her father, even when he gave her good cause to be hostile. Awareness of her anger was warded off at the time of treatment onset.

During one treatment hour, the emotion closest to the surface was anger at the therapist because he would not prescribe sleeping pills for her insomnia. Though the therapist was able to infer this emotion, it was not recognized or expressed clearly by the patient.

We shall now artificially dichotomize the immediate problem of whether the therapist should interpret the anger in terms of the transference or in terms of the stress event. In general, a therapeutic rule of thumb is to focus on negative transference reactions, such as surfacing anger at the therapist. The reason for this rule is that negative reactions interfere with other therapy processes, and the patient might even quit or withdraw. The problem is how not only to deal with negative transference feelings, so that they are reduced enough for the therapy to progress, but also to use the information gained to work through the stress event. One way to decide whether or not to focus on the emergent anger is the therapist's diagnostic impression of the patient's strength. If the patient is capable of tolerating it, the therapist can interpret what is going on. But if the patient is in danger of fragmentation, as in severe narcissistic and borderline characters, the therapist may not interpret the anger directly, but instead may deal with it in a counteractive way or give it a peripheral interpretation in relation to characters outside the treatment situation.

If the therapist decides to interpret the anger in a fairly direct manner, he still must decide which line of interpretation will be the most therapeutic. For example, the therapist can choose among four lines of approach, such as

1. You are angry with me because you feel that I am not taking care of you, just as your father did not take care of you (interpretation of the transference link to father).
2. You are angry with me and are afraid to express it or even know it (interpretation of the fear of being angry).

3. You are angry with me, and so you withdraw (interpretation of the defensive maneuver).
4. You get angry when your dependency needs are not met (interaction of underlying wishes).

These are, of course, not the wordings of the interpretations but a shorthand illustration of the various possible directions. In a full segment of work, each aspect of the interpretation may be made.

Whichever type of interpretation is made first, it may be possible to link the exploration of the anger to the recent stress event, even though the focus remains on working through the immediate negative sentiments toward the therapist. For example, the interpretation may be worded as follows, except that it would be given in short phrases rather than all at once:

"You are angry with me right now because I am not meeting your need for a sleeping pill, just as you are still angry with your father because you feel he took poor care of you by giving you a lousy stepladder."

The principle advantage of this type of wording, which links current transference to the model of the stressful event, is that it maintains a conceptual clarity regarding the treatment's goals and priorities. If the focus is on only the transference meanings of a patient–therapist transaction, the transference will be accentuated as a topic of interest to the therapist. Some transference work creates more transference work because the therapist's interest in the transference aspects of treatment has an intrinsic transference-evoking effect, a paradoxical cycle. The tendency is toward a character analysis (Oremland, 1972) rather than working through the life event and then terminating or establishing some other therapeutic contract.

EXAMPLE OF DEPRESSION AFTER THE DEATH OF A LOVED ONE. During the first three interviews the work focused on a young male patient's feeling that his mother had left him alone by dying. But as a result of this work, his feelings of intense loneliness decreased. The pain and threat of his loss had been reduced to a level at which his available defensive and coping strategies could inhibit further emotional responsivity. During the ensuing interviews, his feelings of sadness and ideas of being left were absent.

Despite the symptomatic relief, the therapist inferred that the stressful event had not been completely worked through but, rather, had only been worked on to the point that denial and numbness had become possible. At this point in treatment, as is common, the patient searched for topics to discuss because he did not want to lose the therapist through treatment termination. That is why in one hour he brought up a current problem, an argument the night before with his girl friend.

There was no doubt that the emotion nearest the surface was anxiety about the argument, and the therapist gave his attention to this situation. But in his interventions he chose not to explore in detail the relationship between the patient and his girl friend because he felt it would deflect the therapeutic path to interpersonal relationships in general and from there into a long-term therapy. Instead, he linked the patient's fears of losing his girl friend to the recent loss of his mother by saying, "Another loss might be very hard for you to contemplate right now."

This remark was enough to link the young man's current emotional state to the incompletely processed stress event. Through such maneuvers, it was possible to avoid diffusion of the therapy to many topics. With this patient, a decision to attempt a general characterological revision might be made after more work on the loss.

These case examples do not mean that the work of relating the meaning of subsequent occurrences to the stress event can be forced. In some patients, especially adolescents or young adults, loss of a parent or sibling may be worked on only to a point that denial can set in. Then the implications of the loss are vigorously inhibited, and attempts at connection, such as illustrated here, will not succeed. In such instances, the therapeutic goal must be reconsidered, the defenses accepted, and the patient either seen over a considerable period of time with a therapeutic strategy or terminated until any later work is indicated.

RESULTS OF BRIEF DYNAMIC THERAPY FOR STRESS RESPONSE SYNDROMES

Along with the brief dynamic therapy described earlier in this chapter, my colleagues and I developed a series of measures useful for assessing the outcome of such treatments, the disposition of patients, the process of therapy, and the interaction of these variables. These include the Impact of Event Scale, which offers specific stress measures for self-report (Horowitz, Wilner and Alvarez, 1979; Zilberg, Weiss, and Horowitz, 1983); the Stress Response Rating Scale, which measures the clinician's assessment of current stress levels (Weiss, Horowitz and Wilner, 1984); and the Patterns of Individualized Change Scales, which assess social and work functions as well as self-esteem and specific stress symptoms (Kaltreider et al., 1981; DeWitt et al., 1983; Weiss et al., 1985).

The therapy-process measures pertinent to this approach to psychotherapy include assessments of the therapeutic alliance (Marziali, Marmar and Krupnick, 1981; Marmar et al., in press) and the assessment of specific therapist interventions on a therapist-actions scale or checklist (Hoyt, 1980; Hoyt, et al., 1981). These process scales, the assessment of patients' motivations for dynamic psychotherapy (Rosenbaum and Horowitz, 1983), and the developmental level of the self-concept (Horowitz, 1979; Horowitz, Marmar, Weiss, et al., 1984) rely on independent opinions of judges reviewing videotapes, audiotapes, or transcripts and have been found to be reliable at satisfactory levels.

Using all such measures in the study of 52 cases of pathological grief reactions after the death of a family member, we examined the results of a 12-session, time-limited brief dynamic psychotherapy of the kind just described (as reported in detail in Horowitz, Krupnick, Kaltreider, et al., 1984). Before treatment, this sample had levels of symptoms comparable with those of other outpatient samples studied in treatment research. The SCL-90 is perhaps the most widely used measure of symptomatic distress and thus provides a valuable benchmark. The mean total pathology score at intake on the SCL-90 for the sample was 1.19 (SD, 0.59). This level is almost identical with the figure of 1.25 (SD, 0.39) reported by Derogatis et al. (1976) for a sample of 209 symptomatic outpatients analyzed in a validation study of this measure. The mean depression subscale score in our sample at intake was 1.81, and in the Derogatis et al. study it was 1.87. The scores for anxiety were also comparable: 1.39 in our sample and 1.49 in the sample of Derogatis et al.

A significant improvement was seen in all symptomatic outcome variables when pretherapy scores were compared with follow-up levels. These findings are given in Table 7-5. The results are also expressed in terms of the standardized mean difference effect size coefficient recommended by Cohen (1979) for before-after data. He defined a large effect as 0.80 or greater. Our large effect sizes were in the domain of symptoms and ranged from 1.21 to 0.71. Changes in work and interpersonal functioning (PICS relationship composite) and the PICS capacity for intimacy were more moderate.

Table 7-5. Outcome Variable Means at Time of Pretherapy and Posttherapy Follow-up Assessments[a]

PRIMARY DISTRESS MEASURES	PRETHERAPY SCORE, MEAN	(SD)	POSTTHERAPY SCORE, MEAN	(SD)	NO.	t	p	EFFECT SIZE (SD UNITS)
Self-report								
Stress specific								
Intrusion (IES)	22.1	(7.6)	12.9	(8.0)	48	8.53	<.001	1.2
Avoidance (IES)	19.1	(9.8)	8.7	(8.5)	49	5.15	<.001	0.9
General								
Anxiety (SCL)	1.4	(0.8)	0.7	(0.6)	48	6.40	<.001	0.9
Depression (SCL)	1.8	(1.0)	1.0	(0.8)	48	6.41	<.001	1.0
Total pathology (SCL)	1.2	(1.6)	0.7	(0.5)	48	6.90	<.001	0.9
Evaluating clinician report								
Stress specific								
Intrusion (SRRS)	17.6	(9.9)	9.7	(8.1)	49	5.15	<.001	0.7
General								
Total neurotic pathology (BPRS)	15.6	(5.4)	11.0	(6.2)	49	5.03	<.001	0.7
PICS, independent clinician judgments								
Stress symptoms composite	3.6	(0.6)	4.7	(1.1)	43	−6.56	<.001	1.0
Relationship composite	4.2	(1.1)	4.6	(1.0)	44	−2.29	.027	0.4
Intimacy capacity	3.4	(1.6)	4.1	(1.6)	42	−3.65	.001	0.6

[a]IES indicates Impact of Event Scale; SCL, 90-item Hopkins Symptom Checklist; SRRS, Stress Response Rating Scale; BPRS, Brief Psychiatric Rating Scale; and PICS, Patterns of Individual Change Scales.

TIME-UNLIMITED PSYCHOTHERAPY

Complex, delayed, or chronic stress response syndromes are probably best treated with a time-unlimited format, for there will usually be an extended treatment time required. This also applies to persons with post-traumatic stress disorders in the context of a personality disorder, especially those personality disorders characterized by vulnerability to the coherence and stability of self-organization. Even in such extended psychotherapies, however, a focus on working through the traumatic events and the reactions to them may be usefully preserved. This brings into question the level of interpretation to be used during such therapies.

In general, the approach advised is one that begins at the surface, is anchored to the traumatic events, and gradually extends to related issues at a pace that is tolerable and useful to the patient.

LEVELS OF INTERPRETATION

Levels of interpretation range from surface to depth, as shown in Table 7-6. At the top of the table the first of eight levels from surface to depth is called "Stressors and Stress Responses" and at the bottom of the table is "Unconscious Scenarios and Schematic Affective Agendas." In general, the shorter the therapy is and the more disturbed the patient is in his or her organizational level of inner working models of self and relationships, the longer one will have to deal with the surface levels.

Any of the levels of attention that the therapist uses in helping the patient establish a focus and aim for the treatment and in organizing sequences of his or her own interventions may focus on current situations, the in-treatment situation, and/or on past historical and developmental events. Some aspect of the focus at a given level is also offered for each of these sectors in Table 7-6.

Crisis intervention (Caplan, 1961; Jacobson, 1974; Kutash, Schlesinger, et al., 1980) often successfully enables a patient to get through a crucial strain while staying at the top level of Table 7-6. Establishment of the connection also enables the patient to examine experiences in a way that was too overwhelming to do alone or in an existing social network. Usually, dynamically oriented psychotherapy, however brief, advances to at least the next level of analysis, at which pending coping choices and conscious scenarios are examined. This includes a

Table 7-6. Levels of Interpretation

CONTENT AREAS	LEVEL OF ANALYTICAL FOCUS		
	Current Situation	Therapy Situation	Past
Link between external situation and personal responses			
1. Stressors and stress responses	Intentions of how to respond	Expectations of treatment	Relevant experiences of previous stress events
2. Pending coping choices and conscious scenarios	Conflicting aims of how to respond	Dilemma analysis of what to deal with first	Long-standing goals and habitual conundrums
3. Avoidance of adaptive challenges	Threat and defense	Resistance to working through a conflicted issue	History of self-impairing character traits
4. Repertoire of states of mind	Triggers to entry into problem states or exit from symptomatic states	States of therapeutic work and nonwork	Habitually problematic and desired states
5. Expressed irrational beliefs	Differentiation of realistic from fantastic associations and appraisals		
Link between current problems and long-standing, individualized personality patterns			
6. Repetitive maladaptive interpersonal behavior patterns	Interpersonal problems and self-judgments	Difference among social alliances, transferences, and therapeutic alliances	Abreaction or reconstruction of traumas and strains in relationship
7. Self-concept repertoires and role relationship models	Views of self and others	Differences among social alliances, transferences, and therapeutic alliances	Development of role relationship models
8. Warded-off unconscious scenarios and impulsive agendas	Urges, dreams, and creative products	Regressive, intense transferences	Episodes of regression that uncovered warded-off aims in the past

variable attention to current situations outside and inside the therapy
and to varied clarifications of previous patterns. However it is done,
this level of interpretation requires confrontation with conflicts: conflicting aims regarding how to master and integrate the recent stressors,
dilemmas regarding how much to expose to the therapist, and possibly
how goal conflicts and habitual conundrums relate to a current impasse
in progressing toward the completion of reaction to a recent trauma.

As the patient can tolerate it and requires it to achieve maximum
adaptation to a traumatic event, the therapist can deepen the analysis
of conflicts. Frequently, especially in chronic or blocked passage through
the phases of response to stressful life events, the patient will require
some interpretation and confrontation with avoidance of the adaptive
challenges carried from the event to current life-plan decisions. The
threats projected to occur, were these avoidances set aside, can be
analyzed with a focus on external situations. The resistances to discussing topics and emotions during the therapy can be interpreted, and
when indicated, these defenses and resistances can be related to enduring and self-impairing character traits. Often, with the development
of a sense of safety based on evolution of a therapeutic alliance, the patient alone will set aside many avoidances and resistances, but the linking of these to enduring character traits usually requires accurate observation and labeling by the therapist as the facilitator.

Unless the stress response syndrome is relatively simple, most dynamic psychotherapists will find it advantageous to deepen the level
of interpretive work to include the patient's repertoires of mental state,
irrational beliefs, and repetitive interpersonal behavioral patterns, in-
sofar as these relate to (1) predispositions to the person's reaction to
the event, (2) the actual current signs and symptoms of the stress
response syndrome, and (3) current impediments to maximum adaptive gains in life changes set in motion by the event.

Examining the patient's repertoire of states of mind allows the patient to put the symptoms of the stress response syndrome in a broader
personal context and to study the specific triggers to activating the state
of mind that contains the symptom. The importance of doing this in
instances of chronic stress response syndromes cannot be overempha-
sized, because it leads the way to understanding the link between the
past trauma and current realities and the occasional use of the past
trauma as a screen that both depicts current conflicts and yet symbolically obscures aspects of their immediacy.

EXAMPLE OF A SCREENING FUNCTION. The patient was a 70-year-old man who had been a civilian worker in the Philippines at the time of the Japanese invasion in World War II. He was interned in a concentration camp throughout the war, where he both experienced and witnessed atrocities. For several periods he helplessly anticipated his own death with panic and anguish. He also felt murderous rage states well up in him, but he had to contain any sign of hostility in response to provocations, in order to increase his chances of survival. Periodically, in the nearly 40 years that had passed since his release, he had nightmares in which he relived aspects of these experiences. These usually were accompanied by panicky feelings but occasionally had surges of raw hatred as their affective components. Recently, the nightmares had increased in frequency, and he had other depressive symptoms. When these mental states were analyzed, he was found to vary in the degree to which he would enter a state of anger in which he struggled to control hostile expressive urges. His retirement had placed him in family circumstances in which he was goaded and humiliated by a son-in-law who wanted him to move out of the room he had in his daughter and son-in-law's house. When this happened, he was more likely to have the nightmares of his World War II experiences. Treatment did not eliminate these nightmares but did attenuate the overall situational difficulty, symptom picture, and frequency of sleep disruption.

The longer the time is from the stressor event to the present therapy, the more likely it is that the stress event syndrome will involve complex problems of maladaptive interpersonal behavior patterns. There is a lock-in across levels of interpretative work, so that work at the surface levels will help maladaptive patterns based at the organizers of meaning at deeper levels. Early work in therapy may lead to improved interpersonal relationship patterns, even when present, without proceeding to interpretive work at the level of self-concepts, role relationship models, and unconscious fantasy scenarios, scripts, and life agendas. Nonetheless, in complex cases this is often necessary, and complex cases are the ones most often seen by dynamically trained psychotherapists: the simpler ones have already been treated. Thus, in the middle phase of therapy, the therapist may reformulate the case in terms of what has been learned thus far and deepen the level of interpretative work. This will mean exploring the usually unconscious meaning structures involved in forming views of self and others, including self-critical functions and their derivatives from developmentally important relationships.

SUMMARY

To recapitulate, the treatment of stress response syndromes is centered on completing the information-processing cycles initiated by the stress event. The phase of stress response is recognized in an informed interview for signs and symptoms, and the treatment techniques are used according to the current phase, in order to move forward. Sometimes this includes facilitation of warding-off maneuvers, just as at other times the patient will be helped to set aside unconscious defensive operations. Transference and core neurotic conflicts will be a part of the therapeutic work but will often be interpreted according to their real relationship to the current stress. This will permit a clear focus for brief therapy. The nuances of the therapy technique, beyond the general strategies, will depend on the patient's and the therapist's character styles.

Part III

Individual Variations

INHIBITORY OPERATIONS: REACTIONS TO STRESS AND PSYCHOTHERAPY WITH HISTRIONIC (HYSTERICAL) PERSONALITIES

The next three chapters model the defensive maneuvers used to counter the tendency to intrusion and painful emotional response after trauma, which are inhibition, switching, and sliding to alter valuation. Because inhibition has been frequently associated with hysterical styles, switching with obsessional styles, and sliding of meanings with narcissistic styles, we shall begin with the historical backgrounds of these neurotic character patterns.

HISTORICAL BACKGROUND: HYSTERICAL STYLE

The concept of hysterical character, now called histrionic personality disorder by many, was developed in the psychoanalytic studies of hysterical neuroses, even though these neuroses may occur in persons without hysterical character, and persons with hysterical styles do not

149

necessarily develop hysterical neurotic symptoms. We shall discuss the ideal typology of hysterical style, assuming that most persons will have only some of the traits and no person will fit the stereotype perfectly. The development, diagnosis, and treatment of this type of personality are described in more detail elsewhere (Horowitz, 1977a, b; Horowitz, Marmar, Krupnick, et al., 1984).

The main symptoms of hysterical neuroses are either conversion reactions or dissociative episodes (Janet, 1907). Both symptom sets have been related to dynamically powerful but repressed ideas and emotions that would be intolerable if they gained conscious expression (Breuer and Freud, 1895; Freud, 1893). In classical analytic theory, the intolerable ideas are a wish for a symbolically incestuous love object. The desire contradicts the moral standards and so elicits guilt and fear. To avoid these emotions, the ideational and emotional cluster is warded off from awareness by means of repression and denial. Because the forbidden ideas and feelings press for expression, there are continuous threats, occasional symbolic or direct breakthroughs, and a propensity for traumatization by relevant external situations. Although later theorists have added the importance of strivings for dependency and attention ("oral" needs), rage over the frustration of these desires, and the fusion of these strivings with erotic meanings, the correlation of hysterical symptoms with efforts at repression has been unquestioned (Easser and Lesser, 1965; Marmor, 1953; Ludwig, 1972).

Psychoanalysts view hysterical character as a configuration that either predisposes toward the development of conversion reactions, anxiety attacks, and dissociative episodes or exists as a separate entity with similar impulse-defense configurations but different behavioral manifestations. The hysterical character is viewed as typically histrionic, exhibitionistic, and labile in mood, and is prone to act out unconscious fantasies without awareness.

Because of a proclivity for acting out oedipal fantasies, clinical studies suggest that hysterical persons are more than usually susceptible to stress response syndromes after seductions, especially sadomasochistic ones, after a loss of persons or of positions that provided direct or symbolic attention or love, after a loss or disfigurement of body parts or attributes used to attract others, and after events associated with guilt over personal activity. In addition, any event that activates strong emotions such as erotic excitement, anger, anxiety, guilt, or shame is more than usually stressful, even though an hysteric may precipitate such experiences by means of these behavior patterns.

Clinical studies also indicate the kinds of responses that may be more frequent in the hysteric during and after the external stress event.

Under stress the prototypical hysteric becomes emotional, impulsive, unstable, histrionic, and possibly disturbed in motor, perceptual, and evaluative functions.

Styles of thought, felt emotion, and subjective experience are relevant to our discussion and have been described by Shapiro (1965) and Horowitz (1977a, b). Shapiro emphasized the importance of impressionism and repression as part of the hysterical style of cognition. That is, the prototypical hysteric lacks a sharp focus of attention and arrives quickly at a global but superficial assumption of the meaning of perceptions, memories, fantasies, and felt emotions. There is a corresponding lack of factual detail and definition in perception, plus distractability and incapacity for persistent or intense concentration. The historical continuity of such perceptual and ideational styles leads to a relatively nonfactual world in which the guiding schemata of self, objects, and environment have a flat quality.

Dwelling conceptually in this nonfactual world promotes the behavioral traits of hysterical romance, emphasis on fantasy meanings, and *la belle indifférence*. For example, the prototypic hysteric may react swiftly with an emotional outburst and yet remain unable to conceptualize what is happening and why such feelings occur. After the episode he or she may remember his or her own emotional experiences unclearly and will regard them as if they were visited upon him or her rather than self-instigated.

This general style of representation of perception, thought, and emotion leads to patterns observable in interpersonal relations, traits, and communicative styles. A tabular summary of what is meant by these components of hysterical style is presented under these headings in Chart 8-1.

Shapiro's formulations differ from clinical psychoanalytic opinion in terms of the stability of such patterns, regarding them as relatively fixed, perhaps the result of constitutional predisposition and childhood experiences. Other analysts regard these patterns as more likely to occur during conflict. Our discussion will not contradict either position, as both allow us to assume a fixed baseline of cognitive emotional style and an intensification of such patterns during stress.

CONTROLLING THOUGHT AND EMOTION: HARRY AS HYSTERIC

We shall now consider Harry as if he responded to stress and treatment in a typically hysterical manner. One of his six conflictual themes, as described earlier, will be used to clarify the hysterical mode of con-

Chart 8-1
Patterns in the Hysterical Typology

INFORMATION-PROCESSING STYLE

Short-order patterns—observe in flow of thought and emotion on a topic.

- global deployment of attention.
- unclear or incomplete representations of ideas and feelings, possibly with lack of details or clear labels in communication, nonverbal communications not translated into
  words or conscious meanings.
- only partial or unidirectional associational lines.
- short circuit to apparent completion of problematic thoughts.

TRAITS

Medium-order patterns—observe in interviews.

- attention-seeking behaviors, possibly including demands for attention, and/or the use
  of charm, vivacity, sex appeal, childishness.
- fluid change in mood and emotion, possibly including breakthroughs of feeling.
- inconsistency of apparent attitudes.

INTERPERSONAL RELATIONS

Long-order patterns—observe in a patient's history.

- repetitive, impulsive, stereotyped interpersonal relationships often characterized by
  victim–aggressor, child–parent, and rescue or rape themes.
- "cardboard" fantasies and self-object attitudes.
- drifting but possibly dramatic lives with an existential sense that reality is not really real.

---

trolling thought and emotion. This theme is Harry's relief that he was
alive when someone had to die (see Table 7-1, a1).

Considered in microgenetic form, Harry's perceptions of the dead
woman's body and his own bodily sensations of being alive matched
his fear of finding himself dead. The discrepancy between his perceptions and his fears led to feelings of relief.

In the context of the woman's death, his relief was incongruent with
moral strictures. Harry believed that he should share the fate of others
rather than have others absorb bad fate. This discrepancy between current and enduring concepts led to guilt. Harry had a low toleration for
strong emotions, and the danger of experiencing guilt motivated his
efforts to control the representations that generated the emotions (see
Figure 8-1).

Although controlling helped Harry escape unpleasant ideas and
emotions, it impeded his information processing. Were it not for con-

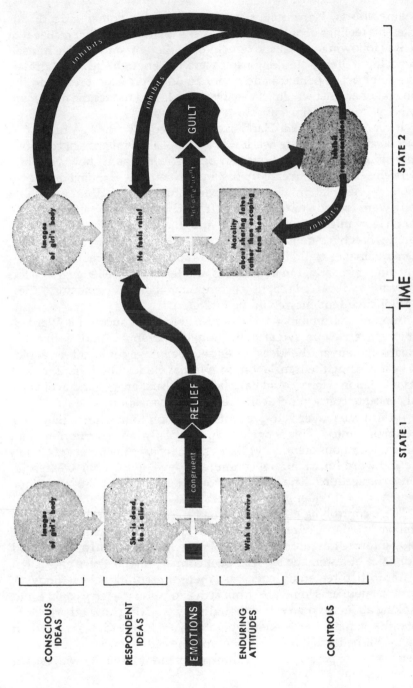

CONSCIOUS IDEAS

RESPONDENT IDEAS

EMOTIONS

ENDURING ATTITUDES

CONTROLS

STATE 1

STATE 2

TIME

Figure 8-1. Harry as Utilizing Hysterical Modes of Control by Inhibition of Representation

153

trolling efforts, Harry might think again of the woman's death, his relief, his feelings about surviving at her expense. He might realize that he was following unrealistic principles of thought and forgive himself for feeling relief. If thinking itself were not enough, he could undertake some act of penance and remorse. But repression prevented the thought or act that would change his attitude and reduce the discrepancy between his feelings and his sense of morality.

If repression is *what* Harry accomplished, one can go further in microanalysis to indicate *how* it was accomplished in terms of cognitive operations. These operations can be abstracted as if they were in a hierarchy. The maneuver to try first in the hierarchy is inhibition of conscious representation. The initial perceptual images of the woman's body were too powerful to ward off, and immediately after the accident, Harry might have behaved in an "uncontrolled" hysterical style. Later, when his defensive capacity was relatively stronger, the active memory images could be inhibited, counteracting the repeated representation. Similarly, the initial ideas and feelings of relief might be too powerful to avoid, but later, as components of active memory, their reproductive tendency could be inhibited.

Suppose this inhibition failed or was only partly successful. Warded-off ideas were expressed in some modality of representation. In a secondary maneuver, the ideas' extended meanings could still be avoided by inhibiting the translation from initial modes into other forms of representation. Harry could have only his visual images and avoid verbal concepts concerning death, relief, and causation.

A third maneuver is to prevent association to meanings that have been represented. This is again, hypothetically, an interruption of an automatic response tendency. Harry might conceptualize events in image and word forms but not continue to develop the obvious associational connections. The purpose would be avoiding a full conscious awareness of threatening meanings.

These controlling efforts are three typically hysterical forms of inhibition: avoidance of representation, avoidance of translation of threatening information from one mode of representation into another, and avoidance of automatic associational connections. If these efforts fail to ward off threatening concepts, there are additional methods. A fourth maneuver is to reverse from active to passive. Harry could avoid thinking about his own active thoughts by studying how other factors (fate, the woman, the listener to his story) are involved. He could then change his belief that he is alive because he actively wished to be alive even if another person died, by thinking of one's passivity with regard to fate, of the woman's activity in hitchhiking, and of how she got herself into the accident.

The fifth and last "hysterical" maneuver is altering the state of consciousness. Metaphorically, if the hysteric cannot prevent an idea from gaining consciousness, he or she removes consciousness from the idea by changing the organization of thought and the sense of self. Harry used alcohol for this purpose, but no outside agents are necessary to enter a hypnoid state, with loss of reflective self-awareness. These five cognitive maneuvers can be listed as if they were a hierarchy of "rules" in the hysterical style for avoiding unwanted ideas (Horowitz, 1977a, b).

1. Avoid representation.
2. Avoid intermodal translation.
3. Avoid automatic associational connections (and avoid conscious problem-solving thought).
4. Change self-attitude from active to passive (and vice versa).
5. Alter state of consciousness in order to (1) change hierarchies of wishes and fears, (2) blur realities and fantasies, (3) dissociate conflicting attitudes, (4) alter the sense of self as instigator of thought and action.

The hysteric has further maneuvers, but these extend into longer time periods. Harry could manipulate situations so that some external person could be held responsible for his survival. This would reduce the danger of a sense of guilty personal activity. In regard to very long-range maneuvers, Harry could characterologically avoid experiencing himself as ever fully real, aware, and responsible. He could identify himself with others, real or fantasied, which would make any act or thought of crime their responsibility and not his.

CLARITY IN THERAPEUTIC INTERVENTIONS: AN IMPORTANT NUANCE WITH PERSONS WHO HAVE HYSTERICAL STYLE

If the person of hysterical style enters psychotherapy because of stress response symptoms, the therapist will try to terminate the state of stress by helping him or her complete the processing of the stress-related ideas and feelings. This activity will include thinking through ideas, including latent conflicts activated by the event, experiencing emotions, and revising concepts to reduce discrepancies. The interpretation of defense may help remove impediments to processing, but the main goal in this model is to end or reduce a state of stress rather than to alter the character style. Even with such limited goals, character style must be understood and the usual therapy techniques used with appropriate nuances.

The nuances are versions, variations, or accentuations of major techniques such as clarification. One example is simple repetition of what the patient has said. The therapist may, by repeating a phrase, exert a marked effect on the hysteric, who may respond with a startle reaction, surprise, laughter, or other emotional expressions. The same words uttered by the therapist mean something different from those thought or spoken by the hysteric himself or herself; they are to be taken more seriously.

Additional meanings accrue, and some meanings are also stripped away. For example, a guilty statement by Harry, repeated by the therapist in a neutral or kind voice, may seem less heinous. More explicitly, to call this "repetition" is to be correct only in a phonemic sense. Actually, the patient hears the meanings more clearly and also, hears new meanings, and the previously warded off contents and meanings may seem less dangerous when repeated by the therapist.

Simple repetition is, of course, not so "simple." The therapist selects particular phrases and may recombine phrases to clarify them by connecting causal sequences. At first, when Harry was vague about survivorship but said, "I guess I am lucky to still be around," the therapist might just say "yes" to accentuate the thought. A fuller repetition, in other words, such as "you feel fortunate to have survived" may also have progressive effects; it "forces" Harry closer to the potential next thought: "and she did not, so I feel badly about feeling relief."

Left to his own processes, Harry might have verbalized the various "ingredients" in the theme, might even have painfully experienced pangs of guilt and anxiety, and yet might still not have really "listened" to his ideas. In response to this vague style, the therapist may pull together scattered phrases: "You had the thought 'Gee, I'm glad to still be around, but isn't it awful to be glad when she's dead'?" Harry might listen to his own ideas through the vehicle of the therapist and work out his own reassurance or acceptance. This seems preferable to giving him permission by saying, "You feel guilty over a thought that anyone would have in such a situation," although this is, of course, sometimes necessary.

As we shall see, these simple everyday maneuvers are not so effective with persons of obsessional style.

Other therapeutic maneuvers oriented toward helping the hysteric complete the processing of stressful events are equally commonplace. To avoid dwelling further on well-known aspects of psychotherapy, some maneuvers are listed that apply to specific facets of hysterical style (Chart 8-2). Each maneuver listed has additional nuances. For example, with some hysterics, interpretations or clarifications should be very short and simple, delivered in a matter-of-fact tone that counters their vagueness, emotionality, and tendency to elaborate any therapist activity into a fantasy relationship.

NUANCES OF RELATIONSHIP WITH HYSTERICAL PATIENTS IN A STATE OF STRESS

Hysterical persons have a low toleration for emotion, although they are associated with emotionality. One emotion is often used as a defense against some other emotion, but even the substitute may get out of control. Because motivations are experienced as inexorable and potentially intolerable, the ideas that evoke emotion are inhibited. If tolera-

---

Chart 8-2
Some of the "Defects" of the Hysterical Style and Their Counteractants in Therapy

FUNCTION	STYLE AS "DEFECT"	THERAPEUTIC COUNTER
Perception	Global or selective inattention	Ask for details
Representation	Impressionistic rather than accurate	"Abreaction" and reconstruction
Translation of images and enactions into words	Limited	Encourage talk Provide verbal labels
Associations	Limited by inhibitions Misinterpretations based on schematic stereotypes, deflected from reality to wishes and fears	Encourage production Repetition Clarification
Problem solving	Short circuit to rapid but often erroneous conclusions	Keep subject open Interpretations
	Avoidance of topic when emotions are unbearable	Support

---

tion for the unpleasant emotions associated with a stressful event can be increased, then the cognitive processing of that event can be resumed. The therapeutic relationship protects the patient from the dangers of internal conflict and potential loss of control and so operates to increase tolerance for warded-off ideas and feelings. The therapist effects the patient's sense of this relationship by his or her activities or restraint. How this is typically done is also a nuance of technique.

After a stress event, the hysterical patient often manifests swings from rigid overcontrol to uncontrolled intrusions and emotional repetition. During these swings, especially at the beginning and with a desperate patient, the therapist may oscillate between closeness and distance, always staying within the boundaries that characterize a therapeutic relationship.

The hysteric may consider it imperative to have care and attention. This imperative need has been called, at times, the "oral," "sick," or "bad" component of some hysterical styles (Easser and Lesser, 1965; Marmor, 1953; Lazare, 1971). During the period of imperative need, especially after a devastating stress event, the hysteric may need sympathetic concern and support from the therapist. Without it, the therapeutic relationship will fall apart, and the patient may regress or develop additional psychopathology (Myerson, 1969). During this phase the therapist moves, in effect, closer to the patient: just close enough to provide necessary support but not so close as the patient appears to wish. This is not an endorsement of transference gratification, countertransference, or what has been called a "corrective emotional experience." It is simply a matter of the degree of support extended.

As the patient becomes more comfortable, he or she may begin to feel anxious at the degree of intimacy in the therapeutic relationship because there may be a fear of being seduced or enthralled by his or her own dependency wishes regarding the therapist. The therapist then moves back to a "cooler," more distant, or less supportive stance.

The therapist thus oscillates to keep the patient within a zone of safety by modifying his or her manner of relating to the patient. Safety allows the patient to move in the direction of greater conceptual clarity (Sandler, 1960; Weiss, 1971). Naturally, the therapist's manner includes his or her nonverbal and verbal cues, what the therapist allows himself or herself to do in the context of his or her own real responses and qualities of being. This is not role playing; rather, the therapist allows or inhibits his or her own response tendencies as elicited by the patient.

If the therapist does not come in from a relatively distant position, and if the patient has urgent needs to stabilize his or her self-concept through relational support, then the discrepancy between need and supply will be so painful that the patient will be unable to expose problematic lines of thought. Inhibition will continue. If the therapist does not change from a relatively close position to a more distant one, then conceptual processing will begin, but transference issues will cloud working through the stress response syndrome. Neither clarity nor oscillation by the therapist may be a suitable nuance of technique with the obsessional. A detailed exposition of the psychotherapy with a person with a histrionic personality and a stress response syndrome is found in Horowitz, Marmar, Krupnick, et al., 1984.

Chapter 9

SWITCHING MANEUVERS: REACTION TO STRESS AND PSYCHOTHERAPY WITH COMPULSIVE PERSONALITIES

Inhibitory controls are a capacity. Some persons may have different predispositions or learning opportunities and, therefore, different abilities to inhibit emergent information. Even with a strong inhibitory capacity, other avoidance operations may be necessary to ward off a powerful theme. Another common defense is switching to alternative themes, which jam the representational systems and prevent painful recognition of the warded-off contents. This type of operation is commonly linked to a style that has been called compulsive, obsessional, and rigid (Salzman, 1980; Shapiro, 1965, 1981).

HISTORICAL BACKGROUND: CONCEPT OF COMPULSIVE OR OBSESSIONAL STYLE

The contemporary theory of obsessional style evolved from analysis of neurotic obsessions, compulsions, doubts, and irrational fears. Abraham (1942), Freud (1909), and Fenichel (1945) believed the obsessional neuroses to be secondary to regressions to or fixations at the anal-sadistic phase of psychosexual development. The manifestations of the neurosis were seen as compromises between aggressive or sexual impulsive aims and defenses such as isolation, reaction formation, intellectualization, and undoing. Underneath a rational consciousness, ambivalent and magical thinking were prominent. Common conflicts were formed in the interaction of aggressive impulses and predispositions to rage, fears of assault, and rigid and harsh attitudes of morality and duty. These conflicts led to the coexistence and fluctuation of dominance and submission themes in interpersonal relationships and fantasies.

Salzman (1968, 1980) emphasized the obsessional's sense of being driven, strivings for omniscience and control, and concerns for the magical effects of hostile thoughts.

Vagueness seems less possible for compulsive personalities than for histrionic personalities. Because obsessionals are often more apt to have an acute awareness of ideas, their staying with one position threatens to lead to unpleasant emotions. Seeing the self as dominant is associated with sadism toward others and leads to guilt. And seeing the self as submissive is associated with weakness and leads to fear of assault; hence either position evokes anxiety. Alternation between opposing poles, as in alternation between dominance themes and submissive themes, serves to undo the danger of remaining at either pole (Sampson and Weiss, 1972; Weiss, 1967).

To avoid stabilizing at a single position and to accomplish the defense of undoing, obsessionals often use the cognitive operation of shifting from one aspect of a theme to an oppositional aspect and back again. The result is continuous change. At the expense of decision and decisiveness, obsessionals maintain a sense of control and avoid emotional threats (Barnett, 1972; Shapiro, 1981; Schwartz, 1972; Silverman, 1972).

Although obsessionals move so rapidly that their emotions do not gain full awareness, they cannot totally eliminate their feelings. Some obsessionals have intrusions of feelings either in minor, quasi-ideational form, as expressed in slips of the tongue or intrusive images, or in major forms, as expressed in attacks of rage. Even when this occurs, however, the event can be undone by what Salzman (1980) called "verbal juggling." This process includes alterations of meaning, use of formulas to arrive at attitudes or plans, shifts in valuation from over- to underestimation, and, sometimes, the attribution of magical properties to word labels.

Shapiro (1965, 1981) described how the obsessional persons' narrowed focus misses certain aspects of the world while engaging others in detail. The ideal flexibility of attention is smooth shifts between sharply directed attention and more impressionistic forms of cognition. But the obsessionals lack such fluidity. Shapiro also explained how the thoughts, emotions, and behaviors of obsessionals and rigid characters are driven by "shoulds" and "oughts" dictated by a sense of duty, by their fears of loss of control, and by their need to inhibit recognition of their "wants." Despite their usual capacity for hard work, productivity, and will power, obsessional persons may experience difficulty and discomfort when they must make a decision. Instead of deciding on the basis of wishes and fears, obsessionals must maintain a sense of omnipotence and therefore must avoid the dangerous mistakes inherent in a trial-and-error world. The decision among possible choices is likely to rest either on a rule evoked to guarantee a "right" decision or else is made on impulse, to end the anxiety. The result of these cognitive styles is an experiential distance from felt emotion. The exception is feelings of anxious self-doubt, a mood instigated by the absence of true cognitive closure. These aspects of cognitive style are summarized with the common traits and patterns of behavior in Chart 9-1.

OBSESSIONAL TENDENCIES OF RESPONSE TO STRESS

Stressful events may so compel interest that there may be little difference in the initial registration and experience of persons with histrionic or obsessional styles. But, short of extreme disasters, obsessional persons may remain behaviorally calm and emotionless, in contrast with the emotional explosions of hysterics. There are exceptions, of course, to such generalizations. During some events, obsessionals may become quite emotional, and hysterics may remain calm. The difference is in the quality of the person's conscious experience. Hysterical persons can have a "hysterical calm" because it is based on the inhibition of some aspects of potential knowledge, and there is no emotion because the implications of the stressful event are not known. If and when obsessionals behave emotionally, they may experience it as a loss of control, one to be "undone" by retrospective shifts of meaning, rituals, apologies, or self-recriminations.

After a stressful event, obsessionals and hysterics both may exhibit similar general stress response tendencies, including phases of denial

---

Chart 9-1
Patterns in Obsessional Typology

INFORMATION-PROCESSING STYLE

Short-order patterns—observe in flow of thought and emotion on a topic.

- sharp focus of attention on details.
- clear representation of ideas, meager representation of emotions.
- shifting organization and implications of ideas rather than following an associational line to conclusion as directed by original intent or intrinsic meanings.
- avoiding completion on decision or a given problem, instead switching back and forth between attitudes.

TRAITS

Medium-order patterns—observe in interviews.

- doubt, worry, overly detailed productivity and/or procrastination.
- single-minded, unperturbable, intellectualizing.
- tense, deliberate, unenthusiastic.
- rigid, ritualistic.

INTERPERSONAL RELATIONS

Long-order patterns—observe in a patient's history.

- develops regimented, routine, and continuous interpersonal relationships low in "life," vividness, or pleasure. Often frustrating to be with.
- prone to dominance-submission themes or power and control struggles.
- duty filling, hardworking, seeks or makes strain and pressure, does what one should do rather than what one decides to do.
- experiences self as remote from emotional connection with others, although feels committed to operating with others because of role or principles.

---

and intrusion. But they may differ in their stability in any given phase. Obsessionals may be able to maintain the period of emotional numbing with greater stability, and hysterics may be able to tolerate phases of episodic intrusions with more apparent stability and less narcissistic injury.

During the oscillatory phase, when the uncompleted images and ideas of the current stressful concepts are often repeated and intrusive representation, hysterics are likely to inhibit representation to ward off these unwelcome mental contents. Obsessionals may be precise and clear in describing the intrusive images but may focus on details related to duty, for example, and away from the simple emotion evoking meanings of the image's gestalt. Although the compulsive personality style is one of the most common, it is least adaptable to the emotional accessibility and centrality of focus desirable for effective brief therapy (Malan, 1979; Sifneos, 1966).

It is during the oscillatory phase of both intrusions and warding-off maneuvers that these styles stand out the most. Instead of, or in addition to, the repressive maneuvers, as listed earlier, obsessionals respond to threatened repetitions with cognitive maneuvers such as shifting. By shifting to something else, obsessionals are able to jam their cognitive channels and prevent emergence or endurance of warded-off contents, or to shift meanings so as to stifle emotional arousal. That is, by shifting from topic to topic or from one meaning to another meaning of the same topic, they can avoid the emotion-arousing properties of one set of implications.

CONTROLLING THOUGHT AND EMOTION: HARRY AS OBSESSIVE

To model Harry as using switching operations to avoid the hazard of strong emotions, a time in psychotherapy was considered when Harry began to talk of the unbidden images of the woman's body. At this period in therapy he began to associate to his memory of feeling relieved to be alive. The next conceptualization, following the idealized line of working through outlined earlier, would be association of his relieved feelings with ideas of survival at her expense. This cluster would be matched against moral strictures counter to such personal gain through damage to others, and Harry would go on to conceptualize his emotional experience of guilt or shame (Chapter 7, Table 7-1, a1). Once this was clear, he could revise his schematic belief that someone had to die, accept his relief, feel remorse, even plan a penance, and reduce incongruity through one or more of these changes. But Harry did not follow this idealized route because he determined the potential of these emotional experiences as intolerable at a not-fully conscious level of information processing. Thus he switched to another ideational cycle in order to avoid the first one. He also associatively related to the images of the woman's body.

A common element in both ideational cycles allowed a pivotal change and reduced Harry's awareness that the subtopic had changed. The pivot for the switch was the idea of bodily damage. In the second ideational cluster, Harry's concept was that bodily damage could happen to him, perhaps at any future time, as it had now happened to her. Through the comparison between his wishes for invulnerability and his dread of vulnerability, his fear was aroused (Table 7-1, b1 and Figure 9-1).

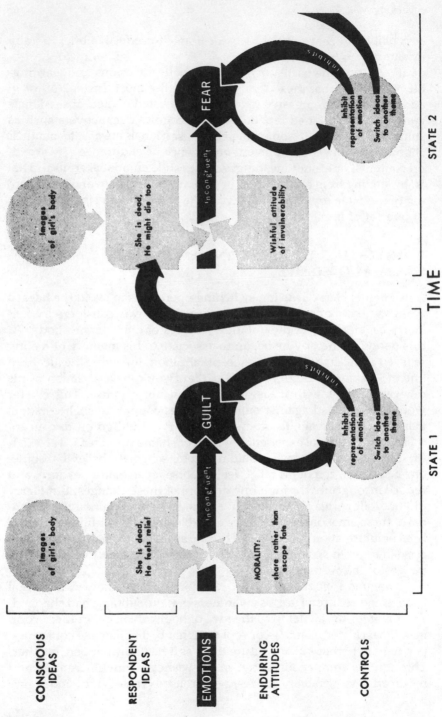

CONSCIOUS IDEAS

RESPONDENT IDEAS

EMOTIONS

ENDURING ATTITUDES

CONTROLS

Images of girl's body

She is dead, He feels relief

MORALITY: share rather than escape fate

Incongruent

GUILT

Inhibit representation of emotion

Switch ideas to another theme

inhibits

Images of girl's body

She is dead, He might die too

Wishful attitude of invulnerability

Incongruent

FEAR

Inhibit representation of emotion

Switch ideas to another theme

inhibits

STATE 1

STATE 2

TIME

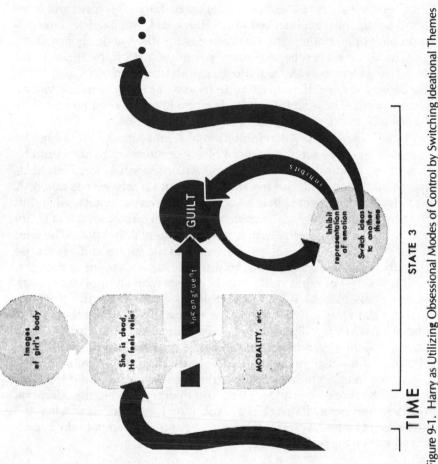

Figure 9-1. Harry as Utilizing Obsessional Modes of Control by Switching Ideational Themes

167

Although fear is unpleasant and threatening as a potential experience, the switch allowed movement away from the potential feelings
of guilt (theme a1). When the second theme (b1) becomes too clear, fear
might be consciously experienced. The procedure can be reversed with
return to a1. Harry could alternate conscious and communicative meanings between a1 and b1 without either set of dangerous ideas and emotions being fully experienced. But Harry did not need to limit his
switching operations to the two contexts for ideas about bodily damage; he could switch between any permutations of any themes and
could transform, reverse, or undo guilt with fear or anger (Jones, 1929).
He could see himself as a victim, then as an aggressor, then a victim,
and so forth. These shifts would dampen his emotional responsivity
but reduce his cognitive processing of themes.

This does not imply that inhibition of representation would not be
found in an obsessional version of Harry or shifts of theme would be
absent in hysterical versions of Harry. An obsessional Harry might attempt inhibitions and use his shifts when inhibitory efforts failed. A
hysterical Harry might shift from active to passive, as noted earlier, but
the timing and quality of the shifts would differ. An obsessional Harry
would shift more rapidly, with less vagueness at either pole. The shift
could occur in mid-phrase, between an utterance of his and a response
from the therapist, or even as virtually simultaneous trains of thought.

It is because of rapid shifts that therapists who attempt clarity with
obsessionals may be thwarted in their task. Suppose the therapist
makes a clarifying intervention about a1, the survivor guilt theme. The
obsessional Harry might have already shifted to b1, his fear of body
injury, and thus hear the remarks in a noncongruent state. The clarification procedure might not work well because Harry was clear in the first
place, was not listening from the earlier position, and undid the therapist's intervention by further shifts. An interpretation to the effect that
Harry feared bodily damage as a retribution for his survivor relief and
guilt would be premature, at this point, because he had not fully experienced either the fear or the guilt.

HOLDING TO CONTEXT: AN IMPORTANT NUANCE WITH PERSONS WHO HABITUALLY USE SWITCHING MANEUVERS

Holding a person who shifts to a topic or a given context within a
topic is equivalent to clarifying for the person who typically inhibits
ideas. Metaphorically, the switcher avoids conceptual time, whereas

the inhibitor avoids conceptual space. The goal of holding is a reduction of shifting so that the patient can progress further along a given conceptual process. The patient must also be helped to tolerate the emotions that will be experienced when he or she cannot quickly divert ideas into and out of conscious awareness.

Holding to context is more complicated than clarification. One begins with at least two current problems, such as the dual themes of a1 and b1 in Harry. When the patient is not shifting with extreme rapidity, the therapist may simply hold the patient to either one or the other theme. But the patient will not comply with this maneuver, and the therapist must not confuse holding with forcing. Ferenczi (1926), in an effort to speed up analysis, experimented with various ways to make the obsessional stay on topic until intensely felt emotions occurred. For example, he insisted that his patient develop and maintain visual fantasies relevant to a specific theme. During this technical maneuver his obsessional patients did experience emotions, and they even had affective explosions, but the transference complications impeded rather than enhanced the therapy.

The therapist thus must shift, even though he or she attempts to hold the patient to a topic. That is, the therapist must shift at a slower rate than the patient does, like a dragging anchor that slows the process. This operation increases the patient's progress in both directions. That is, with each shift, he or she is able to go a bit further along the conceptual route of either theme, even though he or she soon becomes frightened and crowds the theme out of mind with an alternative.

The therapist may use repetitions, as with the hysteric, in order to hold or slow the shift of an obsessional patient. But this same maneuver is used with a different nuance. With the inhibitor, the repetition heightens the meaning of what the patient is now saying. With the switcher, the repetition goes back to what the patient was saying before the shift away from the context occurred. With the hysteric, the repetition may be short phrases. With the obsessional, greater length may be necessary in order to state the specific context that is being warded off. For example, if Harry were talking about bodily damage and shifts from a survivor guilt context to his fears of injury, then the therapist's repetition must link bodily damage specifically to the survivor guilt theme. With an hysteric, such wordy interventions may only diminish clarity.

At times, this more extensive repetition in the obsessional may include the technique of going back to the very beginning of an exchange, retracing the flow carefully, and indicating where the patient introduced extraneous or only vaguely relevant details. Reconstruction may add warded off details. This technique has been suggested for long-term character analysis (Weiss, 1971; Salzman, 1968), during which defensive operations are interpreted so that the patient increases conscious control and diminishes unconscious restrictions on ideas and feelings. In shorter therapy, aimed at working through a stress, this extensive repetition is still useful, because during the review by the therapist, the patient attends to the uncomfortable aspects of the topic.

Increased time on the topic allows more opportunity for processing and hence moves the patient toward completion. Emotions aroused by the flow of ideas are more tolerable within the therapeutic relationship than for the patient alone. Also, time on the topic and with the therapist allows continued processing in a communicative state, emphasizing reality and problem solving rather than fantasy and magical belief systems. Identification with and externalization onto the relatively neutral therapist also allows temporary reduction in rigid and harsh introjects that might otherwise deflect thought.

Focusing on details is sometimes a partial deterrent to shifting in the obsessional, just as it may also aid clarity with the hysteric. The nuances of focusing on details differ because the purposes differ. In general, the aim with the hysteric is to move from concrete, experiential information, such as images, toward more abstract or more extended meanings, such as word labels for activities and things. The aim with the obsessional is to move from abstract levels, at which shifts are facile, to a concrete context. Details act as pegs of meaning in concrete contexts and make shifts of attitude more difficult. This maneuver uses the obsessional's predisposition to details but allows the therapist to select them. Again, the nuance of asking for concrete details is part of the general aim of increasing conceptualization time.

In states in which the shifts are so rapid as to preclude simple repetition or questioning, the therapist may use a more complex form of repetition. The therapist repeats the event, for example, Harry's intrusive image of the woman's body, and then repeats the disparate attitudes that the patient oscillates between in a single package. For example, the therapist might tell Harry that the image of the woman's body led to two themes. One was the idea of relief at being spared from death that made him feel frightened and guilty. The other was the idea of bodily harm to himself. Were the rate of oscillation less rapid, this form of "packaged" intervention would not be as necessary, as simpler holding operations might be sufficient and the therapist could focus on a single theme.

These efforts by the therapist encroach on the patient's habitual style, and the patient may respond by minimizing or exaggerating the meaning of the intervention. Obsessionals are especially vulnerable to threats to their sense of omniscience, especially after traumatic events. If the therapist holds them on a topic, obsessionals will sense their warded-off ideas and feelings and develop uncertainties that cause their self-esteem to fall.

To protect the patient's self-esteem, the therapist uses questioning to accomplish clarification and topic deepening, even when he or she has an interpretation in mind. The questions aim the patient toward answers that contain the important warded-off but now-emerging ideas. Obsessional patients can then credit themselves with expressing these ideas and experiencing these feelings. With hysterical persons, the therapist might, in contrast, interpret at such a moment, using a firm, short delivery, as a question might be followed by vagueness.

To obsessionals, incisive interpretations often mean that the therapist knows something that they do not know. A transference bind over dominance and submission arises as the patients rebel against the interpretation with stubborn denial, acccept it meekly without thinking about it, or both.

Timing is also important with obsessionals working through stress-activated themes. After experience with a given patient, the therapist intuitively knows when a shift is about to take place. At just that moment, or a bit before, the therapist asks the question. This interrupts the shift and increases the conceptual time and space on the topic about to be warded off. These technical nuances are shown in Chart 9-2.

NUANCES OF RELATIONSHIP WITH OBSESSIONAL PATIENTS IN A STATE OF STRESS

The oscillation in degree of support described as sometimes necessary with the hysterical style in extreme stress is not as advisable with the obsessional style. Instead, therapists should create a safe situation for the patients by remaining stable within their own clear boundaries (e.g., objectivity, compassion, understanding, concern for the truth, or whatever are their own personal and professional traits).

The patients learn the therapist's limits within this frame. It gives them faith that the therapist will react neither harshly nor seductively, and this trust will increase the patient's breadth of oscillation. They can express more aggressive ideas if they know the therapist will not

Chart 9-2
Some of the "Defects" of Obsessional Style and Their Counteractants in Therapy

FUNCTION	STYLE AS "DEFECT"	THERAPEUTIC COUNTER
Perception	Detailed and Factual	Ask for overall impressions and statements about emotional experiences
Representation	Isolation of ideas from emotions	Link emotional meanings to ideational meanings
Translation of images into words	Misses emotional meaning in a rapid transition to partial word meanings	Focus attention on images and felt reactions to them
Associations	Shifts sets of meanings back and forth	Holding operations Interpretation of defense and of warded-off meanings
Problem solving	Endless rumination without reaching decisions	Interpretation of reasons for warding off clear decisions

submit, be injured, compete for dominance, or accuse them of evil. Harry could express more of his bodily worries when he knew the therapist would not himself feel guilty or overresponsible.

If the therapist changes with obsessionals' tests or needs, then they will worry that they may be too powerful, too weak, or too "sick" for the therapist to handle. Also, obsessionals may use the situation to externalize warded-off ideas or even defensive maneuvers. The therapist shifts, not they. This is not to say that obsessionals do not, at times, need kindly support after disastrous external events. But their propensity for shifting makes changes in the degree of support more hazardous than does a consistent attitude, whether kindly supportive, neutrally tough, or otherwise.

Suppose the therapist became more kindly as Harry went through a turbulent period of emotional expression of guilt over survival. Harry might experience this as an increase in the therapist's concern or worry about him. Or he might shift from the "little" suffering position that elicited the therapist's reaction, to a "big" position from which he looked down with contempt at the "worried" therapist.

Similarly, if the therapist is not consistently tough-minded, in the ordinary sense of insisting on information and truth telling, but shifts to this stance only in response to the patient's stubborn evasiveness, then the patient can shift from strong stubbornness to weak, vulnerable self-concepts. Within the context of this shift, the patient experiences the therapist as hostile, demeaning, and demanding.

Unlike hysterics, then, obsessionals' shifts in role and attitude within the therapeutic situation are likely to be out of phase with changes in the therapist's demeanor. Obsessionals can chance further and more lucid swings in state when they sense the therapist's stability.

Transference resistance will occur despite the therapist's efforts to maintain a therapeutic relationship. Patients will exaggerate the therapist's stability into an omniscience that they will continually test. When negative transference reactions occur, the therapist will act to resolve those that interfere with the goals of therapy. But some transference reactions will not be negative, even though they act as resistances. Hysterics may demand attention and halt progress to get it. Obsessionals may take an oppositional stance not so much out of hostility or stubbornness, although such factors will be present, as out of a need to avoid the dangerous intimacy of agreement and cooperation. Because the therapist is not aiming at analyzing the transference to effect character change, he or she need not interpret this process. Instead, with an obsessional patient in an oppositional stance, he or she may word the interventions to take advantage of the situation. That is, interventions can be worded, when necessary, in an oppositional manner. Suppose Harry were talking about picking up the woman and the therapist knew he was predisposed to feeling guilty but was warding it off. With an hysterical Harry, the therapist might say, "You feel badly about picking up the woman." With an obsessional and cooperative Harry, he or she might say, "Could you be blaming yourself for picking up the woman?" With an oppositional obsessional stance, the therapist might say, "So you don't feel at all badly about picking up the woman." This kind of Harry might disagree and talk of his guilt feelings.

To summarize, holding to a topic or subtopic is a nuance of technique used to help persons disposed to switching types of warding-off maneuvers to complete the processing of stress related ideas. Clarity, though useful with those who inhibit, is not as directly helpful with the switcher who may require both clarity and holding to a topic. Distortion of meanings, a third type of control maneuver, is used frequently to avoid conflicting ideas triggered by stress events and requires other nuances of technique, illustrated in the next chapter.

Chapter 10

SLIDING MEANINGS: REACTION TO STRESS AND PSYCHOTHERAPY WITH NARCISSISTIC PERSONALITIES

Narcissism has been regarded as an important aspect of human character throughout recorded history, and it was summarized in Ecclesiastes: "Vanity of vanities, all is vanity." Freud's (1914a) explorations of the unconscious led him to emphasize the compensatory nature of such vanity, and Adler (1916) centered a psychology on inferiority and narcissistic compensations for deflated self-concepts. Recently, there has been a major resurgence of interest in the psychodynamics of the narcissistic character (Kohut, 1966, 1968, 1971, 1972, 1977; Kernberg, 1970, 1974, 1975, 1976). Pertinent to such interest is the question of how persons of narcissistic character respond to the inevitable stresses of life such as injury or loss. The typical narcissistic response of sliding meanings is contrasted with the classical typologies of the hysteric and obsessional, as are the nuances of therapy that help change this defensive avoidance.

BACKGROUND

Freud (1914a) used the concept of narcissism as a polarity between self-centeredness and relationships with others. He characterized some syndromes as *narcissistic neuroses*. This now-defunct term meant syndromes characterized by a withdrawal of interest in others. The contrasting set of syndromes were called *transference neuroses* in which interest, however distorted, remained centered on other persons. This duality was based on the theoretical position that psychic energy, in the form of libido, was distributed either to the self or to objects; that libido therefore was in limited supply; and that the increased self-concern would mean decreased concern with others (Hartmann, 1964).

This theory has since been rejected because it does not conform well enough with clinical observations. Instead, the development of self-interest and self-concepts is now seen in two simultaneously related but partially independent series. In one series the self-representation and self-regard gradually become an independent function. In the other series there is an interdependence of one person with another, that is, self-representation and self-regard gradually develop object representations, object interests, and patterns of self- and object transaction (Kohut, 1971). Increased narcissism can be motivated by either a need to compensate for a deflated self-concept, without the associated withdrawal of interest from objects, or by a problem in relationships with others that must be handled by increased self-interest (Kernberg, 1970).

In the narcissistic character, damaged self-concept underlies a more superficial self-love, grandiosity, or idealization of others regarded as appendages to the self (self-objects). In psychoanalytic reconstructions, vulnerability of the self—the tendency toward discohesive self-concepts under stress—has been traced to difficulties during the period of differentiating the self from the mother or other early parenting figure (Mahler, 1968). Dominance of narcissistic traits in either or both parents may predispose a child to difficulties in developing a flexible, accurate, and independent self-presentation because the parents may treat the child as if he or she were a function of themselves rather than a separate entity.

Being an only child or having a real or "special endowment" projected by a parent may build a sense of unusual importance into the child, one that is doomed to a rude awakening when he or she moves socially beyond the nuclear family. That is, any atmosphere that encourages and gratifies inflated self-representations will also predispose a child to traumas when realistic limitations, inability to perform, or depreciating types of interpersonal treatment are encountered. Such encounters will also occur in the family when the child develops enough will and ability to contest parental superiority and power and to feel betrayed and let down when his or her own power is insufficient to achieve his or her own goals.

NARCISSISTIC RESPONSES TO STRESS

When the habitual narcissistic gratifications that come from being adored, given special treatment, and admiring the self are threatened, the results may be depression, hypochondriasis, anxiety, shame, self-destructiveness, or rage directed toward any other person who can be blamed for the troubled situation. The child can learn to avoid these painful emotional states by acquiring a narcissistic mode of information processing. Such learning may be by trial-and-error methods, or it may be internalized by identification with parental modes of dealing with stressful information. The central pillar of this narcissistic style is a polarization of good and bad, with externalization of bad attributes and internalization of good attributes in order to stabilize grandiose self-concepts and avoid entry into states of mind organized according to deflated self-concepts. These operations demand distortion of reality and imply either a willingness to corrupt fidelity to reality, a low capacity to appraise and reappraise reality and fantasy, or a high capacity to disguise the distortions. The disguises are accomplished by shifting meanings and using exaggeration and minimization of bits of reality as a nidus for fantasy elaboration.

The narcissistic personality is especially vulnerable to regression to damaged or defective self-concepts on the occasions of loss of those who have functioned as self-objects. When the individual is faced with such stress events as criticism, withdrawal of praise, or humiliation, the information involved may be denied, disavowed, negated, or shifted in meaning to prevent a reactive state of rage, depression, or shame. If such measures should fail, in addition to externalization of bad attributes and internalization of good qualities, there may be a shift not only in affect but also in global being. This change in state includes changes in demeanor and style. If the stress event—for example, criticism of the person—leads to a mild level of threat, then the behavioral response may be an increased effort to obtain external "narcissistic supplies." That is, there may be a search for other persons to erase the criticism, supply praise, or provide through idealized power, a useful umbrella that can be extended over the self. Much like the hysterical personality, the narcissistic personality will try to woo or win attention from sources that enhance self-esteem.

If the stress event is of greater magnitude or if the restorative efforts outlined above should fail, then narcissistic types of deviation from realistic information processing will be more prominent. The goal of these deflections from knowing reality is to prevent a potentially cata-strophic state in which a cohesive sense of self is lost. The hazard is not simply guilt because ideals have not been met. Rather, any loss of a good and coherent self-feeling is associated with intensely experi-enced emotions such as shame and depression, plus an anguished sense of helplessness and disorientation. To prevent this state, the nar-cissistic personality slides the meanings of events in order to place the self in a better light (Horowitz, 1975b). What is good is labeled as be-ing of the self (internalization). Those qualities that are undesirable are excluded from the self by denial of their existence, disavowal of related attitudes, externalization, and negation of recent self-expressions. Per-sons who function as accessories to the self may also be idealized by exaggeration of their attributes. Those who counter the self are depre-ciated; ambiguous attributions of blame and a tendency to self-right-eous rage states are a conspicuous aspect of this pattern (Kohut, 1968; Horowitz, 1981).

Such fluid shifts in meanings permit the narcissistic personality to maintain apparent logical consistency while minimizing evil or weak-ness and exaggerating innocence or control. As part of these maneu-vers, the narcissistic personality may assume attitudes of contemptuous superiority toward others, emotional coldness, or even desperately charming approaches to idealized figures.

Reality testing and reality-fantasy differentiation are not as readily lost in the narcissistic personality, as they are in borderline or psychotic personalities. But the distorted meanings force further distortions as cover-ups. The resulting complications lend a subjectively experienced shakiness or uncertainty to ideational structures. Lapses in these defen-sive arrangements of ideas may occur during states of stress. Paranoid states and episodes of panic, shame, or depersonalization may also oc-cur. Self-destructive acts may be motivated by wishes to end such pain, to achieve a "rebirth," to harm the offending self, to feel something, and to achieve secondary gains such as obtaining sympathy or enact-ing a "wounded hero" role. These and other attributes of the nar-cissistic personality are summarized in Chart 10-1.

Chart 10-1
Patterns in the Narcissistic Typology

INFORMATION-PROCESSING STYLE

Short-order patterns—observe in thought and emotions on a topic.

- Slides meanings of information that might damage self-concept. Also uses denial, disavowal, and negation for this purpose.
- Attention to sources of praise and criticism.
- Shifts subject-object focus of meanings, externalizes bad attributes, internalizes good attributes.
- Occasionally dissociates incompatible psychological attitudes into separate clusters.

TRAITS

Medium-order patterns—observe in interviews.

- Self-centered.
- Overestimates or underestimates self and others.
- Self-enhancement in accomplishments real or fantasied, in garb or demeanor.
- Avoids self-deflating situations.
- Variable demeanors depending on state of self-esteem and context:
  - charm, "wooing-winning" quality, controlling efforts, or charisma.
  - superiority, contemptuousness, coldness, or withdrawal.
  - shame, panic, helplessness, hypochondriasis, depersonalization, or self-destructiveness.
  - envy, rage, paranoia, or demands.

INTERPERSONAL RELATIONS

Long-order patterns—observe in patient's history.

- Often impoverished interpersonally or oriented to power over others or controlling use of others as accessories (self-objects).
- Absence of "I-thou" feelings.
- Social climbing or using others for positive reflection.
- Avoidance of self-criticism by goading others to unfair criticism.
- Discarding of persons no longer of use.
- Pseudo twinning relationship.

CONTROLLING THOUGHT AND EMOTION: HARRY AS NARCISSISTIC

During Harry's psychotherapy, several conflictual themes activated by the accident became apparent. Prominent among these were his feelings of fear that he might have been killed, guilt over his own sexual ideas, guilt for "causing" the death of the hitchhiker, remorse for feeling relieved upon realizing he was alive and she was dead, and anger at her and the other driver for causing the accident.

Let us consider one of these various themes, worked through in different phases of therapy. The presumed context, now, was the time in psychotherapy when Harry was talking about the intrusive images of the woman's body and the association between these images and his ideas about his own vulnerability to death. Conceiving his possible death was highly incongruous with Harry's wishful attitude of invulnerability. The hazard of the incompatibility of these ideas is especially great for narcissistic personalities, as they have to maintain a brittle, but inviolately ideal, self-concept.

Conceptually experienced, the incongruity tends to evoke fear beyond a level of toleration. Controls are instituted to prevent continuation or enlargement of such felt emotion, for two reasons: to prevent the threatening levels of fear and to avoid representation of fear because it would also be a "narcissistic injury" for Harry to admit that he was scared. This "double jeopardy" of the narcissistic personality makes insight treatment difficult, as will be discussed shortly.

A microanalysis of the ideational-emotional structure begins, in State 1 of Figure 10-1, with a repetition of an image of the woman's dead body. This is the intrusive symptom Harry developed after the accident as part of a general compulsive repetition syndrome. The associated and responsive idea was that because she was dead, he too might die. The concept of personal death vulnerability was grossly incongruous with an enduring concept of personal invulnerability, and this discrepancy evoked anxiety.

Defensive maneuvers are motivated by such signal anxiety. Subject designation is inhibited, leading to a more abstract idea, "someone dies," a less frightening concept than that the self may perish. Thus, by means of externalization and disavowal of the death construct, Harry slid the meaning of personal mortality into personal immortality, a version of undoing. Instead of anxiety, the shifts of meaning allowed a sense of triumphant excitement by State 2. The very image that evoked anxiety now led by a slight irrationality into a more positive emotional experience. State 2, because of its defensive nature, is essentially unstable, and so Harry would probably tend to repeat Step 1.

Meanwhile Harry disavowed any similarity between himself and the hitchhiker. Narcissistic Harry exempted himself from this group membership by thinking, in effect, "She is the kind who dies; I am not." To use an exaggerated version of this prototypical narcissistic defense, Harry classified himself as an exception, perhaps with an extension of

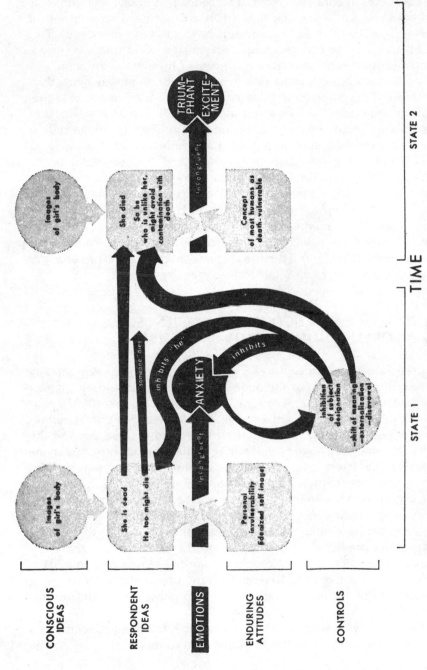

Figure 10-1. Harry as Utilizing Narcissistic Modes of Control by Sliding Meanings

181

the idea that someone had to die. If someone had to die, then someone had been chosen to die, and it was she and not he. This then meant he was saved by this selection, presumably because he was special. This membership in the chosen group is like a sign of immortality, and it is incongruent with the enduring concept of humans as vulnerable to death. This is a positive affect kind of incongruity: things are better than anticipated. As diagrammed, Harry felt a kind of triumphant excitement in responding to this set of ideas. Thus a complete reversal of emotions was accomplished by shifting and undoing meanings and externalizing mortal contaminants such as death and vulnerability.

This sliding meaning maneuver is similar to an obsessional device that uses one train of thought to block out another. But unlike a prototypical obsessional, a narcissistic Harry experienced emotions, perhaps both fear and triumph. Also, the narcissistic Harry would not as readily go back and forth in endless undoing operations. In pure narcissistic form, he would not have to undo the triumph by feeling scared, even though he remained vulnerable to fear and might repeat the sliding of meanings whenever fear-related ideas reemerged.

TACTFUL RECONSTRUCTION OF EXPERIENCE: AN IMPORTANT NUANCE WITH NARCISSISTS

In cognitive-emotional processing, a useful counteractant in therapy is reconstruction, and for the nuance of relationship in therapy, tact is important (Kohut, 1971; Ornstein, 1978; Goldberg, 1978, 1980). Narcissistic personalities present a double problem, as mentioned before. There is both the threat of warded-off ideas and experiences and the realization that they have been warding something off. Interpretations of defense and latent content are intolerable for narcissistic personalities unless they are tempered by the proper dosage, timing, nuance of delivery, and context in the therapeutic relationship. Otherwise the patients recognize that they have distorted the information in unrealistic ways and can have three traumas: (1) recognition of the self-threatening information previously avoided by distortions, (2) shame that they needed to be told and were "caught" distorting something, and (3) experiencing a reactive need to relinquish the unrealistic but sustaining gratification of seeing themselves as persons chosen by destiny for immortality.

Tact is also vital because, like hysterics, the narcissistic personalities may be more attentive to the therapist than to topical meanings. The therapist is an important current source of praise or criticism, and the real or fantasied observations of the therapist's degree of interest or disinterest will affect the patient's general equilibrium.

In the psychotherapy of a narcissistic Harry, during his expression and avoidance of the death themes just discussed, it would be helpful to recover and reconstruct the sequence of his fear of dying, including his memories of conceptual experiences during the accident. This procedure should be done as slowly as necessary to help Harry avoid a threat sufficient to throw him into a state of self-fragmentation.

During the reconstruction the therapist should also be unusually careful to agree with Harry's self-experiences as an instigator and as an object. This is similar to the importance of scrutinizing activity and passivity in hysterical styles. Both therapist and patient would sort out ideas about how involved Harry was in every aspect of action and what happened for external reasons. This sorting out would include discriminations among realities, real probabilities, and fantasies about his personal vulnerability. In the sorting out and reconstruction, some particular externalizations would be reversed, although the general tendency to externalization might not necessarily be interpreted.

For example, suppose a narcissistic Harry expressed rage at the other driver who forced him off the road. This externalizing of blame would be an effort to symbolize to all that the fault lay with the other driver, not with Harry. Underlying this are not only threatening ideas of his realistic faults but also unrealistic potential accusations regarding his full culpability. The reconstruction contains every possible element of ''blame'': how responsible he was for picking her up, for the cars in near collision, for pulling off the road in the way that he did, for his actions after the crash. Some end point of realistic decision, reached for each topic, would relieve Harry of the unrealistic components of blame. In the narcissistic personality these blame components are not necessarily an unconscious or conscious sense of guilt but, rather, are criticisms that may come from any source and demolish self-esteem. The therapeutic action of review and reconstruction would allow Harry to come to a conscious decision about his degree of culpability and would offer him the experience of not being assaulted with criticism by the therapist (even when the therapist was goaded to make such assaults by the patient's flagrant externalizations).

Reconstructions and reviews include the fear-evoking theme used for illustration. Working through this vulnerability theme would be especially difficult for the narcissistic Harry. Realistic threats to the self-integrity were his Achilles' heel, probably already lacerated by earlier traumas that might be revived and reopened in this context. These recollections, when seen, would also require reconstruction in the light of the present. These reconstructions with narcissistic patients need special extended efforts clarifying self- and object distinctions among motives, beliefs, actions, and sensations.

During this process there will be shifts in topical meaning, and so holding to a given aspect of a topic, as with obsessional patients, may be indicated. The nuance common with narcissistic personalities is to arrive at more stable meanings by encouraging the one meaning that has implications of current importance. For example, the "someone dies" idea has multiple meanings such as "each may die" or the salvation of one through the "sacrificial death" of another. The grandiose idea of the sacrifical absolution is deflated by holding and discussing the more important fear themes around "each may die." If necessary, interpretation of the corruption in reality adherence, as implied by the sacrifice-exemption theme, may be necessary but can be possible only if the therapeutic situation in some way provides adequate support for the patient's self-esteem.

NUANCES OF RELATIONSHIPS WITH NARCISSISTIC PATIENTS IN A STATE OF STRESS

Treatment of narcissistic personalities is often difficult for the therapist because the relationship with the patient is less infused by the real therapeutic alliance and the transference-countertransference colorations than with hysterical and obsessional patients. The narcissistic patient uses rather than relates to the therapist.

Despite feeling unimportant as a real person, or distant, or bored, the therapist must understand what is going on and provide a closer relationship with the patient. The therapist may have to be supportive for a period, as with the hysterical patient in great stress. With the narcissistic patient, support and closeness may not be so much a matter of warmth as of accepting externalizations without interpretations. This will not be done without consequence, however, because later in therapy it may be necessary to interpret and discourage such externalizations.

Narcissistic personalities achieve the sense of safety necessary to experience and express usually warded-off ideas and feelings through three types of quasi relationships. One form is characterized by personal grandiosity with the expectation of admiration, another by idealizing the therapist with the expectations of being all right because he or she is related to by an ideal figure. The third is to regard the therapist as a twin who restores the self by simply being there, in the here and now, together (Kohut, 1971, 1977).

The grandiose quasi relationship usually occurs either at the beginning of treatment or during recovery from an initially defeated state of mind precipitated by the stress event. Bragging and self-endorsements come in subtle or gross forms and take away conceptual time from stress-relevant topics. Tact, as emphasized earlier, takes the form of allowing these efforts to restore self-esteem, rather than insisting on staying with core conflicts or interpreting the grandiose effort as compensatory.

This tact and forbearance may be unusually difficult for therapists who are used to relying on the therapeutic alliance or positive transference to tide the patient over periods of hard work on threatening ideas. It is difficult to remember that the relationship with narcissistic patients is not stable and that their need is imperative but not coordinated with the usual concerns, however ambivalent, for the person toward whom they direct their needs.

In idealizing the therapist, the second most common form of quasi relationship, the damage is repaired as the patient imagines that he or she is once again protected and given value by a powerful or attractive parent. The stress response syndrome becomes a ticket of admission for this kind of self-supplementation. Again, tactful tolerance is necessary early in the treatment when the person is still partially overwhelmed by the stress response syndrome. It would be an error to see behavior, such as giving exaggerated testimonials about the therapist's unique ability, as equivalent to the transference-motivated seduction gambits of some hysterical patients or to the undoing of negative feelings by obsessional patients. The testimonials simply indicate idealization that provides a momentary repair of damage to the self, a safer time during which there may be some work on processing and integrating stress events.

Even externalizations can help patients gain sufficient emotional distance from loaded topics so that they can tolerate thinking about them. For example, if a patient projects a feeling of disgust about death onto the therapist, the relevant nuance would be to ask the patient to talk further about how the therapist feels. This allows the patients to work along the ideational route as if it were the therapist's route. A direct interpretation, such as "you are disgusted by death," should come only later.

Chart 10-2
Some "Defects" of Narcissistic Style and Their Counteractants in Therapy

FUNCTION	STYLE AS "DEFECT"	THERAPEUTIC COUNTERACTION
Perception	Focuses on praise and blame	Avoids being provoked into either praising or blaming but is realistically supportive
	Denies "wounding" information	Uses tactful timing and wording to counteract denials by selective confrontation
Representation	Dislocates bad traits from self to other	Repeatedly reviews in order to clarify who is who in terms of the sequence of acts and intentions in a recalled interpersonal transaction
Translation of images into words	Slides meanings	Consistently defines meanings; encourages decisions as to most relevant meanings and how much to weight them
Associations	Overbalances when finding routes to self-enhancement	Holds to other meanings: cautiously deflates grandiose beliefs
Problem solving	Distorts reality to maintain self-esteem	Points out distortion while (tactfully) encouraging and supporting reality fidelity
	Obtains illusory gratifications	Supports patient's self-esteem during period of surrender of illusory gratification (helped by the real interest of the therapist, by identification with the therapist, and by identification with the therapist as a noncorrupt person). Finds out about and gradually discourages unrealistic gratifications from therapy
	Forgives self too easily	Helps develop appropriate sense of responsibility

Narcissistic considerations are present in every character type, not just narcissistic personality, and some of these nuances of treatment might be pertinent at any time. The "defects" commonly found in the typical narcissistic personality and comparable therapeutic counters are summarized in Chart 10-2.

Chapter 11
TREATMENT VARIATIONS

The previous chapters discussed the therapy of stress response syndromes using a psychodynamic approach. The theory of stress response also offers a basis for the rationale and effects of therapeutic techniques of other points of view such as learning theory. Once again, we shall use Harry as a pliable model to try our ideas.

BEHAVIOR THERAPY OF HARRY

Behavior therapy is problem oriented.* In the first discussions with Harry, the most important problems were crystalized as the behavior to be modified. Choosing those behaviors to be shaped would rest, final-

---

*The author is indebted to the work of Stewart Agras, M.D., professor of psychiatry at Stanford University, who discussed the behavioral treatment of "Harry" in a conference on multiple therapeutic approaches to this same case (University of California, June 1974).

ly, with Harry but would evolve through discussion with the therapist. The relevant problem list might be as follows:

Problems to be solved that relate to the acute episode:

1. The recurrent unbidden images of the woman's body and the associated anxiety.
2. The secondary reactions such as irritability and alcoholism.
3. The fear of driving.
4. The avoidance of thinking about the accident could be a problem, as Harry had had a period of denial. Even during the period of intrusive images, he tried to ward off other memories or reactions to the accident.

Problems that existed before the acute episode and continue:

1. Communication difficulties with his wife, probably including sexual impairments.
2. Drinking as a problem.

In typical behavior therapy, one problem would be selected for the first work. In Harry's case, the central issue might well be recurrent images of the woman's body. One hope would be that if this symptom were relieved, other problems, such as his driving phobia, might also be helped. If not, *in vivo* exposure to driving situations would be the technique of choice (Marks, 1978).

The recurrent unbidden images would be regarded in behavior therapy as a failure of extinction. That is, under normal circumstances, the mind's natural and automatic processes would lead to a gradual reduction in the images' power to arouse fear. The purpose of the therapy therefore is to aid these natural processes leading to extinction of the conditioned association between a given stimulus idea and the unpleasantly strong emotional responses.

Two kinds of behavior techniques, both using images, would be the main choices for first work on the problem. These would be implosion or flooding (Stampfl and Lewis, 1967) and systematic desensitization (Wolpe, 1958). Both techniques aim to sever the association between the stimulus idea and the emotional response, although the operations are quite different.

In systematic desensitization, the therapist and patient construct a hierarchy of images from a mild to a maximal fear stimulus. The patient is then taught systematic relaxation of the body, on the grounds that fear or anxiety cannot be as readily experienced in a state of relaxation. For example, the stimulus is suggested to the patient, who silently images this content and tries to maintain bodily relaxation. If she feels anxious, she may signal the therapist by raising a finger. The therapist at once tells her to stop the image, then deepens relaxation by suggestion, and tries again. Later, the therapist may discuss the patient's subjective experiences and accessory ideas with her.

The patient is praised as she progresses. Gradually it becomes possible for her to form deliberately the most feared images without emotional arousal. In addition to deconditioning the idea-emotion associational bond, the patient has learned two others kinds of control. Through practice she has learned to invoke images volitionally and also to terminate them at the therapist's suggestion. One hopes that she then can generalize by herself this effect to dispel the images (Singer and Pope, 1978; Horowitz, 1983).

Although the aim with implosive technique is similar, the approach is strikingly different in terms of emotion. Instead of starting with a mild stimulus and a relaxed state, the therapist suggests the most lurid and frightening forms of the feared stimuli. The goal is to evoke so much anxiety that the idea-emotional system will "implode" inward upon itself. Less metaphorically, the technique operates on the assumption that fantasy and reality can be differentiated. Hence comparisons between imagination and actuality will reduce the patient's anxiety. When using implosive or flooding techniques with Harry, he would be asked to visualize not only the woman's mangled body but perhaps also to enlarge upon this in "dynamically oriented" ways, such as imagining being covered with blood, killing the woman, being blamed by her, having intercourse with her, and so on (Stampfl and Lewis, 1967). Every phase of the story would be used as a stimulus, elaborated into highly charged and conflictual forms.

A behavior therapist would evaluate the problem in the light of Harry's character and the nature of the initial relationship between Harry and the therapist. With an hysterical Harry the first choice might be systematic desensitization; with an obsessional Harry the first choice might be flooding, implosive, or *in vivo* exposure techniques (Agras, 1974).

SYSTEMATIC DESENSITIZATION OF AN HYSTERICAL HARRY

Systematic desensitization can use either a realistic or an image approach. That is, slides of accidents and bodies can be shown, or else visual images can be suggested. Suppose the latter in what follows. An hysterical Harry would be encouraged by this technique to imagine what he has attempted to inhibit. Because the image period is usually one minute long, there is an opportunity for many associations, as demonstrated by Brown (1969) and suggested by others (Breger and McGaugh, 1965).

The associations would be extended, and the images would be translated into words in the discussion with the therapist that would follow the period of silent relaxation and directed imagery. Thus the first three defenses on the hysterical style list of Chapter 8 would be counteracted indirectly through the suggested technique. Representations would be encouraged, the translation of images into words would be fostered, and the associations would be extended.

Harry would also be encouraged to maintain a steady state in relation to passivity and activity. He would be instructed and practiced in controlling his level of relaxation and even his state of consciousness. First the therapist would describe a sequence of procedures to the patient and obtain his consent to undertake these procedures. Harry would then be reassured that the sequence of procedures would be gradual, that the therapist were in charge, that he would announce each small increment as it was about to happen and initially would be the source of ideas.

The therapist would suggest to Harry the images to form, when to form them, and when to stop them. The partial passivity required of the patient would reassure an hysterical Harry, who would feel that the responsibility lay with the therapist. Free of responsibility, Harry could change his state of consciousness, as in entering a relaxed state and allowing the images to come to mind. He could make the therapist "order" him out of that state by signaling his anxiety with a finger movement. Thus although the patient causes the cessation by signaling the therapist, he or she experiences the situation within a role model in which it is the external authority figure who tells the patient to start and stop mental contents that are fearsome and out of control. There is a permitted passivity and a moratorium on responsibility that fits well with the typical hysterical maneuver of externalizing the source of activity in guilt-arousing situations.

Similarly, systematic desensitization has a "good fit" with hysterical styles of selective inattention and impressionistic reporting of perception, in that the procedures tend to counteract such styles. The instructions point the patient's attention in a specific direction, and the selection of images demands detailed reports and considerations.

The various conformities of the patient's style to the desensitization procedure explain why this technique, rather than the implosive technique, might be used for persons with hysterical defensive styles. Of course, the fit is not perfect. Other aspects of the hysterical personality, such as the tendency toward misinterpretations based on schematic stereotypes and the short circuits to rapid but erroneous conclusions are not particularly well handled by the desensitization technique. But a clinically experienced and well-trained behavior therapist can probably use the methods of psychoanalytically oriented brief treatment to supplement the desensitization procedure (Feather and Rhoads, 1972; Marmor and Woods, 1980).

Systematic desensitization does not fit as well with the defensive styles of Harry as an obsessional character. Obsessionals can often image without emotional reaction because they can focus on emotionally irrelevant or counterrelevant details of the conscious experience. The images suggested in the hierarchies might not be unusual conscious experiences but; rather, images already reviewed in dozens of ruminations. Warded-off stimulus ideas might not be revealed to the therapist in the first place and not included in the procedure.

RELATIONSHIP PROBLEMS IN THE
BEHAVIOR THERAPY OF AN HYSTERICAL HARRY

In conducting systematic desensitization, the therapist shows a kindly concern for the patient's anxiety, manifesting comfort through the instructions in muscle relaxation and terminating images that arouse too much tension. After each period of image contemplation, the therapist asks about the patient's own experiences. The therapy contract is very clearly demarcated and has been explained in detail to the patient. Each person has defined roles. Within this safe context, patients with hysterical personalities can experience the warmth, attention, and personalized support they usually crave, with some desperation, in moments of stress.

The role relationship with obsessionals may be less favorable. Relaxing by order of the therapist or imaging on instructions may seem too much like submission, but resisting such threats may interfere with the treatment. There may, however, be a balance: the orderliness of the procedures and the details of what to expect may be appealing and add a sense of safety. Thus with an obsessional Harry, the therapist might emphasize these aspects of the technique. Thus nuances of techniques of treatment in behavior therapy might evolve with hysterical and obsessional character styles, just as they did with psychodynamic therapy.

An analogous, nurturing, supportive, and directive role would be preserved in another behavior technique that might be used to treat an hysterical Harry. Suppose the driving phobia continued and the therapist elected the techniques of *in vivo* exposure, graded practice, and positive reinforcement. Harry would be encouraged to drive an increased distance each day, to keep track of his performance, and to report to the therapist. The therapist would react neutrally to disappointing performances and praise Harry for good performances. Harry would be in a state of anticipated accusations from an introject of the dead woman, from his wife's attacking him for picking up a woman, or from his superiors. The responsible, supportive, and praise-giving therapist thus would counteract the importance of these punitive introjects. In some instances, a companion during the *in vivo* exposure could serve this role.

IMPLOSIVE THERAPY OF AN OBSESSIONAL HARRY

A behavior therapist might select implosive treatment with an obsessive Harry on the grounds that the treatment would both counteract the defense of isolation and control the patient's tendency to shift away from emotionally evocative aspects of memory and fantasy. The therapist would learn of Harry's anxiety-provoking images of the woman and elaborate on them. The elaboration would be based on general theory, intuitions about Harry, and observation of Harry's ongoing responses (Stampfl and Lewis, 1967). The therapist would infer that Harry had wanted to have sex with the woman, felt guilty over his own survival, and feared his own bodily damage. He would tell Harry, in detail, how to image himself vividly completing the scenario of sex with the woman, his wife's expected reactions, his own dismemberment, and the woman's damaged body.

To my knowledge, implosive therapy has not been tried on real stress response syndromes of this sort. A behavior therapist would probably restrict the use of lurid imagery to the more fantastic expectations of the patient. For example, if Harry were encouraged to imagine the woman accusing him of causing her death and were to become excruciatingly anxious during this procedure, then he would also become aware of the discrepancy between the fantasy of such an accusation and the reality that no accusation is justified or possible. He had not deliberately done anything to harm her; he had attempted to help her with a ride; he had tried to avoid the collision; and he would have helped her if she had been injured and not dead. The woman cannot return to accuse him except in his fantasies.

Harry might not yet have faced such fantasies as his own, but the story lines might have been initiated in his associations. In implosive therapy, the therapist would put these fantasies into words, which might allow Harry to confront them and also react against them as if they were the therapist's ideas. Harry might thus reach a point of relative, if partially disavowed, completion.

The therapist would be quite forceful in the direction of imagery in the implosive technique. Harry, provided that he followed the main instructions, could not shift from fearsome ideas to guilty ideas. When the therapist talked about Harry being impaled by the pipes, breathing and vomiting his own blood, it would restrict Harry to imaging his own potential harm. He must become frightened. Because the therapist in implosive therapy would go right on talking because Harry would be expected only to imagine as instructed, not to reveal his thoughts, he could tolerate the fear. He would be supposed to be afraid; it would be his "duty" in the therapy, and he also would not expose himself by doing it wrong, as the obsessional would usually fear. Similarly, when the therapist imposed imagery regarding guilt, Harry could not shift back to the fear images because he would not be given conceptual space for such a maneuver. In this manner, the therapy would counteract the prototypic defensive maneuvers of the obsessional, as discussed in Chapter 9.

RELATIONSHIP PROBLEMS IN THE BEHAVIOR THERAPY OF AN OBSESSIONAL HARRY

In implosive therapy, the therapist seems sadistic; he or she is deliberately and forcefully making the patient anxious. Of course the effect is paradoxical. The therapist is cruel to be kind. This seeming cruelty may have two effects: it may counteract the obsessional patient's guilt, and it may evoke a counterreactive aggression by the patient. For example, the therapist might tell Harry to visualize the guilt-activating imagery. Harry might do this in imagery, but in word representations he might defy the therapist by saying mentally "I am not guilty," "It was not my fault," "It was an accident."

The therapist's activity pushing aside defenses and bringing ideas into the open, also modifies the self and object schemata situation. For instance, instead of internalized aggressive presences (introjects) telling Harry he was bad, here would be a real person describing bad images and making him feel uncomfortable. Harry could resist. In a sense, he could progress as he simultaneously agressively resisted, submissively cooperated, was punished, and was cared for in a tough way. Oddly enough, obsessionals may feel comfortable in this interpersonal situation. The increased safety may help them work through many of the conflicts triggered by the stress event. In contrast, hysterical patients may feel punished, seduced, and overwhelmed by implosive therapy.

Guided practice may also be used with obsessionals. Following the principles outlined here, the appeal to obsessionals is not so much the praise as the feedback and documentation that also accompany the procedure. That is, they can see how they are doing, do a little better, and feel very much in control.

COGNITIVE THERAPY OF HARRY

Cognitive techniques as described by Ellis (1973), Beck (1976, 1985), Meichenbaum (1977), and others are likely to approach the problem of intense negative affective states during the intrusion phase of stress response. The aim is to clarify and alter the cognitive contents that arouse and perpetuate the painful and overwhelming emotions. The approach is dual: to reduce pathogenic cognitions and to enhance alternative, adaptive ones. For example, the therapist might point out that Harry spoke repetitively to himself in sentences such as "I killed that woman and deserve to die myself" and then develop and rehearse an alternative view such as "I am entitled to live."

Harry was a truck dispatcher. He took a run because he was short-handed. But he did not ordinarily drive a truck. If Harry had anticipatory anxiety and phobic avoidance behavior regarding resuming work, especially driving trucks, he might be helped in cognitive therapy to clarify an inner dialogue in which he would be making statements like "It will happen again." After clarification of such pathogenic cognitions, the cognitive therapist might instruct Harry to try to stop such episodes of negative ideation and to talk positively to himself, replacing his irrational views by deliberately rehearsing statements such as "This time the trip will go smoothly," "Don't make negative statements, just think rationally about what you have to do next," or simply "I can do it."

The identification of pathogenic cognitions is similar to the clarifications and interpretations of dynamic therapy. The activity of stating these specific ideas clarifies themes for which vagueness, ambiguity, and short circuiting have permitted avoidance in hysterical personalities. At first, obsessional patients will hail suggestions of preferable ideas. Such patients often wish to obtain rules by which to live, but later on they often resist being controlled by the therapist's ideas of what may be adaptive. Narcissistic patients may use the focus on one cognitive theme to mask other themes, thus escaping from conflicts by idealizing the work on a limited sector.

Whatever the type of therapy or the combination of techniques from different schools of psychotherapy to suit an individual patient, it is useful to formulate the case according to the three sets of issues presented in the preceding chapters: (1) the nature and implications of stressor events and reality situations, (2) the phase of the patient's current response, and (3) the patient's habitual states of mind, self- and object concepts, motives and agendas, defenses, and style of thinking, feeling, and communicating.

Part IV
Clinical Examples

Chapter 12

LOSS OF A LIMB

With the assistance of Robert Nadol, M.D.

A single external event can trigger divergent reactions. These separable yet interconnected responses may occur in different phases at any given moment in time. One set of ideas and feelings may be warded off, resulting in a period of relative denial; another set may be intrusive in terms of conscious experience. Xalia's story is presented here to illustrate such phasic differences and to show how these differences can orient a therapist in his or her intervention strategy.

Xalia is a 19-year-old woman. Her left leg and knee joint were mangled in a car accident. The injury was severe, but the doctors at her local hospital attempted immediate restorative surgery. Gangrene set in after the emergency operation; consultation with specialists led to a hospital transfer and an amputation. She was then discharged to recuperate at home.

Dr. Nadol is currently Clinical Assistant Professor of Psychiatry at Brown University.

Six weeks later, Xalia reentered the hospital so that the stump could be fitted with an artificial leg. She received intensive physical therapy to strengthen the stump and learn how to use a prosthesis. During this hospitalization, she asked for a psychiatric consultation. Initially, the surgical staff resisted her request because she seemed to be doing well. But they decided to comply with it when she persisted. Xalia was seen by a resident psychiatrist. She told him she had requested the consultation because she had become aware of a lack of appropriate emotional response to the loss of her leg. In the physical therapy exercise room and on the ward she met other persons with amputations. She recognized their losses often as less severe than her own. They grieved for the loss of part of their body, whereas she remained cheerful. She felt that she had not faced her situation and was going on as if nothing had happened.

The psychiatric consultant agreed that she was avoiding the implications of the amputation and explored some of the circumstances of the accident. He recognized the defensive operations of thought stopping and inhibition of communication but did not know what thoughts and feelings she might be warding off. Moreover, he felt uncertain about disrupting her denial at this time. She was in the midst of active physical treatment and cooperating well with it. True, for a young, attractive, unmarried, and unattached woman to lose a leg would necessitate psychological work in reorganizing her body image, self-concept, and future plans. But should this work be done now or after she learned to use her prosthesis successfully? When is denial useful, and when does it impede adaptation? After talking with her and with the staff, the resident psychiatrist referred the patient to a stress unit therapist for further exploration and formulation.

This therapist then interviewed Xalia on the orthopedic ward. She was pleasant but urgent in her self-presentation. She communicated a feeling of pressure that could be verbally described as, ''You really must help me right now.''

Below is a transcript of that interview and the one that followed, interspersed with commentaries on meanings and implications of what is being communicated. The psychiatrist has already introduced himself and obtained consent to tape the interviews.

FIRST SESSION

T: (Therapist) Why don't we start with you telling me why you asked for a psychiatric consultation?
X: (Xalia) What I asked for a psychiatrist for?

T: Yes.

X: Because, um, I think that I need somebody to help me.

T: Uh-huh.

X: Um, because uh (pause) well, since the accident and my stepbrother was driving, I start hating him later (pause), and I don't want to hate him.

Note that almost at once, Xalia presents a new topic that was not mentioned to the consultant. This hatred of her stepbrother is a complex of ideas and feelings that intrude upon her: "I start hating him later, and I don't want to hate him." She had told the first consultant about a complex of ideas in a denial phase, that is, her intellectual observation of the absence of appropriate reactions to missing a limb. This psychiatrist had, of course, not heard about the hatred theme from the first consultant. He listens attentively to her further development of this theme.

T: Yes.

X: I don't want him to think that, um, it was his fault, but (pause) or, um, something 'cause, um, well, I don't want him to. And, ah, sometimes, well, I feel like yelling it to him and telling him it was his fault and, uh, that he can get out of that game (pause), so, um, so I just don't want to tell him never.

T: Yes.

X: Not even to my family 'cause I'm the only one who knows.

T: That's something we might be able to talk about. Anything else?

X: Mm Mm.

T: Well, tell me what happened. I know you've had an accident, but I don't know anything else.

X: Well, um, we went to a dance (pause); I was, um, two of my step-sisters and me, we went with my stepmother and father. It was a dance for Andy, my stepbrother. So, after the dance, my parents were going to go somewhere else, so they told us to go with Andy in the car, and, um (pause) oh, yeah, and then when we were, we were going just to (pause) go in a street, it was a blind intersection. It was like this.

T: Yes.

X: And, uh, and, uh, he, he was, um, my, I think he was drunk, and um, I was, I was talking with my stepsisters in the back, I was in the front seat, and, um, and then I saw that, that he didn't put no brakes on and we were going to, getting to the corner. So, um, I saw him, I was thinking that was really strange. We were almost at the corner. He didn't put the brakes on, and we were going to crash. He didn't; he was just smiling; that's all I remember, and then l, I woke up in the hospital (long pause). Well, they were trying to save my leg for two weeks. And Dr. Smith told me that he was going to amputate it, and, uh (long pause) well, my parents didn't tell me nothing, you know, about Andy. After, only when I was over here, about a month and a half later since the accident, she told me that (pause) he was very, very, um, very bad, that he was (pause) um, crying all day in his room (pause), that he wasn't eating or nothing, that he thought it was his fault. And she told me it wasn't his fault, it was the brakes' fault (pause). But I knew it wasn't the brakes. I mean, I told, I told the police, I told the (pause) the, um, insurance man, everybody, that it was, uh, it was the brakes. 'Cause I didn't realize before; I still don't realize that I, I don't have my leg. And um, more, I guess I feel funny about it.

T: Yes.

X: See, I don't realize, I don't care. Right now I don't care about it, 'cause I don't realize that I need it.

T: Yes.

X: But when I was at home last month for a couple of weeks, and, uh, Andy was going out (pause), he was going to take the car, and, uh, and then I was thinking that, uh, how could, how could my parents let him drive again. How? And how was he going out and I was staying, it was his fault. And I felt like yelling and telling him it was his fault, but I don't want him to blame himself.

T: Yes. But you're one of the only people that realizes how much he was at fault.

X: Yeah. I'm the only one who knows that it was his fault.

T: Yes.

X: See, 'cause I told the other people that it was the brakes' fault too.

T: Yes.

X: 'Cause I didn't want him, you know, if I'm, if I'm like this right now, I don't want another person to get (pause) hurt, or losing his feelings.

T: So, then, there are two things that you recognize might be helpful to talk out. One would be that you don't quite realize all the implications of what's happened.

X: Mm.

T: And then, you have this load about your stepbrother. You want him to be punished, but you don't want him to be punished. When did all this happen?

X: September 12th.

T: Uh-huh. And how long were you in the hospital the first time?

X: I was in the hospital there three weeks. Then I came (pause) for about, for about a month, then I was home for a month, then I came here.

T: And you've been here for 15 days now. Does Dr. Smith see you here?

X: Yeah. He's my doctor.

T: I'll give him a telephone call and see if it's all right with him that I talk with you. Would that be all right with you?

X: Oh, he's on vacation.

T: Well, I'll do it when he comes back, and we'll just talk anyway.

X: Yeah.

T: Now, what's your mood been like all that time?

X: My, um, what do you mean?

T: Oh, what has it been like for you day in and day out when you go home? Have you been cheerful or sad or numb or waiting, or . . . ?

X: No. That's strange. I live with my father and stepmother.

T: Uh-huh.

X: I lived in Canada, but I came two years ago here to study. And, uh, I don't know, I feel like, a little like, right now, I don't want to go home.

T: Yes.

X: My real mom was here since the accident. But right now, I don't want to go home. I would prefer to stay over here and, now, not to go away. I don't know why, and, well, sometimes I start to get angry at my father and my stepmother, even my stepsisters, and I feel guilty for it.

T: Just since the accident?

X: Mm-hm.

T: You get angry at them and irritated?

X: Yeah, it's funny because they think that, that Andy's very innocent and he's a very good boy and like he is sometimes, but (pause), I don't know.

T: Yes. You know something they don't know.

X: Mm-hm.

T: Okay. Well, you get around pretty well in a wheelchair and on crutches too?

X: Yeah.

T: I can't stay too long now. I just came up to see you. But could you come next door to my office? Would you mind coming over there?

I think we'd have a quieter room. We could just set up a time, and then we can just have a little longer to sit and talk this over.

X: Yeah.

SECOND SESSION

T: I'd like to know more about what you've been thinking about.

X: (Pause) Well (pause), I already told you, well, (pause) mm (pause), I think that I love my father and stepmother, but at the same time I don't. I don't know.

T: Uh-huh. You get angry with them.

The therapist has already noted that instead of saying she is hostile and instead of describing family members as bad, she will inhibit her communications and presumably her thoughts by trailing off and saying "I don't know." She has, of course, made critical remarks about her brother, but she regards such revelations as lapses in control. Knowing that she has such feelings is experienced as a threat to her sense of well-being. The therapist wants her to discuss her conflicted feelings so that they can examine them together in the therapeutic situation. He knows hostile ideas are at the surface because they intrude into her awareness. He refrains from questioning her about her warded-off ideas and feelings. If he were to say here, "I wonder if you are possibly angry at your father and stepmother?" it would be her style to answer either "I don't know" or "Yeah, I guess so" in a passive manner. Instead, the therapist labels her thoughts in a brief, firm, and direct way. He does this in order to clarify the thoughts and to establish a ground rule that in this situation there is to be open communication of those ideas and emotions that are usually suppressed in social situations.

X: A lot, yeah. (pause)

T: And yesterday we talked about your stepbrother and you.

X: Yeah.

T: How old is he?

X: Eighteen.

T: So he's a little younger than you are.

X: Mm-hm.

T: And what's he like?

X: (Pause) He's very tall, strong (pause), mm (pause), very nice guy. Mm (pause). Kinda crazy (pause), mm.

T: Kind of crazy? How?

X: Well, you know, always drinking and, uh, with me, I mean, he was my favorite.

T: Uh-huh.

X: And I was his favorite too.

T: Uh huh.

X: So, we were always going together; well you know, when I first came from Canada, then, uh, well, he was, uh, the first one, that, um, if one of my stepsisters came and started fighting with me or something, he came and told them to leave me alone, that, you know. And then, uh, he taught me how to drive, he taught me how to get around.

T: Mm.

X: The city and all that, uh, well he was—(trails off).

T: He was very close to you.

X: Yeah (pause). Sometimes.

T: Right. So maybe right now we could talk about the business with your stepbrother not pressing the brakes and then telling the police and everyone else that he did press the brakes. Maybe we can just see where we can get with that right now. That seemed to be a problem that you had coming back into your mind.

The therapist seeks to explore the more intrusive theme. He watches her facial expression as he talks. He slowly adds each new phrase until he sees that she is ready to take up the topic.

X: Yeah, I just remember that, um, that I, um, I thought that it was kind of strange when we were going to turn around the corner, he didn't put the brakes on (pause). And then, I suddenly saw he was smiling, and, uh, well, at the dance, I don't (pause), or I was sitting with some friends, so I saw that he was drinking. But, well, he always, he always drinks, but he never got, gets drunk; you know what I mean?

T: Yes.

X: So, then we get—got out, um (pause), then, uh, some friends were outside, and, and they told him to, you know, how 'bout a race? He goes, ''Oh, okay.''

T: Mm-hm.

X: So, we left from the dance, and the car was working pretty good. So then, we left them, and we were going to go home and, um (pause), well, he didn't put the brakes on.

T: Uh-huh.

X: And he was going very fast.

T: Was there a race going on, a play race?

X: No, yeah, well it's kinda, it's kinda a park and, uh, it's named Boyle Park.

T: Uh-huh.

X: And, um (pause), they have a big place where they have bands some and, uh, oh, yeah, they have a space to drive there (laughs) and, uh (pause), well, when we were coming back home, um, he was going kind of fast. Well, he, he admitted, he told everybody he was going very fast (pause). He was going over 80 miles, close to 85. So, um, then, uh, well, I didn't get scared or nothing; nobody did and, 'cause he always goes that fast (pause). But then, um, like, my stepmother told me, um, later that, and, uh, asked them when the car was there and then I w____ a lot of, you know, uh, the police and fireman, doctors came to take me out of the car and then, that he went out running into the car kind of crazy and that he was crying and all that, that it was his fault. So, partly because of that, I didn't tell them nothing 'cause I felt, I don't know, that, like, um, I was going to blame myself forever if I, I tell them the truth or something.

T: Yes.

X: So, uh, I didn't say nothing, and, uh, oh, when I went home, he was very nice with me. He didn't tell me nothing, though. One time when I was here in the hospital, I called home and he answered the phone, so he knew it was me and he started crying, telling me that it was his fault, to forgive him, and all that. And, uh, I told him it wasn't his fault and (pause), you know, to realize that it was an accident. But I, I wasn't thinking that.

T: Yes.

X: I would think that it was his fault, but I shouldn't tell him. And then when I'm home, I feel like yelling at him, telling him, you know? And I'm always in a bad humor sometimes, and I, I never was like that.

T: But you haven't told him?

X: Mm-mm.

T: Now there's something there, because, you see, while everyone else may not know, he knows. He knows what happened. And you've been very close with him.

X: Yeah.

T: So, you must be the kind of people who talk to each other. And you know something, and he knows something, but you don't tell him.

X: Yeah, but he knows this, but I think that right now he thinks that it wasn't his fault.

T: Ah!

X: Because, you know, everybody was telling him that it was the brakes. But it wasn't.

T: Yes.

X: The brakes were okay, and he didn't even put the brakes on.

T: Yes.

X: So, it wasn't the brakes. Now he probably doesn't remember because, oh, yeah, he said that, uh, well, yeah, it sounded like he was drinking, so he's probably been remembering.

T: Yes.

X: And, uh (pause), well, everybody's saying, you know, nobody mentions it anymore.

T: Well, do you have the feeling that maybe they're trying to protect him?

X: Yeah.

T: And you want to protect him too. . . .

X: Mm-hm.

T: But, there are different levels of protecting. He's actually feeling very badly.

X: It doesn't sound like it (angry outburst).

T: It doesn't? He's not feeling very badly now?

X: Mm-mm.

T: You told me that he was crying?

X: That was at first.

T: That was at first, so he's forgetting about it now?

X: He forgot all, all of it.

T: Uh-huh.

X: That was about two weeks, three, a month. About a month. But now, well, he doesn't remember or nothing. That time, that time when we, we go out, I told them, well, everybody was kind of afraid that if they told him to take me out that I was going to say no, or tell him I wasn't going to go with him because I was afraid and all that. So my parents and, um, everybody, every time that I had to go out, they took me, and they didn't tell him. Even though I told them I was—that I want to go with him.

T: Driving in the car?

X: Yeah.

T: So you don't get to have as much time with him.

X: Yeah. And then that, um, well, one time when we were alone, then I told him, "Why don't we go over there, you know?" And he goes,

"Okay, you want to; you want to, okay." So we left. He was very happy, I mean probably because he knew that I was trusting him again.

T: Yes.

X: And then, he started asking me when I was going back to Canada, what I was planning to do, and, uh, how I felt. But he didn't say nothing about the accident or anything; he didn't mention it.

T: Yes. Well, the accident is kind of like a taboo subject right now, isn't it?

X: Yeah.

T: No one's supposed to mention it.

X: Nobody (laughs).

T: But I guess what I'm wondering is if your father and stepmother don't want you to talk about it, if they want it to be all over and done with.

X: Mm-hm.

T: But I wonder if that's the way your stepbrother feels. I'm just wondering about the idea of you and him having a very private kind of conversation about this.

In what may be too rapid an approach, the therapist is trying to suggest a move toward completion by interpersonal working through. He believes she is torn between her anger at the stepbrother and guilt if she expresses her resentment.

He has not picked up the clues, at this point, that she is also feeling that the local family wants to get rid of her, as in "he started asking me when I was going back. . . . "

One problem will be that she is conscious only of resentment based on her limitation of activity, being forced to tell a lie, and at being no longer rewarded for going along with the story. She is not yet in touch with her rage at her stepbrother as the cause of her loss of a limb. The loss complex is still being warded off by inhibitory processes.

X: (Long pause, voice very soft) Be very painful. I mean he was— (pause).

T: I'm not sure you should either, but I'm just entertaining the idea. We'll just think about it; you don't have to do it or anything. What do you think would happen if you were to, in some very private way, have an opportunity to just talk it over with each other?

X: He'll probably tell my stepmother that I was thinking it was his fault. And then that was going to be a big problem because they were going to, um, going to tell me that it wasn't his fault, then I was going to get mad. I was going to tell him the truth (voice intense), and then, my mom was going to come and tell them, and then there was going to be a big ton of trouble.

T: Yes. You've already thought about what would happen.

X: Yeah (pause). So I don't want it to; I don't want it to happen (laugh).

T: But let's just see what that would be like if it were like a script, you know, written out for a television program. You would have this talk with your stepbrother. He'd get mad, I guess, and he'd go tell his mother that you were blaming him for the accident, and then they'd make life miserable for you?

X: Mm-hm.

T: And then what would happen? Would you have to go home to Canada? They'd kick you out? Or they'd be mean to you?

The earlier clues have now registered in the therapist's mind.

X: (Laughs) No, well, they're not mean with me. We only don't, um, you know have a good relationship; well, we do, but (trails off).

T: You do and you don't.

X: Yeah, we do and we don't. Well, I was always, I was always thinking that they prefer, well, it does (pause) that's, um, logical, that she prefers her sons and daughters, well, yeah. I was the stepdaughter only. And, uh, well (pause), they didn't let me do nothing, not even to go someplace, because they said that they were responsible for me and that if something happened to me, they were, it was going to be their fault, their responsibility. That's, that's right; they don't like it.

T: Yes.

X: So, mm (pause), you know, they wouldn't tell me to go back to Canada, but I would (laughs). I would feel—

T: You would feel you had to go back?

X: Yeah, 'cause I, if I, I won't feel good staying there.

T: Well, what would going back feel like? What would you go back to?

X: My real mother.

T: Yes, well, I don't know what that's like.

A sign of this patient's immaturity and dependency is seen in her talking to the therapist as if he knew her history. The telling of her story to many persons in a university hospital contributes to this effect, but she reveals in many other ways a psychological, developmental level of less than her chronological age. Her deportment, posture, and mannerisms are those of an early adolescent. The therapist believes that this is not merely a regression due to stress and hospitalization but, rather, a continuation of a preevent character structure. Other thoughts strike him: that she probably has an incompletely developed feminine self-concept and body image, is sexually conflicted, may use the injury as an excuse to avoid sexuality, and may have unusual problems in working through the sexual and other implications of the body loss. The stress, were this substantiated by later material, would be a complex of the new event, earlier conflicts, and impeded psychosexual development.

The patient gives her background history at this point, which indicates that she feels like a second-rate child with both her real mother, who remarried and had more children, and with her stepmother and real father. She left Canada when she had difficulty in high school and felt excluded from her family there. She hoped to make a better home with her father and to form an attachment with her stepmother and stepsiblings.

The accident disrupts the refuge she found, and she is frightened that they will exclude her because she "knows too much." She must stifle her rage to avoid this threat. She reveals this story but is not actively aware of the psychological meanings, a relatively hysterical style of "not knowing." Nonetheless, this material is at the surface and is clarified by the telling process.

The therapist then summarizes, as the transcript continues:

T: There are kind of two things that are problems for you now, that you wanted to talk over. One is the business with your stepbrother, you know, your anger where you can't win, no matter what you do.

X: Mm-hm.

T: And the other was your feeling that you don't quite realize what it means that you were in the accident and that you lost your leg. And that's probably going to be a pretty gradual thing as you get used to using your new leg. It may feel artificial and funny at first before you get used to it. Do you want to talk at all about that today?

X: Well, you know, lots of people, they lost their leg too, and they were very sad and, uh (pause), even, because I saw a man down in physical therapy who lost his finger. He was crying (pause).

T: Yes.

X: And he was very sad, and I lost my leg and I didn't realize it. I was very happy. Well, I always have been happy; I never get mad or anything and, um, well, I was thinking that probably I'm not normal (slight laugh).

T: Uh-huh.

X: Simply 'cause I don't realize it.

T: Well, you know, I've seen people who've lost different parts of their body, and everyone doesn't get sad about it. It's not necessarily abnormal or crazy or anything like that. Some people just take it and go on with their life.

The therapist has made a quick decision to support her denial of the limb loss complex for the time being and focus on the family support system, establish a therapeutic alliance, and then see what happens.

X: Yeah, but I mean, not even crying? Not even that?

The therapist realizes that by her response he may have erred: Supporting the denial sets up a therapeutic misalliance that will perhaps disrupt the therapeutic possibilities. He thus tries to reverse himself.

T: Well, let's find out more about it, though. Do you find yourself having any dreams about yourself?

X: Yeah (as if disappointed).

The therapist persists in his error by asking too peripheral a question. Dreams are important to the self-concepts contained, but the timing of this question is poor and based more on the therapist's discomfort than on the need for this information at this point. It would have been better to have ended the remark with, "Well, let's find out more about it."

T: What are you like in your dreams?

X: (Long pause) Like I was before.

T: Uh-huh.

X: Dancing again, and then, uh, I see myself in a place and all my friends over there.

T: Uh-huh.

X: And then, they don't go over there to ask me for a dance 'cause they know that I have an artificial leg or something like that.

The therapist obtains useful information. Despite his procedural error, the patient goes ahead.

T: Yes.

X: And then, I see my stepbrother dancing (pause), and I don't know, I feel something against him. It's not, it's not only 'cause I don't have my leg. It's because I don't like the way it looks either.

T: Yes.

X: To say to me they had to do two, some operations and I didn't li____. I don't like the way it does.

This is a typical avoidance of words to clarify her repugnance at how her leg looks. The therapist decides to ask for details to see how deep seated this defense is.

T: Would you describe it to me? Of course, I haven't seen your leg.

X: Well, it's kind of, um, well, they took skin from here to go over here.

T: Yes.

X: So, it's kind of, uh, looks black and all that.

T: Mm.

X: And, uh, well, I thought I was going to be, you know, there was, they were just going to amputate my leg and that's all.

T: Yes.

X: It wasn't going to look like that, but it does. And every time that I, I w____, I just saw it last month. The doctors wanted me to see it, but I didn't want to, and I said well, if they're going to do another operation, plastic surgery, it's not gonna look the same; it's not necessary for me to see it right now. So, I wait. And I thought I was going to look better.

T: So you didn't look at it then?

X: Only one time, and I, I didn't want to, but I did. And I didn't, I didn't like it.

T: Yes.

X: That's the only time that I cried for it and then, uh—

T: You did cry, though?

X: Yeah (pause). Only because it looked like that (voice tone insistent).

T: Yes, but that's part of the sadness. It's partly there. These things come in doses. But tell me more about it.

The therapist means the sadness is partly there and will occur in doses, but as often happens, his own primary process echoes the patient. "It's partly there" is what is wrong with the leg. These slips are not uncommon when treating persons with stress response syndromes. The therapist unconsciously sides with the patient's avoidances, feeling that the loss is so real that reminders will hurt the patient. He also, at a primary process level, explores his own reactions to the universal threat of body injury. The conflict in the therapist to express and to avoid expressing the loss leads to parapraxes.

X: I will cry, too, because, uh, well, I am (pause), all the time, you know, when I saw people in the streets on crutches and things, I felt (voice very soft) ashamed.

T: Yes (empathically).

X: You know that? And, uh (pause), when I was, when I was over, I didn't want to go to the store or something like they were going to bring me, just that I don't want to, people to feel ashamed of me; something.

T: Yes.

X: That's why I didn't go to graduation, either.

T: Oh, you didn't?

X: Mm-mm. Well, I wasn't, I didn't have to.

T: Yes, but you didn't want to go because you thought—

X: No. (Interrupts)

The patient gets the incipient thought and wants to prevent the clear statement, but the therapist persists.

T: —people would look at you and—

X: Well.

T: —think you didn't look nice?

X: Y-y-y-eah, but (pause) I didn't like myself, you know, people staring at me 'cause I only had one (pause) leg.

Possibly identifying with the therapist, the patient does add the descriptive word *leg*, after a pause. Previously she had used the label *it*.

T: Yes.

X: So, um (pause), well, I didn't want to go.

T: Yes (pause). So this is something that's still tender emotionally for

you (pause). And you don't like to look at it, don't like how it looks.
X: I do now.
T: A little better now?
X: (Laughs) Yeah, I guess.

The interview ended with their agreeing on a brief therapy to extend beyond the point of discharge from the hospital. During the therapy, the discussions were similar to the above material in that more time was spent on working through Xalia's rage and only a little time was devoted to the sadness and shame over her loss of the limb. In other words, Xalia's accident and amputation set in motion at least two main cycles of thought and feeling, both incomplete when the treatment began. One was more intrusive, and the other was still in a phase of denial and numbing.

All such statements are relative. For example, Xalia did have thoughts about looking different after the amputation or finding the stump ugly. But many more reactions lie ahead before she can adapt to an altered body. In comparison, the impulses to castigate her stepbrother are urgent and conscious, as is the opposing desire to maintain family harmony at the price of silence and thereby avoid both guilt over harming her stepbrother and fear that she would be sent back to her real mother and stepfather in Canada. The discussion and working through of this conflict thus meant recognizing the implications of losing a leg.

One explanation for the inhibition of personal loss and the emergence of interpersonal anger is the association of personal loss with a more profound threat. There was a brief emergence of this theme during the therapy when Xalia told of intrusive ideas that came very briefly into her awareness, of wanting to be dead, and of persons on TV who killed themselves. The implication was that if she were to realize fully her personal losses (of her leg, and her family closeness), she was afraid she might commit suicide. The profoundness of this threat is one reason that techniques that would thwart or skirt her defensive denial would not be advised. The time to master these issues will come later, when her rehabilitation is more advanced, her social support system is stabilized, and she has a well-established relationship with a therapist.

The rage at her stepbrother, a theme dealt with immediately in therapy, was not instigated solely by the accident. Though very close to him, Xalia also resented his being the complete child of her stepmother and the prize male in a family that prized sons. In addition, ambivalence and competition among the siblings was a major theme in the extended family, going back three generations. Work in this area meant recognizing the major themes of conflict present before the stress event.

SUMMARY

The case of Xalia illustrates both intrusive thoughts and denial. Two complexes, activated by the accident, were described, and at a given moment in time, one was more emergent, and one was more successfully inhibited. The inhibited complex, revolving around sadness and shame over bodily loss, was not purely denied but was partly recognized and contributed some intrusive thoughts. Nonetheless, therapy focused mainly on the more emergent themes, which involved preexistent conflicts, and followed the patient's leads.

Chapter 13

VISUAL SHOCK AND THE COMPULSION TO LOOK

With the assistance of Erik Gann, M.D.

A young man walks down a Chicago street. A woman jumps to her death from a window high above him. Her body smashes into the pavement just behind him. He turns to find her mangled corpse in full view, her brains spattered on the cement and on him. Stunned, he has a compelling impulse to stare at the woman's remains. Simultaneously, as he continues looking at the body, he feels an equally disturbing sense of transgression.

Experience of this event did not result in a stress response syndrome of sufficient intensity to motivate this man to seek consultation. Instead, other events led to an interview two years later and provided an opportunity to see what happens to such a memory, independent of treat-

Dr. Gann is Clinical Assistant Professor of Psychiatry and Faculty, the Psychoanalytic Institute, New York University Medical Center.

ment issues. The result is an illustration of (1) the enduring intrusion of images from traumatic perceptions; (2) the interaction of the repetition tendency with aims to inhibit such intrusions and pangs of emotion; and (3) the compulsion to look at stressful scenes, even though it conflicts with social taboos against doing so.

Daniel, the young man, had been interviewed by a physician as part of the admission procedures for a medical school in Chicago. During the interview, he described the incident as it had occurred two years earlier in Chicago. A young Latin American secretary working for the same firm as he did threw herself from a window in the building, landing very close to him as he passed on foot below her. The memory of this event was still vivid in his mind. He often found himself talking about it or thinking about it. He had not sought psychiatric help, however, for the recurrent, disturbing memories or for any other problems. The physician was impressed with the intensity and peremptory emergence of this memory during the entrance interview. She suggested, and he agreed to, an interview with a psychiatrist who had a research interest in this type of situation.

During the interview, it became apparent that this event had had several ramifications for Daniel. First, he had been immediately thrust into the midst of several universal responses and conflicts. He had found it imperative to look, to discover what was going on, and to attempt to comprehend the meaning of what were highly unusual and disturbing visual perceptions. There seems to be a quasi-instinctual need to look at such things; e.g., the uncanny fascination of observing accident victims, looking at executions, watching horror films. In addition, he became aware of his concern about the woman who was essentially unknown to him. This appears to have been connected to a common response of identifying with the victim. Finally, another conflict was aroused; the survivor's guilt. These universal conflicts became enmeshed with his own personal conflicts.

After an initial agreement concerning the exploratory and investigative nature of the interview, Daniel was asked to tell the incident in any way he wished. He responded as follows:

"I've talked about this a lot (pause). I was very upset when it happened (pause). A woman jumped out of a ten-story building; she landed next to me. I don't really remember. I didn't see her. She landed about 10 feet away from me. I don't remember any sounds except the blood rushing in my ears, which I guess didn't happen 'til I turned around and saw what happened. She was lying on the ground with her head facing me. There was a large hole in the top of her head (pause). My first reaction was that she had fallen down, that she had tripped on the sidewalk or had a heart attack. My first reaction was, what could I do to help her? You know, what's the smartest thing to do—cover her up with a blanket, give her artificial respiration? That was my immediate thought, even though I saw that there was nothing in her head . . . just a big, empty hole (pause). I stood and stared for quite a long time. I remember one of my thoughts was that I shouldn't be looking at that, but for some morbid reason, I wanted to look at it and kept staring at it. Then I noticed her brains were all over the sidewalk. Some was on me too, and that upset me. Initially, people just walked by . . . (pause) that really upset me too. Nobody stopped, and I started crying. I walked closer and looked more (long pause). I noticed her right leg was split open. She was wearing big, black boots about up to here, and her right leg was split open through the boot, and the next thing I remember was that people started to gather around. I walked off quite a good distance and then stared again, again for a while; I don't know how long. It seemed that what happened was that everything stopped, and I couldn't hear anything except the blood in my ears. I wasn't aware of anything going on except this one scene with nothing moving, and then I turned around and stared again, and the same thing happened, and then I left. I got on the bus and kind of looked at people; I'd been in Chicago about eight months then. It was starting to bother me because people were so unfriendly there. And I looked at them (on the bus) like, well, at least now, be friendly; at least now, open up, but I didn't say anything to anybody.''

He then added that all this did not hit him at that time, and at first, talking about it did not affect him very much; he just forgot about it. However, not long after the incident, talking about it made him nervous, and in fact, the phone conversation to set the appointment had also left him feeling nervous.

One aspect of the scene that still bothered him was an image of a passerby stepping on a piece of her brains. He stated, ''That still bothers me. I don't think I've accepted that. It upsets me when it comes into my head; I immediately shove that out of my mind. I say, 'How could that have happened' and then say, 'Okay, that happened; forget about it.'''

At this point, still early in the interview, Daniel spontaneously reported a dream he had had approximately two weeks before (between the medical school interview and this one). He was reminded of it in this context only because his girl friend, an aspiring psychologist, told him that it was related to the suicide incident.

''I saw a man get killed in a car accident in the dream. Something that I flash on when I see, picture what happened, was that hole in her head (the woman in the stress event). That was empty, and in this accident, the man had his legs cut off, but I could see all the way up into his body cavity and it was all scooped out. I could see all his bones and everything; it was as if the legs were part of the actual body cavity.''

At this point, he paused and remained silent for a minute or two. The psychiatrist asked if that were the whole dream and he replied, ''Yeah; there's more detail, but I don't know if you want to hear the whole thing.'' When interest was indicated, he proceeded.

''I was walking over an overpass; there had been an accident. There were police around and I saw the man lying there, and he looked kind of plastic, like he had black, plastic hair, very smooth olive skin but looked like he was android or plastic. He had a shaft in his chest; it looked like a metal shaft had gone into his chest and had broken off about there, (gesturing). And blood, kind of, on his chest. And when I walked by, I noticed that his legs were cut open; of course, I just saw a cross-section of his legs, the muscles and the bone, and then it turned into the part where it was all hollow. And I could see his spinal—his backbone and his rib cage, but it was covered with—you ever see the inside of a fish? It's kind of silvery, a silvery coating? Well, it (the man's backbone) was all covered with that kind of silvery coating. And then the man started squirming and blood started gushing out of his mouth and would kind of cover his face and run off very smoothly, and I could kind of put myself in his position, and I knew he was in a great deal of pain, and I knew he was saying to himself, 'I just wish this would be over.' And I knew he knew it would be over very soon.''

He continued immediately by reporting that his girl friend had said that the dream was probably related to his having observed a similar occurrence. When asked for his thoughts about this comment, he replied, ''It (his girl friend's statement) didn't click with me; I don't think it (the dream) had anything to do with it (the stress event), but it might. I've never had a dream like that before, where I've seen somebody actually in the process of dying. And when I saw the woman jump out of the window, it was about two years ago—so I think that was a pretty long time ago. The dream doesn't bother me, though when I had it, I just said, 'Okay, you've had this dream.'''

The remainder of the interview focused on the immediate and long-range impact of the event. Daniel reported that the time spent in Chicago came during a period in his life when he was somewhat depressed and lonely, and he was struck by the city and its inhabitants as being indifferent, cold, and uncaring. The woman's suicide was ''the last straw'' for him, and he decided to leave for the West after that.

Immediately after observing the body and the ensuing scene, Daniel had gone home. While on the bus, he caught himself staring intently at a young woman across the aisle and became ''self-conscious'' and felt he "shouldn't have been staring" at her. For the next several days, he felt numb and somewhat withdrawn and then began noticing a need to tell people about it. There followed a period of intrusive thoughts about the accident, which he kept trying to push out of his mind. After approximately a month, he would not think about the event unless something brought it to mind.

Daniel became essentially free from intrusive images of the scene, unless he heard specific topics mentioned that triggered a series of images. He would then feel compelled to review this set of images in his mind and would often feel the need to describe the whole memory to someone. He was aware that hearing of an incident in which someone was hurt or mutilated or hearing anything concerning Chicago would initiate this conscious and compulsive repetition of the imagery. However, hearing about death, suicide, or accidents in general would not have the same effect.

When his memory was triggered by one of these cues, Daniel would envision the following sequence: first, an image of the woman lying on the ground with the hole in her head; then he would see "her face, which was flattened because she landed on the back of her head." This was followed by an image of the leg, "split, with no blood in there either, and white"; and finally he would see "a piece of brain on the sidewalk, and I remember thinking, it must be a part of her medulla because of the convolutions." The images would make him "nervous" and "depressed" because they were "close" to him and occasionally evoked his own vague thoughts of suicide.* Over the two-year period, Daniel felt that he had achieved some conscious control over reexperiencing the imagery at any given moment. That is, he could choose either to push the thought out of his mind or to think about it and, inevitably, to recreate the above cycle of images.

In general, Daniel had not noticed the onset of any other symptomatology since the event. He was not aware of any other intrusive imagery or any difficulties with sleeping, eating, or sexual functions. The only behavioral disturbance he remarked upon was his reactions after talking about the incident, when he would invariably feel "spaced out . . . my mind just goes out of focus . . . feel emotionally like being about to faint; conscious, but as if there are no stimuli coming in." This feeling would persist for about 30 minutes after having described the scene and the unbidden images, and he reported having felt this sense of dissociation during this interview.

*Although Daniel experienced episodes of mild depression, he never seriously entertained suicidal notions, nor did this depression ever interfere with his functioning.

In addition, he reported two other significant consequences of his experience. The first involved driving past an automobile accident about six weeks after the stress event. He saw a man on the side of the road holding his bleeding head in his hands. He then noticed that the top of the car was smashed in and that there was a baby crib in the back seat. Upon observing the crib, he suddenly became upset and began to fantasize about the baby or the man's wife being trapped in the car. Then he was struck by the thought that "it was unnecessarily morbid to fantasize about it and I should stop." Whereupon, he consciously and with difficulty, forced himself to cease thinking about this episode.

The second consequence was an extended fantasy, a story that he had evolved over time about the suicide victim and her reasons for killing herself. She had many children and was working hard to support them. The children were too much to handle, and her husband had left her. She felt alone, alienated from her children, and as if she were fighting the whole world alone. This was too much for her, and so she killed herself.

In fact, the subject did not know her and knew none of this to be necessarily true, but he told me, "I had to give myself an understandable reason why she'd do that."

In the final minutes of the hour, Daniel spoke of his fears about this interview. He found that he was more nervous discussing the incident in this instance than at any time in over a year. He was worried that the psychiatrist would notice something that was bothering him but that he was unaware of and would not care to admit, such as the idea that the incident had affected him more than he thought it had.

The psychiatrist observed aloud that Daniel had been able to continue his life with a minimum of disturbance, despite the occasionally troubling thoughts. He offered him a chance to return to talk about it and to be treated briefly for help with the recurrent distressing visual images. Daniel thanked the psychiatrist and said he would call if the need arose.

DISCUSSION

From his own subjective memory report, one can reconstruct the behavioral and ideational contents of Daniel's immediate response to this terrible scene. Perhaps it would be best to begin by placing the whole stress event in the context of this lonely period in his life when he was mildly depressed. A manifestation of that mood was his thought that one is not cared for in Chicago. In this frame of mind, he had an incredible experience.

Suddenly "something" made him turn around as he walked along the street. He reports not remembering any sounds except "the blood rushing in my ears." One must surmise that he heard the awful sound of the impact of the body which probably would have resulted in an explosive noise. But Daniel either repressed this entirely or else did not record the initial impressions in memory. He was then presented with an awful sight—a dead, mutilated, female body with a gaping, empty hole in her cranium. The shock of this visual perception may have eroded preliminary codings of the auditory percepts. Next he was aware of a thought—"she has fallen down (perhaps), has tripped on the sidewalk, or has had a heart attack." He wondered what he should do to help her and yet was aware of the irrationality of these thoughts while observing simultaneously "that nothing was in her head." His mind rapidly appraised alternatives along multiple lines of associations. He tried to disavow the terrible finality of bodily destruction but concluded by recognizing its reality.

He was frozen into a state of staring. Then after a moment, he became acutely uncomfortable with his awareness that he was staring, and he thought, "I shouldn't be looking at that." Then he found himself caught in a conflict; he "shouldn't" look, "but for some morbid reason, I wanted to look at it and kept staring at it." A large part of what followed, according to Daniel's description, involved both his looking and what he saw.

One source of disturbance stemmed from the incongruity between Daniel's ordinary schema of how bodies should look and the way this particular body looked. Bodies are supposed to be intact, shaped in an ordinary manner, and the insides invisible. But this body was misshapen, and the insides were visible. In order to resolve this incongruity, he instinctively needed more information, and his eyes were glued to the body by an automatic tendency to obtain that information. In addition to this automatic tendency, there may have been psychodynamic factors such as a body schema developed around fearsome but unconscious castration fantasies.

The compulsion to look is thus an adaptational function based on a need to find out about any possible danger in novel situations. But self-awareness gives new meanings to automatically instigated staring. Daniel felt that looking was socially taboo. Customarily, eyes are averted from dead bodies; corpses are covered up as rapidly as possible; and children are protected from them. He thus felt guilty for having looked and wanted social confirmation of his act. Since the event, he relived the horror of looking, the compulsion to look, the aim never to look at such things again, and the wish for social sanctions.

Another facet of the scene was his observation that other potential onlookers were not looking, an aspect of the general tendency to deny threat. People walked by, stepping on pieces of the brain, and, incredibly enough, disregarding the body. These other people, then, represented the opposite, or mirror, response: the need to not look. For Daniel, cognitive and emotional processing of the event included not only appraisal of the meaning of the woman's body but also understanding, integrating, and accepting his own immediate responses and those of other persons who, in a sense, socialized his reactions.

While riding the bus, he caught himself reenacting what had just occurred as he stared with tears in his eyes at the young woman opposite him. Perhaps he was identifying with the dead woman as he thought, ''Well, at least, now, be friendly'' (to him). He was also asking, nonverbally, if looking was all right.

Despite his identifying with the dead woman's plight as being depressed in Chicago, there was probably a countertheme of relief that it was she who died and not he, that she was mutilated and he was intact. This thought could only serve to reinforce his sense of guilt.

By this time, Daniel was already manifesting a stress response syndrome. Over the next several days, he forgot about it but felt vaguely depressed. This represented an initial period of denial and numbing, which soon began to alternate with a need to tell what happened. He also began to experience intrusive imagery and was most aware of this when exposed to one of the trigger stimuli, like hearing one of a set of words or seeing events such as the automobile accident. In general, he was preoccupied with the presence of the memory of the event and with his efforts to prevent it from coming to mind. He was also trying to ward off the guilt, fear, and depression associated with this memory, and one would imagine it was the discomfort of these potential emotions that prompted him to try actively to suppress the images. But two years later, he still had intrusive images of the event after certain specific triggers, such as the word *Chicago*.

THE MEANING OF THE INTERVIEW AND THE DREAM

Daniel's dream occurred some time after the medical school interview, at which he had somewhat impulsively told his story and while he was anticipating the interview reported here. It occurred probably as these stimuli activated unworked-through aspects of the memories and represented a continued ideational cycle responsive to the stress event. His decision to follow the medical interviewer's suggestion and to come for the interview with a psychiatrist may also have included a covert wish to continue with and complete the cycle of thought initiated by the stressful perceptions. He continued to deny, however, that he was bothered very much at this point by the memory of the event. Accordingly, he did not view the dream as connected to this memory or to the recurrent, disturbing, intrusive imagery he still experienced. Instead, his girl friend suggested it, and he found that the suggestion "didn't click." He maintained his denial despite his report of an association in the initial part of the dream presentation that confirmed his feeling that the dream was related to the stress memory. He associated the man's exposed body cavity with the hole in the woman's head. However, after adding more detail in the second part of the dream, he told of his disagreeing with his girl friend's interpretation.

It will be helpful to examine briefly the form and content of the interview in this context. Daniel began with a description of the stress event. He emphasized the impact on him of the woman's empty cranium, the brains splattered about, and his own behavior, looking and staring—first at the body and then later at people on the bus. He immediately presented the disturbing conflict as his desire to look and his guilt about doing so.

Soon afterwards he mentioned having had the dream and offered a description, concentrating on the part concerning the body cavity that was "all scooped out" and the association to the woman's empty cranium. Then he stopped and was silent. The interviewer asked whether that was the whole dream, and he replied, "There's more detail in it, but I don't know if you want to hear the whole thing."

Interactionally, he was asking if the interviewer could stand hearing more detail, as the interview process was a reliving of some aspects of the stress situation with the externalization of some of his quandaries to the therapist. He presented the distressing images to the interviewer in a forceful way and watched his response. If the interviewer preserved his equanimity, then, by identification, Daniel too could remain unperturbed. If the interviewer did not criticize or reprimand him for staring, then the compulsive looking would be made socially acceptable. If the interviewer expressed his own wish to see and know more, then Daniel could feel less guilty about looking.

Several references have been made linking his dream to the stressful event. What is the evidence for this? A connection between the man's body cavity in the dream and the woman's cranial cavity in the perception has already been mentioned. The view is reversed, from above and downwards to below and upwards. Daniel said the man in the dream had been in an accident, a term he used during the interview to refer to the woman's fall. The man's legs had been severed, and the bones could be seen, an image similar to what he had received when looking at the woman with her leg split open.

After learning that the interviewer wanted to hear the details, Daniel reported the second part of the dream: "The man looked kind of plastic, like he had black, plastic hair . . . looked android or plastic." The woman had worn black (patent leather or plastic) boots, probably had dark hair, and her face, flattened from the impact of the fall, may have looked "android" or unreal and plastic. The man had "very smooth olive skin"; the woman was Latin American. In this second telling, Daniel again described the man's legs as "cut open . . . I saw a cross-section of his legs, the muscles and bone." This is an even stronger suggestion of his image of the woman's leg "split open." He saw the man's "spinal—his backbone." He had described a part of the woman's brain as being quite identifiable as her "medulla." The "silvery coating . . . like the inside of a fish" in the dream is probably associated with the luminescent quality of the meninges, which he might have observed on the brain parts. Finally, in the dream, he spoke of putting "myself in his position." The woman has become a man in the dream, as her suicide was "very close to home" for him. The dream's manifest content contained images derived from the original stress event and occurred in expectation of reliving the event in the forthcoming interview.

To recapitulate, two years after a frightening experience, images of that experience continued to have an intrusive quality, emerging despite suppressive efforts when there were certain associational triggers. In addition, there was a continued need to retell the story while both awake and asleep. Even the process of the interview itself had aspects of reenactment. This is by no means an unusual story and illustrates the endurance and intensity of a response to stressful events in a normal person.

Chapter 14

AN AUTOMOBILE ACCIDENT

With the assistance of Richard Olsen, M.D.

Jane is a 23-year-old woman who developed a relatively severe reaction to an automobile accident. Her therapy was completed in five interviews which will be reported in detail here to illustrate the process of treating stress response syndromes. The relevant issues are the succession of intrusive and denial signs and symptoms, a technique of limited abreaction, and the interaction of the external stress event with Jane's current tasks in life and personal development.

Six weeks after her automobile accident, Jane called asking for immediate help because she was tense, nauseated, and unable to eat or sleep. She had been seeing a doctor for neck and back pain and been placed on medications for pain, muscle spasms, nausea, and insomnia.

Dr. Olsen is presently Assistant Professor of Clinical Psychiatry at the University of California, San Francisco.

Nothing helped, and her physician had called in to see whether psychiatric hospitalization was in order. It was suggested that she be referred to the stress clinic for evaluation. When she telephoned, she sounded tearful and desperate and complained of extreme nervousness and preoccupation with the accident. An appointment was made for later that same day. After discussing the research and teaching aspects of the clinic service, Jane gave an informed consent for participation. The following interviews then took place.

FIRST SESSION

Jane appeared for the first session looking pale, tense, and wearing a protective collar around her neck. A slender and moderately attractive person who dressed modestly, her face was rigid, and she moved in a guarded and halting manner.

T (Therapist): What's up?
J (Jane): I'd rather you didn't ask me that leading question (she appears to be very tense).
T: Well, you called this morning.
J: My doctor thought I'd better call because I was getting more and more anxious and I couldn't eat. He knows— he's treating me for a whiplash . . . (long pause).
T: Yes.
J: . . . and it brings on the pain . . . (long pause).
T: What does the not eating . . .
J: What does it do?
T: Well, how does it come upon you?
J: Well, whenever I get upset, I slow down on whatever I'm eating. I never have had an appetite too much. And when I got upset this week, I just began to vomit in the morning and couldn't keep anything in my stomach.
T: Well, that was just this week that you got upset?
J: Well, yeah, but this is like I've been upset before.
T: When did it seem to start, being upset?
J: I've never calmed down since the accident, not completely. I've been on the medication ever since.
T: What medication is that?

Ordinarily, at the very beginning of a contact, the therapist would not focus on a detail such as medications but would instead encourage reports of more central material. This focus is made in order to help the patient establish a therapeutic alliance as well as to evaluate the current situation. She is quite tense, resistant to the idea of communicating with the therapist, and focuses on somatic issues. She has not presented psychological reasons for coming. At the same time, she is indicating nonverbally that she is in great need and wants to be taken care of. A somewhat tangential discussion thus may establish a model of successful communication, provide a calming effect to counteract the extra stress of a first therapeutic contact, and pave the way for freer communication of the more central details.

J: It depends on what week you're talking about. He's been changing it as I change.
T: Uh-huh. Have you been taking tranquilizers?

Her remark, "it depends on what week" is sarcastic, and the therapist knows that the state of her relationship with her doctor may be important. Her dependence on and her irritation toward her physician already impress the therapist. He expects that there may be a potential for this sort of transference in the therapy and considers the possibility of its being related to her reactions to the stress event. He chooses to persist in finding out the answer to his earlier question "What medication?" in order to establish the model for the therapeutic communication mentioned above.

J: Tranquilizers, pain killers, and a joint deflamatory medication 'cause I messed up my hips as well. I have to wear a lift on my shoe now.
T: Who is your doctor?
J: Doctor Smith.
T: What kind of a doctor is he?
J: He's an M.D., internist.
T: Uh-huh. Are you seeing him privately, or are you a clinic patient?
J: Privately. He is the one who I went to after the accident 'cause he was my doctor.
T: And he suggested you come here?
J: Yeah.
T: When was that?
J: I went to him Tuesday because I had missed work. I just started substituting as a nurse's aide, and I was really upset with some nurse, and I had to have a head nurse find another substitute at the last minute because I got all the way down to Zone City where I'm working and I couldn't stay. And I went to his office and I slept

there for three hours while I was waiting for him to come. The receptionist let me sleep there. And then he changed my medication, and by Thursday, I was in the same state all over again. I got through Wednesday somehow, but by Thursday I couldn't so I didn't even leave and go to Zone City. And I called him, and he started making arrangements, so he contacted the clinic.

T: Yes, right. So here you are. Well, this is what we'll do now. I'll just try and find out what I can about you this time and maybe another time. Then, we'll try and assign you for appropriate treatment. It already sounds like something is indicated.

J: What?

T: I don't know, but something.

J: Something?

Her rejoinder is subdued sarcasm and is provocative. The therapist again has the impression that Jane will set up a passive dependent or passive-dependent-aggressive type of transference situation. She is challenging him to do something before he knows what is going on. She has not said clearly that she is in psychological distress but has presented only physical complaints. He is comparatively certain that she is in psychological distress and chooses to focus on this issue. His next remark will, therefore, be made as a statement. This again points toward developing a therapeutic contract. The therapist illustrates his intentions here; he will clarify and interpret but not assume responsibility for her life. He already has a hunch that her physical complaints are both real and used as a defensive denial of emotional responses to the accident. He is, in a mild way, undercutting that defense by focusing attention on the area of warded-off experiences. These early choices are often quite important, but unfortunately, they have to be made on very few data.

T: It sounds like you are in psychological difficulty.

J: Yeah, I know, it has to be psychological. There is no other reason to have all these problems at once (long pause).

T: Well, I'd like to know much more. Where do you think would be a good place to start; would it be to tell me about the accident, or—? (trails off).

The patient is still resistant to telling the therapist what kind of difficulty she is experiencing. The therapist now senses that this is not simply a high level of anxiety or inarticulateness but that there is also an element of defiance. Perhaps he is being equated with the referring physician. She may be covertly communicating an accusation that would go something like this were it to have been expressed verbally rather than nonverbally: "You see, you won't help me enough: I still hurt, and so I won't cooperate with you. Let's have you make me do what you think will help. Then we'll see that it won't help either. That will prove that if anyone is to blame, it is you, and not me." To avoid this type of transference, the therapist backs off a little from the firmness of his earlier remark, "It sounds like psychological difficulty" and places the responsibility for choosing their next topic partially with her.

J: Well, the accident stopped me from doing all kinds of things. On the day of the accident, I was on my way to an assignment to substitute in Zone City. And I took Banning Road because the school was near Banning. I never take it unless I have to, and in the fog, someone rear-ended me at a stop light. And after that, after I gave out flares and told everybody that my neck hurt, we moved the cars because other cars were bearing down and nearly hitting them again. And a policeman came and passed out flares and put them out on the highway, and another car came and smashed into my car and I went into shock. And I was just like a robot from there until a few hours later when I came down again.

She does not mean physiological shock but, rather, a direct entry into a numbing phase of response to stress.

T: Uh-huh. You were driving alone?
J: Yeah, I was on the way to work. I have to be alone to get there because substitute nurse's aides never know where they're going to be. But the doctor kept me off work for a month. And that same day, I was supposed to go to an interview for a regular job, and they were good enough to hold the job open for me. And I had to wait until I could find out whether I would be able to work. They decided that I could work and so I went to work with my collar on, about two and a half, three weeks ago. But they placed me in another ward, with new people because there was a rule about two people in the same family on the same service and my sister-in-law was working on that service. I'm supposedly teamed with two other aides, but they are very, very close and are roommates as well so that they are together all of the time, and they are actually teaming and I am way off, and I see them only during report.

T: Yes, so you are kind of isolated?

J: Yeah.

The theme of people's letting her down is repeated again: the nurses, nurse's aides, her doctor, and (by inference) this therapist. The therapist gently affirms this feeling by saying that she is isolated, and so she continues with a freer description of how tough things are at work. She says she broke down one day recently but does not reveal what that means. Only in later hours did she describe what had happened. She had grown so irritated with a complaining, senile patient that she slapped him. She was terrified that she would be reported and lose her registration as a paraprofessional, as well as the immediate job. After adding details about work, which seem to smooth out the communicative feeling with the therapist, she continues as follows:

J: But after I got myself upset Tuesday, I couldn't get myself calmed down, and I dragged through Wednesday, and I couldn't make it Thursday, and I stayed off today.

T: Yes. Well, can you tell me what being upset and nervous is like inside you? How is it going in there?

J: It changes. It started just to be stomach trouble, but along with it, my stomach would hurt and my bowels would be loose. The stress would go into my back, and now the small of my back and my hip joints and my neck all hurt, and just about every single muscle hurts by now. I haven't eaten enough in so long that I'm just exhausted, and—

T: How long has it been since you've eaten anything?

J: I eat little bits 'cause every day is like a cycle. In the afternoon, I'm pretty good, and by evening, I might even be able to eat solid food. But in the morning or the middle of the night if I wake up, I can't stomach anything, and I'll just be sick.

T: Will you throw up if you try to eat?

J: Yes. Or right now, I was throwing up on Wednesday before I went to work, and I got it into my nose and I always get sinus problems anyway; and I was sneezing all day and I didn't think about it, but that evening, it drained back down and burned my throat. I haven't been able to shake that yet; I'm still—like I was crying all day yesterday and the night before, and the more I cry, the worse it got. So, last night, I woke up hysterical; I couldn't breathe 'cause I couldn't clear my throat and I had a pain in my chest, and it turned out to be that I was sleeping on my side and a muscle had tightened.

During the therapy, this patient has symptoms related to her joints, bones, muscles, gastrointestinal system, eyes, and upper respiratory system. None of these are malingering; she tends to develop psychophysiological reactions under stress. Such symptoms should never be regarded unsympathetically. It will be seen that Jane has conflicts between dependency wishes and strivings for independence. She has already presented herself to the therapist as both needing to depend on someone and not wishing to depend on anyone. The somatic symptoms are presented as a reasonable basis for obtaining sympathy and attention, but they are presented in such quantity that the therapist is made uncomfortable with the load. He changes the topic, perhaps too abruptly, but does try to find out more about what may be real aspects of her dependency-independency conflict.

T: Are you staying alone?
J: No, I'm with my father and my stepmother.
T: Yes.
J: But I don't get on with my father. He is an alcoholic, and we have what he decided is a mutual agreement: we talk to each other as little as possible because if we say more than three words, there is an argument.
T: I see. Then it's somewhat of a tense living arrangement.
J: I wanted to get out of it before the accident. I had planned to leave in either August or in October, depending on whether I could sign a contract for September or not or get some other kind of work. I was taking typing lessons in case I couldn't find a job as an aide. But now, I have to stay home until I'm well 'cause I have no place to go and no money.
T: Did you finish training just recently?

The therapist notes with interest that the accident has forced her to stay on with her father. She had planned to separate from him, a more-than-appropriate move for a 23-year-old. The psychodynamic possibilities demand further exploration, but the therapist delays this because a therapeutic alliance is not yet established and because she is so distraught. He already believes that her dependency-independency conflicts may be important and that the establishment of a therapeutic alliance in itself will offer enough support to enable the patient to improve and not require hospitalization and probably not need medications. After details about her current work and training situation, the therapist tries gently to return to the situation of living with her alcoholic father.

T: Do I gather that you had a kind of plan of getting a job and then moving out?

J: Uh-huh; pretty soon.

T: Yes, well (long pause), so there seems possibilities of that, but getting into the accident really set you back?

J: Yeah, right after the accident when I was pretty medicated, I felt really, really good because the pain hadn't set in; it took a few days. A job possibility came up for just the kind of job I wanted. Only it was a rumor; it was something the nurses were pushing, and the nursing director hadn't set her mind on it yet, and she had just asked around for nurses and aides to transfer into those positions who were already employed in the hospital. And so several people contacted me who had been contacted by her saying, "You really fit into this one." But in the days after that, my neck got tighter. I couldn't drive myself down to Zone City, so I couldn't go to an interview. And since that time, the woman who would have interviewed me committed suicide.

T: Now, what's been on your mind in terms of the accident itself? Does it come back to you at all?

It is advisable to ask directly about intrusive phase symptoms, as the patient knows them consciously but often does not know how to report them.

J: The only time I really think about it is when we're commuting on the freeway and someone changes lanes or does something stupid. Then I feel that it's about to happen because I saw the guy coming when I was hit. I could see him in the rearview mirror, and he was coming too fast. That's the only time I really think much about it.

T: Yes. And you said you don't drive now?

J: Yes, I do. I don't drive to Zone City because it's too far to go, but I drive around the city. Today I'm not driving because I haven't eaten in so long that I'm too weak.

T: And what is keeping you from eating? Is it lack of appetite?

J: Well, I don't have any appetite, and my throat was really sore, and my stomach wouldn't take food except for a few hours, and then it won't take much. But I talked to my doctor again; I talk to him every day, and he has prescribed something so that my stomach will remain calm so that I can eat. I just picked it up before I came here.

T: What is that?

J: I'd have to look; it's in my purse. Do you really want to know?

T: No, just if you knew. Are you taking any other medicines besides this one you're going to be taking?

J: Uh-huh; I was taking Valium right after the accident, with the other medications, and then I went off of it last Tuesday. Then he put me on Compazine. That Compazine puts me to sleep. When it hits, I'm out. So today, he put me back on Valium, and he doubled the dose.

T: Does that help you?

J: Yeah, the only thing that bothers me is that it dulls my mind. After having studied medical stuff like anatomy, that just freaks me out because I like to be able to think clearly and know stuff. Like I couldn't even keep my charts. I had them all messed up as to which patients had what temperatures, which had movements, and all like that.

T: So it would be important to get through this stage that you're in—

J: Right. I really don't like to be on any kind of medicine at all, and I usually have to be coerced by the doctor to keep on it. I keep wanting to go off of it and stay off of medication. It scares me because I've seen too many people with problems.

T: And what did you do at home yesterday?

J: Well, first I typed a couple of letters, and the phone was going all day with the doctor trying to find out where he could put me in. And the people were calling me who were concerned.

T: Where he could put you in?

J: For psychiatric help.

T: Oh, I see.

J: He had thought he could put me in Acme Hospital. And I'm—

T: That didn't work out at Acme?

J: No, I'm out of the district. I'm reading a book and was watching TV. And I've got a dog and I usually walk her every day, but when my hip joints hurt, I don't want to walk. Yesterday, by late afternoon, I was feeling good, so I took her for a walk.

T: And do you have difficulty concentrating, like when you try to read or watch television?

J: It depends on what it is. Like I was reading a medical book the other night, and I kept having to put it down because I couldn't imagine the parts that you should imagine as you're reading. But when I'm reading really light stuff, like from the *Reader's Digest* or something, then I have no trouble concentrating.

T: And do you see anybody?

J: My family keeps coming in and out, but most of my friends are— like when I was working full time and she's (her girl friend) stay-

ing hopped up on uppers to keep working. And she doesn't really
want to see me* because I make her unhappy and mess her up. And
another friend just took off* for the country, and another one is leaving* for back East, and she claims that she is really busy. And really,
those are the only people I see much of; I don't see a lot of people.

T: No boy friends?

J: Not right now.

T: In the past?

J: Not lately, but yeah.

T: So, you're feeling pretty isolated except for your family? Why does
your girl friend say that you mess her up?

J: We act rather strongly against one another; we have different beliefs, but we're willing to be friends. She, right now, is kind of selling what she wants to be and what she wants to do and trying to
convince herself. She's going around spouting it out to everybody.
She has already tried it out on me and knows that I disagree with
it. She doesn't want to be near me because she's trying to convince
everybody that the things she's going to do next are right, and I
don't believe her.

T: How would you characterize—or how would she characterize you;
what are your strong attitudes?

The therapist is after more information about her character and level
of psychological development.

J: Most of my friends, including her, say that I'm stable. Doesn't
sound like it now, but I'm usually stable and very—if I do something
one way, like help out in a strange situation, I can figure out ways
to get out of them. And I'm always there when anybody wants to
get out of that kind of situation. Like the car breaking down; I'm
really mechanically inclined, and if it broke down and I was there,
I would probably open the hood, and if it was simple, I would put
it together or I'd know how to call for help.

She seems proud of having independent skills.

T: Right. Any other strong attitudes your friends would say you had
that would characterize your personality?

---

*More desertion themes.

J: People who don't know me very well think I'm an egghead or that I'm cold.

T: But it's not true?

J: Well, I've got other friends who say they thought that and then when they got to know me, they found out that I wasn't. So I don't think it's true.

T: Okay, let's go back; do you mind talking more about the accident? It's seems like it's really centrally important.

This is a firm attempt to set a focus for a brief therapy. The therapist has gathered some general data and tried to foster a therapeutic alliance in the conversation so far.

T: You were going to work, and you saw this car coming at you, and you knew it was going to hit you. Could you, could you just tell me all the details from there?

J: I had come to a red light, and one car had stopped in front of me, and I was stopped and waiting. And while I was waiting, I caught an action in the mirror, and so I watched it and saw the car coming at me too fast and tensed up, and then he hit. And the first sensation after the numbness, the first numbness, went away was that my shoulder and neck hurt. And after the person in the front had seen my car jump, he came back and said, "Are you hurt?" I said, "Yes," and he stayed to help us. And the man behind me, the one who had hit me, he took a look around and came up to see me and says, "Are you hurt?" I said, "Yes, my neck is hurt." But I had checked myself out, and I could tell that was the only thing hurting; nothing else was hurting at all. So, I got out of the car and looked at the situation, then I crawled into the back seat and got some flares out 'cause nobody had anything to mark off this accident, and it was in heavy commute traffic and deep fog. So, I used the flares and said, "Has anybody called the police yet?" Nobody had; nobody knew where a phone was; it was really eerie because we were completely fogged in. You could see the road, but you couldn't see anything else because it was really, really fogged in.

Both her willingness to relate the details and her pride in taking charge of the situation (independence) are noteworthy. But she became vague and distracted as she said "fogged in," and that prompted the therapist's next remark. She seemed, in a way, to be reenacting the accident.

T: You probably started feeling unreal.

J: Yeah, yeah. Then the man who had hit me decided that I was shaking, and we couldn't decide whether it was cold or pain. I didn't
even know which it was, so he put me in his car, and we traded
information. Then he left me in his car and went to use the phone,
and after he came back, I decided we'd better move the cars, because
I kept hearing cars braking to avoid my car. We moved them and
I left the engine running and lights on and I moved it into a zone
that was painted off, a safety zone next to an island, a right-turn
island. And he moved off to the shoulder, and we got back into his
car to keep warm. My car was still in a more dangerous position.
And a police car came, and he said they had trouble figuring out
what county we were. So a police car came and didn't seem to see
us. It came from the other direction, and it made a left turn and
stopped. And then after a long time, the policeman that we saw
came, and he pulled around and came and talked to us and pieced
together the accident. Then he put out his flares and was going back
to get this report book when we could hear this other car approaching, and we all turned and watched the next collision, which threw
the car about 8 feet out into the intersection, because he was going
mighty fast. And then that man got out of the car and exploded,
and he just ran and he swore all over the place. He stomped around—

T: Angrily?

Her facial expression and vocal inflection indicate a great emotional
involvement in this new person, and the therapist intuitively picks out
a central aspect.

J: Yeah, he was as mad as he could be. I wanted his name before he
went anywhere. He said, "I'm going to find a phone." I insisted,
and so he threw his license at me and stomped away (she is very
indignant). And the officer was out of hearing range by then, and
he came back, and they started calling tow trucks and stuff and then
they had to decide whether to send for an ambulance for me or
whether I knew someone I could notify, because I was the only one
that was hurt. I said, "I'm really not hurt bad enough to call an
ambulance; I can walk around, and I can sit without hurting myself.
If I think for a minute, maybe I'll figure out somebody I know who
can come and get me." And I thought about it and tried my brother-
in-law, and he was home because it was finals week and he didn't
have a final that morning. So he came to get me, and he handled

my towing service and some of the policeman's questions about me and stuff while I wrote out a report. Then after we had checked the car and left it in an empty lot, we called my doctor and took me in. But my doctor had two other emergencies that morning in his office, and they left me sitting in the waiting room for an hour and a half. Then they decided after he looked at me for one minute, he needed an X-ray before he could decide anything. So he sent me over to X-ray, which is in the same building. I'd been there before because I had had back trouble before, and I had X-rays and retakes and stuff. And I went back, and he decided there were no fractures and no nerves pinched; it was just a severe strain. He prescribed tranquilizers and pain killers and a prescription for the collar, and I went downstairs and got the collar, and I got the medications and stayed home. But my insurance company sent a field representative to my house that afternoon. And I was really, really—not the same as I am anxious now—but excited more, and I called a friend to stay with me, and my family kept dropping in, and the house was full of people, and they had like a party and joked a lot, having a good time. And then the guy with a tape recorder came and taped my version of the accident, and he wanted a medical release and—

T: And so your family didn't realize, because there was not any big deal like bandages, they didn't realize that you'd been hurt.

The therapist is picking up on her vocal tone which indicates her hurt and anger that she got so little attention.

J: Right. And then when I started to hurt, it really scared me 'cause I didn't know it was going to start to hurt.

T: Right, and that was really frightening.

J: And then the following Tuesday, I started therapy, physical therapy. But a few weeks later, I had to call my doctor about pains in my hip joint. It was just one at first, and I've had something related to that before, but it wasn't the same; this was stronger. And he didn't understand what it was and couldn't find out, and so he looked up my old X-ray and found out it was in my other hip, so he went for another X-ray. And he then said that the joint didn't show anything, but in the days that followed, it got worse and has gone to the other side. It turned out that I was sleeping on my side. I always slept on my side before this, and so I was sleeping on my side. I was sleeping on my hip, and it was getting irritated. And then I'd turned over to the other side and done it to the other one. So—

T: How did you feel about seeing your doctor repeatedly?

J: Well, he had me down once a week, and it turned out that I made the once-a-week appointment. I might not have a new complaint every week, but I just got in on a once-a-week appointment until this week.

T: How did the relationship go between you and your doctor? Do you know what I mean?

J: Yes. Well, he is almost argumentative in manner, but not that strong. I don't know where—well, if I ask something, then he asks something back, and we go back and forth. And it isn't as if he's trying to explain the whole thing to me; I need to ask him to find out how things are going to go.

T: Right, just like being surprised that it was going to hurt. Doctors sometimes feel, "Well, I won't say anything because I don't want people to imagine it." And then what happens is what usually happens in these things. Delayed symptoms come up, and then you're surprised. But I get the feeling throughout that your feelings are badly hurt, as well as your neck.

For her, this is a major interpretation and also a second round in trying to establish a therapeutic contract for exploring her ideas and feelings.

J: Uh-huh.

Her response is vague, and so the therapist tries gently to rivet her attention to the issue. She has not yet fully agreed to the exploration of psychological issues.

T: Does it make sense to you?

J: My feelings hurt?

T: Yeah.

J: I'm awfully disappointed that all my plans got wrecked.

T: Yeah, but I don't think you've been able to tell anyone that.

J: But I talk to my sister-in-law all the time. Only thing is that she is talking about other things when she talks back, so I don't know if she's hearing (long pause).

T: Well, I think there's some working through to do about talking over these things. That, at least, I see as being real essential for you to do. Anything else?

The therapist is once again working toward establishing a therapeutic contract centered on psychological issues.

J: Oh, on the day before the accident, I hadn't been called to work. And I have a choice; I can call in at the City Hospital where I used to work and say I'm there, or I can do what I please. So, I decided it was about time I got myself another car 'cause I had sold my car about a month before when it was beginning to give me trouble. It was a '60 Toyota, and parts were really hard to get 'cause mine was made for the Canadian specifications. So I sold it and was still convinced that Toyota makes a good car for an economy car. It is big enough not to scare me. I know that Volkswagens blow around on the freeways; that scares me, and being in an accident scares me. This is before the accident; I went down—I saw an ad in the paper and I made phone calls; then I went down to Danville where there was a good dealer. I won't trust the guy locally 'cause I've heard what happens. And I test drove a car, and I said, "Yeah, I'll put a down payment on it." Then I told him that there were a couple of things that needed work before I would pay for the car, and he wrote them up and then I had the accident the next day. I was supposed to pick it up on Saturday, and I had arranged financing independently on my own through their bank which they had set up for me. But it was my own financing. I got home, and my father said, "Oh, no, I'll pay the whole thing for you; you can just pay me back." Which is the arrangement he did with my sister, and since I'm financially in a rotten position anyway, I decided, well, money is going to help me get out of the house faster; I'll do it. And so I canceled the loan financing, and I got all their correct numbers and had my father write up a cashier's check 'cause he has the money in the bank.

Dependency on her father and the link of cars to her father turns out to be an important dynamic issue in working through the stress event.

Saturday, I really freaked out about picking up a car 'cause I couldn't drive; I had the collar on, and the pain was getting bad, and I was taking codeine and was too doped up to drive. I convinced my brother and my brother-in-law to come along. They took me down, and they were really nice; and they took me in a car with back rests in it, shoulder harness, and drove real careful. And when we got there, they test drove it for me. They said they'd take it on a rough road and really see how it was doing but the salesman who was selling it to me and told me he'd be there wasn't there, and he turned me over to the manager.

The desertion theme emerges again. Note that she is talking more openly to the therapist and in a pressured manner.

And the manager needed all the details because the salesman had left in a hurry. And we made the arrangements finally and signed the papers and gave him all the money and took the car home. And since then, problems that I stated on the first form weren't solved. Today was the day we finally had an appointment to have it done, so I sent my brother down again, and he just got the car back, but I haven't had a chance to ride in it or drive it myself yet to see if it really is repaired or not.

T: So you have that hassle. Well, look, we have to stop. I'd like to see you again before we decide anything. But you know, I think we've already decided that whatever else, there is some talking to be done.

Yet another effort to reach agreement on a therapeutic contract.

J: Okay.
T: You know, I hope this won't interfere with you working.

A suggestion that she is well enough to work and should go on rather than regress.

J: I work in the morning only.
T: Oh, well, let's see what we can do in the afternoon.
J: It would have to be after 1:00 o'clock.
T: Um. I could see you if you could come Monday at 2:30. Would that be okay?
J: Okay.

SECOND SESSION

Jane began by saying that she had done quite well over the weekend. She felt that the first hour had helped her: "It just worked; I don't know what it did. I know afterwards, I kept thinking, 'I sure didn't say a lot of details that were there that I could have said,' but at the time, I didn't think." This suggested to the therapist that she was in a denial phase of response. The hour helped both in the sense of socialization, discussing the accident with a therapeutically oriented person, and in a general way, raising her concerns to a reality-oriented rather than fantasy-oriented level.

She went on to add that she had moved out of her father's house. She had asked her pregnant sister to take her in, and that had been an improvement over eating with her father who often vomited at mealtimes because of his alcoholism. She indirectly attributed the idea of this move to the therapist's remark in the first hour that the situation at home was tense. Probably the therapist's repetition of what she herself had been saying acted as a permission for her to become more assertive.

She was worried about being a burden on her sister but said, "I'm going to turn it around, and I'm going to help her, and I'm helping because I don't have to be the one that everyone else is helping. It puts me one block away from the person I was commuting with, my sister-in-law. And I'm going to see if I can commute alone pretty soon, 'cause I don't like to be driven. I'm going to try it one time with her sitting beside me and if that doesn't have any problem at all, then I'm just going to commute by myself."

The therapist is pleased to see the reassertion of her striving for independence and activity. He has also been impressed by both regressive forces leading to searches for dependency as a secondary gain from the accident and the loaded but unexplored issue of her deterioration at the accident when yelled at by the driver of the second car. Also, she was at the point that her doctor was considering psychiatric hospitalization, and she was showing many somatic as well as psychological complaints. He favored further work rather than a termination at this point. His feeling that the improvement was in a way a relationship cure added to this decision to continue. First, he asked more about what seemed to be a fear of driving and then asked an open-ended question.

T: Well, what about cars and driving? How has that been on your mind the last few days?
J: Well, I drove here. I drove all over this morning doing stuff, getting keys made and stuff.
T: Alone?
J: Sure. Ever since the accident, I'm always able to drive short dis-

tances alone; no problem at all. The only problem that still scares me is getting on the freeway in heavy commute traffic, where mergers are going on. That part scares me. But I think if I was behind the wheel and not having to watch somebody else do it, I could handle it fine, because I did it since January and never had an accident or even a close call. You know, I know how to do it; just whether or not I'm scared or not.

T: Okay. Well, where should we go from here?

J: I don't know. I'd kind of like to find out why I get into such deep depressions and can't get—well, this time I couldn't get myself out, because I wouldn't want to go into it again. If it ever happened again, it would screw up my career in nursing, being unable to attend or just breaking down like that. I mean, if I couldn't have pulled out this week, my contract probably would have been torn up and destroyed, and my record would have been messed up, you know. And I really would like to get to the root of why I throw myself into depressions.

T: Okay. That's something then that we should explore a little bit more. Maybe we'll have time now. But I wanted to ask you also where the memory is with you right now about the accident.

J: I can remember it fine.

T: Uh-huh. Does it come back to you when you don't want it to at all?

As mentioned earlier, patients often do not spontaneously report intrusive phase symptoms. Risking the danger of suggesting a symptom, the therapist asks pointedly about a common response to accidents.

J: No. I think—I don't usually remember what I dream. But since, like the last week or so, I have had nightmares, usually right when I wake up I remember something, some piece of it, and I think sometimes I have nightmares about the accident because it scared me so bad.

T: Yes. But you don't remember what they are?

J: No. Never have (laugh).

T: Do they sometimes wake you up out of your sleep?

J: Well, it is a combination, because I move around if I'm having a nightmare, and then I don't know whether it's the nightmare or laying on a hip joint or bending my back or what it is that wakes me up. But I wake up, and I can remember a piece of bad dream and being in pain at the same time. So, I don't know, is it the night—

you know, I'm so wrapped up in too many things at once—I can't say. Like last night, I slept fantastic—no problem at all. And I know I woke up on my side which is supposed to be a no-no until the hips get better. And this morning, this hip joint was irritated, but after I was up and moving around and took a hot shower, after about 45 minutes, it's okay now. So I think pretty soon I'm throwing the book away and forget about it, so I can sleep like I want to sleep.

T: Uh-huh, and during the day, you don't find you're having thoughts about the accident coming in on you when you don't want them to?

J: The only time they'd come in on me is if I associate with something happening right now, like in the car—

T: That might trigger it?

J: Yeah, trigger it.

T: Well, you know, thoughts like that are always surprises.

This is a "moving closer" type of remark, meant to reveal empathy with the patient. The patient responds with associative memories.

J: Yeah, definitely. Well, I know, well, I mean, I kind of compare it with my mother's death a long time ago, and for a long time after that, things would trigger that memory, you know. And now it's so long that—and I used to counsel at the York Avenue place with the kids who had a lot of trouble. A lot of them had fathers who disappeared and people in the hospital dying and things like that, and I could handle that fine for them, too, you know. And I got out of that, and I'm confident that I'll be able to get out of the accident myself. But something else is still triggering depressions on me because I still get into them.

T: Well, there may have been a clue to that in our discussion Friday. It may not be the right one, but it might be there. I kind of got the idea that you experienced the accident, in one way, as just another insult.

J: Yeah.

T: Does that seem to fit with you?

J: Uh-huh.

T: And maybe there have been a number of other ones in your life, and this was just. . . .

J: Another one, yeah.

T: . . . just another one to hit you. Of course, it had that kind of rippling effect in that it interfered with so many of your plans.

J: Yeah. It meant nothing in particular. My car, I hadn't paid for it;

I was right in the middle of it. And that afternoon, I was supposed to go for planning for the summer. That particular day, I was doing a million matters of business, and none of them could be done . . . (long pause).

In an event-centered therapy, one may not wish to stray too far afield. But she calls her psychological reaction a depression and seems to recognize a recurrent pattern. The therapist believes this must be explored to understand her character, preexisting conflicts, and the meanings attached to this recent event. As she pours out a tale of losses, the therapist realizes the importance of accumulated stresses and the ''last straw'' effect in this case.

T: Okay. Well, tell me a little bit about some of the other depressions that you've had. What kind of things seem to trigger them?
J: I think most of the other ones were triggered by people dying, because I've watched my mother go into a depression when her mother died. That was when I was 5; I was just a kid, and I don't know what I was doing. I used to throw tantrums, but I don't know what else I was doing. But when I was 12, she was ill, and she had been ill for years and died of cancer and that threw me. They had to take me to a doctor and start giving me vitamin shots to pull me back out because I was wasting away, losing too much weight.
   A few years after that, my favorite aunt died, and I went into another one. Shortly after that, one of my best friends died, and then I went into one again. One summer, in fact, I think it was the summer my aunt died, there was a dog we bought the year after my mother's death—and she always thought a dachshund would be a nice kind of dog because they're clean. So my sister helped find one and everything, convinced my father who was against it, and we bought a dachshund. It turned out that the dachshund was pedigreed, and he was overbred, and he had come out with a mean temperament. If a professional had been the breeder, he probably would have been destroyed because of his temperament, but it was a nonprofessional person who sold it to us, and he was like a one-man dog and we didn't know it. He could have been trained maybe to be a watchdog; otherwise, he should have been destroyed because he was mean. But we kept him for six years, and we had to do all kinds of things all over the house so that the family could protect people from him because he was moody and temperamental. He hurt people, and I got into all kinds of trouble because I was sit-

ting for people at the time. I had to take a little girl to the emergency hospital and nearly landed in a lawsuit because her eye got scratched and all kinds of problems with him.

But anyway, that summer he fell down the back stairs and dislocated his back and paralyzed himself from the shoulders back with some control of his internal organs. I had to take care of him 'cause I was the only one home, and I nursed him and nursed him and nursed him, and finally I was just getting really tired of it. My parents were going to be on vacation, and I said, "Is it okay with you if you'll take along the dog? I'm going to take two weeks off and visit a friend in Tahoe." They said fine. And I call, and they say everything is fine, and I came home and found that they had run out of pain killers and didn't know that pill was important and hadn't gotten any, and the dog had been in pain for eight days and just shaking with the pain. So I took him to the vet, and we had to have him destroyed.

We had two dogs at the time—my other dog caught one of the infections that the dachshund had, and she had to be nursed back to health. After all that happened, after I went into a depression—it wasn't very long or very strong, because I had to do so many things right then and get back to school and stuff, but it seems they're all tied up with someone dying.

T: Losing something you like or are attached to?

J: Yeah. And then after that, there was—last summer was different. Last summer, I was taking courses; that's the last thing before you student nurse and go out. One of the people in the courses said, "I know you're really good" 'cause I was helping her out. She said, "I've got a job possibility for you," so I went and followed it up and got the job, only the job was really something I wasn't quite ready for, and it threw me for a loop. I was tense because I had to learn how to deal with unusual patients and all of this as a semi-volunteer, possibly with money coming through and me in debt for a car that I had just bought, all at once.

And so I got all upset, and Dr. Smith treated me then with tranquilizers, and I got through it and we had a glorious summer, no matter what (laughter). But about a week before the end of it, my mother's last surviving sister died of a brain tumor, and her daughter is a dwarf, who is slowly becoming—well, now I guess you'd call her a hermit. She has withdrawn from just about every living soul in the world. I happen to be one of the few people alive that she'll talk to. There is a handful of people; my sister, her sister, her brother, and a couple who she'll talk to on a very superficial level. I was trying to see if I could help her out, but of course, she wouldn't accept it. And also having lost my aunt, I went into another tailspin, but I came out of that one quick; it was short. I just got mad at the whole thing and said, "I've got to live for me and get out of this mess."

Since that time, there's just been like little short things like the pressure of substituting. I'd get myself worked up in the morning waiting for that phone to ring and wouldn't be able to eat breakfast until after the phone rang, and I knew what the day was going to be. I was just waiting because at 6:00 A.M. when it could ring, I'd have to wait until 8:30 to know for sure whether it's going to ring. And then on three occasions, they called me for emergencies, so I really was never sure. So, I made it a policy that if it didn't ring by 8:30, I just left and I either did volunteer work or I did something else, 'cause it was driving me crazy to wait for the phone.

T: Well, you're a very strongly motivated person to get out and do things.

J: Yeah, well, I've had to.

T: It is related to what you've said; you've decided that you're going to survive. There are a number of messes in your family.

J: Definitely. Yeah. My mother taught me from the time I was very tiny, because my sister told me not too long ago that my mother had arthritis before I was born. And before she was ever pregnant with me, they told her that she shouldn't carry another child; it would hurt her too much, she had arthritis in her back. When I was very, very small, she would be in bed in the morning, and she would tell me how to do things. I would have to go and do them and then come back to her and see if they were done correctly. Instead of having her show me, she would just tell me, and I would have to go and do them, like getting ready for school in the morning, getting breakfast, and that kind of thing. So, I had to learn how to do things independently.

Then, it got to the point where her arthritis would get worse, and she wouldn't be awake, and I wouldn't want to wake her, so I would do them all by myself, and if something new came up, I would sit down and think and see if I could figure it out so I wouldn't have to wake her up. But the older I got, the arthritis got worse and then—I don't know, something happened when I was about 8. It improved for a while, and she got out and got a job. And then we had to take on the whole thing about fixing dinner and buying food while she was out working. Then the cancer started, and she stopped work. Then she got really, really sick. Finally, because my father doesn't believe in hospitals, he insisted that she die at home, and she died at home from cancer and from all the complications from it.

T: Were you nursing her?

J: No, they wouldn't let me because I was the littlest. They had locked me out. That hurts sometimes (crying). They'd send me away, so I couldn't see her very much. Because she was so sick, they didn't want me to be scared, but it's scary not to know.

T: It can be harder than knowing the worst, sometimes.

J: I don't know. She finally died of dehydration; not from the cancer itself, but from what it caused.

T: I get the feeling that you never had a chance to say good-bye.

J: No. She said something once that sounded like good-bye, but they never told her she had cancer, and we knew for a while. She was smart and knew it. 'Cause she was taking cobalt treatment, and anybody would know. But (silence) one time she did say something that was like good-bye. But that was months before she died. But I always have to—in my own family—I have to fight for the right to be treated my own age because I'm the littlest. My father wants me to be little and protected.

The regressive trend may have an oedipal overtone, as suspected in the first hour. The accident made her ill and a stay-at-home like her mother. Later material will show that she has an ambivalent attachment toward her father in which they each can play either role: he babies her or she nurses him. Her progressive developmental strivings were leading to a healthy separation from this bond, with external sources of potential gratifications providing the enticements that would allow her to leave her father. The accident upset this forward movement and is a variegated type of loss, as later material will show.

J: I usually win, but it's always a big hassle. Like he didn't want me to go to the funeral. I told him—I was going to a parochial school at the time—I told him they're sending 100 school-age children my age to sing at her funeral, and they're my classmates. And if my classmates can go, there's no good reason why I can't go. He was convinced and I went. Had he left me out of the funeral, I don't think I would have believed that she had died.

T: Yes, I think you were quite right to have gone.

In hope of a rapid restabilization at her most progressive level, the therapist has decided to directly support her independence. He means this support also as a counter to the undercurrent of her potential dependent transference.

J: After that, after my father married Joan; she is fabulous; she came in, and we tried to make her fit and she tried to fit. It was a strain for a while, but it all worked out really beautiful. But then Dad began to drink more and more.

T: That's something more recent then?

J: Well, I can't remember how many years they've been married. He drank heavily after my mother died. My aunt, the one who's dead now, was trying to get all the kids placed somewhere else. They wanted to take me away from my house and place me with family or in an institution or something 'cause he was drinking too badly. But we proved to her that we were old enough to run a household whether he was well or not, and we did, 'cause he couldn't do anything. He was drinking really, really bad.

And then, for a while, he sobered up, and he met Joan and.he was well and healthy and doing all kinds of things. Like he's really handy around the house; he fixes everything, or he did. And it was then that she knew him when he was happy, a whole person.

But not long after the marriage, he began to go to pieces again. And a couple of years ago, her son was in Vietnam, and he had a few more months before he came home from Vietnam, and we had a long time to wait before we could see my brother. So we planned a vacation 'cause she was getting so anxious for him to get home. We would drive to Arizona and visit my brother, and by the time we got home, it would be close to the time for her son to get home.

Shortly after we left, they notified our household that her son was killed in action. My sister was the only one there, and she tried to notify us on the road and because it was a military matter, the highway patrol wouldn't help. We got all the way there, and my brother told my father on the phone and Joan collapsed, and we had to carry her to the car. He knew she was upset; she started saying all kinds of things against everybody.

She reports another loss. The therapist notes similarities but cannot be sure whether they are relevant. Joan "said things against everybody," which may be like the second man's anger. In what follows, her father insists on sticking to the cars instead of going with Joan. Cars are very important to him. The therapist recalls that in the first hour, Jane spoke so proudly about taking care of the car, putting out flares, but does not yet know what to make of all this.

J: Then we got to the base, and my father wouldn't let us abandon what we were driving, which was a car with a trailer. I wanted to abandon the whole thing and take a jet home and comfort Joan, and he wouldn't let us do it. So my brother got an emergency leave, and we put my stepmother and brother on a plane, and they got to San Francisco, and they have lots of family and friends here to help them out. But then my father and I had to take the car and trailer back home. I knew how to drive; I had a license and I was experienced; more experienced than he realized because he doesn't hear me when I say things—he discounts what I say. But he wouldn't allow me to relieve him at the wheel.

T: He tried to drive it all himself?

J: He did. And finally, a gas station attendant took one look at him part way down and said, "Hey, you guys need a rest." My dad told him, "Yeah, we have to get home to a funeral, but I guess I do need a rest." One time, we tried to stop and find a motel, but we couldn't. But finally, a gas station attendant let us sleep in the back of the gas station. I could sleep, but he couldn't and he stayed so wound up; he was wide awake waiting for me to sleep so that I wouldn't fall apart. I woke up and I had to talk to him all the way to San Francisco 'cause I was so scared he would fall asleep at the wheel. He wouldn't let me relieve him at all, and he knew I could drive the car even with the trailer on it, 'cause I knew how to drive a car. I knew quite well; I had driven tractors and all kinds of things before that. But when we got to San Francisco and got home, he got sick all over the place and collapsed in a big heap; he had no control over his vomiting, diarrhea, and yelling and screaming, and he just fell to pieces.

An important memory contains cars, yelling, and falling apart. This memory was reactivated by her more current accident. Note how the patient is using the hour to go through an association that she may have been warding off in her own thoughts and that would be difficult to talk through with her family members.

J: And he won't allow any doctor to ever touch him, and we didn't have anything in the house that we could calm him with, except alcohol again. And there he went again on alcohol. From there until now, he's become an alcoholic, only he won't admit it and he won't accept any help of any kind, and he won't see a physician of any kind.

Note the implication that she is partly responsible for his resuming drinking by not driving, needing sleep, and giving him alcohol.

J: But, we went to the funeral, and it turned out that my stepbrother's wife had sent him a "Dear John" letter and he had volunteered for a dangerous mission and that is how he had gotten killed. Right after the funeral, she was living with another guy and getting the money from the government for him and buying a hot rod and just running all over. Joan was so upset that the household was just in a turmoil for months and months and months. She was bitter all the time. And even today, we all know that we can't say President Johnson in front of her or she'll become upset, and we can't say Vietnam in front of her or she'll become upset, or we can't say the name of the girl he married or see anybody drive a red sports car or any of that because she's still very upset about it. When things happen to make her upset, she sits and cries about her son who's gone, because her husband died and her son's gone and he was the last one of their family.

T: So, this kind of series of events you think might contribute to your vulnerability to getting depressed when an event happens? And there's another element in it that sounds like it is very important, which is your determination to survive and get out from under.

J: Be independent, is all I want. That's the one thing my family always hesitates about, always, is for me to try something. They're always beholding me, saying, "Well, are you sure, are you sure, are you sure?" I finally get myself convinced and I'm ready and confident, and they put all the doubt back in me.

T: Yeah, but you seem very successful when you do things. Like just moving out now; it seems like it's really an important step.

The patient has been crying at times during her telling of these stories. This expression of her feelings seems to have been a positive reaction for her. The therapist offers an appointment one week off to see how things are going then, implying by inflection that he expects them to go well.

THIRD SESSION

Jane was to return for her next appointment on Monday. But she called sooner, on Friday, asking to be seen because she did not think she could get through the weekend. A brief appointment was scheduled for later the same day.

T: Well, what's up?
J: I'm getting all keyed up again.
T: Uh-huh.
J: And the thing that scared me really bad is in the pediatric ward. I've hit two patients. The first one was before; I hit an old man who kept touching me. And then it happened again this morning with a child. It is just terrible. But this kid kept picking at his burn. I couldn't get his attention because my voice keeps fading. My hearing is also shot. Doctors say I've got both eustachian tubes blocked, so when I get all frustrated and something is about to go, I overreacted.

She goes on with details about the patients, crying at times and searching the therapist for his facial responses. He responds neutrally.

T: Yes.
J: And I'm physically getting myself tied up again. This morning I couldn't eat anything again (spoken very slowly and deliberately). I don't want to do that Saturday and Sunday and Monday. So when I left work, I decided that I'd call you and see if I could see you. The first time I saw you—after that I could eat again (long pause).
T: Yes. Why don't you just try and tell me whatever comes to you right now?
J: Well, I'm shaking (there are tears in her eyes).
T: Uh-huh; well, you're also crying, aren't you?
J: Yeah. Okay, this morning I told my doctor that I wouldn't take anything that had any depressants in it, 'cause I was scared of getting depressed again. And I have an infection, but he's treating it with antibiotics. He said, "If you won't take any depressants, will you use steam?" I've got an old vaporizer that I used to use when I'd get these things before. I'm staying at my sister's with her husband in their flat. They put me in the spare room that's going to be the nursery in January when the baby is born. It's just an old flat, but the vaporizer last night was too strong and loosened all the dirt

on the wall, and this morning there was just gobs of greasy dirt dripping down on the walls, all around. That's what I woke up to. Stupid stuff that's nobody's fault; just keeps happening, but when it does—

T: Did somebody blame you for that?

J: No, they kidded me about it, but they couldn't laugh about it because I was too tied up already and they knew it.

T: Yeah.

J: And then I woke up even before I saw the walls, with some of the paint which had been doing—and once I saw them, my stomach was out of control. I took stomach medicine that I'd been taking, and I got up and got dressed and went in, and they were having breakfast. I couldn't bring myself to eat anything because I just kept feeling so rotten. After they were gone, I was sick. Then I pulled myself together. My attorney wants me to write a diary, so I wrote an entry in the diary and left for work (silence). That's just today. Today's worse than yesterday which is worse than the day before.

T: You have an attorney?

Litigation is always a concern because compensation can be a secondary gain for continued suffering.

J: Yes, he's on vacation this week.

T: What is he going to be doing for you?

J: He's going to handle the medical costs of my accident.

T: Uh-huh.

J: But it's kind of ripped up; we don't know a lot of things yet. Because I was a substitute, we don't know if there's any way to collect compensation for loss of job.

T: Yes (silence).

J: Other things that keep bugging me is on my own ward I don't—can't think of things far enough ahead—can't plan ahead, so many things, I can see how they should go and can't make them go. Things turn my head in another direction and I can't get back fast enough.

T: Tell me more about your reaction with your patient.

Jane then gives a detailed description of how frustrating the child patient was to care for. She does not label her affect with words, but the therapist provides the label as the transcript continues.

T: You must have felt angry at him.

J: Yeah, repeatedly angry at him. But I have to watch it because he's so destructive of himself and won't let himself heal.

T: Yes, but right now, anger is especially hard for you to control because you're also angry at those people who. . . .

J: Yes, angry at the nurses who won't help enough.

The patient interrupts the therapist. He had intended to link her anger to the auto accident and to the various people who had blamed and deserted her. Deciding this link is probably correct and that she is warding it off by her interruption, he persists with his intent, feeling that she will be able to tolerate this confrontation.

T: Well, you're also susceptible to anger now because you haven't had a chance yet to work through and work out anger at the people who got you into the accident.

J: Yeah. Something happened yesterday that got me started off last night. There was a continuing education thing at the hospital. Yesterday's film was a thing on policemen and first aid. It was how a patrolman saw an accident happen and what happened after it. I really got upset during it, but I got myself all together before the lights went back on and helped clean up and everything. I've been having lunch with the ward clerk and went out to see a friend of mine in another ward and talked with her. She is going to try and help find me someplace to stay besides where I am.

But that accident flashed back on me again last night during dinner. My sister and brother-in-law had been riding in their car. They witnessed an ambulance accident and right in the middle of dinner, they were telling me about it. They didn't know it, but I couldn't take it and I just stopped eating and right then, I began to get sick. And I don't want to make my sister any more upset, so I just slipped away. They know I don't have any appetite anyway, and they weren't very upset.

Jane's intrusive episodes are now very apparent. Although intrusive signs were present before as bad dreams, the earlier interviews basically represented a denial phase. In the first interview, she was in an unstable denial state with loss of concentration, bodily symptoms, anxiety, and tension. In the second interview, the denial phase was more stable. Now, by the third interview, it appears that ideational repetition has become more prominent and is contributing to her discomfort.

T: But you didn't want them to know that their talking about the ambulance triggered the memory?

J: Yeah.

T: Were you ashamed to let them know, or you thought it would hurt their feelings?

J: No, my sister is pregnant with her first child, and we were very, very scared that she would lose it and she wouldn't let us tell anybody for weeks. She's just—I don't want to upset her that much either, because she was upset already about it, worrying about it.

T: Yeah. But last night they were talking about this ambulance, and then you began—

J: Thinking about the morning I reacted in my own accident. And then I stopped eating and (silence) and later—

T: And you were feeling frightened when this happened?

J: Yeah.

T: In fact, very frightened.

J: But I couldn't really say anything because I was also afraid to get her upset.

T: Yes (silence). Well, that may have been a trigger to your reaction today, you know.

J: It acted like a trigger.

T: Do you know that this is the sort of thing that happens after accidents?

J: I figured it would, but I never heard it said.

T: Yes. People often go through a period when things are kind of out of mind. Then they come back, especially if there is something that hasn't been worked through about it. For you, there are a number of things that haven't been worked through. You're frightened. Even though you don't rationally think so, part of your mind thinks that it might just happen again.

This is essentially a supportive remark aimed at reducing her fear of her symptoms and at sharing an understanding of what is going on.

J: Well, it was the kind of accident that could happen again and again because, I was saying, that it was the other man's fault, and I had no way to get out of the way. But I have to commute now because— the only arrangement I had before was riding with my sister-in-law, and I reached the breaking point with that. I can't ride with her anymore because I get just as scared watching her drive as not going at all. I'm better when I'm in control of the car.

T: Yes, I'm not surprised to hear that.

J: But even like coming over here. A couple of times I checked the mirrors and ahead in merging traffic, and I look, and there's somebody too close behind me, and I have no idea how they can get that close unless they are coming up too fast, which is what happened before.

T: Yes, so there is this constant expectancy below the surface that is frightening you. And the other thing I think that will need some working on is your anger. You feel very badly about having it, and you're trying to do things, like with your sister, by not even letting her know that this reminded you of your accident.

J: That's why I want to stay with somebody else besides her.

T: Are you sure she's so delicate?

This is an indirect challenge directed against what the therapist intuits is her own defective or vulnerable self-image. The remark, at an unconscious level, may be received as "maybe you are not so delicate and can see yourself once again as a capable, grown-up woman."

J: Well, she was a few months ago, and she tells me she's not now. But it's hard to believe.

T: Well, for her to know what you're going through might not injure her in any way. You might just let her know what you're going through.

A therapist ordinarily does not give direct suggestions, even in brief therapy. But in this instance he does, because he believes that less-inhibited communication with her sister may help her to work through the meanings of the accident more rapidly. As with his previous statement about the delicacy of her sister, this comment has an indirect meaning: "You can take knowing what is going on, and it will also be all right to let others know how you have responded."

J: The thing is that she's a personnel worker for the phone company, and she's getting people like me all the time and she's always saying she works because she has to. I don't want her to be pressured at home, too. But she really should stay out of that job; it's not doing her any good.

T: Well, we have to stop now. We can continue on Monday at the time we scheduled. So see you then.

J: Okay, at 3:00 o'clock.

FOURTH SESSION

Jane reported feeling gradually better over the weekend, but she was still shaky and awoke early. At the beginning of the hour, she and the therapist again reviewed her reaction to the movie on accidents and her intrusive thoughts about her own accident. She then talked about wanting to avoid discussing the accident because she was afraid that if she did get into it again, she would become upset and not do well at work. The therapist was inclined to deal directly, even abreactively, with the accident memory, again in a denial rather than a completion phase, and he wanted to work the memory through to the point that she would not be upset by reminders. The hour proceeded with the following discussion of whether or not to focus further on the accident:

T: Yes, that's the decision we have to make now. Should we do that [not dwell on it now], while you try and get through, or—sooner or later, I think it has to be talked out.

J: I know it does, because it scares me when it happens.

T: Yes. So I think your intuition might be best. My intuition doesn't say for sure, so let's go on yours. You decide whether we talk about it now or make another appointment and talk more about it.

J: It's kind of weird because it's hanging over my head if I don't do it. And then I might just start thinking that way and go round and round again.

T: Well, I wonder if you're not in enough control so that we could do a little bit, kind of a small dose, and then just stop.

J: Okay.

T: Want to try that? Let's say you can stop any time you want.

J: Okay.

T: Okay? So I'd like you to do this feeling as relaxed in your body as you can. Why don't you try and just see if you can't really relax yourself, okay? Then we can spend a little time talking about it.

The suggestion to relax is used because the therapist believes it will be helpful with this particular person. Other patients tense up with a directive to relax. The implication is that she will be able to talk about the accident with the therapist without getting too frightened. In what follows, the therapist continues talking until he feels the patient is in a mental set in which she can recall and yet retain a sense of control.

T: Okay. Here's what we're going to do and all we're going to do. We're going to go back to the accident and have you remember a little bit of it and just see what springs to mind from it, and perhaps it will be something that will make you reexperience some of those emotions. As it happens, you'll try and keep relaxing, and we'll try and talk about the ideas and feelings as they come to you. You'll try and keep putting the feelings into words, and I'll try and understand them as best I can. We don't have to do a big chunk of it today; we can do a portion. That way, you'll learn it's safe. I think it might help to put it all in your control, keeping it from coming back when you don't want it to. Does it seem reasonable to you? Any questions? Okay, let's just go back to the accident. One thing that struck me about it was that man who came out yelling at you.

J: Yeah, he was the second guy.

T: Yes, I thought maybe that was upsetting you, especially upsetting. Was that so?

J: I could feel myself just going out of awareness when he was doing it. I mean, just slipping into shock or whatever it is; just the more he yelled, the farther away from him I got until I finally just yelled at him, "You're not leaving the scene of this accident until I get your name!" So he threw his license at me and left anyway. But that was a long, long time because that collision was a half hour after the first collision.

T: Now, try and just go back and remember what he said, and let's just see what comes to you.

J: His thing was how he had appointments to keep, and I couldn't hear a lot of it. He sees the wreck and yelled and screamed, and then he turned to us. But to us, he just says, "I have to go find a phone as fast as I can." And it turned out that he was in very much the same situation as I was in: he works in a hospital the same as I.

T: He was going to work?

J: Uh-huh. He wasn't a nurse, he was a student lab technician. But it's hardly any different. He had the same need to be on time that I had. But then he stomped away from the scene, and I don't even know where he went because you couldn't see in the fog. I was mad because I had stuck to the scene of the accident, and I wanted to see a doctor because my back was hurting, and he stomped away right away! We had the policeman; we could have settled it, and I could have been on my way if he had stuck around. And I was standing around shaking and hurting, and he was gone.

T: And what's this; he threw the license—

J: Threw it at me.

T: At you?

J: Because I was the one that protested.

T: And where did it hit you?

J: I think I caught it.

T: And then what happened to his license? He drove off without his license?

J: No, he couldn't drive his car; his car was demolished. He walked away fast from the scene, but you couldn't see more than 20 feet in the fog, and he went to a phone, which I should have done long before that. But since my neck hurt and I knew I was numb every place else, I was afraid to walk as far as it was to a phone. I didn't know how badly I was hurt.

T: And you never saw him again?

J: No, he came back. In fact, a few minutes later, the policeman had his report and stuff together. I got confused then, and I gave him the other man's license instead of my own because he wanted a license. And then I left to phone Zone City to tell them I couldn't come. By then, they had already talked to me about an ambulance, and I told them I didn't think I needed one. So I called my brother-in-law to come and take me to a doctor.

T: But this other man came back?

J: Well, I missed him somehow. I'm not sure if he came back by the time I came back.

T: And did you have any more to do with him?

J: Yeah. We climbed into the back of a patrol car to fill out all the forms because it was really cold and he kept borrowing pens and being obnoxious to everybody. He had to ask his questions whether you were in the middle of saying something or not, and this kind of thing. I was the last one to finish the report because I had the two collisions to report.

T: How was he obnoxious to you?

J: It was just his general attitude, I would suppose. His standard behavior. Instead of asking for anything politely, he would just demand it. Like if another officer asked a question about the tow cars—I called for a 3-A truck because I know 3-A's come faster and I'm personally in 3-A, even though my Dad's not. So they had three different trucking companies, two trucking companies coming. A tow truck arrived, and he assumed automatically that it was his. And I listened and understood that it had to be mine. But he butted in already, and I couldn't outspeak him; I had to wait until he was finished and then explain it to them that it was my tow truck. Every time there was a question, he was right there for himself.

T: So you feel he was being selfish?

J: Yeah.

T: And his selfishness was hurting you worse.

J: This was the wrong time to be selfish. He should have been—like the police officers; there were two of them there, let them direct it. And before that, when they weren't there and they weren't in charge, he didn't take any effort to lead it, you know, like direct the traffic or put out the flares or that kind of thing. But when somebody else was there, he would compete with them—just standing in our way.

T: So, he was obstructing your getting help?

J: I wanted to get out of there as fast as I could and find out why my neck hurt so bad.

T: Let's try and go back then. We know a lot more about your neck now than then, but let's go back then; let's see if we can reconstruct your thoughts about your neck.

J: Right after the collision, I was numb and in a few seconds, the only feeling I had was my neck on the right side and in my shoulder. And it hurt; I couldn't feel anything else at all. Then the driver in front came back 'cause he could see I was just dazed and looked straight ahead. He had seen through his mirror my car hit. He came back and said, "Are you okay?" And I said, "No." He said, "How bad?" I said, "I think it's only my neck, but I'm not sure." Then I waited and I could tell that the rest of me was okay. I felt okay

T: What thoughts were going through your mind?

J: Well, I know that if you're hurt and you get into shock far enough, you can be badly hurt and not know it and walk around with it. That's what was going on in my mind. It just feels like my neck, but I'm not sure.

T: So you were thinking that you might be badly hurt and you might not know it, and you might walk around and hurt yourself more.

J: Uh-huh. But then, I looked at the situation and I thought if I don't move this car from where it is right now, somebody is bound to collide into it again. So I got out of the car anyway and got into the back of the car and gave them some flares to pass out. Then I looked at the situation and said to the other man that I think we'd better move our cars because we're at the top of a grade by a red light on a really foggy morning and it's going to be a ten-car pileup if we

don't. So I moved into a safety zone near an island, and he moved
all the way off to the shoulder. I left my car running with the lights
on so that people could see it.

T: Could we go just a little way in your imagination and imagine what
didn't happen, but what you might have thought might happen?
Which would be that you would walk around and your neck would
get hurt worse. Just imagine—

J: My neck or my back?

T: Yeah, imagine that. What would you imagine would happen?

J: Well, I've had back trouble before, and when it got bad enough, I
was told not to move until it relaxed. And I would imagine that I
would get paralyzed.

T: Where would you be paralyzed?

Because of the patient's neck pain, other somatic complaints, and
her mother's severe illnesses, the therapist wishes to explore for cognitive elements of somatic localization that occurred at the time of the
accident.

J: I don't know.

T: Your legs?

J: Well, before it would have been my legs, but I don't know about
this one.

T: What was the back trouble before?

J: I have one leg shorter than the other, and I repeatedly strained
muscles because of the imbalance, so it's been different muscles getting strained. One time I did it real good, strained it on the job and
had to stay still for a while until it eased up.

T: And if you didn't, you might get paralyzed?

J: No, just that it would stay, the pain.

T: The paralyzed idea was during the accident?

J: Yeah.

T: Okay. Any other thoughts about your body, anything you can remember? Try and go back in your mind to the accident.

J: Well, after the accident, after the first collision when we were waiting, we were sitting in his car, I got double vision. But that's not
unusual for me; I have a muscle problem in my left eye. I wondered
about it, because I didn't think my head had gotten hurt.

T: But it might mean that you had a head injury?

J: Right.

T: At least, that was your thought then?

J: Yeah, but I get double vision under stress, no matter what's causing it. Can't think of anything else.

T: So, you were worried then that you might be—your back might be
broken or something and you might get paralyzed if you moved.
And then you were running around putting out flares.

J: Well, nobody else would do this kind of thing; nobody else was
thinking. You know, I'd ask a question, and there wouldn't be a
response because they couldn't think of an answer for it.

T: Well, maybe you felt that they were fools. You had to risk yourself
because they were so foolish.

From listening to her vocal intonations, the therapist has a growing conviction that she is struggling between impulses to express rage
and a need to inhibit such expressions. He is attempting to provoke
a clear expression of ideas that might lead to anger as well as ideas that
might be threatening, were she fully aware of them. At this point he
is trying out certain labels with her and, more importantly, encouraging continued expression by actively receiving her communications and
not being critical. In a sense, he has just said, "It would be all right
with me if at the time of the accident you thought the people around
you were fools or were afraid they would think you were a fool. I'd
like you to freely tell me that sort of thing, even if you feel badly about
it." As it happens, the label of fool does not exactly hit on a central ideational complex, but the feedback from the therapist sets up a dialogue
that promotes fuller expression.

J: Well, I had to save myself anyway, because they weren't going to
move their car, his car. Nobody else wanted to—like—like direct the
trucks that were bearing down. You know, I said, "Well listen, I've
got a flashlight in the glove box with a red cap on it; if you swing
it, they can see it and get around us." Nobody wanted to do it and
my arm was stiffening up and I was about to stand out and do it
because I—

T: What do you mean, "no one wanted to do it." Who was that?

J: Well, the man in front of us who had stopped and the man who
had hit me.

T: Why didn't they want to do it?

J: One man was ready to leave for work because he said nobody is
really badly hurt. And the man behind me had to leave to telephone
his place of business to tell them he wouldn't be coming in. And
nobody was around who was not busy.

T: So you were just left. Were you all alone?

J: Yeah. I was sitting in the car of the man that hit me because his was in a better position by then.

T: So you were kind of left alone with no one to take care of you?

J: Yeah, but then I could sit up straight and I knew that if I didn't do anything, nothing horrible was going to happen to me like that.

T: Did you feel it was unfair, though?

J: Yeah, and I asked him to make a phone call for me and he came back and said, "Oh, I forgot."

T: He forgot?

J: Yeah.

T: That must have made you angry.

J: I don't know if I felt angry. I felt like desperate—like how can I make that dumb phone call.

T: Yeah, but you'd been left out again. Do you remember that moment, when he came back and said he forgot?

J: Kind of; he was back in the car again.

T: Now you seem pretty relaxed talking about all of this. Any side thoughts?

J: No.

T: How are you feeling right now?

J: A little bit tense.

T: A bit tense? Where is the tension?

J: It's all over.

T: Yeah, describe it, though.

J: I wouldn't know how.

T: Is it in your muscles?

J: Yeah.

T: Do your muscles feel tight? Okay, try and relax them. Does my asking you about it make you more nervous?

J: About relaxing?

T: Yeah.

J: Well, it's just that that's the one thing that everybody is telling me to do.

T: Everyone tells you to relax?

J: Yeah. You can't exactly do it without knowing how.

T: Have you ever learned how?

J: I don't know. I guess I did a little bit. I used to take yoga for a while, but I can't relax myself when my mind isn't relaxed.

T: Well, let's see if we can find where the tension is in your mind right now. What are you doing now? What are you paying attention to?

J: The back of my head.

T: Uh-huh (long silence). Well, one way to find out about such tension, for us to use right here, would be for you to say whatever comes to your mind now.

J: I'm getting scared; I'm not wanting to talk anymore.

T: Yes. What would happen if you were to go on talking? Do you think you'd get more scared?

J: I don't know. This is the same way I feel when I wake up, feeling sick.

T: Uh-huh. Is it a scare that something is going to happen?

J: I think it's more that something is not going to happen that should happen.

T: Uh-huh. That would mean that there'd be no help for you?

J: Yeah.

T: Okay. What do you think should happen?

J: I don't know.

T: You know, the idea of no help for you runs through a lot of this. Nobody being able to help you; your family not being a help to you; the other drivers not helping you; maybe my not helping you.

This labeling of her sense of not being helped seems to make her feel safer, and she continues with considerable additional material, without responses from the therapist.

J: Something else: When I made the phone call, a male operator came on the line, and I didn't recognize the voice as an operator's and I thought it was Bob, which is my brother-in-law and so I spoke to him as if he were, and then we figured each other out. We were both mixed up. He took the message wrong, too. Then I told him the number, and he connected me so fast that I didn't recognize the change in voice. And so when Bob answered, my message was all confused. I know it made him upset, but the more I said anything, the more confused I got and I couldn't get it straight.

So, it turns out that after he had hung up, he didn't know how badly I was hurt, so he called my sister at work, and all he told her was that Jane's been in an accident and I'm going to pick her up. I'll call you later.

After the accident when we were trying to arrange a doctor and stuff, he told me about it, about her being notified. And I said, "Aren't you going to call her back?" He said, "No, we'll wait and see how you are." When I got to the doctor's office, he had two other emergencies ahead of me, and so I waited in the waiting room for an hour and a half and then I waited in an examining room for 15 minutes, and then when he saw me, he sent me to X-ray. The doctor in charge of X-ray had to look at the X-rays that were taken.

And it wasn't until after all of that, that my brother-in-law told my sister. She had been sitting there all morning not knowing, just knowing that I was in an accident. That bothers me because there have been other accidents in the family. There was one when my stepbrother died in Vietnam and my sister was the only person in San Francisco, so when the call came through, she knew and we were on our way to Arizona. Nobody would notify us because it was a military matter, and the highway patrol wouldn't stop us so we had to get all the way there where my brother was and he had to tell us. It was just her sitting there again, waiting and not knowing.

T: So that happened to her with your accident.

J: Yeah.

T: That's upsetting for your sister?

J: It's upsetting for both of us because after that I was in Arizona with my father and we put everybody else on a jet; my brother got emergency leave, and my father refused to let the car sit and go back with his wife. He insisted that we drive back to San Francisco. And I had a driver's license and was perfectly capable of driving, but because there was a trailer on the car, he didn't trust my driving and he wouldn't allow me to drive.

Here is a compulsive retelling of the story of the trip with her father, discussed in an earlier interview. The timing in this hour and her general demeanor indicate the importance of her father in the associations to the accident.

J: So for the whole trip back, I really was tired and very, very worried, so I kept tuning in radio stations and talking so that he wouldn't fall asleep. And he wouldn't pull over and he wouldn't rest until finally I convinced him that we needed to stop, and we stopped in a town full of motels and all of them were closed for the night. So we had to go on or sleep at the side of the road and refused to do that. Finally, a gas station attendant let us sleep in the back of the station, but he didn't sleep all night; he only did it for me, and I barely slept and then had to get up again.

T: How do you know he didn't sleep?

J: He told me he didn't and he'd been sick. He had vomited all over the trailer. He told me he hadn't slept at all. I told him I was in better shape to drive, but he wouldn't let me.

T: That still bothers you?

J: (indignantly) He still doesn't believe I can drive. He won't ride in the car if I'm driving.

Here is an important meaning of her accident. Her father has criticized her driving. Right after the first collision, one association would be something like "Oh, no, my father will say this is all my fault!" This thought would already be on her mind when the second collision occurred and the driver of that car angrily screamed at her. In a larger sense, she anticipates that her accident will give her father reason to say that not only can she not drive well, but also she is not an effective, grown-up woman and must remain his dependent and subordinate little girl. She anticipates his rage and depreciation of her. Responding to this prophecy, she is hurt by him and angry at him. The various rejections and desertions she experiences from other persons involved in the accident and its aftermath serve to justify these feelings. Frustration, sorrow, and anger are also activated by the disruption in her life plan.

Rage at her father cannot be expressed or experienced directly because that would make her feel guilty. She already feels badly at not having rescued her father from his alcoholism relapse after the long drive following her stepbrother's death. This is part of a general ambivalent attachment to her father. Though these formulations are oversimplified and incomplete, they represent the therapist's working hypotheses at this point in therapy. He follows her statement with an exploratory question relating her father to the recent accident.

T: He thought that if you drove, you might have an accident?

J: Uh-huh. Any car that I've bought, he's never stepped foot in.

T: And now you've had an accident.

J: Uh-huh.

T: Maybe you were worried right at the accident about what your father would say. There you'd gone and had an accident, even if it wasn't your fault at all.

J: Yeah! Later that day, I let my brother tell my father; I didn't want to tell him.

T: Why didn't you?

J: Because if I talked to him on the phone, we don't get along very well at all; but if I talked to him on the phone, I would probably get upset enough for him to worry that I was hurt more than I was— just because it's so hard. He doesn't usually hear my voice; he's deaf in one ear and hard of hearing in the other one. He usually—I either shout or he reads my lips. And on the phone, it's impossible with two of us, but it's always a strain for me to talk to him. But on this occasion, I just said, I can't do it at all. Somebody else has to do it.

Her initial response here is probably partly defensive in function. Other evidence suggests that she was primarily afraid of her father raging at her. But she seems to undo that fear by saying that he will worry unduly about her: "I would probably get upset enough for him to worry that I was hurt." This also suggests another defensive operation. If people present signs of physical harm, then one shows concern and does not blame them. She goes on to imply a complaint about her father's neglect: "He doesn't usually hear my voice." After these remarks about her father, she then expresses her own anxiety over confrontation with him: "It's always a strain. . . . I just said I can't do it." The therapist chooses to focus on this self-experience.

T: Were you concerned about what your father would say?
J: Well, I didn't want him to come walking home from the bus stop and see the car all smashed up.
T: Yes, what would he have thought if he had seen the car all smashed up?
J: He would have wondered where in the world I was, what had happened.

Once again, she presents a worried and concerned image of her father rather than that of the enraged accuser. She continues along this line.

J: I didn't think he should do that. I would rather that he be told on the phone than when he comes home—
T: Well, he would think that you'd been in an accident.
J: Yeah. Well, one time before, I messed up the front end of a car, and he went on for hours about "why didn't you tell me." So I knew I had to tell him, otherwise we'd go through that again.

Here is the associative meaning to the man yelling angrily at her. The important and, as yet, undisclosed detail that the car damaged in

the current accident belonged to her father follows after the therapist
clarifies that the car she dented earlier also belonged to her father.

T: Was that his car?

J: Yeah, these were both his cars. Because I had sold my car a few
months ago.

T: Oh, so this was his car in the accident?

J: Yeah.

T: And the new car you bought was going to be yours?

J: Uh-huh (very softly). I sold my car when it started giving me trouble.

T: Yes. So maybe you felt badly that it was your father's car that was
damaged.

J: Yeah. We never agree on that car anyway. He won't keep it up (very
angry)! He won't, like, put the tires on soon enough when they're
wearing out or get stuff done that needs being done. It's always run
down. And like he rebuilt the engine and put it back in; he didn't
put the transmission back in straight so when you start it, you have
to know how to force it into drive to get it started. I usually get frustrated with the engine; you have to sit and wait and then get it
started. I am—every time I get into the car, I'd get mad if I couldn't
happen to get it started right away because of the way he fixed it;
only halfway.

T: Yeah.

J: He did that to the exhaust system, too. It sounded horrible to drive.
They'd give you three clamps; he'd put one clamp on and put the
tailpipe on, and it would rattle all over the place. It'd get a hole in
it and was worn out.

T: Yeah, he really didn't take very good care of the car.

J: He took as little care as he could. He insisted that no work be done
that needed being paid for. He had to do the work.

T: But then he bawled you out when you got in an accident?

J: Yeah.

T: What did he say to you that other time?

J: That was the car before this. That was my fault because I had a sinus
infection and was all run down.

Once again, physical illness is presented as a way to avert blame.

J: I had a choice of public transportation and getting on the medicine
and not being able to drive 'cause it makes me drowsy. So, I decided to drive and not take the medicine, but I got too tired anyway

and I missed a turn in the parking lot and hit a cement wall at a low speed and punched in the front end on one side. So we all knew it was all my fault, but he refused to accuse anybody. He just went wandering around junk yards trying to find a replacement for the front end of the car; and he never found one.

T: Huh. What did he say to you though?

J: Well, by the time that he saw me, I was upset enough and my face was swollen enough that he didn't want to say anything. I loosened my front teeth, and I couldn't talk by the time he saw me, 'cause my whole face was swollen.

T: But he was angry?

J: He didn't show anger or anything; he just stomps away and gets a drink because he's an alcoholic, but he doesn't say anything.

It is possibly relevant that she uses the same word, *stomping*, to describe her father as she did to describe the driver of the second car that hit her car, because this accident is a repetition of the earlier accident. Because she is physically hurt, she does not receive the direct brunt of her father's anger but, instead, is made to feel guilty that she has hurt him and caused his drinking.

T: But did you feel worried about how he would react before he reacted?

J: Yeah.

T: Were you very concerned in your mind?

J: But then he doesn't really react; he runs away from it.

T: But beforehand, you were worrying about how he would react?

The therapist is holding here to the topic and trying to clarify her feelings about her father's potential or actual anger at her.

J: Yeah.

T: I wonder if you had any thoughts about your father right during this current accident?

J: I don't remember thinking about him. I do remember thinking, "Well, at least this car is gone now; nobody can drive it; he'll be forced to get rid of it." And it turns out he's not; he's taking money for it and says he's going to put it back together again. Since then, when we got it home, he made me drive it one afternoon. I told him that the doctor told me to leave the collar on and if I needed to drive, to only go a short distance and take the collar off to drive so I'd be able to turn my head. I said I didn't feel like turning my head enough to drive that day, but he insisted.

She is talking about how her father hurts her. The role structure is that of one person hurting another, and she can place herself in either position. She is afraid both of her accusations that he hurts her and of the possibility that he will accuse her of hurting him. Her communication is devoted to obtaining a verdict from the therapist that she is "not guilty," has been hurt more than enough, and deserves tender attention. She may also want the therapist to be angry at her father. This would be anger on her behalf, and she could avoid guilt. She continues with evidence that her father gave her a bad car.

J: So I drove it and I'd been complaining about the car downshifting suddenly on hills 'cause the transmission still needed work. It took a really good hill to do it, and there weren't any near the house, so I took it to the best hill nearby and it didn't do it. He still doesn't believe me, and he's not going to work on that part of it. But what used to happen was if I took it to work in Zone City, it doesn't have enough speed to make merging easy, so I would go wandering freeway to freeway in a way that I wouldn't need to merge so much. I would get onto highways that weren't freeways. And one of them was Pickwood Drive, which is really steep, and up near the top of it, the car would downshift suddenly and then shift back up and just jerk really, really bad. He had never experienced it because he doesn't drive at all like I drive. I kept telling him that it would happen and that it needed something so that it wouldn't happen, but he wouldn't fix it. So that's why he wanted me to drive it. He said there's nothing wrong with the car. The whole tail end of the car now is out of alignment; it doesn't even travel on a straight line anymore, but according to him, there's nothing wrong with the car anymore. He's going to drive it that way.
But every time his job makes him travel, because his job changes, he takes the other car.

Throughout these sections, she is expressing anger at her father, as shown by her tone of voice and her nonverbal communications.

T: Which other car, the new one?
J: There's another car that he owns.
T: He owns two, a better one and this clunkier one?

J: Yeah.

T: And you got to drive the clunkier one?

J: I was not allowed to drive the better one.

T: Why not?

J: He didn't want me to.

T: He wasn't using it at the time; he was taking the bus.

J: That's right.

T: So why doesn't he want you to use it? Is the idea that you'd get in an accident?

J: I'll do something to it. I'll scratch it in a parking lot or whatever. That one was special; this one is the one that I was allowed to use. It was the one I had driven before that, anyway.

T: But you resented it.

J: I hate that car to begin with! And every time I had car trouble, they'd tell me it's just because you don't like the car and are not willing to put up with it. I said, "Why can't you get me in the situation where I can get another car and I could put up with that." Like I'd wear the battery out trying to start it, and I couldn't keep the transmission in drive long enough to get it started.

T: Okay; well, it seems to me that we were able to talk about the accident, and it wasn't too dangerous to talk about here, so we might go on and schedule another appointment to do that a little bit more.

J: Okay.

T: Does it seem reasonable to you to do that?

J: Yeah.

T: Okay. How about next Monday at this time?

J: I can make it any time; I'm out of work by then. My job ends Friday.

T: Okay, let's make it 3:00 next Monday.

FIFTH SESSION

During the fifth session, Jane indicated that she felt she was back to normal. Her physical symptoms were much improved. She was sleeping and eating well and no longer felt tense and anxious. She did not have intrusive episodes or moments of intense irritability, though she still had some pain in her neck and in her hip joints. She felt that things were going smoothly for her. Three topics occupied the session: her relationships with her father, her mother, and her therapist.

During the week she had begun a dispute with her father that, because of her assertiveness, was resolved to the satisfaction of both of them. Her father wanted her to sign a release so that the payment for damage to his car could be obtained from the insurance company of the other driver. She refused to do this, pointing out that the medical liability was as yet undetermined. She consulted her attorney, who backed up her position. Her father became "pleased that someone more responsible than he or she was looking into it." She felt relief at living out of the house, as her father drank heavily during their discussions. She had resolved her guilt feelings over living with her sister by making maternity clothes for her.

The therapist felt that the restoration of Jane's equilibrium was the result of many factors. Time had passed; there had been some working through in the therapy; and with this, her improvement might have been motivated by a desire to reduce the need to explore the relationship with her father. The presence of unresolved conflicts and ambivalent attachments would not, however, indicate the continuation of a brief therapy aimed at restoring a balance disrupted by a stressful life event. She had moved out of her home environment and was continuing her work; she could pursue her life plan. The therapist continued the interview by asking about the status of memories about the accident in order to see whether there were further intrusive episodes. This would be an additional sector of information relevant to a decision about termination.

T: Any memories come to you about the accident?
J: Today's weather reminds me of it: looks the same.
T: But have there been any other events, like the conversation with your sister that triggered it?
J: No. I've been feeling people being more sympathetic because—even though, like I've had to miss some days at the hospital, one of the other aides came up to me and said that her mother had had the same thing. Only she said that her mother had to have special shoes made, and I kind of smiled and said, "I'm wearing special shoes, too." Other things—we had a ward party and people came and talked to me and stuff.

She went on to talk of how her body was feeling better, though she was afraid that any tension might make her stiffen up again. The therapist offered a kind of summing up of one aspect of what had happened:

T: One of the psychological problems for you was that the accident let you know in a way that your body was vulnerable to injury. When

you didn't get better rapidly, you got frightened that your body was
even more vulnerable.

J: It made me think of something. My mother used to have arthritis
in her back and stay in bed in the mornings. I found myself doing
the same thing, just like her. I was staying in bed because it was
the most comfortable place to be. I didn't want to get up and move
and walk around. I just kept thinking of all the things I was doing
then and that she was doing that when she hurt from arthritis in
her back.

T: Yes. She kept on going also?

As before, this is an implicit encouragement and support of her attempt at independence.

J: Yeah, until she had cancer and she died of cancer.

The therapist believes that one function of this remark is to test him
for a transference potential. If he feels sorry for her and gives her attention for being sick, then she may be tempted to adopt that role more
durably in order to obtain the gratification of sympathy. The therapist
believes Jane is indirectly asking whether she really has to get better.
He wants to give her the support of saying "yes," which he does with
a repetition of the same type of remark he made when he said, "She
kept on going."

T: So you feel kind of brave at times?

J: Sometimes, but sometimes I feel dreadful because I know, uh—she
used to send us away when she was feeling badly so that she could
rest. I can't send my responsibilities away.

T: Okay. Now, have you had any other thoughts, you know, since we
talked a week ago, about getting upset because of the accident?
Have any other explanations for that occurred to you?

J: I think it was a huge disappointment that stopped me from everything I was trying to do. It was at a time when I was trying to plan
moving out of the house and getting a permanent job and just
changing everything around me. And all of a sudden, I was frozen
where I didn't want to be.

The remaining part of the hour dealt with the idea of termination
and the possibility of a transfer to long-term therapy if she wished to
explore further her vulnerability to depressions after losses. Because

she did not express feelings about the separation other than gratitude, the therapist asked her directly:

T: Well, maybe you'll be sad not to see me anymore?
J: I think so (pause). Yeah (pause). That's been happening this month to everyone I'm around, though. Well, one friend who took me out to dinner really doesn't want to see me. It's happening all around me. I'm beginning to get used to it. The patients, you get to know them and they leave. It's okay.

She later accepted the idea of long-term therapy and continued to see another therapist twice a week for five months. By the onset of that therapy, she had essentially recovered from all symptoms related to the immediate stress event. The physical symptoms that had gone into remission remained absent. The residual pains in neck and hips improved by the end of one month. An exception to this marked improvement was continued difficulty with her eyes, a symptom corrected by a new prescription for glasses. The central issue of the therapy was loss and neglect with the attendant fear of not getting enough care in her relationships with other people, though she kept her angry reactions to frustrations in tight check. These themes were worked on in regard to medical treatment for the eye symptoms, legal manipulations to recover medical costs after the accident, relationships with her family members, and the transference.

DISCUSSION

Had it not been for the accident, Jane would most likely have continued her progress toward independence. By establishing social and professional ties, she would have been able to continue her development throughout her young adulthood. If not beset by stress and the disruption of interpersonal relationships due to her neurotic potential, she probably would not have sought psychiatric treatment. At a crucial time, however, the accident activated unresolved conflicts about her own bodily integrity, degree of dependency, and the validity of what might be called her "self-righteousness."

Her concept of bodily integrity was related to her mother and other relatives who had severe bodily misfortunes. She herself had a slight leg deformity and a tendency, when stressed, to a disruption in optic focusing that was also apparently based on a mild congenital anomaly. She was the baby of the family and was raised during a period when her mother was an invalid. Thus, she had a special vulnerability to feeling a defective identity and body image. The physical trauma and fears of even greater injury forced on her awareness by the accident reinforced her defective self-concept as it conflicted with more recently developing womanly and intact self-concepts. Such an accident threatens the sense of invulnerability of all persons, but Jane had a less stable adult self-organization to use to master this threat. Working it through on her own was impossible, and the therapist supported her more competent self-concepts by encouraging her continued efforts to work and cope.

The ambivalent ties with her father were rapidly conceptualized by the therapist in establishing a working model for the therapy. This rapidity carries more risks of error than do the more temperate inferences possible in a long-term psychoanalytic therapy in which more associations, memories, and fantasies are gradually accumulated. Basically, it seemed as if a variety of factors had combined to develop a self-schemata as "hurt, little, and in need," one that conflicted with her developmental progress toward a more mature self-concept.

Jane's mother had been too ill to provide complete maternal care or even a stable identity model. She might have turned to her father, not only as an oedipal love object in a normal, developmental sequence, but also as a source of preoedipal gratification. She probably developed a role model of an ambivalent sort at this stage of early childhood. On the one hand, she conceptualized herself as "little and in need" and her father as taking care of her with the development of a mutual, loving attachment. But at times, she probably felt insufficiently cared for and had a role relationship model in which she was "little and in need" and her father was neglectful. Rage at her father stemmed from this latter version.

Because of such rage, she also developed a model of herself as destructive in her relationship with her father. In conflict with her ideals and morals, this role relationship generated a tendency to feel guilty if she were placed in the role of hurting her father. To avoid guilt, to gain the stronger role for herself, and quite likely also to replace her mother, she often conceptualized herself in the care-taking role and her father in the role of being in need. Later material supported these formulations. Her father turned to her for care at various times, but he also rejected her when she assumed a care-taking role. During her adolescence, he fostered her regression to a preadolescent stage of life and rejected her efforts to care for him. He belittled her attempts at this and, in general, undermined her efforts to gain a sense of womanly competency.

The accident heightened the not-so-latent ambivalence between them that already had "cars" and "accidents" as a theme because of the previous dented fender, the long, traumatic drive he refused to share with her, and his reluctance to let her drive the "good" car. As soon as the accident happened, she knew that blame would enter the picture. Her father would blame her and she would blame him for blaming her and for giving her a bad car. The second man, who yelled angrily at her, became a symbolic father image for her and gave the ambivalent role fantasy a terrifying reality.

The accident thus became an event that produced fear over her bodily integrity, rage and sorrow over the loss of her plans for independence, and anger and guilt, entangled with a wish to remain attached to her father. Perhaps the most important conflict was that of dependency and independency wishes. The bodily symptoms gave her an excuse to resume dependency and yet led to the frustration of not being taken care of properly. The bodily symptoms also could punish her for her aggressive feelings toward her family. Working through the stress event meant processing these themes. She had to reassure herself, by reexamining the current reality, that her body could still work and was not under continuing threat. She had to consider the possibilities for resumed dependencies and ties to her father (or father substitutes such as her doctor) and reject them. She had to reexamine her work and living situation and continue toward independence. She had to evaluate the accident and decide that it was just an accident, that the angry man was just a nasty stranger who behaved badly, and that it was over.

The therapist fostered this working-through process by providing a temporary relationship and encouraging continued efforts toward independence. The various themes were not interpreted at a deeper level. Rather, there was an effort to process the details and immediate associations to the accident so that reality could be clarified and separated from fantasy elaborations. The major theme of dependency-independency surfaced in the transference as a tension between an "I don't want any help; I can do it myself" attitude, presented largely through her demeanor, and a subsurface clamor for excessive worry and concern by the therapist. This was countered with a steady insistence on working on the immediate meanings of the stress event. That is, the therapist did not appear worried about the patient, guilt driven by her remaining symptoms, or neglectful in offering her help and sympathy.

SUMMARY

Jane drove her father's second, poorly cared for car to a job that she hoped would enable her to gain her own independence. She was rear-ended on a foggy day. The man who drove into her was so polite that she could not be angry with him, but a second car piled into her already-damaged vehicle as it stood by the roadside. That driver, a man, exploded angrily at her. This seemed to induce a dissociative state. Later she had difficulty obtaining medical attention. She then felt that her family neglected her by turning a postaccident visit (to check up on her) into a party that ignored her condition.

She developed a progressively debilitating syndrome combining somatic and psychological signs and symptoms. She had neck and hip pains, eye difficulties, nausea, upper respiratory infections, and sleep disturbances. She was also affected by dazedness, difficulty concentrating, irritability, intrusive and repetitive thoughts, and episodes of anxiety. Her brief psychotherapy began when she was in an unstably defended denial phase, in regard to conscious ideas, and then entered an intrusive phase.

When viewed retrospectively, the accident can be seen as an activator of unresolved conflicts. Before the accident, these conflicts caused episodes of what might be a depressive disorder, not severe enough as yet to motivate her to seek psychotherapy. Rather, she was moving forward in her psychological and sociological development. After a turbulent childhood and adolescence, she had successfully completed school and training and was about to engage in a career that would allow her to separate from her family and, especially, to diminish the ambivalent ties binding her to her father. And the therapy enabled her to continue this forward course.

Chapter 15
MULTIPLE STRESS EVENTS

With the assistance of John Bebelaar, D.S.W.

Laura had suffered many losses in her young life. Such accumulations of sorrow sometimes seem so self-instigated that the person is said to have "traumatophilia," not so much "love of trauma" as a seeming attraction for it. Laura used her youthful appeal in an impulsive manner, to compensate for earlier losses, her limited capacity for interpersonal relationships, and her impoverished self-concept. Her actions escalated in desperation and culminated in the equivalent of a suicide attempt. She entered therapy in an extreme state; her ability to cope with life had been virtually exhausted.

She improved during brief psychotherapy. Her story illustrates how inhibitory operations can lead to a phase of denial so pronounced that

Dr. Bebelaar is now a social worker and Assistant Clinical Professor, Department of Psychiatry, University of California, San Francisco.

it resembles organic brain disease. In addition to repression, suppression, and denial, Laura used transference provocations to avoid awareness of ideas and feelings associated with the stressful event, to compensate for an immature level of ego development, and to continue a
pseudoactive but actually passive-dependent life trajectory.

Laura was a slender, well-formed 25-year-old woman who was
deeply involved in the counterculture and drug scene. Two months
before the present therapy began she had been in an automobile accident. Speeding up a narrow mountain road, she tried to pass a slower
car. Unable to complete the turn back she careened over a cliff. Fortunately, there must have been only a modest incline at that embank-
ment. Her car came to rest, totally destroyed, with Laura intact but unconscious from a concussion. She remained dazed for three days.

She recovered quickly in all physical respects while under observation at a hospital. A neurological examination showed her to be normal. Her mental status showed her to be dazed and dull, but she was
correctly oriented for time, place, and person. Her memory was not
consistently impaired, but at times, her wandering attention made ex-
aminations and communication difficult. A neurological puzzle, she
was subjected to extensive diagnostic procedures. An absence of abnormal physical findings led to a discharge to the home of her grandparents.

Over the next few weeks, she seemed to become even more dazed,
disoriented, depersonalized, and limited in conceptual functioning. She
was then reevaluated for brain damage, but the results were again
negative.

Remaining with her grandparents, she felt somewhat better, although she described herself during this period as being disturbed by
intrusive thoughts of worthlessness. She felt tense and restless and impulsively left for San Francisco to live with a male friend who would,
she felt, play the role of a good father and not pressure her for sex. This
was important because although she had been very active sexually for
several years, she now felt "freaky" at the prospect of being touched
by a man and had not engaged in any sexual activity since the accident.

The man, Hans, had indeed taken care of her. He noted her continued withdrawal, chronic tension, emotional constriction, and cognitive limitations. As she was ordinarily vivacious and dramatic, the
change was marked. He urged her to have a psychiatric consultation,
and she agreed.

She was seen three times. The consultant felt that her mental status
was so decompensated that psychological tests for brain damage were

indicated. He also considered in the differential diagnosis that she might have an unusual form of schizophrenia. The psychological tests did not conform to any pattern typical of brain damage but suggested the use of inhibitory defenses such as repression and denial to ward off possible sexual impulses and/or a sense of extreme worthlessness. The outcome of this conflict was believed to verge on an illness of psychotic proportions.

Despite the communicative difficulties imposed by the patient's blurring, vagueness, and inhibition of thought, additional data had been obtained. A neurological examination was again normal. During the interviews she indicated that the accident had happened on the anniversary of two events. One year ago on that day, she had taken a hallucinogenic drug, inadvertently knocked over a candle, and set her house on fire. Exactly two years before, her ovaries had been removed because of benign tumors, and she indicated some sorrow over her inability to have children. (It later turned out that she had already borne a child and placed it for adoption.) With such clues and a persistent concern about a possible neurological basis for her inability to think coherently, she was referred for a trial of psychotherapy in the stress clinic.

Her history unfolded very slowly, but it is helpful to have a summary of it in advance in order to grasp some of the issues in her psychotherapy. Laura described herself as rebelliously separating from her morally rigid and lower socioeconomic-class parents when she was 15 years old. A crucial incident was a sexual affair with an older boy at that time. She had always done poorly in school, and dating was her main interest. They married when she was 18. Two years later, they were introduced to hallucinogenic drugs. After several "good trips," her husband developed a paranoid psychosis. A turbulent period ensued, and she left him when she felt he was a menace to their infant son.

Laura was able to maintain a job as a clerk in the daytime. She spent her evenings in bars, where her encounters with men led to a series of very brief affairs. One more extended episode involved her in masochistic practices with a sadistic man. It was to suit his preferences that she placed her son, then 2 years old, for adoption.

Thereafter, although irrevocably committed to the loss of her son, she felt very guilty and remorseful. She had recurrent fantasies of kidnapping him from his foster parents but was frightened by the prospect of life without her lover and without a constant supply of drugs. When her lover deserted her, she entered compulsively into brief sexual liaisons. She was used and abused while seeking pathetically for care, tenderness, and romance. At the depths of this period in her life, she had intercourse in rotation with each member of a fraternity house. Following this, she met Antonelli, a member of the drug scene who was also experimenting with body energetics and meditation. She began living with him in the most enduring relationship she had yet achieved. One weekend after they had been together for several months, he went out of town on an urgent family matter. She felt lonely while he was gone and slept with one of his coworkers. This man told Antonelli immediately upon his return. Infuriated, he called her a whore and ordered her to leave his apartment.

The "accident" occurred after a frenzied month of searching for fun and, indeed, any sensation to purge from her mind a sense of guilt, gloom, and worthlessness. The night of the accident, she was given Cinzano to drink. It was Antonelli's favorite beverage, and the bar also reminded her of him because it had an Italian name. It was in this state of mind that she borrowed a car and the accident occurred.

After the three-visit consultation described previously, Laura accepted the therapy referral. During the initial hour, a contract for time-limited therapy was set up. She agreed to be seen for 20 hours and, if further therapy were indicated, to be referred to another therapist.

FIRST SESSION

Laura presented herself in a seductive manner conveyed by bodily means. She had "cute" and receptive facial expressions and coquettish postures, gestures, and vocal inflections. Her first words to the therapist were, "Ooh, you look nice." Such a self-presentation was not due so much to any active sexual interest as it was a habitual and stereotyped way to attach herself. For her, to be sexy was to be worthy and was perhaps the only way she knew. This demeanor was a way to reduce the threat of being rejected and feeling defective.

She and her therapist covered four topics in their first hour of work together. These included her symptoms, her recollections of the accident and hospitalization, some references to her lifestyle, and expectations from the therapeutic arrangement. During the hour, her states varied suddenly and considerably. While describing her symptoms she was able to communicate relatively clearly and concentrate on the subject. But on all other topics she was vague, changing from confusion and daze to sudden episodes of uncontrolled sobbing and flirtatious interest in the therapist. This lability was determined by both her character and her response to stress. The sudden instigation of inhibition in order to avoid painful topics led to communicative blockage and alterations of consciousness. These changes in state of consciousness were minor equivalents of dissociative reactions. She used global and relatively undifferentiated controls to regulate ideas and feelings. She had historically not developed more differentiated, discreet, and defensive manners. This tendency to dissociate presented a therapeutic problem. Although it indicated the degree of threat of a given topic, it limited the information, and the reception of communications from the therapist. If the therapist were to say something dangerous, she might inhibit awareness globally and change to a dissociated state of consciousness. Interpretations of warded-off contents would not be processed but, instead, would appear to traumatize the patient. Even clarification, as we shall see, could have such effects.

In this session Laura described her current syndrome, and it appeared to the therapist to be a period of oscillation between denial and intrusive phases of stress response. Her principal signs and symptoms seemed to be an extreme form of the denial phase. She described her most pervasive feeling state as "spaciness." It became gradually clear that in this state she was minimally responsive to others, had no sense of reflective self-awareness, little memory for her immediate thoughts, and hence no sense of continuity of experience. Connections between one event and another or one idea and another were not made or, if made, were not retained.

She did report waking two or three times a night but was unable to remember whether a dream had preceded the awakening. During the day, despite a stuporous or languid appearance, she was startled by sudden noises. Occasional painful and intrusive thoughts of being worthless popped into her mind and motivated her to follow through on treatment arrangements. She dramatically stated that she must change or die.

As mentioned, her initial self-presentation was seductive, an opening that represented one type of transference test. If in response, the therapist were flirtatious or charming, she would either strive to use him as an object substitute or be too frightened to continue. Again, she had never been able to achieve a stable, independent existence. Her dependency relationships were also unstable. Sexuality was used to attract a man, but consummation was followed by rapid dissolution of any bond established. Whenever troubled, she initiated the pattern, a character trait of hers that was repeated in the therapy. Were she successful in enticing the therapist, the therapy would be subverted in order to act out a fantasy of rescue. But she was also extremely vulnerable to rejection, and a profound feeling of worthlessness underlay her efforts to engage interest. A therapist who was frightened by her overtures and withdrew from her would be experienced by her as too cool and as hiding behind a caricature of the ground rules of psychoanalytically oriented psychotherapy.

The present therapist was less reactive than the patient seemed to wish, but he carefully maintained a steady interest and connection with her. "Closeness," as discussed in the chapter on hysterical personalities, was present in the steadiness of attention and in a gentle (not cooing or seductive) approach, as the therapist used simple questions and repetitions to encourage continuity. Thus the main interventions in this hour were an effort to maintain a focus during a communicative process. This therapeutic alliance eventually allowed Laura to encounter the train of thought avoided by massive numbing and denial, for by herself, she could not tolerate the thoughts.

SECOND SESSION

As is often the case, during the second hour the patient presented herself as more decompensated than during the first hour. The establishment of a therapeutic relationship apparently allowed her to loosen her efforts at controlled self-presentation. Though dressed seductively, she impressed the therapist as "blurred" throughout the session. Her speech was slow, halting, and weak. Her thoughts were vague, and except for a repeated description of her symptoms, no train of thought was continued for any appreciable length of time. The therapist was more convinced that she had very weak cognitive functioning and extreme vulnerability. The undertone of seductiveness in the first hour had been replaced by one of helplessness, and the therapist sensed that he should be extremely gentle.

The hour began with the patient confused about what to do. The therapist quietly told her that her job was to tell him what was going on and that his job was to help her understand what it meant. She then repeated the description of her symptoms as given in the first interview. This reduced her anxiety because she had already repeated the story in several medical settings. The therapist accepted this and occasionally asked questions to obtain details or keep her going when she trailed off. Her descriptions then included a report of recurrent, intrusive, and "almost real" images of Antonelli.

The process of questions and repetitions from the therapist plus further details from the patient clarified the phenomena and led to the first associations not directly linked to symptoms. Laura talked vaguely of her current relationship with Hans, her sexual inhibitions since the accident, and her feelings of gullibility. The therapist found these relatively diffused comments to be centered on the theme of "Can I be a good woman?" Laura then said she had been having impulses to try an overdose of street drugs.

Work on this theme led to a murky connection between her current suicidal ideas and those at the time of the accident. A relatively "close" interaction between patient and therapist followed the theme of her feelings of worthlessness. As the reasons for this were approached, she became more diffuse, spoke in a detached way of "needing to sort out the past," and gave scattered information about putting her child up for adoption. She then said, in a seemingly disconnected manner, "Who am I?" paused and continued, "Why not kill myself?"

As the therapist, in a simple way, connected the adoption (i.e., desertion) theme and the suicide idea, she expressed her feelings of worthlessness more clearly. The therapist suggested that she call him between appointments if she became too frightened of suicidal impulses. Perhaps intimidated by the implied closeness of the relationship, she then denied the seriousness of all she had been telling him and ended the hour by saying she might not come to the next scheduled appointment because of a pleasure trip.

During both hours, her expressive style had been mostly vague and inhibited. She spoke very softly and slowly with many pauses and sighs. Her inflection gave an indefinite quality to what she said. It was as if her words evaporated and had no meaning for her after she spoke them. This style provoked the therapist to label and clarify for her. By doing so, he moved closer when the patient was very vulnerable. During this early phase, the therapist's labeling or repetition encouraged Laura to go on for a few more sentences. But to continue doing this for her later, when she was less vulnerable, would have been an error. Below is an example of what this was like at the beginning:

L (*Laura*): I fool myself (pause)—there is nothing to be said (pause)— haven't been able to talk, there is nothing to be said (pause) —nothing a person can relate to (pause)—before the accident.

Despite the vagueness and scattered ideas, the therapist developed an inference based on the repetition and juxtaposition of the "nothing

to say" statements and the "before the accident" allusions. He therefore suggested a connection.

T (Therapist):   Are you saying that "before" you felt there was nothing
                 to say?
L: (perks up) Yes (pause)—my thoughts go to Antonelli
                 (pause)—I imagine his voice, his looks.

A story line was gradually pieced together in the therapist's mind
as follows: Before the accident, Laura and Antonelli reached a point
at which they had nothing to say to each other. She was grieving for
him. This event remained unclear and was slowly clarified through each
repetition during the therapy.

THIRD SESSION

The patient arrived quite early and was dressed unusually conser-
vatively. She seemed stronger and more alert than at any previous time
and later said she had been experiencing more capacity for thinking
and was feeling less "spaced out."

On entering the room, she said, "How are you" in an intimate and
engaging way. Remarks about whether therapy was or was not going
to be of use followed. She revealed that she had polished her nails while
preparing to come to the session but then removed it so as not to appear as if she had carefully dressed up. Later during the hour and seemingly unconsciously, she started reapplying the nail polish. She also
said offhandedly that she could make men happy.

These episodes were also transference tests. As before, if the therapist were too responsive, even with a shy smile, then she was deflected toward seeking a transference gratification by using the therapist
as a substitute for lost love objects. The therapist could not be too cold
either—for example, waiting impassively for her to go on. This patient
was so fragile that she did not have a secure idea of the nature of the
therapeutic alliance, and to her, silence meant a rejection that was
beyond her current capacity to tolerate. The therapist avoided either
hazard by speaking simply of the therapeutic alliance.

After saying that she could make men happy, she paused and then
said provocatively, "What good is this doing?" The therapist replied,
"So far, we have learned that we can talk together in order to clarify
what happened to you before and after your accident." The patient

abruptly ceased her efforts to engage the therapist in talking or responding to her, assumed that she had his attention, and spoke clearly of her
current symptoms, the absence of sexual desire. She referred to three
important relationships with men, one of whom was Antonelli. She
asked herself whether he would want her back and then drifted into
an abstract consideration of right or wrong. Below is a transcript of that
segment.

L: Is there a right and wrong? It seems like if you do things for the right
   reason, you'll get a good reaction. Like the accident and the changes
   I've gone through—maybe I was doing things the wrong way, or
   not taking full account of everything (laugh). So, I want to think
   right and do things right. But who decides what's right? I'm beginning to think more concretely. I don't feel spaced out. I feel capable
   of most anything.
T: Sometimes you think the accident was the result of wrong things
   you were doing?
L: Yeah, I'm sure. The accident seems funny to me: I was madly in
   love with Antonelli. And I almost kill myself by getting drunk on
   Cinzano, his favorite booze, living . . . er, leaving a place called
   Luigi's right before the accident. Seems funny to me.
T: Like it's too much to be coincidence?
L: It could be coincidence. When I look back at it, I think I lost my touch
   with reality a long time before that—probably when he told me
   . . . you know . . . ah . . . or maybe before then, maybe years ago
   (laugh). I don't know (laugh) . . . but, uh.

An emergent thought about what he told her threatened to evoke
too much emotional pain and a characteristic type of inhibition set in,
clouding both her conscious experience and the communicative process.

L: And the accident was right . . . uh, like a final way. Because over
   this past weekend, I was more aware of what was happening around
   me than I was the first time.

She had not shifted the topic but continued to inhibit aspects of the
topical complex. What she meant by "the first time" was the period
just before the accident. This vague labeling was also both stylistic and
immediately defensive.

L: So, I don't know what I was doing the first time—just living it up, I guess. Just like I think about right and wrong, I think about what's important to do.

It was very hard for the therapist to know what she meant because of the vague and somewhat mislabeled concepts. From later material, it was evident that she meant that before the accident, she was feeling confused and seeking as many experiences as possible in order to jam her mind and avoid ideas and feelings about the loss of Antonelli and those of her actions that led to that loss. Thus the "wrong" ideas were allusions to these actions.

T: So you were living it up and feeling out of touch with some part of reality.
L: People can become carried away by their idea of who they are and what's going on, not as aware or thoughtful as they can be of what's happening.
T: You think you were ignoring things you wanted to ignore?

The patient depersonalized the reference: "People can become carried away." The therapist labeled her as the subject of the incipient ideas, "You think, etc." As will be seen, even though she went on with "I," she was not yet ready or able to experience or communicate the idea that she felt badly about doing something wrong that ruined her relationship with Antonelli.

L: I wasn't really ignoring, I was forming my own opinions. For example, I saw what was going on in the house of one of the people in the place where I was staying. The girl wasn't as aware as she should be of what was going on. She was on her own trip too and wasn't able to understand why her old man was (vaguely) with her. Or just forming opinions of things, (pause) I'll probably do that again. But it's better not to just accept everybody as exactly who or what they are. That's how I want to be accepted. Like before I was just being a pretty girl. I wasn't thinking about anything. I was just (pause), you know. And the accident just made me take a really heavy look at myself, and maybe I don't like what I've seen. My 25th birthday is next Wednesday. I think about age a lot. I feel like I've aged a lot physically since the accident. I don't feel 16 anymore (laugh). Um. Ooh (long pause in which she lights a cigarette). I don't like my smoking, but it's hard to quit (pause). Sometimes I suspect smoking cigarettes keeps me from another level of thinking. But then I think the "other levels" idea is just my imagination. But then, I know that's not true (very long pause). Hans told me he can't wait 'til I find out who I am (mumbles) (extended silence).

The patient circled closer to a repetitive theme of having done something wrong. The therapist attempted to move closer to expression and clarifications of what this was when he asked about what she wanted to ignore. Laura used inhibition and a scattering of generalities to ward off such mental contents. Nonetheless, each episode of approach to the warded-off contents advanced toward clarification. At the same time, each approach was a check on the situation for safety. Alone, the patient dared not dwell on "it." But in the therapeutic relationship, she learned that she could think about "it" and feel the painful, emotional responses it evoked, without the pain's exceeding her limits of toleration. Thus the avoidances illustrated here do not indicate that the therapy was not moving along. After the above interchange, the patient paused and then denied that she was either crazy or unhappy. She paused again and then remembered her intensive images of Antonelli. She imagined the future in terms of how she might act if she met him once more. But she again dropped this theme, spoke in a trivial way about recent activities, and idly began to polish her fingernails and glance at the therapist.

Her warded-off pain included both feelings of guilt that she had betrayed Antonelli and, perhaps more intense right here, her sense of hunger for attachment. She could not represent this in words but, instead, behaved seductively in order to replace what was lost and to avoid grief. The therapist, in effect, waited her out calmly and steadfastly. She suddenly seemed to become more alert, emerged from a blurred state, and talked of how men "came on to her on the street." This was followed by thoughts of an impending earthquake, a cataclysm during which the unworthy would perish, and how devils existed inside people. Her thoughts returned to the theme of wrongdoing. But the return of this repressed theme instigated further defensive efforts. She then said defiantly that the accident had changed her outlook and that she did not want to be fooled again.

This meant she did not want to be seduced or enthralled by the therapist, tell all, and then be left in the lurch. Her basic self and object schemata led her to expect that this would happen. She repeated the sequence of discussing the accident a little, feeling wrong in herself, blocking, externalizing, and talking philosophically and vaguely on the topic of who she was. The therapist then said that she both wanted new awareness and was afraid of the emotions that it would bring.

FORMULATION

After the hour, the therapist reconstructed in his own mind the sequence of thoughts that Laura had and also had been warding off. She had suggested that the automobile accident was a suicide attempt caused by her feelings of desolation, and she also felt despair because of the difficulty of mourning for and recovering from the loss of her lover. Thinking about it made her feel intolerably and abjectly remorseful for having caused the separation by her infidelity. Preexisting conflicts included guilt and anxiety over sexuality and counterphobic promiscuity; guilt, sadness, and rage over separations and inadequate supplies from others; and shame over a defective, worthless self-image. The therapist's goal was to help her work through the three recent events: the "act of infidelity," the loss of Antonelli, and her suicide equivalent in terms of these conflicts. This therapeutic effort had to proceed through the filters imposed by her hysterical style, her immature developmental level, and her continued search for parent substitutes.

FOURTH SESSION

During the hour, the patient told the therapist about her experiences with Antonelli. She had lived with him for several months. When he was called away on a necessary trip, she felt lonely and deserted and slept with a mutual friend. The friend told Antonelli as soon as he returned. Antonelli called her a worthless whore and asked her to leave his apartment. She cried for hours and drove wildly about the city, narrowly missing having a wreck that night. She then became blurred over implications of this story.

FIFTH SESSION

Laura reported taking a hallucinogenic drug the previous day, which is reminiscent of the hierarchy of defense described in the chapter on Harry as a hysteric: inhibit representation, do not translate images into word memories, dissociate, become passive. Here Laura used a drug to help her dissociate and also, perhaps, provoke the therapist into rescuing her.

She told of having feelings of worthlessness and thoughts of suicide during the hallucinogenic "trip." She had expected the drug to make her feel free and to allow her to be sexual with Hans. Her manner indicated anger with the drug and the therapist. She changed in a labile and partly uncontrolled manner, from feeling worthlessness and guilt to anger, seductiveness, and a feeling of being "spaced out." She ended by observing her own low control and plaintively questioned her lack of control when Antonelli was away and she slept with his friend. The therapist commented that, in itself, asking this question showed that she could begin to control herself. The purpose of this comment was to increase Laura's sense of self-esteem. It also contained a covert suggestion that she rouse herself to a sense of active responsibility and that the therapy was helpful.

SIXTH SESSION

Laura was able to assemble her story in its sequential order and in a coherent manner. She experienced guilty feelings and checked the therapist to see whether he would be either critical or warmly encouraging. Her eroticized transference overtures became increasingly overt, and she became clearly angry at feeling rejected, allowing herself to pout when the therapist did not take the candy she had offered during the hour. She went on conceptualizing her story with Antonelli, adding some associations that included warded-off oedipal attachments toward her father and an unresolved sense of symbiotic attachment with her mother.

SEVENTH SESSION

Laura seemed much more energetic, and there was little in the way of eroticized transference acting out. Instead, she reported pleasurable flirtations with men and generally avoided talking about the entire stress event. She did, however, add historical material about her earlier flight from her family into promiscuity and her growing sense of worthlessness at that time.

EIGHTH SESSION

Laura again talked about her relationship with Antonelli. She was more emotional and also more deliberately evasive. She inhibited ideas but did not dissociate. She reported feeling sexually aroused by Hans, making an overture, then having intrusive thoughts of Antonelli, and crying. She became anxious as the therapist repeated this sequence, but her thinking was generally much improved. The question of organicity was set aside in the therapist's mind, and he helped her clarify cause-and-effect sequences in the story.

REMAINING SESSIONS

Laura continued to feel more energetic and forgave herself. She imagined meeting Antonelli again and not begging him to take her back at any price. She also discussed her drug history, her feeling of using sex and drugs to escape growing up, and her sadness over the disruption of her marriage and over giving up her child.

She was seductive at times, which led to memories of her anger with her father when he appeared to lose interest in her as she developed sexual, womanly attributes during adolescence and when he accused her of trying to show off her breasts in a sluttish way. She then grew angry with the therapist and displaced this onto anger at needing therapy. She then cried and talked of her sense of inner deadness. Transference gambits of an erotic sort continued whenever she felt especially vulnerable, but she was more able to control them. For example, she could joke about her feelings: "If I thought the world was coming to an end, what would I do? Seduce you? No" (laughs).

This thought about the world coming to an end referred to the therapy's impending termination, a topic dealt with in many of the ensuing hours as it related to (1) fears of relapse without the therapist, (2) the loss of Antonelli and previous losses, and (3) anger that the "price" of getting better was giving up the therapist. As the termination approached, her seductiveness emerged again in a more peremptory manner and led to further work on her need for attachment, her tendency to offer sex in order to be cared for, and her feelings of inadequacy that were both the cause and the effect of such behavior.

DISCUSSION

The therapy was terminated after 20 sessions. There was a marked improvement in Laura's mental status. Her interpersonal relationships were restored to the maximal level she had achieved before the accident. She felt better about herself, was not suicidal, and had worked through several aspects of the loss of Antonelli and her related actions. She had also learned to think about her life and decisions in the context of the psychotherapeutic situation. Some aspects of longing and rage had been touched on in relating Antonelli to her earlier life and in working through the prospect of separation from the therapist. Her core neurotic conflicts and incompletely developed character structure had not changed, although she had more insight into their existence. Now that she was relatively asymptomatic, she could either resume her life as it was before the flurry of recent events or accept a recommendation for long-term psychotherapy aimed at working through her characterological problems.

Chapter **16**

DEATH OF A PARENT

With the assistance of Frederick Parris, M.D.

Margaret, a 25-year-old woman, illustrates denial and the resumption of mourning during psychotherapy and the communicative problems imposed by a style in which isolation and undoing are prominent.

She telephoned the outpatient clinic for an "evaluation of depression" because of suicidal thoughts during a period shortly after her mother committed suicide and because of fear that "she might do as her mother did." She was referred to the stress clinic, and an appointment was made. She phoned and canceled this appointment, explaining that she was feeling much better. Contact was renewed several weeks later when Margaret called again, saying she had been feeling better but now wanted help.

Dr. Parris is presently Assistant Clinical Professor of Psychiatry at the University of California, San Francisco.

FIRST SESSION

She presented herself as composed, unemotional, controlled, intelligent, and personable. As part of obtaining informed consent, she signed a statement containing the words "Research on Stress Response Syndromes." She began the first session by commenting on this phrase.

M (Margaret): It is important to, uh, to study that, and I think the greatest impact has of course, been on my father.

She was referring to her mother's suicide.

M: And ah, I read a research study recently in the paper that said that sudden deaths are extremely hard to get over for a spouse, for him, and after they've been married for 33 years and were very, very close in the relationship, so it affects me most when I'm with him but when I—where as I'm living my own life out here, and I was living my own life when she died, although we were very close (pause).

She said again that her father is the one affected by her mother's suicide. As is often the case, the first minutes of therapy indicate a character trait of the patient. She used alternative facts ("he is upset") as a way to ward off threatening facts ("I am upset"). She went on to say how days could pass without thinking of it, before disclosing her own distress.

M: So I was just thinking recently that sometimes I'm, I'm pretty sure I, I go whole days without thinking about it—and I'm feeling the more direct problems that I'm confronting, you know in my work, which is difficult. I was standing talking on the phone at work yesterday, and there was this girl behind me who was cracking up, saying to her girl friend she felt like committing suicide, and you know, everything was going wrong. And all the machines weren't working, and you know, I was identifying very strongly because that happened to me a couple weeks ago.

Her identification with one who commits or might commit suicide was inscribed on the therapist's mind as a possible key issue. The "universal" stress response theme of fear of merger with a victim is here colored by another "universal" theme, identification with the parent of the same sex.

M: . . . 'cause all the machines I wanted to use weren't working, or I was doing really stupid mistakes. And ah, it was just before Easter and I had to get something done and, and I was just starting to shake, I was just so uptight, and so when I first called here I, ah, was in a very, uh, very bad situation, you know, emotionally, I just didn't know what was going on, and I was, I was feeling suicidal and ah, just, for the first time in my life that I just couldn't cope with the things that were happening to me. And I couldn't cope with my own feelings, and I was just, I felt like I was getting out of control. And when I started realizing what I was doing to myself and to the people around me, notably to the guy I'm living with, um, I realized I had to get a grip on myself, and I have been, I don't feel like I'm freaking out that much anymore. Sometimes I feel, this is why I didn't follow up too closely after I called, I called and, and ah very very urgent at the time and then, you know, then I got a grip on myself and ah, I, I couldn't really make up my mind whether or not I should come ah, or whether I was getting back on the road, and I didn't have to worry too much any more and still feel alternately one way or the other. Sometimes I feel fine, I feel sane, and sometimes I still feel that ah, I need new perspectives and I really need somebody to um, help, you know put my head right back where it should be, you know. I don't know if I've ever, my head has ever been where it should be. So, um, it, it's also hard. I got kind of nervous this morning when you first saw me because I suddenly tried to put all my problems together, and sometimes I feel I can talk about them very coherently, and I like to, and then it comes out to somebody, whoever I happen to be with at the moment, and then, there, I was just afraid this morning on account I wouldn't be able to talk and I wouldn't be able to put anything together. So, I don't know if I can (pause). But I guess it's also hard for me just to sit here and keep talking without any sort of direction, I suppose. So (laugh) do you have any advice for me?

She became diffuse and repetitive at an abstract level over the issue of whether or not she was all right.

The therapist asked her to go on with whatever she felt most distressed about. She talked of her current love relationship with Ned but quickly shifted the topic to her work in photography. She graduated from college with a major in literature and then decided to leave her home in suburban New York to come West. She got a very promising job in movie production. It required that she plan her own original work in addition to carrying out certain editing-room routines. For the first time in her life she felt that she was embarked on a satisfying and self-fulfilling career, but she had difficulty concentrating in the darkened editing room. She retraced her history in order to illustrate her feelings during earlier periods, continuing as follows:

M: You know, I really hated myself all through high school. I thought I was ugly and nobody liked me and I went through all these very unstable things, um, that I started getting over finally when I went to New York State and um, I had a couple of relationships and I met a girl who is now very very close to me. I'm very close to Alice, and we lived together for about a year and a half and have been friends for nearly three years now. And then after I graduated from N.Y.S. as a lit major, um, I worked for a year as a secretary in Central Bookstore which was, it was fun, it was nice, but I felt I wasn't doing anything with my life, and I wanted to do something more creative and interesting. So I came out here because a friend had this movie studio that was really moving, and then, um, my father, who is a computer designer, he was working for General Labs in New Jersey, and he was pressured into taking a big important job which would mean moving to Philadelphia for two years, and my mother said absolutely no, I won't go, I'd die sooner. You know, she's very strong willed, independent person, and, ah, that upset me a whole lot, like (laugh) my god, my parents are splitting up after 29 years, and there was no way my father could get out of it, so, um, my mother would go back and forth. She finally decided to go with him, but she was going to stay home in New York for the summer, and, ah, then she killed herself; it was just as sudden as that. You know, it's very, in a way it's very like her because she wasn't a person to make a big show of trying to ah commit suicide. You know, just she did it (ha, ha).

Margaret's laughter was not simply nervousness; it was a way of undoing and averting negative emotional responses. She later revealed that her mother was strongly committed to being "not only a housewife." She had had her own career as a free-lance illustrator and had earned substantial sums for many years. For a period immediately preceding her suicide, she had received an unusual number of rejections in competitive circumstances and was not earning any money. Her mother loved their home, friends, and community. She hated Philadelphia and the idea of tagging along with her husband and was sure that he would have a second and fatal heart attack from the enormous pressures of the new job to which he had committed himself.

M: —you know just a total shock to everybody, and so I stayed with my father for a month. Just every day, just trying to see him through every day, and, ah, then I spent the next month seeing him and going, arranging things in New York and, and, ah, relaxing and then going down to Philadelphia, and, and then I came out here, ah, about five and a half months ago, um, and started work. I was going to work full time, but I didn't, I'm working part time instead. I'm working two days a week, taking some courses, um, and that's about it. I don't know if it's given you any insights. It's been a, you know, I feel it's been a pretty normal middle-class existence, and, ah, up till now I feel I've been coping with everything fairly well (pause). So I don't think it's anything unusual; I don't even think my problems are anything unusual, and you said it was, um, it was good I realized that it was all going on inside my head, and I do know that. I don't feel that the world is doing anything to me. Um, I feel that the way I see life is that life is to me, and I can sort of make it whatever I want to, ah, so I'm, I just feel, I know that whatever I'm doing with my life is totally up here (pause). So I don't know where to go from here.

Margaret was in a denial phase. After her mother's death she devoted herself to her father's grief, and then she continued with her plans. She was having difficulty at work and with her boy friend, though she played down these problems in order to maintain her sense of esteem. At this point she was not experiencing sadness over the loss of her mother, although the need to ward off such responses may have contributed to her problems at work and with Ned.

The therapist then asked a series of questions exploring for signs of depression, suicidal potential, and any abnormalities in her current mental status. When no material of consequence emerged, he requested more details on her present interpersonal relationships. She responded by telling of her difficulties with Ned, her periodic feeling of jealousy, and her worries about losing him. The therapist sensed, because of clues in the flow of her remarks, that it was she who wished to leave Ned but that for some reason she felt badly about this and could not acknowledge it. But he did not verbalize this, and she continued to describe how Ned moved in with her.

M: Just after Ned and I started getting a little, very, very slightly involved, um he was, he was forced to move out of his apartment, and, ah, so in a moment of rashness, you know, of generosity, I said, well, you know, stay with me if you can't find any other place to stay, as a temporary thing. That's how (laugh), that's how it started. It was really weird, and for a long time, for about a month, I guess, I said, ah, you'll just have to find your own place as soon as you find a job and can pay for it. And he was saying after a while, after we'd been living together for a couple of weeks, he was saying, "No, I want to keep living with you," and I said, "No, I don't want that. I want to live by myself." Um, and so finally, you know, we worked out things to the point where I decided, after about a month and a half or something, that if if we found different living quarters our relationship, which had built to a certain point, that point would just be thrown out the window because it wasn't the kind of thing that could survive on, ah, two totally separate, um, things. It would be a regression, if we lived in different places; it would be putting our relationship on a lower level, which neither of us thought it would survive. So I decided I wanted to continue with it rather than just completely throw it out. And that's why we got a larger apartment and moved about two months ago.

T: And that's about the time you began to become jealous, had fantasies, and worried?

M: Well, it was also the sort of time when I stopped being in control of the situation, because as long as Ned was saying, "I want you," and I'm saying, "Well I'm not sure," you know, I was more in control, and as he was always the one who was making the efforts to, to adapt to my needs and wants and I needed more time by myself. And, ah, once I, once I, you know, sort of made a turn around and said, "I want you, too," then sort of like the balance shifted, and, ah, he became, he wanted to become more in control. I've always, I, I, you know, always resist him being in control, you know, and I said I'm the one who's suddenly having to make all the adjustments. I want it to be 50–50, and, ah, that's when it started, um, resisting the security of, the security of the relationship, and, and sort of subconsciously trying to dump on it, and that was when we moved. So now, now I, I sort of resent feeling that I'm the one who has to make most of the adaptations and most of the changes. You know, because he's, he's still, he says, "Well that's the way I am you know. If you don't like it, that's too bad."

T: How do you feel about having to make the changes? Are you feeling very frightened that if you don't, you'll lose him?

The therapist was aware of the parallel between Margaret and her mother. Both were threatened by lowered controls, possible loss of a man, and a loss by moving. He groped for this connection and her possible identification with her mother in what follows.

M: Yeah (pause).

T: I'm struck also—I'm trying to tie this in with the "Why now" question I have in my mind. You came West involved with yourself. Everything was going fine. You had your independence, but for some reason things have regressed.

M: Mm-huh.

T: Perhaps you feel now the way you did back in high school, that you doubt your own value.

M: No, not, God forbid if I could ever doubt that again. No, I still have a basic sense of my own value and my own worth, and, and the person I am. I still have, you know, about 300 percent more self-confidence, down basically than I, than I, did, then, um.

T: What I was really driving toward was closing the circuit. I was wondering if your mother's death had any effects on you. Here was this case where *she* wanted to retain some control, in a sense of not having to make the move, was forced into a corner, and as you said, "She wouldn't make the move even if it killed her," and that's apparently how it occurred. Would you identify with this part, or would you prefer to—

M: Ah, I respect her a lot, and ah, ah, I respect, you know, the, the strength that she always had and the independence and the, the person that she was. You know, she was just a really beautiful person, and, ah, I suppose the fact that I had to come to terms with her suicide, the fact that she deliberately took her life in the sense that I respect her so much. You know, so I got to respect what she did, you know.

Margaret did not quite connect with the therapist's communication about identification. Instead she reacted as if the therapist had suggested that she might feel critical of or angry at her mother for committing suicide. She was protesting too much about how wonderful her mother was and how much she respected her. She not only was avoiding negative feelings, but she also was avoiding them by stating opposite ones. This was a characteristic style for her, akin to the switching described in Chapter 9. She did this so emphatically and repetitiously, while seeming ill at ease, that the therapist approached it in a very gingerly manner.

T: In fact you almost had to respect what she did, so as not to interfere with your image of her as a . . .

M: Mm-huh.

T: Not to place a value on suicide, but you had it in your mind as respecting her suicide because if you didn't respect that, you would have to question the image. . . .

M: Yeah. Also, um, like she couldn't, you know, I can see how after decades of of living with one man and loving him and having a very close, good relationship that they did, she couldn't turn around and say, I'm leaving you. You know that. I don't see how any person could really do that.

Hence she also could not break up with Ned, although later in therapy she felt able to do so. One reason for coming to therapy was her conflict over how to terminate an unsatisfactory but close relationship.

M: Whereas knowing how much she hated Philadelphia and the pressure-cooker existence, that and the fact that she, she was also very sure that my father, you know, was going to die of a heart attack because he almost did five years ago. And put in a similar situation, she was positive he was going to drop dead anyway, once he did that, once he moved, um. So having made that decision, and she, she also felt that he betrayed her by doing this when he knew that she, she would hate moving so much. But I respected that fact that she wanted to retain her independence and, and that it was hurting her pride to have to follow somebody else. You know, like just to be an appendage to my father um (pause). So she, she wrote in her note, you know, to my father, "You did what you have to do. I'm doing what I have to do." And uh, I, you know, I've never, I haven't thought of suicide at all since I was about 16 years old. And you know, the fact that, you know, my mother's, you know, doing it brought it to my attention so much and having to respect the fact. Like I, I'm, I'm almost positive that's why it seems like an alternative to me now. Um—although I'm, I'm, I'm pretty positive that I wouldn't do it. Because I, I don't think that I could face hurting my father that much. I mean, I wouldn't have to face it, obviously, but um, I just don't think I could. You know, knowing, you know, how much it hurt him for her to die. You know, I just feel it would be another blow that he couldn't bear.

T: I wonder if what makes it even triply hard for you, as sad as you feel, just trying to respect and love your mother, is the fact that she did hurt your father very much in the final analysis.

This was a fairly direct interpretation of her hostile thoughts toward her mother and of a warded-off hostile component in her reaction to her mother's suicide.

M: No. I know she was a very selfish person, and I knew that when she was alive, and I knew it when she was dead. Um, it was a selfish thing to do, you know, and she was a very self-centered person, and she, I knew, I always knew that (pause). So I don't respect her for being so, you know, that self-centered, you know. I certainly don't blame my father, either (pause).

The therapist inferred here an unspoken thought, "I don't blame my mother" before she said, "I don't blame my father either." This was a sequence of undoing: "I don't respect her (I do blame her). (I don't blame her), (I blame father), I don't blame my father." She ended by denying the impact of her mother's death.

M: But I do feel that I've come to terms with, you know, with her death about as much as I ever will. I don't feel that it's, it's really disturbing me so much now, you know, emotionally, except that there are situations that I find myself in now that I, I just say (laughing) you know "I wish you were here." You know, because she, you know, she was always a great support for me. She was somebody who really, really did believe in me and always said so. And she always tried to put some backbone into me, you know, and she really did. I absorbed a lot of things from her. When I was in a situation where I'd say, "Oh mommy I like this guy, and he won't ask me out," and she'd say, "Well go ask him out. What are you waiting for?" You know, she was a very aggressive person, and she, she pounded that into me. Um, and she was, she was an extremely proud person, and she pounded that into me as much as she could too (pause).
T: Okay. We're going to have to end for today.

SECOND SESSION

Margaret came in expressing ambivalence about her need for therapy. She denied any relationship between her problems and what had happened to her mother and said that she had come back only because she felt obligated to discuss whether or not she needed therapy. She did not like the way the therapist just listened to her and offered

nothing of himself. In various ways, she asked for support and friendship. However, in doing so she became provocative and accusatory.
The therapist felt that she was testing him to see whether he would
collapse (have a heart attack as her father did), become angry and wish
to be rid of her, or approach her more intimately and socially (which
would frighten her), or try to control her. But he continued with the
same concerned, tactful, and objective professional manner as in the
first interview. She announced that she was going on a visit to see her
father for a few days.

THIRD SESSION

Margaret dealt superficially and unemotionally with the visit to her
father. She felt that she was much better and believed that her fears
of being flooded were related to "a period of identity problems in
adolescence." She gave additional history, including a suicidal gesture
as an adolescent, when depressed. She was agreeable and intellectual
during the hour, using undoing, negation, and disavowal to avoid
anxiety.

FOURTH SESSION

Margaret spoke of an episode of sadness that occurred while she
was developing her own pictures in the darkroom at work. She had
taken these pictures during a recent visit home and had also brought
back a picture of her mother that she had found there. She talked long-
ingly of missing a girl friend, but to avoid intensifying her sad feelings,
she switched to discussing both difficulties and successes with her
editing work, focusing on mechanical issues. In summarizing her remarks over the hour, the therapist mentioned an idea she had spoken
of earlier in the hour, about going home to be closer to old friends of
hers and her mother.

She responded that introspection on such ideas made her "massive-
ly oversensitive to any little thing." She related this oversensitivity to
Ned and continued as follows:

M: . . . like, um—even if, if I feel, a, I feel affectionate toward Ned and
   he just doesn't happen to feel that way at that moment, it just sends

me, I mean, right to the bottom, or just looking, you know, at a picture of my mother will just send me into a fit of crying, and this doesn't happen normally. But things that don't normally upset me do, things that I just can't, I can't deal with them rationally. I can't shrug them off, and I feel—in a way I feel a huge loss of self-esteem—whereas on the other hand, if somebody said, "Do you like yourself"—I would say "yes." It's just one of, one of the main characteristics of my depression is just feeling unable to cope with the complexities and the demands of life and the future and making a living and achieving something or accomplishing something. It just seems too complicated and too difficult, and the whole thought of it just appalls me.

T: It's only a hunch, but I would think some of those feelings come to mind when you look at a picture of your mother and have some realization of her loss and talent.

The therapist noted the defensive maneuver of abstract generalization, attention to peripheral details, and expansion to issues too large to contemplate, such as "the complexities and the demands of life and the future." By giving this interpretation, he tried to hold her to a topic she had brought up and was also warding off.

M: Well, one of my, one of my strongest fantasies, or actually I have very, very few fantasies that, that I wish, but one of the things that has been recurring since she died is wishing that I'm little again—very little—you know like about 5 years old. And I brought back from the East two pictures, one was of my mother when she was in college, and one was of me when I was 5 years old, and I'm, I'm planning to put them together in a frame because that is my strongest fear (a slip of the tongue), ahh, fantasy, you know, I want to go back to the time that everything was taken care of for me and I didn't have to worry about finances and supporting myself and, and, ah, trying to accomplish something in life. Although I suppose you know, the little things I was going to try and survive were just as traumatic as the things I, I might go through now. But that's, that's how I feel. You know, it's not so much that I hate myself, I hate myself, but a feeling of just being unable to cope with all these things because I, I think that the self-esteem, and the, ah, the feeling I like myself, or I wouldn't be anybody else, um, I think that those feelings are very solid in myself. I don't question them, I, I feel in that sense, I always feel very together. . . .

She was switching from her wish to be little and dependent, an idea that made her feel too infantile, self-critical, and controlled, to assertions that she liked herself. When this undoing operation restored a sense of safety, she could resume her self-critical statements.

M: . . . But my main, the the main characteristic of my depression is just I hate to get up. I hate to face each day. I hate to—um, I feel that every single day is a struggle, and I never want to wake up in the morning, or when I wake up, I never want to get up. I just dread every day. And that's, those are, that's the massive feeling that my depression consists of. And, ah, I relate this to the pressure that has been put on me by my father to succeed—it's not that he's pressuring me. . . .

She was using her characteristic switching maneuver again. She switched to describing her father and was also using the topic of her father to switch away from ideas and feelings related to her mother. As will be seen, the "mother" topic will return.

M: . . . but (sigh) he wants me to, you know, for my own sake, be, because he knows, or he's instilled in me, I suppose, the need to feel that I'm accomplishing something in life. But at the same time I've gone through four years of liberal arts college, and movies are such an overloaded market that it's very difficult, and you have to be extremely aggressive to be able to succeed, and ah, much as I want, I still have these ambiguous feelings. I have tremendous fear of not being able to. And ah, it's just really, that is, that is another thing that's very, very difficult for me to cope with. And you know, when I got these feelings from him, my mother was always the person I was able to go to. She wanted the same things from me, but she, she didn't express them in a pressurized way. She expressed them in a much more sympathetic way that I could identify with, and I've, you know, I always turned to her. And in the years when I was closest to her, I was farthest from my father.

T: When were those years?

The therapist, sensing she was about to switch away from the train of thought involving her mother, tried to hold her to this topic by asking a relevant question about her mother.

M: Oh, my college years and, and, ah, up until she died—well after

I'd left home. She was, ah—um, I feel a lot of sympathy for her, because she, I don't think she was a very good (pause) mother. . . .

This "I feel a lot of sympathy" was a kind of premonitory undoing of the angry feelings that were incipient and emerged clearly in her voice when she subsequently spoke of her mother's terrible temper. Both feelings were really present.

M: . . . She didn't want to be really (a mother). My father told me this after she died. Especially when both my sister and me were little. She hated having two little kids around, and, I mean, she loved us, but I remember she had the worst temper, you know, she used to—I remember when she grabbed me by my hair and shook me like that. Um, I mean she never beat me or, you know, anything like that but she, you know, she had a terrible temper. And this died away very, very much after I left home. And she and my sister, ah, my sister was very unstable and really hated my mother for years even after she went to college, and ah, I don't think their relationship ever really got close, even after that. But after I left home, very quickly I started growing back closer to my parents, and, and my mother always, um (pause), she, she always needed me, and I, I understood that, you know, without ever really talking about it. And you know, sort of a feeling she really wanted me to have all the freedom that I could possibly have, even though she needed me, and she wanted me to be near, you know, on vacations and stuff like that. You know, and she urged me to move to California, even though you know, she would've much rather had me (pause) closer (pause).

The therapist tried to hold her to this topic with another question, but she deflected to other topics until the end of the hour.

FIFTH THROUGH SEVENTH SESSIONS

The next two hours, the fifth and sixth sessions, dealt with ordinary matters at work and with Ned and avoided mention of her mother. In the seventh hour Margaret talked in a general way, about everyday work frustrations. She then told of how strongly she had felt that she had to get away from Ned and be with a girl friend, not to "sob on her shoulder but to get her energy." She "accepted it with equanimity" when the girl friend was too tired to have her come over. She immediately returned to work topics and expressed righteous anger with her boss. She then criticized her editing machine for being defective and talked abstractly about artistic tasks. One purpose of discussing the boss and the equipment was to show that she was not at fault or to blame for her anger.

She then talked, dejectedly, of eventually showing her film work. The therapist said that she might be asking if it were all right to show not her work but her feelings, for he could sense that she was depressed. She said she was sad that she had only her work to attest to her worth, and she was uncertain about it. She came close to tears at the end of the hour, but the cause was unclear, concealed by intellectualized generalizations.

EIGHTH SESSION

Margaret began the next session by saying that she had been feeling unstable for the last two days. She had been reluctant to do darkroom work because she was afraid she would be unable to focus her thoughts while there. The first half of the interview was occupied with a long soliloquy about the uncertainty of her future plans and her ambivalence toward accepting financial support from her father. When the therapist attempted to focus her attention on the unstable feeling, she deflected toward continuing these generalizations and abstract ruminations. But she then went on to mention her mother, as illustrated in the following transition:

M: . . . ah, like last night I got terribly depressed about what I was saying, and I was going through one of my sort of panics, and this time I said, "I'm not going to run over to anybody," and in a way I didn't want to, I wanted to just figure it out. And I couldn't. I mean, I just couldn't figure out why I was feeling so completely down. I knew when it started though, and, and I have an absolute progression of what happened because I'd been sort of down for two days. It all started with a thought of my mother, and, ah, I mean everything was fine. I was feeling really good one evening, and Ned and I were just sitting around talking and a song of Joni Mitchell's came on the radio, and all of a sudden I flashed back to this conversation I had with my mother about Joni Mitchell about two or three years ago, a long time ago, when, um, my mother was

just saying, "Oh, it's just her publicity people that say she writes
and sings and plays the guitar and she does everything." I said,
"Mother, cut it out, she really does." And my mother said, "Oh."
You know, she was, she was just thinking I was being naive. And
I flashed on that, and I got really depressed and into my own
thoughts and I sat down and I wrote a long letter to this woman
back East, who, um, was my mother's closest friend, and who's
like, you know, another mother to me. I just haven't, I haven't been
writing letters lately, but I wrote her a long letter, and (sigh) it was
just, you know, I just went into the bedroom and, and sort of sat
and thought for a long time. I was, I was feeling down but not, not
really terribly bad. I was just thinking and I wanted to be by myself
(sigh), and I was still down with the flu, and I was sick of being
sick and, ah, and so on. And the next day, the next evening, a couple of friends of Ned's came over. I've talked to you about the problem I have of relating to his friends, and this is his friend Tom,
who's a total freak and Tom's, a woman that he lives with. I mean
it's a really weird situation; she's a call girl.

T: Can I ask you what the letter was like that you wrote to the friend
of your mother?

Although the associations may possibly be relevant, the therapist
noted the reference to her ambivalence about her mother, and so he
chose to help Margaret hold onto that aspect of the topic, that is, the
issue of missing her mother, feeling frustrated, and wishing for a substitute mother. If Margaret were on her own, as she would be alone
at home, she would probably not continue to develop this ideational
line because it evoked painful feelings.

M: Oh, yeah, um (pause). I wanted to explain to her, you know, what
was going on between Ned and me because I'd talked to her about
it when I was back East. What I mainly, what I expressed right
away, was the fact that I needed, um (pause), ah, somebody sort
of to function as my mother, and, you know, she is the closest to
me. But she doesn't have the background in my life, and the, the
things that you always go through with your parents (pause)
(sounds about to cry).

T: I asked you that very directly because I think you're experiencing
a lot of feeling right here and now.

M: (Long pause) (sigh). I just don't know if I can really talk about it
(almost crying) (sniff) (long pause).

T: What sort of thoughts are you having?

M: I'm not really having any thoughts. I'm just trying to pull myself
back together again so that I can talk. You know, it's like I said,
I don't want to come in here and and break down, you know,
although you said that does serve a purpose (cries). Um, I really
want to use these sessions very constructively for my head (sniff).
But we are getting very close to my emotions recently, because I've
noticed this several times when I've come in here and started talking, just talking, you know, but not about my mother, not about
anything, but I feel like crying, and it's not as as hard, I mean it's
not hard to hold back, but, but I feel that I'm very close to my emotions (sigh) (pause) (sniff).

T: I think that there's something very constructive going on, expressing emotions here.

This patient had been warding off crying, not only because her
sadness is painful, but also because she believes it is humiliating to give
way to her emotions. The therapist said this to counter her humiliation. With other types of patients it would be a gratuitous remark that
could be used transferentially.

M: (Pause) um, it's not that I've been holding back. The emotions that
I'm feeling are reactions to what I'm saying, um. Thoughts of my
mother have been very much with me. Well, one way of showing
this is a photograph I wanted to make, a self-portrait for my father.
What I chose to do (sigh), was use time exposure on my camera,
you know, you can set it, and about ten seconds later it goes off
so you have a chance to get into a pose or something, do it by
yourself. So I chose to try to take a picture of myself studying
myself in the mirror and in the mirror are two pictures; the two pictures that I mentioned once to you very briefly before; one of my
mother and one of myself when I was little, and the one of my
mother was was when she was about say 20. And to show that I'm
looking at myself very strongly these days and that these two pictures are, um, well, pictures of the little girl, I mean myself as the
little girl because that's, as I've said before, that's sort of almost
how I wish that I were, was, and the picture of my mother, and
it's an old picture. She'd, she just didn't like to have her picture
taken so we have very few pictures of her that are recent and of
those my father has them. My father's coming this weekend, by
the way. . . .

She was expressing the thought "I miss my Mommy, I wish I were a little girl with her again." She modulated the rate of the idea's emergence by using other thoughts. In effect, these thoughts partially filled cognitive channels so that the previously warded-off thought could not rush out all at once and overwhelm her sense of control. The other thoughts, such as "my father's coming" might also have been antidotes to her compelling sense of loss. She continued talking about her father, using his sadness as a vehicle to externalize her own similar feelings, identifying with both his feelings and his capacity to cope with them and savoring the continued attachment. Note that she will say that she warded off ideas of her mother for his sake.

M: . . . So, I'm hoping that we, as always I'm hoping that we'll, we'll just enjoy each other's company and not (sigh), um, bring too many old ghosts back in. Um, this past week was their anni____, their wedding anniversary, and ah, I was afraid my father was going to be really down, so I called him up, and he was, he had friends over for dinner, which really made me happy, he wasn't by himself and depressed. He had been very depressed lately. I knew that, but he was really pleased and touched that I had remembered and that I had called and that made me really happy, and we're both looking forward to seeing each other. But, um, when we're together, I try to keep as far away from any mention and thoughts of my mother as possible because it (sigh) amplifies the feelings so much when the two of us are together. I mean I can talk about my mother, and I can cry about my mother in front of Ned or you or any one of my friends. . . .

As far as the therapist knew, this was the first time she had cried. To reduce her embarrassment she declared that she was comfortable with crying and did it all the time.

M: . . . but with my father, his pain is just so great and so is my own that we just increase each other's feelings. So with him, I just try to avoid every mention of her, every thought, and whether this is good or bad I don't know. . . .

One reason that she might feel badly is that she might have been predisposed to feeling guilt over an oedipal victory. She now had her father and excluded (mention of) her mother. This would be only one factor in an overdetermined behavior pattern.

M: . . . (sniff) (pause). There are, there is this one lady, ah, Marion, who is my mother's closest friend. I've known her all my life. She has a daughter who's a year younger than I am, and (pause) you know, it's like back home. I have a lot of people who who want to function as my special friends and parents, and they do, but she's, she's very much the closest . . . (pause) (cries) (clears throat).

Stabilized by discussing her father and perhaps growing anxious about that topic, she returned to her wish to attach herself to a woman friend as a mother replacement. The woman could not replace her mother; she must give up her mother, and so her sadness came out again.

M: . . . But what I feel that she has been, she's missing in in her role with me (cries) is, you know, all the things that are, that go between a mother and a daughter when they're growing up. All the little problems, all the, you know, the adol____, especially adolescence, which has got to be the worst period of anyone's life, but all the things that, you know, I went through with my own mother, and I have never experienced with Marion (pause). So one of, I expressed that in my letter to her, saying that I wanted, that there were questions that I wanted to ask my mother about her experiences in life that I had never had a chance to or had never run up against and ah . . . (sniff) (pause).

T: What sort of questions would those be?

M: Well they're mainly, ah, with regard to, ah, her marriage. Like I know that my parents went through difficult times, and I, I wanted to know how much do you, should you go, I mean it's crazy, nobody can tell you this, but I wanted to know from my mother's experience (sigh) how do you, how long do you hold on to a relationship when it's not good? How hard do you work for it? How, like, like Ned said to me once that there are going to be times in our relationship when we'll hate the sight of each other, you know, and, and trying to show that that's, you know, that if you really, that a relationship will go through good times and bad times—and the bad times will be awfully bad, but if you can hold on, I mean, the relationship will be very much strengthened, and this is something that my mother had also said to me. She'd, when we'd discussed the relative merits of marriage you know, I've said, you know, what am I supposed to push marriage for, you know, for nothing (said rapidly and vehemently).

She continued talking in generalities about one person's hurting another. She then recalled a family scene in which she had said she did not want to have children. Her mother took her side, but her father was horrified. She went on to talk of her parents' ambivalence toward each other. The therapist summarized by saying that she was talking about expressions of both tender and angry feelings between persons and added that she too may have angry feelings that cannot now be shared with her mother. She denied this:

M: Um, not so much share feelings with her because I always did, and I always did tell her how much I loved her. But I think that's I (sigh), when my mother died, I must have been the only person on earth who didn't have guilt feelings, who didn't say "If only I had done this" or, um, I had no feelings that I could have prevented or, or, ah, I don't know, just plain guilt that, that she had done it, she had committed suicide, and I still don't have any. I don't have any feelings that I wish that I had said that I loved her because, you know, I did. I said it many many times you know, starting I remember even years ago. Must have been when I was just about 17 or 18 and, and, ah, about to either just off to college, or about to go off to college, I said, I remember very distinctly saying to her, that she had given me so much love and understanding and it was the kind of love and understanding that you can't give back. I mean, I can't turn to her and say "Now, you know anytime you want advice, come to me," but it was some, something that I could, that I had learned and could hand on to somebody else. And, ah, even way earlier than that I remember when I was about probably 12 or 13, I had said something meaning to be funny, and it was actually very malicious. I said, she was, no I, I must have been about 14, 'cause I remember the house we were living in, and it's one of my really clearest memories (cries). She was, she was doing the laundry and I was sitting at the table and she was singing and I said, "Mother have you ever listened to yourself sing" and she said "no," and I said, "Well you're lucky," and I was just, it was a stupid joke, and years, I remember, for years later, I always said if there was one thing that I could call back in my life it was that, because it started her crying. I had made my mother cry, and I was just, I, I apologized, I said I'm sorry, I didn't mean it that way; that was really stupid.

She continued with memories of her mother and then spoke of wanting to talk to her father about her mother but being afraid to do so. Finally she talked again of longing to see her mother's friend Marion and of being envious of Ned, who could still call up his mother whenever he had a problem. At the end of the hour she gestured to the box of tissues and said, "Do you always keep these by the chair?" The therapist suggested that she was asking him to say that it was all right with him that she cried during the hour, and it was all right.

REMAINING SESSIONS

This stress-oriented treatment continued for seven more sessions. The above session marked the beginning of Margaret's open mourning for her mother. Her grief process was marked by her loving attachment as well as her resentment and fear of overidentifying with her mother. She had a model of her mother that she had never before clearly conceptualized; she saw her mother as superficially strong and powerful but as weak underneath. The refusal to move with her father, for example, she saw as strong in her first conscious thoughts, but she was warding off ideas that it was weak to have to commit suicide. Her mother was dependent on her father and could not live independently from him. But the attachment was ambivalent and unsatisfactory; her mother did not feel fulfilled by the marriage or by the children or her creative work.

SUMMARY

Margaret was afraid that she was too much like her mother. Her relationship with Ned was a psychological parallel for the relationship between her parents. Like her mother, she believed, she could not give up Ned because she would then drown in a sense of abandonment. On the other hand, she feared marrying Ned because he was self-centered and in some ways unstable, and she did not love him enough. As she could deal more authentically with her separation and independence from her mother, while also accepting the painful reality of the loss, she could risk separation from Ned. She engineered this separation and tolerated it well, while using the therapist as an interim relationship.

In the therapy she also worked through her feelings of being neglected by her father, especially when she heard of his plans to remarry a woman younger than himself, who was about her age. Rage at all abandoning figures, including the therapist, with whom termination was impending, was an important topic for working through in the therapy, in which she continued to use her style of switching topics or attitudes toward the same topic. This characterological defensive style was not interpreted systematically as it would have been in a psychoanalysis. The therapist's awareness of it allowed him to help her temper its use, that is, to use it when her emotions were too threatening at a given moment or to not use it and stay with a topic when her emotions were anticipated to remain within tolerable limits.

Chapter 17

THE SUICIDE OF A FRIEND

With the assistance of Robert Hammer, M.D.

Tim is a 31-year-old single man whose friend committed suicide shortly after a plea for help. During the weeks that followed, Tim felt so haunted by his dead friend that he was motivated to seek treatment. He was unable to sleep, was afraid of the dark, and had startle reactions and unbidden images. During a brief psychotherapy these symptoms were relieved. The suicide of his friend was also linked associatively with the death of his father several years earlier. When the therapist established a situation of safety through a tactful maintenance of Tim's self-esteem, it initiated a mourning process not begun at the time of the father's death.

Jack was Tim's friend and in some ways his leader for several years. His was the role of a man who knows women and is successful at work.

Dr. Hammer is presently a candidate at the San Francisco Psychoanalytic Institute.

Then for about a year while each was involved in other affairs, they seldom met. Recently, Jack had called Tim, and they had spent a long evening together. Jack spoke of feeling depressed and meaningless. He asked Tim to spend more time with him and hinted at moving in with Tim. Tim inwardly recoiled. He was aware of a strong feeling that he did not want to be sucked in. He did not want to rescue Jack; they had not been that close recently. But on the surface he presented a friendly demeanor and tried to cheer Jack throughout the evening.

A few days later, Tim received a telephone call from Carol, a woman who was a close friend of Jack's and a person Tim had recently dated. Carol was worried. Jack was missing and had left a note that suggested a possible suicide. Once again, Tim was concerned but did not want to become involved. Over the next four days Tim periodically felt anxious that Jack might be playing some type of trick to get back at him for not being more concerned. Then on the fifth day Carol called again to say that Jack had shot himself and that his body and been found in some nearby hills.

Carol asked Tim to join some friends in a funeral service. Feeling pressured, he refused but then felt that he had acted in an aloof and callous manner. Within days he developed insomnia, a phobia of the dark, and intrusive thoughts about Jack that at times were so vivid that he could feel his presence as a menace within the room. Below is the opening of the first interview in which he described some of these symptoms.

FIRST SESSION

Tim: A friend of mine shot sh-shot and killed himself; I don't know, about ten days ago; since that time I was afraid of the dark and I'd keep a light on. At first it took me forever to get to sleep; I kept, I'd keep wanting to open my eyes to look around to see if anyone were around in the apartment. I experienced periods during the day when I was frightened, felt very empty, extremely alone (pause); every time I drive by the hills I hate to look in the direction to where I think he was when he shot himself (pause). I don't even want to know the specifics, but I have general information about it (pause). His body was taken to a funeral home which happens to be very near where I live. Every time I go by there I hate to. I just get very uncomfortable, and (pause) I don't like dealing with a woman whom he was involved with, who I happen to work with somewhat now. I felt like she was going to suck me in this thing, into a funeral and extend it, and that was very upsetting. I had a talk with her last night about how I don't want to have anything else to do with her whatsoever (pause), and then on top of that, I started thinking about my own life and how I am not happy with it. I dislike it, how I want to change certain things in it (pause), how I'm lonely, want to get closer to somebody, thinking about having a family, and having a job that I would like to put energy into (pause), but mainly right now I just want to get rid of all these feelings about him (pause). I can't stand it, it's hard for me to, he crops up when I'm alone all the time. . . .

T (Therapist): You mean sort of intrudes on your mind?

Tim: Yeah, this morning, washing my face, I have soap in my eyes, with my eyes closed, I keep thinking all of a sudden somebody is going to touch my arm, and there's no one in the apartment (pause). I don't know why I freak out on that; I just force myself to finish washing my face, and then I open my eyes and I'm okay, look around; it's daylight, and everything's fine. . . .

T: How have you been sleeping lately?

Tim: I was sleeping a little better—at first I had all the lights in the apartment on; now I'm down to one in the living room which I'm very much aware of from my bedroom. Until last night I was definitely sleeping much better each night. I wasn't feeling much. I was better, and then I had this confrontation with this mutual friend, this woman, and that upset me and I felt nervous in my stomach, and it was hard for me to get to sleep. It makes me a little angry, the whole thing, that it should bother me.

T: It makes you angry.

Tim: Angry. I figure the way to get rid of the stress, for me, is to start doing things I want to do that make me happy and to stop sitting around on my ass 'cause then I just think about him. But I feel I move like a snail toward things I want to do.

During the beginning of the first hour, the therapist noted that Tim was seductive in his display of earnestness, readiness for "therapy," and a kind of charm that invited smiles, nods of agreement, and reassurances. There were unusually frequent requests for the therapist's interpretations and personal responses, all of which would have been premature or inappropriate. The therapist thus found it necessary to make some effort not to react with either a feigned warmth or a withdrawal from the patient.

Tim had obtained psychotherapy on several previous occasions. He had entered both individual and group treatment after his father's death, several years before, when he had felt not so much sad as empty, alienated, and aimless. These therapies had focused on his difficulties in maintaining intimate attachments with both men and women. Since developing the intrusive images of Jack, Tim had already gone to a gestalt therapy group. There he had worked on this symptom, and he described it during the interview.

Tim: I took a gestalt therapy group which I haven't found helpful. I wanted more personal attention.

T: You wanted what?

Tim: I wanted more personal attention. This thing was so stressful for me; I felt that I had to get on it now and work on it closely, work on improving my life closely with somebody, and I felt that it wasn't going to happen at the gestalt therapy.

T: Have you been able to talk about this in the gestalt therapy?

Tim: I talked about it yesterday. I had Jack on a pillow, you know, this guy on a pillow, and I yelled at him. I said: "I don't want to think about you anymore. I want to get on to living." Did that whole thing. And I didn't get what I wanted out of there. I was leaving, and one of the senior consultants there, I went up to him and I had wanted to ask him for a hug, but I hadn't been able to in the group, well, he said, that was fine, he would give me a hug afterward, anyway. And then he said, you know—he didn't know what to say. And I interpreted that to mean that he couldn't offer me any help about this thing. And that was, I didn't like that; I felt lonely. I felt like saying (angrily): "Hasn't anyone died in your life or something, and haven't you had to work it through? Can't you even tell me that?" I didn't say that, though.

Tim criticized the gestalt therapist for behavior he felt badly about in his own relationship with Jack. "He couldn't offer me any help." Tim also seemed to denigrate the gestalt therapy in order to win the approval of the present therapist, to whom he related rapidly, superficially, and projectively. Tim appeared ready to idealize the present therapist as a shaman who would exorcize Jack's ghost and diminish Jack as a person with the power to hurt him.

Tim watched the therapist intently. If he talked about his problems to an extent that might be embarrassing, he would then switch to another version of the story that put him in a better light. In telling of his relationship with Jack, Tim spoke alternately of caring and not caring, as if trying to move from a blameworthy to a praiseworthy position. The danger of an uncaring and strong self-concept was that he would in that model of self be to blame for hurting or using others. The danger in caring was the associated sense of weakness and personal vulnerability. The therapist did not comment on these shifting self-concepts. He concentrated instead on trying to develop a shared model of the sequence of events and a therapeutic alliance in which his role would be defined as giving neither blame nor praise but, rather, clarification of what had happened and was happening now.

Later during the first hour, the therapist was surprised by Tim's expression of intense anger toward Carol, the gestalt therapist, and others in general. In essence, Tim regarded Jack's death and its aftermath as an imposition on him, which had weakened him by depleting his energies. This imposition was personified by others who made demands on him or did not contribute to his well-being. He was especially intense in his anger with Carol, who he felt was trying to "milk Jack's death for all it was worth" and to "move in on him" in doing so. He minimized all of his own questionable attitudes and displayed Carol in a bad light.

SECOND SESSION

The second hour can be summarized as one of transference testing. Tim reported feeling much better. His phobia of the dark had improved, and he could sleep with fewer lights on in the house. This was followed by a eulogy about Jack's good qualities. He then attempted to engage the therapist in sweeping theoretical reviews of his current life problems and to communicate a nonspecific readiness for an "in-depth" approach. His wish to please the therapist was clearly apparent but, because of his vulnerability to shame, was not interpreted. Instead the therapist diligently leaned toward a continued reconstruction of the stress event, Tim's state before it happened, and the sequence of subsequent events. His benevolent nonreaction to the patient's provocations for expressions of closeness seemed to be reassuring. Tim then went on to review his life history, commenting on various patterns and meanings himself.

THIRD SESSION

In the third hour Tim seemed to be dejected and closer to the therapist, and again solicited sympathy. He described general feelings of fear and helplessness and gradually related these to an identification with Jack. The next associations led to Tim's first discussion of his father, who had died of cancer some years previously, and from whom Tim had inherited some money. His mother had tried to get closer to him and also felt that she should have a greater portion of the money from the father's will. His feelings that his mother was "trying to suck him in and being selfish" the therapist linked to Tim's reactions to Carol as trying to suck him in after Jack's death.

FOURTH SESSION

During the fourth hour Tim was more defensive than he had been throughout the first three hours, and he seemed aloof. He talked earnestly and somewhat glibly about his conflicted attitudes toward women. He enjoyed fantasies replete with sadistic but harmless play. But in his actual relationships with women, he tended to be so submissive that he felt they soon lost interest in him. There was a certain exhibitionistic quality about his stories of sexual relationships, as if he were saying pointedly that he was heterosexual rather than homosexual. The therapist accepted these demonstrations at face value and did not interpret them. Rather, he worked to maintain a steady and nondirective interest in Tim in order to stabilize his self-esteem.

FIFTH SESSION

A few weeks had now passed since Jack committed suicide. Carol called to invite Tim to join several friends at the site of the death, where they would have a final farewell ceremony for Jack. But Tim was determined not to go and tried to make other plans for that day, of a concrete and defiantly pleasurable nature. In this, the fifth hour, Tim spoke with some pressure of how he wanted to avoid thinking of Jack because it "would drive him crazy." The therapist sensed that it was necessary to ask him, indirectly and gently, what this meant. Tim, with embarrassment bordering on a sense of deep humiliation, reported that although he had said he was feeling better, he had still been having recurrent intrusive images of Jack. Though he could not describe this quite as directly as it is stated here, he had not talked about these intrusions because he was afraid the therapist would not be interested or would withdraw from him because he had not improved rapidly enough.

In the intrusive images Tim saw Jack, still alive and bleeding from his wound, having second thoughts and crying out for help. The therapist quietly said, "Jack felt alone." Tim then related "alone" to himself and talked of his own suicidal ruminations and his identification with Jack. He then worked on the association to himself of "having second thoughts." He had second thoughts that he ought to have been more willing to reestablish his closeness to Jack and thereby prevent Jack's need for such a desperate escape from loneliness. This line of thought was repeated throughout subsequent therapy sessions, and as Tim reviewed his acts and decisions, he confirmed for himself that though he did feel guilty, he was not responsible for rescuing either Jack or Carol.

As he returned to the idea of suicide and whether or not persons should be rescued, Tim revealed for the first time that his father had contemplated suicide and had himself entered therapy with a psychiatrist. Tim had felt then the way he had felt with Jack, that he should give more affection to his father but did not want to drain himself. He used the treatment as an excuse; he did not have to get close to his father because it might interfere, in some nebulous way, with the therapeutic process. His father had, at this time, tried to get closer to Tim, but in a needy rather than paternal way. This abortive effort at intimacy or, as Tim experienced it, at using him, had been repeated after the diagnosis of cancer.

In more normal times, the father had treated Tim imperiously. A successful businessman, he regarded Tim as an appendage rather than a successor whom he might groom to take on adult work. Tim thus had been placed in a need-fear dilemma. He felt dependent on his father and lonely without his love, but whenever he got close to him, he felt used.

SIXTH SESSION

At the sixth session, Tim reported that he was depressed. After the last hour he had felt like talking with his mother. In a long telephone conversation with her, he had had both positive and negative feelings.

His mother seemed to make herself more available to him and to want more contact, but he was uneasy about becoming closer to her and being used. The similarity of his images of his mother and Carol and his fears of being ''sucked in'' were worked on. Although he feared being used, he also had bad self-images when he backed off from people. He then spoke of also feeling badly when he approached the women. He felt as if he were too strong, inappropriately taking over his father's or Jack's woman. The emotions of these ''strong'' images were isolated; he did not feel virile and competitive, only vaguely disturbed over issues of right and wrong. Avoidance of the imagined blame in the therapist's eyes seemed to Tim to be an important motive for how the information about these meanings was processed. For example, he readily changed the designation of attributes, sometimes labeling the one in need as himself and other times as Carol. The therapist's interventions were to clarify gradually who had any given attribute in a specific interchange.

Tim became uncomfortable talking of his mother and Carol and, as an avoidance, began to discuss sports. He described his enthusiasm and vitality while playing ball. He imagined that the therapist was ''a fellow jock'' who empathized with this and felt warm and close. The therapist asked if this reminded him of anyone. He then spoke of how he and his father had played ball and of how it was the only time of sharing between them. He cried and spoke of continuing with sports as some kind of celebration of his father's memory.

SEVENTH SESSION

The following hour was characterized initially by flat affect. Tim talked vaguely of current work and dating problems. The therapist commented that he ''seemed to have more difficulty getting started this hour'' and asked in a kindly way if they might reflect on it together to see why this might be. With hesitation, Tim reported that he was having ''difficulty thinking about his father.'' This acquisition of the therapist's work usage (difficulty) was noteworthy. The implicit shield of certification seemed to enable him to contemplate warded-off ideas without feeling like a bad person for having them.

He went on to say that he had been stopping himself from thinking about his father when he was alone. As he spoke, Tim checked the therapist with penetrating glances to see whether he felt that such avoidance of therapeutically endorsed topics was blameworthy. When he seemed reassured that the therapist was not angry with him, he expressed anger with his father. He questioned the need to let himself feel sad; his father did not deserve his positive and sad feelings because he had given Tim so little during his life. Tim should be selfish too, a person who needs no one. The same held true for Jack. Tim was angry that he had been made to feel as though he ought to be a rescuer. He did not know how to be of help to anyone else and did not want to be expected to try.

REMAINING SESSIONS

In the nine ensuing hours, Tim and his therapist worked through his fear of being "sucked in," his anger, and his fear of retaliation for neglecting Jack. A mourning process had been initiated, a process with certain narcissistic qualities. As part of this process they worked on his feelings toward his father and his father's death, as well as on the symbolic connections between his father and Jack and between Carol and his mother. The process in relation to his father can be summarized as follows.

DISCUSSION

During Tim's mourning process, the threat of injury to his self-concept was prominent in the themes that were warded off and in the transference attitudes that were activated by approaching these themes. Rage at neglect was the central theme, and it had to be viewed in terms of self-experience as both the neglected person and the person to blame for the neglect. Tim placed himself in both roles in relation to Jack and his father.

When Tim saw his father as healthy and powerful and when he saw Jack as the masterful leader, he felt anger at their lack of interest in him. When he saw his father and Jack as in need, Tim felt withdrawn and even found them repugnantly weak. He then feared that they would in turn be angry with him. If he were to give of himself, he feared that he would be drained, lose independence, and be doomed to serve the identity of another. By dying, his father and Jack seemed to confirm to Tim that he was at fault.

His problem was warding off this blame. He expected the rage of others in the form of either angry demands on him or revenge for neglect. This fearful expectancy was represented in the intrusive images of Jack who had, symbolically, come back to haunt, assault, or trade places with him.

As Tim recalled and related memories of being with his father during his terminal illness, he realized that he felt badly that he had not been more giving to his father, just as he regretted not being more supportive of Jack. But this awareness emerged in stages. He softened the potential injury to his self-esteem by first presenting material about how others were to be blamed. By implication he was then not to blame, or not completely to blame. For example, he explained to the therapist that the reason he had not told his dying father that he loved him was because his mother had told him not to do so. Her rationale was that if he told his father that he loved him, it would be an unusual event, and so his father would then realize that he must be terminally ill.

As he spoke of his regret for not telling his father of his feelings, he expressed rage at his mother. He pointed out to the therapist that she was also to blame for making his father uncomfortable when, because she was worried about money, she would not provide luxuries for the hospital room. Only when he was further along in the working-through process could he acknowledge that as a person in his late twenties, he was independent enough to decide for himself what to say or to do for his father and that his holding back was related to his own discomfort with his closeness to his father and his fear of his father's illness.

As Tim dealt with the issues of himself as self-centered and related this to his mother's and father's selfishness, he experienced the therapist in such roles. He felt that the therapist would be critical and angry with him for neglecting the therapy and at times tested the therapist for this countertransference potential.

At the height of this tranference, Tim usually regarded the therapist's interpretations as reprimands rather than insights. He would feel more aloof from the therapist when he thought the therapist was enthralled with the theory that Tim's reaction to Jack's death was connected with his reaction to his father's death. Tim could then disavow that such feelings were his own, by believing that he was manipulating the therapist as he continued the theme only in order to make the therapist happy. If he did not feel praised for such continuation, then he would feel that the therapist was angry with him. During this period, he felt that he and the therapist were each, in some way, neglecting the other. Rage would be vaguely in the air, never fully attached to either person.

It was necessary for the therapist to avoid direct interpretation of the externalization of blame during the period when Tim's defense to preserve his self-esteem was paramount. A premature comment that Tim blamed his mother for what he blamed in himself would have been taken as a slur, as Tim was not yet ready to tolerate the experience of bad attributes in himself. He first had to contemplate the idea of blame for neglect at a distance, to see whether it was safe. Then, gradually the attribution could move from others to himself.

Although the therapist avoided overly direct interpretations, he did encourage this working-through process. For example, when Tim talked about not saying that he loved his father, the therapist helped clarify which persons communicated what ideas, what his mother said about not telling his father, what Tim felt like saying but did not say, what he said to his mother, what he said to his father, and so on.

With such work Tim made contradictory statements. When he felt too badly about not expressing affection, he said that he had shown his father that he cared. But when he felt less threatened, he said that he had not expressed himself to his father. A tactful approach meant avoiding confronting Tim with contradictions but, rather, encouraging a gradual movement along a train of thought that he had been inhibiting and distorting.

SUMMARY

With this rudimentary outline of some themes, it is possible to put them into a sequence of thought. This omits some psychodynamic themes, including oedipal competitions, separation anxiety and object loss, and fears of homosexual love, but it conveys the quality of working through a given cycle of ideational and emotional responses. Some of the principal concurrent defensive operations are indicated below in parentheses.

- My father (and Jack) is a powerful man. He does not do enough for me; I like him but I hate him for that.
- I would like to be powerful like father (and Jack); then I would not need him.
- I will model myself after him while watching out for the danger of being used by him or being sucked in by him.
- He (father, Jack) is not omnipotent; he can feel pain, weakness, and death.
- I must move further away from him (father, Jack) to avoid contamina-

tion with death or extreme need. I am afraid it is too late; the same thing may happen to me.

- By moving further away, I did not save him (father, Jack) or even help him during his suffering.
- Jack, like my father, will be enraged and get back at me.
- These images and my feeling that he is present are either evidence he is out to get me or show I am weak and going crazy.
- But I am not to blame. I refuse to believe I should have done more. People are wrong to expect anything of me. I refuse to think any more about this (denial, suppression, disavowal).
- It is not true that I moved away from Jack or my father (slides meanings to alter the story).
- Even if it is true, then others did it too, more than me. They are to blame (externalization).
- Even though others moved away and bear their responsibility, I am responsible that I moved away from him (father, Jack).
- Although I did not do all that I might have, I am still not a terrible person. My neglect did not directly kill them.
- I miss my father and am sad that it was not better between us.
- I am sorry that he (father, Jack) died; I wish I had done more. But even though I did not do as much as I would have liked, it is not true that they are now enraged at me.
- Even though it is true that I felt an inner rage that my father did not do more for me, that rage did not kill him (or Jack). So I do not have to bear total responsibility for his death (father, Jack).

As indicated by the later items in this condensed ideational line, Tim began to grieve not only for the father he had lost but also for an ideal father he had never had. As one example of this mourning process, he had a kind of restitutional fantasy in which he was a surgeon operating on his father and saving his life. This fantasy condensed many feelings: his anger (cutting open his father), his rescue wishes (saving him), his need to be strong and admirable (the brilliant surgeon), and his need to be omnipotent against death.

Tim's symptoms were relieved. With the cessation of intrusive images of Jack entering or being present in his apartment, he was able to go to bed with the lights off and to sleep through the night. His anxiety attacks stopped, and he felt confident that he had worked through the stress event. He had shown a readiness to deal with his character problems and a wish to advance from his less-than-optimal prestress level of ego development. For these reasons, long-term psychoanalytic psychotherapy was recommended after termination of the brief therapy.

References

Abraham, K. (1942). A short study of the development of the libido, viewed in the light of mental disorders. In K. Abraham, *Selected Papers*, pp. 418–501. London: Hogarth Press.

Adler, A. (1916). *The Neurotic Constitution: Outline of a Comparative Individualistic Psychology and Psychotherapy.* Trans. B. Gluck and J. Lind. New York: Moffat Yard.

Agras, S. (1974). Behavior therapy of stress response syndromes. Talk given at the symposium *Stress: Psychotherapy of Stress Response Syndromes*, June 1, 1974, University of California, San Francisco.

Aldrich, C. K. (1974). Some dynamics of anticipatory grief. In B. Schoenberg et al., eds., *Anticipatory Grief*. New York: Columbia University Press.

Antrobus, J. S., Singer, J. L., and Greenberg, S. (1966). Studies in the stream of consciousness: Experimental enhancement and suppression of spontaneous cognitive processes. *Perceptual and Motor Skills* 23:399–417.

Archibald, H. C., Long, D. M., Miller, C., and Tuddenham, R. D. (1962). Gross stress reaction in combat—A 15-year follow-up. *American Journal of Psychiatry* 119:317–322.

Archibald, H. C., and Tuddenham, R. D. (1965). Persistent stress reaction after combat. *Archives of General Psychiatry* 12:475–481.

Axelrod, J., and Reisine, T. D. (1984). Stress hormones: Their interaction and regulation. *Science* 224:452–459.

Baker, G. W., and Chapman, D. W. (1962). *Man and Society in Disaster*. New York: Basic Books.

Barnett, J. (1972). Therapeutic intervention in the dysfunctional thought processes of the obsessional. *American Journal of Psychotherapy* 26:338–351.

Barr, H. L., et al. (1972). *LSD: Personalities and Experience*. New York: John Wiley.

Bartheimer, C., et al. (1946). Combat exhaustion. *Journal of Nervous and Mental Disease* 104:359–525.

Basch, M. (1980). *Doing Psychotherapy*. New York: Basic Books.

Beck, A. T. (1976). *Cognitive Therapy and Emotional Disorders*. New York: International Universities Press.

———. (1985). *Cognitive Therapy of the Anxiety Disorders*. New York: Basic Books.

Becker, S. S., Horowitz, M. J., and Campbell, L. (1973). Cognitive response to stress: Effects of demand and sex. *Journal of Abnormal Psychology* 82: 519–522.

Berliner, B. (1941). Short psychoanalytic psychotherapy: Its possibilities and its limitations. *Bulletin of the Menninger Clinic* 5:204–213.

Bibring, E. (1943). The conception of the repetition compulsion. *Psychoanalytic Quarterly* 12:486–519.

Bilodeau, C. B., and Hackett, T. P. (1971). Issues raised in a group setting by patients recovering from myocardial infarction. *American Journal of Psychiatry* 128:73–78.

Bion, W. (1940). The "war of nerves": Civilian reaction, morale and prophylaxis. In E. Miller, ed., *The Neuroses in War*, pp. 180–200. New York: Macmillan.

Boehnlein, J. K., Kinzie, J. D., Ben, R., and Fleck, J. (1985). One year followup study of post traumatic stress disorder among survivors of Cambodian concentration camps. *American Journal of Psychiatry* 142:956–959.

Bourne, P. (1970). *Men, Stress and Vietnam*. Boston: Little, Brown.

Bourne, S., and Lewis, E. (1984). Pregnancy after stillbirth or neonatal death: Psychological risks and management. *Lancet* 2:31–33.

Bowlby, J. (1961). Process of mourning. *International Journal of Psycho-Analysis* 42:317–340.

———. (1969). *Attachment and Loss*. Vol. 1. New York: Basic Books.

———. (1980). *Attachment and Loss* Vol. 3: *Loss: Sadness and Depression*. New York: Basic Books.

———, and Parkes, C. M. (1970). Separation and loss. In E. Anthony and C. Koupernik, eds., *International Yearbook for Child Psychiatry and Allied Dis-*

ciplines. Vol. 1: *The Child in His Family*, pp. 197-217. New York: John Wiley.

Breger, L. (1967). Function of dreams. *Journal of Abnormal Psychology Monographs* 72(5), Whole No. 641.

———, Hunter, I., and Lane, R. (1971). Effect of stress on dreams. *Psychological Issues* 73:1-213.

———, and McGaugh, J. C. (1965). Critique of reformulation of "learning theory" approaches to psychotherapy and neurosis. *Psychological Bulletin* 63:338-358.

Brett, E. A., and Ostroff, R. (1985). Imagery and posttraumatic stress disorder: An overview. *American Journal of Psychiatry* 142:4, 417-424.

Breuer, J., and Freud, S. (1895). Studies on hysteria. *Standard Edition* 2:1-17. London: Hogarth Press, 1954.

Brill, N. Q. (1967). Gross stress reactions II: Traumatic war neuroses. In A. M. Freedman and H. J. Kaplan, eds., *Comprehensive Textbook of Psychiatry*, pp. 1031-1035. Baltimore: Williams and Wilkens.

———, and Beebe, G. W. (1955). A follow-up study of war neuroses. Veteran's Administration Medical monograph. Washington, D.C.: U.S. Government Printing Office

Broadbent, D. E. (1971). *Decision and Stress*. London: Academic Press.

Brown, B. M. (1969). Cognitive aspects of Wolpe's behavior therapy. *American Journal of Psychotherapy* 124:854-859.

Burgess, A. W., and Holstrom, L. (1974). Rape trauma syndrome. *American Journal of Psychiatry* 131:981-986.

———. (1976). Coping behavior of the rape victim. *American Journal of Psychiatry* 133:413-418.

Caplan, G. (1961). *An Approach to Community Mental Health*. New York: Grune & Stratton.

———. (1964). *Principles of Preventive Psychiatry*. New York: Basic Books.

Cartwright, R. D., Bernick, N., Borowitz, G., and Kling, A. (1969). Effect of an erotic movie on the sleep and dreams of young men. *Archives of General Psychiatry* 20:262-271.

Chodoff, P. (1970). German concentration camp as psychological stress. *Archives of General Psychiatry* 22:78-87.

Christianson, S., and Nilsson, L. (in press). Functional amnesia as induced by a psychological trauma. *Memory and Cognition*.

Cobb, S., and Lindemann, E. (1943). Neuropsychiatric observation after the Coconut Grove fire. *Annals of Surgery* 117:814-824.

Coelho, G. V., Hamburg, D. A., and Adams, J. E., eds. (1974). *Coping and Adaptation*. New York: Basic Books.

Cohen, F., and Lazarus, R. (1973). Active coping processes, coping dispositions, and recovery from surgery. *Psychosomatic Medicine* 35:375-389.

Cohen, J. (1979). *Power Analyses for the Social and Behavioral Sciences*. New York: Academic Press.

Dahl, H. (1977). Considerations for a theory of emotions. Introduction to J. DeRivera, A structual theory of emotions. *Psychological Issues* 10:1–8.

Danieli, Y. (1982). Families of survivors of the Nazi holocaust: Some short and long term effects. In C. Spielberger, N. Sarason, and N. Milgram, eds., *Stress and Anxiety*, vol. 8, pp. 405–423. New York: Hemisphere Publishing.

Davis, D. (1966). An Introduction to Psychopathology. London: Oxford University Press.

De Fazio, V. J. (1975). Vietnam era veteran: Psychological problems. *Journal of Contemporary Psychotherapy* 7:9–15.

De La Torre, J. (1972). The therapist tells a story: A technique in brief psychotherapy. *Bulletin of the Menninger Clinic* 36:609–616.

Derogatis, L. R., Rickels, K., and Rock, A. F. (1976). The SCL-90 and the MMPI: A step in the validation of a new self report scale. *British Journal of Psychiatry* 128:280–289.

Deutsch, F. (1949). *Applied Psychoanalysis.* New York: Grune & Stratton.

DeWitt, K., Kaltreider, N., Weiss, D., and Horowitz, M. (1983). Judging change in psychotherapy: The reliability of clinical formulations. *Archives of General Psychiatry* 40:1121–1128.

Diagnostic and Statistical Manual of Mental Disorders 3rd ed. (1980). Washington, D.C.: American Psychiatric Association.

Dimsdale, J., and Hackett, T. (1982). Effect of denial on cardiac health and psychological assessment. *American Journal of Psychiatry* 139:1477–1480.

Easser, R. R., and Lesser, S. R. (1965). Hysterical personality: A re-evaluation. *Psychoanalytic Quarterly* 34:390–405.

Eaton, W. W., Sigal, J. J., and Weinfeld, M. (1982). Impairment in Holocaust survivors after 33 years: Data from an unbiased community sample. *American Journal of Psychiatry* 139:773–777.

Egendorf, A., Kadushin, C., Laufer, R., Rothbart, S., and Swan, L. (1981). Legacies of Vietnam: Comparative adjustment of veterans and their peers. Washington, D.C.: U.S. Government Printing Office.

Eisenbruch, M. (1984). Cross-cultural aspects of bereavement. I: A conceptual framework for comparative analysis. *Culture, Medicine and Psychiatry* 8: 283–309.

Eitinger, L. (1969). Psychosomatic problems in concentration camp survivors. *Journal of Psychosomatic Research* 13:183–189.

Ellis, A. (1973). *Humanistic Psychotherapy: The Rational-Emotive Approach.* New York: McGraw-Hill.

Engel, G. L., and Schmale, A. (1967). Psychoanalytic theory of somatic disorder: Conversion specificity and disease onset situation. *Journal of the American Psychoanalytic Association* 15:344–365.

Erickson, K. (1976). Loss of communality at Buffalo Creek. *American Journal of Psychiatry* 133:302–305.

Fairbairn, W. R. (1952). *War Neuroses: Their nature and significance.* Boston: Rutledge, Regents, Paul.

———. (1954). *An Object-Relations Theory of the Personality.* New York: Basic Books.

Feather, B. W., and Rhoads, J. M. (1972). Psychodynamic Behavior Therapy: I. Theory and rationale; II. Clinical aspects. *Archives of General Psychiatry* 26:496–511.

Fenichel, O. (1945). *The Psychoanalytic Theory of Neurosis.* New York: W. W. Norton.

———. (1954). The concept of trauma. In *The Collected Papers of Otto Fenichel,* Vol. 2, pp. 49–69. New York: W. W. Norton.

Ferenczi, S. (1926). *Further Contributions to the Theory and Technique of Psychoanalysis.* London: Hogarth Press and Institute of Psychoanalysis, 1950.

Festinger, L. (1957). *A Theory of Cognitive Dissonance.* New York: Row, Peterson.

Figley, C. R., ed. (1978). *Stress Disorders among Vietnam Veterans: Theory, Research and Treatment.* New York: Brunner/Mazel.

———. (1984). Trauma and Its Wake. New York: Brunner/Mazel.

Figley, C. R., and Leventman, S., eds. (1982). *Strangers at Home: Vietnam Veterans since the War.* New York: Praeger.

Finn, J. D. (1972). *Multivariance: Univariate and Multivariate Analysis of Variance, Covariance, and Regression.* Ann Arbor, Mich.: National Education Resources.

Fischer, R. (1971). A cartography of the ecstatic and meditative states: The experimental and experiential features of a perception-hallucination continuum are considered. *Science* 174:897–905.

French, T. (1952). *The Integration of Behavior,* Vol. 1: *Basic Postulates.* Chicago: University of Chicago Press.

Freud, A. (1936). *The Ego and the Mechanisms of Defense.* New York: International Universities Press.

Freud, S. (1893). On the psychical mechanism of hysterical phenomena. *Standard Edition* 3:24–41. London: Hogarth Press, 1962.

———. (1899). Screen memories. *Standard Edition* 3:302–322. London: Hogarth Press, 1962.

———. (1909). Notes upon a case of obsessional neurosis. *Standard Edition* 10:155–318. London: Hogarth Press, 1955.

———. (1914a). On narcissism: An introduction. *Standard Edition* 14:69–102. London: Hogarth Press, 1957.

———. (1914b). Remembering, repeating and working through. *Standard Edition* 12:145–150. London: Hogarth Press, 1958.

———. (1920). Beyond the pleasure principle. *Standard Edition* 18:1–68. London: Hogarth Press, 1962.

———. (1926). Inhibitions, symptoms and anxiety. *Standard Edition* 20:77–175. London: Hogarth Press, 1959.

———. (1937). Constructions in analysis. *Standard Edition* 25:255–269. London: Hogarth Press, 1964.

Friedman, O., and Linn, W. (1957). Some psychiatric notes on the *Andrea Doria*. *American Journal of Psychiatry* 114:426–432.

Furst, S. S. (1967). Psychic trauma: A survey. In S. S. Furst, *Psychic Trauma*, pp. 3–50. New York: Basic Books.

Gifford, S. (1964). Repetition compulsion. *Journal of the American Psychoanalytic Association* 12:632–649.

Glass, A. (1953). Problem of stress in the combat zone. *Symposium on Stress*, pp. 90–102. Washington, D.C.: National Research Council and Walter Reed Army Medical Center.

———. (1954). Psychotherapy in the combat zone. *American Journal of Psychiatry* 110:725–731.

Glick, I., Parkes, C., and Weiss, R. (1975). *The First Year of Bereavement*. New York: Basic Books.

Glover, E. (1929). The "screening" function of traumatic memories. *International Journal of Psycho-Analysis* 10:90–93.

———. (1931). The therapeutic effect of inexact interpretation: A contribution to the theory of suggestion. *International Journal of Psycho-Analysis* 19:457–459.

Goldberg, A. (1973). Psychotherapy of narcissistic injuries. *Archives of General Psychiatry* 28:722–727.

———, ed. (1978). *The Psychology of the Self*. New York: International Universities Press.

———, ed. (1980). *Advances in Self Psychology*. New York: International Universities Press.

Goldstein, M. J., Alexander, F. G., Clemens, T. L., Flagg, G. W., and Jones, R. B. (1965). Coping style as a factor in psychophysiological response to a tension arousing film. *Journal of Personality & Social Psychology* 1:290–302.

Gorer, G. (1965). *Death, Grief, and Mourners in Contemporary Britain*. New York: Doubleday.

Grayson, H. (1970). Grief reactions to the relinquishing of unfulfilled wishes. *American Journal of Psychotherapy* 24:287–295.

Green, B. (1982). Assessing levels of psychological impairment following disasters. *Journal of Nervous and Mental Disease* 170:544–552.

Green, B. L., Grace, M. C., Glesser, G. C. (in press). Identifying survivors at risk: long-term impairment following the Beverly Hills Supper Club fire. *The Journal of Consulting and Clinical Psychology*.

———, Wilson, J. P., and Lindy, J. D. (1985). Conceptualizing posttraumatic stress disorder: a psychosocial framework. In Figley, C. R. (Ed.) *Trauma and its Wake: The Study and Treatment of Post-traumatic Stress Disorder*, pp. 53–69. New York: Brunner/Mazel.

Greenacre, P. (1949). A contribution to the study of screen memories. *Psychoanalytic Study of the Child* 3–4:78–84.

———. (1952). *Trauma, Growth, and Personality*. New York: W. W. Norton.

Grinker, K., and Spiegel, S. (1945). *Men under Stress*. Philadelphia: Blakeston.

Haan, N. (1977). *Coping and Defending*. New York: Academic Press.

Hackett, T., and Cassem, N. (1970). Psychological reactions to life threatening illness. In H. Abram, ed., *Psychological Aspects of Stress*. Springfield, Ill.: Chas. C Thomas.

Haley, S. A. (1974). When the patient reports atrocities. *Archives of General Psychiatry* 30:191–196.

Hamburg, D., and Adams, J. E. (1967). A perspective in coping behavior, seeking and utilizing information in major transitions. *Archives of General Psychiatry* 17:277–284.

Hartman, E. (1967). *The Biology of Dreaming*. Springfield, Ill.: Chas. C Thomas.

Hartmann, H. (1939). *Ego Psychology and the Problem of Adaptation*. New York: International Universities Press.

_____. (1964). *Essays on Ego Psychology*. New York: International Universities Press.

Hendin, H., and Haas, A. P. (1984). *Wounds of War*. New York: Basic Books.

_____, Haas, A. P., Singer, P., Gold, F., and Trigos, G. G. (1983). The influence of precombat personality on post-traumatic stress disorder. *Comprehensive Psychiatry* 24:530–534.

Higbee, K. L. (1969). Fifteen years of fear arousal: Research on threat appeals: 1953–1969. *Psychological Bulletin* 72:426–444.

Hilberman, E. (1976). *The Rape Victim*. Washington, D.C.: American Psychiatric Association.

Hinsie, L. E., and Campbell, R. J. (1960). *Psychiatric Dictionary*, 3rd. ed. New York: Oxford University Press.

Hoch, P. (1943). Etiology and pathology of traumatic war neuroses. Paper presented to USPHS conference on war neurosis.

Hocking, F. (1970). Extreme environmental stress and its significance for psychopathology. *American Journal of Psychotherapy* 24:4–26.

Horowitz, Milton. (1963). A historical review of the concept of the repetition compulsion. Paper presented at the fall meeting of the American Psychoanalytic Association, New York.

Horowitz, M. J. (1969). Psychic trauma: Return of images after a stressful film. *Archives of General Psychiatry* 20:552–559.

_____. (1970). *Image Formation and Cognition*. New York: Appleton-Century-Crofts.

_____. (1973). Phase oriented treatment of stress response syndromes. *American Journal of Psychotherapy* 27:606–615.

_____. (1974a). Microanalysis of working through in psychotherapy. *American Journal of Psychiatry* 131:1208–1212.

_____. (1974b). Stress response syndromes: Character style and brief psychotherapy. *Archives of General Psychiatry* 31:768–781.

_____. (1975a). Intrusive and repetitive thoughts after experimental stress: A summary. *Archives of General Psychiatry* 32:1457–1463.

_____. (1975b). Sliding meanings: A defense against threat in narcissistic personalities. *International Journal of Psychoanalytic Psychotherapy* 4:167–180.

_____. (1976). *Stress Response Syndromes*. New York: Jason Aronson.

_____, ed. (1977a). *Hysterical Personality*. New York: Jason Aronson.

_____. (1977b). Hysterical personality: Cognitive structure and the process of change. *International Review of Psycho-Analysis* 4:23–49.

_____. (1979). *States of Mind*. New York: Plenum.

_____. (1981). Self righteous rage and the attribution of blame. *Archives of General Psychiatry* 38:1233–1238.

_____. (1983). Post-traumatic stress disorders. *Behavioral Sciences and the Law* 1:9–23.

_____. (in press). Stress, post-traumatic and adjustment. In J. Cavenar et al., eds., *Textbook of Psychiatry*. Philadelphia: Lippincott.

_____, and Becker, S. S. (1971a). Cognitive response to stress and experimental demand. *Journal of Abnormal Psychology* 78:86–92.

_____, and Becker, S. S. (1971b). Cognitive response to stressful stimuli. *Archives of General Psychiatry* 25:419–428.

_____, and Becker, S. S. (1971c). The compulsion to repeat trauma: Experimental study of intrusive thinking after stress. *Journal of Nervous and Mental Disease* 153:32–34.

_____, and Becker, S. S. (1973). Cognitive response to erotic and stressful films. *Archives of General Psychiatry* 29:81–84.

_____, Becker, S. S., and Moskowitz, M. L. (1971). Intrusive and repetitive thought after stress: A replication study. *Psychological Reports* 29:763–767.

_____, Becker, S. S., Moskowitz, M. L., and Rashid, K. (1972). Intrusive thinking in psychiatric patients after stress. *Psychological Reports* 31:235–238.

_____, and Kaltreider, N. (1979). Brief therapy of stress response syndromes. *Psychiatric Clinics of North America* 2:365–378.

_____, Krupnick, J., Kaltreider, N., Wilner, N., Leong, A., and Marmar, C. (1981). Initial psychological response to parental death. *Archives of General Psychiatry* 38:316–323.

_____, Marmar, C., Krupnick, J., Wilner, N., Kaltreider, N., and Wallerstein, R. (1984). *Personality Styles and Brief Psychotherapy*. New York: Basic Books.

_____, Marmar, C., Weiss, D., DeWitt, K., and Rosenbaum, R. (1984). Brief psychotherapy of bereavement reactions. *Archives of General Psychiatry* 41: 438–448.

_____, Schaefer, C., Hiroto, D., Wilner, N., and Levin, B. (1977). Life event questionnaires for measuring presumptive stress. *Psychosomatic Medicine* 39:413–431.

_____, Simon, N., Holden, M., Connett, J., Borhani, N., Benfari, R., and Billings, J. (1983). The stressful impact of news of premature heart disease. *Psychosomatic Medicine* 45:31–40.

_____, and Solomon, G. F. (1975). A prediction of stress response syndromes in Vietnam veterans: Observations and suggestions for treatment. *Journal of Social Issues* 31(4):67–80.

———, and Solomon, G. (1978). A prediction of stress response syndromes in Vietnam veterans. In C. F. Figley, ed., *Stress Disorders among Vietnam Veterans*, pp. 67–80. New York: Brunner/Mazel.

———, Weiss, D., Kaltreider, N., Krupnick, J., Marmar, C., Wilner, N., and DeWitt, K. (1984). Reactions to death of a parent: Results from patients and field subjects. *Journal of Nervous and Mental Disease* 172:383–392.

———, and Wilner, N. (1976). Stress films, emotions and cognitive response. *Archives of General Psychiatry* 30:1339–1344.

———, Wilner, N., and Alvarez, W. (1979). Impact of Event Scale: A study of subjective stress. *Psychosomatic Medicine* 41(3):209–218.

———, Wilner, N., Kaltreider, N., and Alvarez, W. (1980). Signs and symptoms of post traumatic stress disorders. *Archives of General Psychiatry* 37: 85–92.

———, Wilner, N., Marmar, C., and Krupnick, J. (1980). Pathological grief and the activation of latent self images. *American Journal of Psychiatry* 137: 1157–1162.

———, and Zilberg, N. (1983). Regressive alterations in the self concept. *American Journal of Psychiatry* 140(3):284–289.

Hoyt, M. (1980). Therapist and patient actions in "good" psychotherapy sessions. *Archives of General Psychiatry* 37:159–161.

———, Marmar, C., Horowitz, M. J. et al. (1981). The Therapist Action Scale and the Patient Action Scale: Instruments for the assessment of activities during dynamic psychotherapy. *Psychotherapy: Theory, Research, and Practice* 18:109–116.

Jacobson, G. F. (1974). The Crisis Interview. Paper presented to the symposium *Comparative Psychotherapies*, University of Southern California School of Medicine, Department of Psychiatry, Division of Continuing Education, San Diego, June 24–28.

Janet, P. (1907). *The Major Symptoms of Hysteria*. New York: Hafner, 1965.

Janis, I. L. (1958). *Psychological Stress: Psychoanalytic and Behavioral Studies of Surgical Patients*. New York: John Wiley.

———. (1962). Psychological effects of warnings. In C. W. Baker and D. W. Chapman, eds., *Man and Society in Disaster*, pp. 55–92. New York: Basic Books.

———. (1967). Effects of fear arousal on attitude change: Recent development in theory and experimental research. In L. Berkowitz, ed., *Advances in Experimental Social Psychology*, Vol. 3, pp. 166–224. New York: Academic Press.

———. (1969). *Stress and Frustration*. New York: Harcourt Brace Jovanovich.

———, and Leventhal, H. (1968). Human reactions to stress. In E. F. Bergatta and W. W. Lambert, eds., *Handbook of Personality Theory and Research*, pp. 1041–1085. Chicago: Rand McNally.

———, and Mann, J. (1977). *Decision Making*. New York: Free Press.

Johnson, J. E., Leventhal, H., and Dabbs, J. M. (1971). Contribution of emotional and instrumental response processes in adaptation to surgery. *Journal of Personality and Social Psychology* 20:55–64.

Jones, D. R. (1985). Secondary disaster victims: Emotional effects of recovering and identifying remains. *American Journal of Psychiatry* 142:303–308.

Jones, E. (1929). Fear, guilt, and hate. *International Journal of Psycho-Analysis* 10:383–397.

_____. (1953). *The Life and Work of Sigmund Freud*, Vol. 1. New York: Basic Books.

Kaltreider, N., Becker, T., and Horowitz, M. J. (1984). Relationship testing after parental bereavement. *American Journal of Psychiatry* 141:243–246.

_____, DeWitt, K., Weiss, D., and Horowitz, M. J. (1981). Pattern of individual change scales. *Archives of General Psychiatry* 38:1263–1269.

_____, and Mendelson, S. (1985). Clinical evaluation of grief after parental death. *Psychotherapy: Theory, Research and Practice* 22:224–230.

_____, Wallace, A., and Horowitz, M. J. (1979). A field study of the stress response syndrome: Young women after hysterectomies. *Journal of American Medical Association* 242:1499–1503.

Kandel, E. (1983). From metapsychology to molecular biology: Explorations into the nature of anxiety. *American Journal of Psychiatry* 140:1277–1293.

Kaplan, D., Grobstein, R., and Smith, A. (1976). Predicting the impact of severe illness in families. *Health and Social Work* 1:71–82.

Kardiner, A. (1959). Traumatic neuroses of war. In S. Arieti, ed., *American Handbook of Psychiatry*, Vol. II, pp. 245–258. New York: Basic Books.

_____, and Spiegel, H. (1947). *War, Stress and Neurotic Illness*. New York: P. Hoeber.

Keiser, L. (1968). *The Traumatic Neuroses*. Philadelphia: Lippincott.

_____. (1969). Accidents create opportunities. *Contemporary Psychology* 14:434–435.

Kernberg, O. (1970). Factors in the psychoanalytic treatment of narcissistic personalities. *Journal of the American Psychoanalytic Association* 18:51–85.

_____. (1974). Further contributions to the treatment of narcissistic personalities. *International Journal of Psycho-Analysis* 55:215–240.

_____. (1975). *Borderline Conditions and Pathological Narcissism*. New York: Jason Aronson.

_____. (1976). *Object Relations Theory and Clinical Psychoanalysis*. New York: Jason Aronson.

_____ et al. (1972). Psychotherapy and psychoanalysis. *Bulletin of the Menninger Clinic* 36:3–275.

Klein, G. S. (1967). Peremptory ideation: Structures and force in motivated ideas. In R. Holt, ed., *Motives and Thought: Psychoanalytic Essays in Honor of David Rapaport. Psychological Issues* 5:80–128.

Knight, R. (1971). Evaluation of research of psychoanalytic therapy. *American Journal of Psychiatry* 98:434–446.

Kohut, H. (1966). Forms and transformations of narcissism. *Journal of the American Psychoanalytic Association* 14:243–272.

_____. (1968). The psychoanalytic treatment of narcissistic personality disturbances. *Psychoanalytic Study of the Child* 23:86–113.

_____. (1971). *The Analysis of the Self*. New York: International Universities Press.

_____. (1972). Thoughts on narcissism and narcissistic rage. *Psychoanalytic Study of the Child* 27:360–400.

_____. (1977). *The Restoration of the Self*. New York: International Universities Press.

Kolb, L. C. (1982). Healing the wounds of Vietnam. *Hospital and Community Psychiatry* 33:877.

_____. (1983). Return of the repressed: delayed stress reaction to war. *Journal of the American Academy of Psychoanalysis* 11:531–545.

_____. (1984). The post-traumatic stress disorders of combat: a subgroup with a conditioned emotional response. *Military Medicine* 149:237–243.

Koranyi, E. A. (1969). Psychodynamic theories of the "survivor syndrome." *Canadian Psychiatric Association Journal* 14:165–174.

Krueger, D. W. (1984). *Emotional Rehabilitation of Physical Trauma and Disability*. New York: Spectrum.

Krupnick, J., and Horowitz, M. (1981). Stress response syndromes: Recurrent themes. *Archives of General Psychiatry* 38:428–435.

Krystal, H. (1968). *Massive Psychic Trauma*. New York: International Universities Press.

_____. (1985). Trauma and the stimulus barrier. Psychoanalytic Inquiry V. 5 Hillsdale, N.J.: Analytic Press.

_____, and Niederland, W. G. (1971). Psychic traumatization. *International Psychiatric Clinics* 8:11–28.

Kubie, L. S. (1943). Manual of emergency treatment for acute war neuroses. *War Medicine* 4:582–599.

_____. (1958). *Neurotic Distortion of the Creative Process*. Lawrence: University of Kansas Press.

Kübler-Ross, E. (1969). *On Death and Dying*. New York: Macmillan.

Kutash, I. L., Schlesinger, L. B., and Associates (1980). *Handbook of Stress and Anxiety*. San Francisco: Jossey-Bass.

Langley, K. M. (1982). Post traumatic stress disorder among Vietnam combat veterans. *Social Casework* 63:593–598.

Lazare, A. (1971). The hysterical character in psychoanalytic theory. *Archives of General Psychiatry* 25:131–137.

Lazarus, R. S. (1964). A laboratory approach to the dynamics of psychological stress. *American Psychologist* 19:400–411.

_____. (1966). *Psychological Stress and the Coping Process*. New York: McGraw-Hill.

_____. (1968). Emotions and adaptation. *Nebraska Symposium on Motivation* 16:175–266. Lincoln: University of Nebraska Press.

_____, Averill, J. R., and Opton, E. M. (1969). The psychology of coping: Issues of research and assessment. Paper presented at *Coping and Adaptation*, Stanford University.

_____, and Folkman, S. K. (1984). *Stress, Appraisal and Coping*. New York: Springer.

_____, and Opton, E. M. (1966). The use of motion picture films in the study of psychological stress: A summary of experimental studies and theoretical formulations. In C. Spielberger, ed., *Anxiety and Behavior*, pp. 225–261. New York: Academic Press.

Lewin, K. (1935). The conflict between Aristotelian and Galilean modes of thought in contemporary psychology. In *A Dynamic Theory of Personality*, pp. 1–43. New York: McGraw-Hill.

Lewis, C. S. (1961). *A Grief Observed*. London: Faber.

Lewis, N. D., and Engel, B. (1954). *Wartime Psychiatry*. New York: Oxford University Press.

Lidz, T. (1946). Psychiatric casualties from Guadalcanal. *Psychiatry* 9:143–213.

_____. (1946). Nightmare and the combat neuroses. *Psychiatry* 9:37–49.

Lifton, R. J. (1967). *History and Human Survival*. New York: Vantage Books.

_____. (1973). *Home from the War*. New York: Simon & Schuster.

Lindemann, E. (1944). Symptomatology and management of acute grief. *American Journal of Psychiatry* 101:141–148.

_____. (1960). Psychosocial factors as stress agents. In J. Tanner, ed., *Stress and Psychiatric Disorders* pp. 13–17. Oxford, England: Blackwell.

Lindy, J. D., Green, B. L., Grace, M. C., Titchner, J. L. (in press). Prevention of longterm psychopathology following disaster. *The Journal of Preventive Psychiatry*.

Luborsky, L. (1984). *Principles of Psychoanalytic Psychotherapy: A manual for supportive-expressive (SE) treatment*. New York: Basic Books.

Ludwig, A. M. (1972). Hysteria: A neurobiological theory. *Archives of General Psychiatry* 27:771–777.

Luisada, P. V., Peele, R., and Pittard, E. A. (1974). The hysterical personality in men. *American Journal of Psychotherapy* 131:518–521.

Mahler, M. (1968). *On Human Symbiosis and the Vicissitudes of Individuation*. New York: International Universities Press.

Malan, D. H. (1963). *A Study of Brief Psychotherapy*. London: Tavistock.

_____. (1976). *Toward the Validation of Dynamic Psychotherapy*. New York: Plenum.

_____. (1979). *Individual Psychotherapy and the Science of Psychodynamics*. London: Butterworth.

Mandler, G. (1964). The interruption of behavior. *Nebraska Symposium on Motivation* 12:163–220. Lincoln: University of Nebraska Press.

Mann, J. (1973). *Time Limited Psychotherapy*. Cambridge, Mass.: Harvard University Press.

Marks, I. (1978). Behavioral psychotherapy of adult neurosis. In S. Garfield and A. Bergen, eds., *Handbook of Psychotherapy and Behavior Change*, 2nd ed., pp. 493–549. New York: John Wiley.

———. (1980). *Living with Fear*. New York: McGraw-Hill.

———. (1981). *Cure and Care of Neuroses: Theory and Practice of Behavioral Psychotherapy*. New York: John Wiley.

Marmar, C., Marziali, E., Horowitz, M. J., and Weiss, D. (in press). The development of the therapeutic alliance rating system. In L. Greenberg and W. Pinsoff, eds., *Research in Psychotherapy*. New York: Guilford.

Marmor, J. (1953). Orality in the hysterical personality. *Journal of the American Psychoanalytic Association* 1:656–675.

———, and Woods, S., eds. (1980). *The Interface between the Psychodynamic and Behavioral Therapies*. New York: Plenum.

Marris, P. (1958). *Widows and Their Families*. London: Routledge.

Marziali, E., Marmar, C., and Krupnick, J. (1981). Therapeutic alliance scales: Development and relationship to therapeutic outcome. *American Journal of Psychiatry* 138:361–364.

Maskin, M. (1941). Psychodynamic aspects of the war neuroses. *Psychiatry* 4:97–115.

Meichenbaum, D. (1977). *Cognitive-Behavior Modification: An Integrative Approach*. New York: Plenum.

———. (1980). *Cognitive Behavior Modification*. New York: Plenum.

Menninger, K. (1954). Regulatory devices of the ego under major stress. *International Journal of Psycho-Analysis* 35:412–420.

Miller, G. A., Galanter, E., and Pribram, K. H. (1960). *Plans and the Structure of Behavior*. New York: Holt, Rinehart & Winston.

Miller, N. E. (1963). Some reflections on the law of effect to produce a new alternative to drive reduction. *Nebraska Symposium on Motivation* 11:65–112. Lincoln: University of Nebraska Press.

Monat, A., and Lazarus, R. S. (1977). *Stress and Coping*. New York: Columbia University Press.

Moore, B. E., and Fine, B. D. (1968). *A Glossary of Psychoanalytic Terms and Concepts*. New York: American Psychoanalytic Association.

Moos, R. (1976). *Coping with Physical Illness*. New York: Plenum.

Murphy, W. F. (1961). A note on traumatic loss. *Journal of the American Psychoanalytic Association* 9:519–532.

Myerson, P. G. (1969). The hysteric's experience in psycho-analysis. *International Journal of Psycho-Analysis* 50:373–384.

Nefzger, M. D. (1969). Follow up studies of World War II and Korean war prisoners. *American Journal of Epidemiology* 91:123–138.

Nicholson, R. A., and Berman, J. S. (1983). Is follow-up necessary in evaluating psychotherapy? *Psychological Bulletin* 93:261–278.

Niederland, W. G. (1968). Clinical observations on the "survivors syndrome." *International Journal of Psychiatry* 49:313–315.

Nomikos, M. S., Averill, J. R., Lazarus, R. S., and Opton, E. M. (1968). Surprise versus suspense in the production of stress reaction. *Journal of Personality and Social Psychology* 8:204–208.

Noshpitz, J. (1982). Review, *Demography of Invulnerability* by E. E. Werner and R. S. Smith. *Contemporary Psychiatry* 1:253–260.

Oppenheim, H. (1905). *Textbook of Nervous Diseases*. Berlin: S. Karger.

Oremland, J. D. (1972). Transference cure and flight into health. *International Journal of Psychoanalytic Psychotherapy* 1:61–75.

Orne, M. T. (1962). On the social psychology of the psychological experiment: With particular reference to demand characteristics and their implications. *American Psychologist* 17:776–783.

Ornstein, P. (1978). *The Search for the Self: Selected Writings of Heinz Kohut*, Vols. 1 and 2. New York: International Universities Press.

Osterweiss, M., Solomon, F., and Green, M. (1984). *Bereavement Reactions, Consequences and Care*. Washington, D.C.: National Academy Press.

Ostwald, P., and Bittner, E. (1968). Life adjustment after severe persecution. *American Journal of Psychiatry* 124:87–94.

Parad, H., Resnik, H., and Parad, L. (1976). *Emergency Mental Health Services and Disaster Management*. New York: Prentice-Hall.

Parkes, C. M. (1964). Recent bereavement as a cause of mental illness. *British Journal of Psychiatry* 110:198–204.

―――. (1970). The first year of bereavement: A longitudinal study of the reaction of London widows to the death of their husbands. *Psychiatry* 33:444–467.

―――. (1972). *Bereavement*. New York: International Universities Press.

―――, and Weiss, R. S. (1983). *Recovery from Bereavement*. New York: Basic Books.

Pearlin, L., and Schooler, C. (1978). The structure of coping. *Journal of Health and Social Behavior* 19:2–21. Also in McCubbin, H. I., ed., *Family Stress, Coping and Social Supports*. New York: Springer, 1982.

Peterfreund, E. (1971). Information systems and psychoanalysis: An evolutionary biological approach to psychoanalytic theory. *Psychological Issues* 7:Monograph 25/26.

Piaget, J. (1954). *The Construction of Reality in the Child*. New York: Basic Books.

Popovic, M., and Petrovic, D. (1965). After the earthquake. *Lancet* 2:1169–1171.

Pumpian-Mindlin, E. (1953). Conspirations in the selection of patients for short-term psychotherapy. *American Journal of Psychotherapy* 7:641–652.

Rado, S. (1948). Pathodynamics and treatment of traumatic war neuroses (trauma-phobia). *Psychosomatic Medicine* 4:362–368.

Raphael, B. (1983). *The Anatomy of Bereavement*. New York: Basic Books.

Rees, W. D. (1970). Hallucinatory and Paranormal Reactions to Bereavement. M.D. Thesis.

Reider, N. (1953). Reconstruction and screen function. *Journal of the American Psychoanalytic Association* 8:82–99.

Richardson, J. T. E. (1979). The post-concussional syndrome. In D. J. Oborne, M. M. Gruneberg, and J. R. Eiser, eds., *Research in Psychology and Medicine*, Vol. 1, London: Academic Press.

Rioch, D. (1955). Problems of preventive psychiatry in war. In P. Hoch and D. Zubin, eds., *Psychopathology of Childhood*, pp. 146–166. New York: Grune & Stratton.

Robertson, J., and Robertson, J. (1969). *John, Seventeen Months: Nine Days in a Residential Nursery* (film). London: Tavistock Institute of Human Relations, Tavistock Clinic.

Robins, L. N., Smith, E. M., Cottler, L. B., Fischback, R., and Goldring, E. (1985). Impact of Disaster on Mental Health. Paper presented at the Annual Meeting of the American Psychiatric Association, Dallas, May 22.

Rosenbaum, R., and Horowitz, M. (1983). Motivation for psychotherapy: A factorial and conceptual analysis. *Psychotherapy: Theory, Research and Practice* 20:346–354.

Rosenblatt, P. C., Walsh, R. P., and Jackson, D. A. (1976). Grief and mourning in cross-cultural perspective. New Haven, Conn.: Human Relations Area Files Press.

Rosenthal, R. (1966). *Experimental Effects in Behavioral Research*. New York: Appleton-Century-Crofts.

Sachs, O. (1967). Distinctions between fantasy and reality elements in memory and reconstructions. *International Journal of Psycho-Analysis* 48:416–423.

Saltz, E. (1970). Manifest anxiety: Have we misread the data? *Psychological Review* 77:568–573.

Salzman, L. (1968). *The Obsessive Personality*. New York: Science House.

———. (1980). *Treatment of the Obsessive Personality*. New York: Jason Aronson.

Sampson, H., and Weiss, J. (1972). Defense analysis and the emergence of warded off mental conflicts: An empirical study. *Archives of General Psychiatry* 26:524–532.

Sandler, J. (1960). The background of safety. *International Journal of Psycho-Analysis* 41:352–356.

Schank, R., and Abelson, R. P. (1977). *Scripts, Plans, Goals, and Understandings*. Hillsdale, N.J.: Erlbaum.

Schur, M. (1966). *The Id and the Regulatory Process of the Ego*. New York: International Universities Press.

Schwartz, E. K. (1972). The treatment of the obsessive patient in the group therapy setting. *American Journal of Psychotherapy* 26:352–361.

Sears, R. R. (1936). Functional abnormalities of memory with special reference to amnesia. *Psychological Bulletin* 33:229–274.

Selye, H. (1976). *Stress in Health and Disease*. Boston: Butterworths.

Shapiro, D. (1965). *Neurotic Styles*. New York: Basic Books.

————. (1981). *Autonomy and Rigid Character*. New York: Basic Books.

Shatan, C. (1973). The grief of soldiers: Vietnam combat veterans' self-help movement. *American Journal of Orthopsychiatry* 43:640–653.

Shore, J. H., Tatum, E., and Vollmer, W. M. (1985). Psychiatric Findings of Mount St. Helens Disaster. Paper presented at the Annual Meeting of the American Psychiatric Association, Dallas, May 22.

Sifneos, P. (1966). Psychoanalytically oriented short-term dynamic or anxiety-producing psychotherapy for mild obsessional neuroses. *Psychiatric Quarterly* 40:270–282.

————. (1972). *Short-term Psychotherapy and Emotional Crisis*. Cambridge, Mass: Harvard University Press.

Silver, S., and Iacono, C. (1984). Factor analytic support for DSM-III post traumatic stress disorder for Vietnam veterans. *Journal of Clinical Psychology* 40:5–14.

Silverman, J. S. (1972). Obsessional disorders in childhood and adolescence. *American Journal of Psychotherapy* 26:362–377.

Singer, J. L., and Pope, K. S., eds. (1978). *The Stream of Consciousness: Scientific Investigations into the Flow of Human Experience*. New York: Plenum.

Smith, E. M., Robins, L. N., Cottler, L. B., Fischback, R., and Goldring, E. (1985). Psychosocial Impact of a Double Disaster. Paper Presented at the Annual Meeting of the American Psychiatric Association, Dallas, May 22.

Socarides, C. W. (1954). On the use of extremely brief psychoanalytic contacts. *Psychoanalytic Review* 41:340–346.

Solomon, G. F., et al. (1971). Three psychiatric casualties from Vietnam. *Archives of General Psychiatry* 25:522–524.

Spielberger, C. D. (1966). Theory and research on anxiety. In C. D. Spielberger, ed., *Anxiety and Behavior*, pp. 3–20. New York: Academic Press.

Stampfl, T. G., and Lewis, D. J. (1967). Essentials of implosive therapy: A learning-theory-based psychodynamic behavioral therapy. *Journal of Abnormal Psychology* 72:496–503.

Sterba, R. (1951). A case of brief psychotherapy by Sigmund Freud. *Psychoanalytic Review* 38:75–80.

Stern, M. M. (1961). Blank hallucinations: Remarks about trauma and perceptual disturbances. *International Journal of Psycho-Analysis* 42:205–215.

Stevens, S. S. (1966). A metric for the social consensus. *Science* 151:530.

Stone, L. (1951). Psychoanalysis and brief psychotherapy. *Psychoanalytic Quarterly* 20:215–236.

Straker, M. (1971). The survivor syndrome: Theoretical and therapeutic dilemmas. *Laval Médical* 42:37–41.

Strauss, A. (1975). *Chronic Illness and the Quality of Life*. St. Louis: C. V. Mosby.

Strupp, H., and Binder, J. (1984). *Psychotherapy in a New Key: A Guide to Time-limited Dynamic Psychotherapy*. New York: Basic Books.

Sutherland, S., and Scherl, P. J. (1970). Patterns of response among victims of rape. *American Journal of Orthopsychiatry* 40:503–511.

Sutherland-Fox, S., and Scherl, P. J. (1975). Crisis intervention with victims of rape. In L. G. Schultz, ed., *Rape Victimology*, pp. 232–245. Springfield, Ill.: Chas. C Thomas.

Tart, C. T. (1969). *Altered States of Consciousness*. New York: John Wiley.

Tatum, E. L., Vollmer, W. M., and Shore, J. H. (1985). High-Risk Groups of Mount St. Helens Disaster. Paper presented at the Annual Meeting of the American Psychiatric Association, Dallas, May 22.

Taylor, J., and Spence, K. (1952). The relationship of anxiety level of performance in serial learning. *Journal of Experimental Psychology* 44:61–64.

Terr, L. (1981). Psychic trauma in children: Observations following the Chowchilla school-bus kidnapping. *American Journal of Psychiatry* 138:14–19.

———. (1983). Chowchilla revisited: The effects of psychic trauma four years after a school-bus kidnapping. *American Journal of Psychiatry* 140:1543–1550.

Titchner, J. L., and Kapp, F. T. (1976). Family and character change at Buffalo Creek. *American Journal of Psychiatry* 133:295–299.

Tomkins, S. S. (1962). *Affect, Imagery, Consciousness*, Vol. I: *The Positive Affects*. New York: Springer.

———. (1978). Script theory: Differential magnification of affects. In H. E. Howe, Jr., and R. A. Diensbier, eds., *Nebraska Symposium on Motivation* 26:201–237. Lincoln: University of Nebraska Press.

Trimble, M. R. (1981). *Post Traumatic Neuroses*. New York: John Wiley.

vander Kolk, B., Blitz, R., Burr, W., Sherry, S., and Hartman, E. (1984). Nightmares and trauma: A comparison of nightmares after combat with lifelong nightmares in veterans. *American Journal of Psychiatry* 141:187–190.

Veith, I. (1965). *Hysteria: History of a Disease*. Chicago: University of Chicago Press.

———. (1977). Four thousand years of hysteria. In M. J. Horowitz, ed., *Hysterical Personality*, pp. 7–95. New York: Jason Aronson.

Veronen, L. J., and Kilpatrick, D. G. (1983). Stress management for rape victims. In D. Meichenbaum and M. Jaremko, eds., *Stress Reduction and Prevention*, pp. 341–375. New York: Plenum.

Waelder, L. (1964). Statements as reported by S. Gifford, in "Repetition Compulsion." *Journal of the American Psychoanalytic Association* 12:632–649.

Wallerstein, R. S. (1967). Development and metapsychology of defensive organization of the ego. *Journal of the American Psychoanalytic Association* 15:130.

Weiss, D., DeWitt, K., Kaltreider, N., and Horowitz, M. (1985). A proposed method for measuring change beyond symptoms. *Archives of General Psychiatry* 42:703–708.

———, Horowitz, M., and Wilner, N. (1984). Stress response rating scale: A clinician's measure. *British Journal of Clinical Psychology* 23:202–215.

Weiss, J. (1967). The integration of defenses. *International Journal of Psycho-Analysis* 48:520–524.

———. (1971). The emergence of new themes: A contribution to the psycho-analytic theory of therapy. *International Journal of Psycho-Analysis* 52:459–467.

Whitty, C. W. M., and Zangwill, O. L. (1977). Traumatic amnesia. In C. W. M. Whitty and O. L. Zangwill, eds., *Amnesias*, 2nd ed., pp. 104–117. London: Butterworths.

Wilkinson, C. B. (1983). Aftermath of a disaster: The collapse of the Hyatt Regency Hotel Skywalks. *American Journal of Psychiatry* 140:1134–1139.

Wilner, N., and Horowitz, M. J. (1975). Intrusive and repetitive thought after a depressing film: A pilot study. *Psychological Reports* 37:135–138.

Wilson, J. (1980). Conflict, stress and growth: The effects of war on psychosocial development among Vietnam veterans. In C. Figley and S. Levantman, eds., *Strangers at Home: Vietnam Veterans since the War*, pp. 123–165. New York: Praeger.

———, and Krauss, G. (1982). Predicting post traumatic stress syndrome among Vietnam veterans. Paper presented at the 25th Neuropsychiatric Institute, Veterans Administration Medical Center, Coatsville, Pa., October 21.

Windholz, E. (1945). Observations on psychiatric rehabilitation of veterans. *Bulletin of the Menninger Clinic* 9:121–133.

Windholz, M., Marmar, C., and Horowitz, M. J. (in press). A review of research on conjugal bereavement: Impact on health and efficacy of intervention. *Comprehensive Psychiatry*.

Witkin, H. A. (1969). Influencing dream content. In M. Kramer, ed., *Dream Psychology and the New Biology of Dreaming*. New York: Chas. C Thomas.

———, and Lewis, H. B. (1965). The relation of experimentally induced pre-sleep experience to dreams. *Journal of the American Psychoanalytic Association* 13:819–849.

Wolberg, L. (1967). *The Technique of Psychotherapy*, 2nd ed. New York: Grune & Stratton.

Wolpe, J. (1958). *Psychotherapy by Reciprocal Inhibition*. Palo Alto, Calif.: Stanford University Press.

Zabriskie, E., and Brush, A. (1941). Psychoneuroses in wartime. *Psychosomatic Medicine* 3:295–329.

Zilberg, N., Weiss, D., and Horowitz, M. J. (1982). Impact of Event Scale: A cross validation study and some empirical evidence. *Journal of Consulting and Clinical Psychology* 50:407–414.

INDEX

About the Author

Mardi Jon Horowitz, M.D., is Professor of Psychiatry and Director of the Center for the Study of Neuroses at the University of California, San Francisco. He also directs the Program on Conscious and Unconscious Mental Processes, funded by the John D. and Catherine T. Mac Arthur Foundation, San Francisco. He is the author or editor of several books, including *Hysterical Personality*, *States of Mind*, and *Image Formation and Psychotherapy*, and co-author of *Personality Styles and Brief Psychotherapy*.